LANCASHIRE QUAKERS AND THE ESTABLISHMENT

Lancashire Quakers and the Establishment

1760–1830

Nicholas Morgan

Ryburn Academic Publishing

First published in 1993
by Ryburn Publishing Limited
Krumlin, Halifax

ISBN 1 85331 015 8

Composed by Ryburn Publishing Services
Printed by Ryburn Book Production, Halifax, England

Contents

Acknowledgements

This book reproduces without substantive amendment the text of my doctoral thesis. Michael Mullett first suggested that I should study the relationship between the state and the Quakers through an examination of the materials contained in the Friends' Meeting House in Lancaster. He was a thoughtful and stimulating supervisor, and his constant encouragement was in no small part responsible for the completion of the thesis. He and his family also provided generous and tolerant hospitality on a number of occasions. I owe a special debt to Austin Woolrych who whilst teaching me his special subject at the University of Lancaster introduced me to, and awoke my enthusiasm for, the study of history from original sources.

I wish to thank the Friends of Lancaster Meeting, who allowed me access to their archive and their history. The late Ralph Randles was an enthusiastic guide to the materials kept in Meeting House Lane; it is a particular regret to me that he could not read the fruits of my researches. My friends and ex-colleagues at the Library of the Society of Friends in London, who guided me in my first tentative exploration into Quaker archives, continued to be immensely supportive of my work. In particular I should thank them for their willingness to make materials available to me in Glasgow which I otherwise would have had difficulty in consulting. Library staff at Lancaster Public Library, Lancaster University, University College London, the University of Glasgow, the Mitchell Library in Glasgow and the National Library of Scotland generally met my requests for assistance with a patience and good humour which I rarely showed to them, and consequently receive my thanks and belated apologies.

I benefited greatly from conversations with a number of my fellow researchers in the field of Quaker history, and should thank in particular Beatrice Carre, Craig Horle, Richard Clark, and T.A. Davies. Three senior colleagues, Martin Daunton, Tony Slaven, and Archie Duncan, all encouraged me to finish this work, and were each generous in allowing me time to do so. Sandra Walker prepared the typescript with typical efficiency and good humour, whilst her family patiently endured the disruption it caused in their household.

Christine has provided support for me in this undertaking since its inception; I doubt if it would ever have been completed but for her continued encouragement. On a more practical level she has tried to remedy my chronic inability to spell or punctuate correctly: it was an admirable attempt, but any errors of presentation which remain, along with those of content, are entirely my own responsibility.

For helping bring my work before a wider readership, I am grateful to Stephen Constantine at Lancaster University and to everyone at Ryburn Publishing.

Nicholas Morgan

Conventions

For convenience, dates throughout the book are given in the old style. I have followed the general Quaker practice of beginning the year on the first of March. So the 28th February 1688 (new style) would read 28/12/1687 (old style), whilst the following day would be 1/1/1688 (old style). To avoid confusion I have occasionally double-dated (1687–88) where it appears necessary (for a note on Quaker dating, see the new edition of Isabel Ross, *Margaret Fell. Mother of Quakerism*, (2nd ed., York, 1984), pp.vi–viii). Spelling and punctuation from manuscript sources have been modernised except where this appears to detract from the original sense of the document.

Much of the source material for this book originates in minute books or other similarly-dated collections. I have therefore given citations to sources by date rather than by (the not always extant) page number, except on the few occasions where irregular record keeping has made a page number a more convenient form of reference.

Abbreviations

1. General

HMC	Historical Manuscripts Commission
LFMH	Lancaster Friends' Meeting House, Meeting House Lane, Lancaster
LPL	Lancaster Public Library, Market Square, Lancaster
LSF	Library of the Society of Friends, Euston Road, London
PRO	Public Record Office, Kew, Surrey

2. Manuscript Sources

DQB	LSF, Typescript Dictionary of Quaker Biography
GBS	LSF, Great Book of Sufferings
LMMM	LFMH, Lancaster Monthly Meeting Minutes
LQMM	LFMH, Lancashire Quarterly Meeting Minutes
LQMS	LFMH, Lancashire Quarterly Meeting Book of Sufferings
LWMMM	LFMH, Lancaster Women's Monthly Meeting Minutes
LWQMM	LFMH, Lancaster Women's Quarterly Meeting Minutes
LYMM	LSF, London Yearly Meeting Minutes
MMS	LSF, Minutes of the Meeting for Sufferings
Port	LSF, Bound MSS Portfolio series of correspondence
SMMM	LSF, Swarthmore Monthly Meeting Minutes
SWMMM	LSF, Swarthmore Women's Monthly Meeting Minutes
SPMM	LSF, Swarthmore Particular Meeting Minutes
SWPMM	LSF, Swarthmore Women's Particular Meeting Minutes

3. Published works

Apology	Robert Barclay, *An Apology for the True Christian Divinity ... preached by the people Called in Scorn, Quakers ...* (6th ed., London, 1736)
Beginnings	W.C. Braithwaite, *The Beginnings of Quakerism* (London, 1912)
Besse	Joseph Besse, *A Collection of the Sufferings of the People called Quakers....* (2 vols., London, 1753)

9

A Brief Collection	Margaret Fell, *A Brief Collection of Remarkable Passages and Occurrences Relating to ... Margaret Fell ...* (London, 1710)
CSPD	*Calendar of State Papers Domestic*
A Collection	Richard Hubberthorn, *A Collection of the several Books and Writings of ... Richard Hubberthorn ...* (London, 1663)
DNB	*Dictionary of National Biography* (63 vols., London, 1885–1900)
HMC *Fleming*	HMC Twelfth Report, App. pt.VII, *The Manuscripts of S.H. Le Flemming ...* (London, 1890)
HMC *Kenyon*	HMC Fourteenth Report, App. pt.IV, *The Manuscripts of Lord Kenyon* (London, 1894)
Journal	John L. Nickalls (ed.), *Journal of George Fox* (revised ed., London, 1975)
Parliamentary History	*The Parliamentary History of England ...* (23 vols., London, 1812–1820)
Political Associations	Norman C. Hunt, *Two Early Political Associations ...* (Oxford, 1961)
Second Period	W.C. Braithwaite, *The Second Period of Quakerism* (London, 1919)
Stout	J.D. Marshall (ed.), *The Autobiography of William Stout of Lancaster 1665–1752* (Manchester, 1967)
VCH Lancs	William Farrer and J. Brownbill, *The Victoria History of the County of Lancaster* (8 vols., London, 1906–1911)

4. Journals etc

JFHS	*Journal of the Friends' Historical Society*
THSLC	*Transactions of the Historic Society of Lancashire and Cheshire*
TLCAS	*Transactions of the Lancashire and Cheshire Antiquarian Society*
TW&CA&AS	*Transactions of the Cumberland and Westmorland Antiquarian and Archaeological Society*

Introduction

The subject of this book is a study of the relationship that existed between Quakers, or Friends, and the Establishment in the late seventeenth and early eighteenth centuries.[1]

The definition which will be given to the word 'Establishment' as it is used in this book is in need of some clarification, as it does not entirely accord with conventional usage. It will be taken to include the monarchy, Parliament, the law courts and the representatives of central and local government. The Anglican Church, however, is not included within the definition. That is not to say that the relationship between the Established Church and the Quakers will not be considered here, for in many instances Quaker conflicts with the state were a product of the enduring relationship that existed between the secular and spiritual authorities in post-Restoration England.[2] However, a thesis by my fellow-researcher at the University of Lancaster, Richard Clark, covers the broad area of Quaker relationships with the Anglican authorities, whilst the main concern of the present work is to examine the civil and political establishment's relationship with the Quakers.[3]

Moreover, this book is concerned not only with the civil and political establishment, but also with another, the existence of which was not immediately apparent in 1660. This was the Quaker establishment. Its membership originated in those Quaker leaders and ministers who survived the persecution they and their co-religionists underwent in the immediate post-Restoration years. The authority of this Quaker establishment rested in a number of business or executive Meetings, all based in London, which in addition to overseeing the general administration of the Society also acted as an intermediary between Quakers throughout England, Ireland, Wales, Scotland and the Colonies, and the authorities. This book, then, is a study of the multi-faceted relationship which existed between the generality of Friends, the Quakers who made up the body of the various Meetings in London, and the civil and political establishment. In addition, it seeks to explain this relationship by means of a detailed examination of those areas of Quaker behaviour which brought Friends most often into

11

contact (and not infrequently conflict) with the authorities. The book concludes by discussing the state or conditions of Quakerism in the late seventeenth and early eighteenth centuries, and considers to what extent the nature of the relationship that existed between Friends and the authorities was determined by this condition.

Particular attention is given to the interaction between Friends in the North-West of England, their co-religionists in London and the South, and the authorities. Although evidence is presented from a variety of counties in the North-West, the main emphasis is on Lancashire, including that part in Furness, Lancashire 'north of the sands', which came within the compass of the Quaker organisation in the county. The history of religion in the North-West during the early modern period has not gone without notice.[4] Nor has the the the history of the region itself.[5] It was, in the early seventeenth century, an area distinguished only by the gulf which divided it from the South. Poor communications, a backward economy and a totally inadequate structure for ecclesiastical adminis- tration and the provision of religious teaching, condemned the North- West to be a "dark corner of the land".[6] Ironically, however, it was to be from this darkest corner that the "star" of Quakerism arose in the 1650s.

The North of England was the Galilee of early Quakerism.[7] Edward Burrough, the Quaker propagandist who hailed from Underbarrow in Westmorland, likened the North to the description of Bethlehem given in the Book of Matthew (Matt. 2, 6–10). He wrote in 1655:

> O thou North of England who are accounted as desolate and barren, and reckoned the least of the Nations, yet out of thee did the branch spring, and the Star arise which gives light unto all Regions round about ... and out of thee the terror of the Lord proceeded, which makes the earth to tremble and be removed; out of thee Kings, Princes and Prophets did come forth in the name and power of the most High.[8]

In the same year the Yorkshire Quaker, William Dewsbury, wrote of *A True Prophecy of the Mighty Day of the Lord Which is coming, and is appeared from the North of England, and is arising toward the South; and shall overspread this nation, and all nations of the world.*[9] For Richard Hubberthorn, from Yealand Redmayne, "God the Father raised up his own seed according to his promise out of the North to spoil Babylon". "The promised seed of the Lord is come forth", he wrote "and is spreading over the Nations as the morning over the mountains".[10] Looking back on the early years of Quakerism, George Fox wrote of 1654, that "the churches were settled in the north, the Lord had raised up many and sent forth many into his vineyard to preach his everlasting gospel ..." "A matter of seventy ministers did the Lord raise up and send abroad out of the north countries".[11] In London it was reported that "The expectations of our Friends here ... have been and are very great, to have seen some Friends out of the North to come to abide here ..."[12]

This regional aspect of early Quakerism was also recognised by critics; in 1653 Francis Higginson, minister at Kirkby Stephen near Kendal, published *The Irreligion of the Northern Quakers*. "I here present you", he wrote,

> with a brief relation of the execrable irreligion of a sort of people lately started in some part of the north, commonly called Quakers. When you have read it, you will be ready to dream (if you be acquainted with the history of the last century) that you behold the turbulent Exorcists of Germany, revived in England …;

"Sometimes", he continued,

> some of them, men or women, will more like frantic people than modest teachers of the gospel, or like prophets of Munster or John of Leyden's apostles, run or stand in the streets or market place, or get upon a stone and cry 'Repent …'. Kendal, and many other towns in these northern parts, are witnesses of these mad speakings and practices.[13]

In London it was complained in 1654 that the city had been invaded by "plaine North country ploughmen".[14]

The seventy ministers to which Fox referred (and in this reference he was drawing on the scriptural source of Luke 10, 1) in fact numbered sixty-six, and they are known in Quaker history, with a typical perversity, as the "Valiant Sixty".[15] Drawn almost exclusively from the counties of Lancashire, Yorkshire and Westmorland, and frequently recruited from the region's earlier Seeker congregations, these early Friends were responsible for carrying the message of Quakerism south between 1654 and 1655 to London, and south-west to Bristol.[16] Amongst their numbers were also the earliest Quaker missionaries to Scotland, Ireland, Europe and America. The Valiant Sixty were drawn from a variety of backgrounds; over half were described as yeomen or husbandmen, with an equal number, eight, being involved in either trade or the professions.[17] These descriptions, however, undoubtedly hide a wide variety of economic activity, and an equal variety of wealth and status. What they shared most was their regional background, which, according to historians such as Hugh Barbour, instilled in them common grievances and shared assumptions which combined to give Quakerism its "special flavour". Barbour summarised his view thus:

> the self-sustaining farmers and shepherds of the Northwest of England, where Quakerism took rise and gathered its special flavour, felt disinherited by their landowners and gentry, by the church, and by the schools …. When this radicalism was focused and deepened by the religious experience of Quakerism within their own lives, it made them

react explosively against the evils in the social order wherever they found them.[18]

The North's gift to early Quakerism did not end with this "explosive" group of sixty-six ministers. Friends in the North also provided the material and organisational sustenance which maintained the Movement during its infancy. From 1654 material sustenance was provided by the Kendal Fund, a collection raised from Friends in the North which was administered by two Friends in Kendal. Funds were given to aid the travelling ministers and also to relieve the hardships of Quakers who were undergoing imprisonments, particularly in the South. The fund was "servicable", wrote Margaret Fell, "to the whole body, – to those that have been sent forth into the ministry and to them that have suffered imprisonment, and for books and several other things ..."[19]

Monthly Meetings for business, a legacy to early Quakerism from the Seeker past, were established in the Northern counties as early as 1653, according to Fox "to look after the poor and to see that all walked according to the Truth etc."[20] These Meetings also dealt with legal matters.[21] The elders who arranged these Meetings, "friends charged with special duties", also met as county representatives at Yearly Meetings or General Meetings of Northern Friends which were held at Skipton in 1657, Scalehouse in 1658, Skipton in 1659 and 1660 and Kendal in 1661. These Meetings discussed finance, the ministering effort, organisation and discipline, and were attended by elders from the North and South.[22] The first Yearly Meeting for the country as a whole was held at Skipton in 1660; it was attended by "the substantial men and Elders in the Truth ... both from Bristol and London and other places". It did not, however, last for "from thence, it was removed to London the next year, where it hath been kept ever since, as being looked upon a more convenient place".[23]

The North also provided at Swarthmore Hall, near Ulverston, a "safe house" from which operations of the leadership could be directed. Fox's first visit to Swarthmore had been in 1652, when in the absence of Judge George Fell, the owner of the Hall, he had effected the convincement (the Quaker equivalent of conversion) of Fell's wife, Margaret, her three daughters, and many of her servants.[24] George Fell, who had profited from both legal office and shrewd purchases of forfeit estates and fee-farm rents under the Commonwealth, offered protection to Fox and his co-religionists and used his considerable local influence (he was vice-chancellor of the Duchy of Lancaster and an assize judge) on their behalf.[25] Swarthmore became the centre through which all early Quaker correspondence passed, and Margaret Fell became the confidant of all the ministering Friends, who sent accounts of their trials and triumphs to her. She was also responsible for raising money for the Kendal fund and seeing to much of its distribution in the South. She became "a tender nursing mother unto many", adapting to her role as a Quaker matriarch with the ease which one would expect from a leading member of local society.[26]

This infant structure, firmly settled in the North, was swept away in the storm of persecution which broke over Friends in the immediate post-Restoration years.[27] Fuelled on a national scale by a mixture of understandable mistrust of all forms of radicalism, and irrational hatred of Dissent, persecution at the local level was often fired also by personal jealousy and financial ambition.[28] 1661 saw mass imprisonments of Friends following the abortive Fifth Monarchist rising led by Richard Venner in London.[29] The development of Cavalier Parliament legislation directed against either Quakers in particular or Dissenters in general saw Friends caught in a net designed to extirpate any political threat which they or the other Dissenting churches were thought to have posed to the newly restored regime.[30] As far as the future of the Movement was concerned, the most important legacy of this period was the vacuum created by the deaths of the majority of the early Northern Quaker ministers and leaders, many of whom had perished from prison fever or the accumulated effects of long periods of incarceration in cold, damp gaols.[31] This, as Christopher Hill has pointed out, is a "tribute to the efficacy of English gaols in removing undesirables".[32]

The Quaker response to the nationwide sufferings of Friends, and to the deaths of so many of the early ministers and leaders, was encapsulated in George Fox's attempts, beginning in 1668, to rebuild the organisation that had existed before the Restoration.[33] There were to be two major changes of emphasis: the first was the shift to London, "a more convenient place"; the second was the predominance of George Fox. The organisational structure which finally emerged in 1675 was not imposed by Fox without difficulty, particularly in the North, where a separation, led by two Friends, John Story and John Wilkinson, threatened the unity of the whole Movement.[34] The differences that emerged amongst Friends over Fox's organisation have been attributed in large part to the inevitable tensions that existed between church organisation and Christian liberty.[35] But it is clear that many forces combined to cause these differences. One point which W.C. Braithwaite, the foremost Quaker historian of the Society of Friends, certainly underplayed was the extent to which these problems arose out of George Fox's intensely authoritarian attitudes. It was not the principle of a collective discipline which some Friends objected to, or even a discipline arrived at by elders, but rather a discipline imposed by one man whose personal interpretation of the Truth was to stand as a consensus for the whole society. This view of Fox has been forcibly stated by Tom O'Malley. Fox, he argues, was pursuing an "object of suppressing individual inspiration through the erection of the system of church government".[36] Fox and his colleagues wanted to gain a monopoly on the Truth; they were, as one Quaker critic protested, claiming "a Pattent for all Gospel Priviledges".[37] This was a patent, moreover, which firmly rested within the newly created Meetings in London.

Of these Meetings the most important were the Yearly Meeting, the Morning Meeting and the Meeting for Sufferings. The Morning Meeting dealt with Quaker publications, rejecting, as O'Malley has shown, manuscripts which were over aggressive, controversial, or idiosyncratic, in favour of those which conformed to Fox's idea of church uniformity and harmony.[38] The reason for this was the need to smooth the path which Quakers might need to tread to the authorities. The Meeting was also responsible for organising the Quaker Meetings in London, and for supervising the conduct of ministers in the capital.[39] The Meeting for Sufferings, not established until 1675, quickly became the main executive body of the Movement, taking over many of the responsibilities of the Morning Meeting. It acted as, in the words of Eric Evans, an "*ad hoc* legal aid society" to Friends who had fallen foul of the law, and also, as Norman Hunt has shown, as a sophisticated political pressure group, lobbying the authorities in order to gain favours for Friends.[40] The Yearly Meeting, or Friends' annual delegate conference, was as we have seen, moved to London in the early 1660s for "convenience". Its complexion also altered; from 1672 onwards it was decided that the Meeting was

> to consist of six Friends for the city of London, three for the city of Bristol, two for the town of Colchester and one or two from each and every of the counties of England and Wales respectively .... [41]

Thus the capital's advancing domination of the Quaker executive was also reflected in its delegate assembly. Part of the convenience and necessity of being in London was the proximity to the court, Parliament and the law courts, all of which were to be regularly approached for a relaxation of persecution. However, the London base helped to diffuse some of the Northern "special flavour" of Quakerism, a flavour which may not have eased the task of those Friends seeking to approach the highest powers in the land in order to gain concessions for their suffering co-religionists.

The organisation that was established in the counties was based on a structure of Particular, Monthly and Quarterly Meetings.[42] At the head of this structure was the Quarterly Meeting, which was made up of representatives from the various Monthly Meetings within its compass. The Lancashire Quarterly Meeting met four times a year, generally at Lancaster, being preceded by the meeting of the Quarterly Meeting for Sufferings for the county.[43] In Lancashire the Monthly Meetings seem to have originally been Lancaster, Swarthmore, Marsden, and Knowsley (later Hardshaw), servicing respectively the north, north-west, east and south-west of the county.[44]

In the eighteenth century a Monthly Meeting was also established for the Fylde, later becoming Preston Monthly Meeting.[45] The function of these meetings was to provide general oversight of the Quaker community. This included relief of the poor and those imprisoned, keeping a record of Quaker sufferings (the prosecution or persecution of Friends by the authorities of Church and state for matters of conscience), the exercise of discipline against those guilty of disorderly walking (breaches of the

Quaker code of behaviour), the supervision of marriages, and the registration of marriages, births and deaths. To some extent the function of the Quarterly and Monthly Meeting within the county overlapped (as in the matter of discipline); however, as the Quarterly Meeting was the means by which the Friends in the county (officially) communicated with Friends in London (either nominated correspondents at the Meeting for Sufferings or the Yearly Meeting) it remained the senior Meeting.

Making up the Monthly Meetings were a larger number of Particular (later known as Preparative) Meetings. In Lancashire these generally served a small town or village, or a clearly defined rural community. Lancaster Monthly Meeting, for example, originally comprised Yealand, Wyresdale and Wray Meetings. These were joined in the 1670s by Fylde, Chipping, Claughton and Freckleton.[46] During the period under discussion there seem to have been between twenty and twenty-four Particular Meetings in the county, acting as the lowest level of administration for the collection of tithe testimonies and sufferings, and also for collections towards the county "stock".[47] This number of Meetings concurs with Michael Watts' total of twenty-two "congregations" for the county in the early eighteenth century.[48] These twenty or so Meetings serviced the administration of the Quaker community in the county; in addition, Meetings for Worship (held on First-day – Sunday – and on weekdays) were held at a variety of locations, which suggest a broad geographical base of support for Friends in Lancashire. In Lancashire, houses in at least 36 different towns, villages or hamlets were registered by Friends between 1689 and 1700 as places of worship under the terms of the Toleration Act of 1689.[49] A further 27 locations were added between 1701 and 1720.[50]

A demographic reconstitution of the Lancashire Quaker community in the late seventeenth and early eighteenth centuries is beyond the scope of this book, and would more properly be the subject of a work in itself. Nonetheless some general observations can be made as to the numbers of Friends in the county during this period. Data collected relating to tithe sufferings between 1650 and 1700 have identified 509 Friends in the county who suffered either by distraint, illegal seizure of goods, or imprisonment for refusing their payment during this period.[51] Allowing the assumption that the majority of tithe sufferers were likely to be heads of households, and that the average size of the family/household in the county was five, a figure for the total population of Friends in the county over the fifty years can be arrived at of 2,545.[52] This figure does not take into account those Friends (at least 5% of the total) not liable to pay tithes, and nor does it allow for under-recording of sufferings.[53] Data collected relating to tithe testimonies reveal a total number of 630 male Friends and 778 women Friends who made a declaration to their Meeting between 1675 and 1710.[54] The source is incomplete, but the total of 1,408 adult Friends active between 1675 and 1710 is not wildly inconsistent with the figure arrived at for the total population of Quakers in the county between 1650 and 1700.

Data collected by two historians, one in the nineteenth century and the other in the twentieth, perhaps provide a more reliable guide to numbers. J.S. Rowntree, in order to explain a decline in the number of Friends over the eighteenth century, compiled detailed statistics on membership, much of it drawn from data relating to marriages within the Society.[55] These data were collected at ten yearly intervals; using Rowntree's methodology it is possible to arrive at totals for Friends in the county by decade between 1660 and 1760. The average total for each decade was 1,511; the decade with the largest number of Friends was 1690–99 (with a total of 1,694), being closely followed by 1700–1709 (with a total of 1,666). Rowntree's figures show a marked decline in the numbers of Friends in the county from the 1730s onwards. The total for the decade 1720–29 was 1,568, which fell over the following ten years to 1,428. Between 1740 and 1749 the figure fell to 1,113.[56] Broad confirmation of Rowntree's data can be found in the work of Michael Watts, who had calculated membership figures for all Dissenting groups in England and Wales in the early eighteenth century.[57] He gives a total for Lancashire of 1,460 "hearers" (by which I take him to mean active members), some 3.7% of the population of 39,510 Quakers which he identifies for the country as a whole. This national total of Friends represented some 0.73% of the population; in Lancashire, Quakers made up 0.74% of the county's inhabitants.[58]

Watts' figures also allow us to make some comparison between Friends and other Dissenting groups. Although Friends were the second largest Dissenting body in the county they were dwarfed by the Presbyterians, who commanded the allegiance of some 16,630 hearers.[59] However, although Friends were less than a tenth of the numerical strength of the Presbyterians, their organisational structure was far more impressive. Whilst the Presbyterians had forty-two congregations to service their 16,000+ members, the Friends had about twenty-two Particular Meetings and at least thirty-six registered places of worship to service their 1,460 members. The situation supports Watts' conclusion that although Quakers "were less numerous than the Presbyterians or Independents, they had more particular meetings and were more evenly distributed over the country than any of the other Dissenting denominations".[60]

If Friends were distributed evenly both within the county and without in terms of numbers, then how were they distributed socially? Two studies of the social origins of Quakers in Lancashire, by Alan Cole and the late Alan B. Anderson, provide general answers to this most difficult of questions. Cole, who based his research on Quaker marriage registers between their first recorded marriages in the 1650s and 1688, concluded that in Lancashire, Quakerism was "strongest amongst the economically hard pressed but still independent petite bourgeoisie".[62] This reflected his findings for the country as a whole, both in rural and urban areas, where he found "remarkably few members of the 'ruling class' among them".[63] Anderson, drawing on probate data for 273 Friends dying between 1652 and 1690, confirmed that Friends were drawn "largely from the middle ranks of society, the independent landholders and tradesmen", although he queried whether they were "economically pressed", and found that Cole had "seriously underestimated the number of gentlemen" among the Lancashire Quakers.[64] Both concurred in the main occupational concentrations of Friends in the county. Over 40% of Cole's total were involved in the textile or clothing trades, compared with just over 20% of Anderson's. Fifty-six per cent of Anderson's total were either yeoman or husbandmen (a large number of whom we might expect to be also involved in the textile industry) as compared with 33% of Cole's.[65] In all, these two groups accounted, in both cases, for in excess of 70% of the Quaker population in the county.

Research into the social origins of Friends in other parts of the country has tended to support the view that Friends were drawn mainly from the middle ranks of society, although there has been considerable disagreement concerning the exact place of Friends within the middle ranks, and the degree to which this place might have changed during the post-Restoration period. So Richard Vann, drawing on probate records and evidence from Quaker registers of births, deaths and burials for Buckinghamshire, has argued that early Friends were drawn from the "middle and upper bourgeoisie, rather than the petite bourgeoisie".[66] Drawing on a broader base of research he has argued that the social composition of Friends in the late seventeenth century was more "plebeian" (although still bourgeois) than it had been in the founding years.[67] A narrowing of the social base of recruits was combined with a growing urban concentration; Friends were, he concludes, becoming increasingly socially and geographically isolated.[68]

Judith Hurwich has argued against Vann's findings; using hearth-tax assessments she has shown that Friends in Warwickshire had little gentry support at any stage, with an overwhelming degree of their support coming from "artisans and poor husbandmen". Unlike Vann, she finds no evidence of a narrowing social or geographical base, remarking that "what needs to be explained" was not Friends' social change but rather their social stability.[69] Barry Reay has concluded that early Friends were drawn from the "middling sort", although they were "wealthier than the general population"; William Spurrier has found that Friends in Essex "were generally of a modest-to-low social and economic standing" in the early years, with evidence of "increasing prosperity later on".[70] A study of Friends in Cambridgeshire finds that both early and later Friends were, and remained, poor.[71] However, despite these areas of disagreement, (which only serve to stress how subject to regional variation Quakerism was) the findings of Cole and Anderson are sufficiently in accord to allow us to speak with some confidence of the social make-up of Friends in the county at the start of our period. A social profile of Lancashire Friends in 1740 is not available, although the overriding impression is certainly one of prosperity.[72]

If Friends have left us only imprecise data relating to their numbers and social status then they surely compensated for this in leaving an astonishing archive of manuscript and printed material relating to their history.[73] Much of this material was generated to support the sophisticated organisational structure which Friends had created. Minute books were kept by the local Meetings to record all aspects of daily business – when separations occurred among Friends the keeping of minute books seems to have been regarded as a sign of legitimacy – both with the world, within the Meeting itself, and with other local and national Meetings.[74]

In London the Yearly Meeting Minutes recorded both the annual accounts of Truth's prosperity and sufferings which were sent in by the various Quarterly Meetings, and also the debates which took place on major issues within the Society. In addition, the Yearly Meeting acted as correspondent to the various Yearly or Half-Yearly Meetings in Ireland, Europe and the Colonies. A Yearly Meeting epistle, representing the sense of each years' Meeting, was printed annually and distributed to the Quarterly Meetings along with written epistles to counties dealing with more specific matters.[75]

Much of the Yearly Meeting's business was formulated by the Meeting for Sufferings, which met at least weekly from 1675 onwards, acting in effect as Friends' standing executive committee. Its minutes contain detailed accounts of Friends' political activities, and also record the correspondence which passed between the Quarterly Meetings and their executive committee. Much of this related to legal business, frequently cases of prosecution and persecution involving Friends in the counties. Legal opinions were sought from counsel in important cases where precedents might be established, and these were distributed to the counties (and were also recorded in a separate series of manuscript volumes);[76] in addition advice was offered by the Meeting as to how Friends should answer the process of the law. The Meeting also dealt with matters relating to publications in conjunction with the Morning Meeting of Ministers, and with serious matters of discipline.

In addition to these purely administrative records, Friends also kept meticulous records of sufferings, which reveal with graphic intensity the collision between the Quaker conscience and the civil and ecclesiastical authorities. Detailed accounts of sufferings were drawn up and scrutinised by local Meetings, generally being recorded (as in Lancashire) in a Quarterly Meeting Book of Sufferings. In addition, after checking, copies of these accounts were sent to London (normally in the care of those Friends attending Yearly Meeting) where they were again checked for discrepancies before being entered in the Great Book of Sufferings.[77] The reasons for keeping a record of sufferings were threefold. Firstly, they provided raw data from which petitions and pamphlets could be compiled. Secondly, they provided a source of inspiration to Friends and a clear guide to Quakerly conduct. Thirdly, they confirmed Friends' place in Protestant history.

In the first place, the suffering records provided an archive from which examples could be drawn to be presented to Parliament or persons in

authority, with a view to influencing their actions favourably on Friends'
behalf.[78] As an archive it was plundered ruthlessly by Friends in order to
highlight the worst excesses of the legal system against them. Friends had
been advised by George Fox, that

> if any eminent case of suffering hath or does happen, be very p'ticular
> and express therein, and with those cases of your sufferings it might be
> well, as any Friend or Friends have it in their hearts, to write a brief
> epistle to the judges (long ones they'll not like) therein desiring them
> to represent your suffering case to the King upon their return to
> London.[79]

The extent to which Friends produced "eminent" cases from their
records has been highlighted by Norman Hunt, who has shown that the
claims they made to Parliament in 1736 relating to tithe prosecutions were
grossly exaggerated.[80] However, it should be remembered that these
exaggerations were the product of the selection and editorial process
carried out in London by those compiling the pamphlets etc. that were to
be presented to Parliament. The records themselves were compiled only
after thorough checking both at local and national level to ensure that they
contained a true account of the proceedings against Friends.

Even critics of the Quakers, whilst questioning the use to which their
records might be put, did not think to question their accuracy. So,
according to one hostile pamphlet, the Quakers had

> a Register of their Sufferings (which have been inflicted for their
> Breach of the Laws) thereby to render the Governors and Government
> odious for Persecution, to Posterity. And do threaten, in After-ages, to
> publish the same, when the reasons of the things, and the matters of
> Fact, may be forgotten[81]

However, when Friends came to publish a compilation of their
suffering records they were less concerned to render the government
odious than to "exhibit to Posterity a Variety of rare and Singular
Instances of a People remarkable for their Christian Zeal".[82] This was the
second function of recording sufferings, to mould future Quaker
behaviour by reference to the past. It was intended in 1738 that,

> the Example of their Ancestors may reprove the present Degeneracy of
> too many, who by Speech and Behaviour proclaim their Declension,
> from that Plainness and simplicity in both, which those that went
> before them conscientiously practised and suffered for ... [83]

Friends were also to look to the past, not only to find worthy examples
of behaviour, but also to confirm their place in Protestant historiography.
The suffering records showed how the primitive Spirit of Protestantism

reviving among the Quakers, constrained them to testify, and enabled them to suffer under Penal Laws, enacted by degenerate Protestants.[84]

Such sufferings could be compared with those of the "first Reformers in England" at the hands of the Church of Rome (Friends no doubt had in mind those contained in Foxe's *Book of Martyrs*) in order to show how similar they were to those of the early Friends at the hands of a church that was reformed only in name.[85] This sense of historical mission was the main dynamic in Quaker belief. Friends had "incessantly laboured" to carry on the Reformation, and

> do yet stedfastly persist, as becometh a Race of true Protestant Reformers, more zealous for the Extirpation of Popery, than any that ever went before them.[86]

It is from these Quaker administrative and suffering records that the bulk of the source material used in this book is drawn. In order to establish a national perspective I have consulted the first twenty-eight volumes of the Minutes of the Meeting for Sufferings, covering the period 1675–1749, from which it is possible not only to trace the changing conduct of the Society in relation to the political establishment, but also its relationships with the Quarterly Meetings in the counties, particularly Lancashire. It is also possible to judge the degree of interaction between Friends and the Establishment from accounts of meetings with officials and "Persons in Power" contained in the Minutes. They also provide much information on events in the counties which do not appear in the local records. In addition I have consulted the relevant Yearly Meeting Minutes for the period, and also those volumes of the Great Book of Sufferings which include data relating to Lancashire.[87] This corpus of material relating to Friends' central administration has been supplemented by a variety of other manuscript material held in the Library of the Society of Friends, notably the bound manuscript Portfolio series of correspondence.[88] In general the survival of letters and other ephemera from the late seventeenth and early eighteenth century compares poorly with that which has survived from the early years of the Society, which is mainly preserved in the Swarthmore Collection of manuscripts.[89] However, it has been possible to locate some official correspondence in the Portfolio series between Lancashire Quarterly Meeting and the Meeting for Sufferings, and also personal correspondence concerning Friends and events in Lancashire.

Material relating to Lancashire Meetings had, with the exception of the minutes of the various Swarthmore Meetings which are held in London, been drawn from the archive presently housed at the Friends' Meeting House, Lancaster.[90] I have consulted the Lancashire Quarterly Meeting Minutes and the Women's Quarterly Meeting Minutes, which give a clear picture of events throughout the county and provide a useful barometer of Northern Quaker sentiment towards London during the period under discussion.[91] The Quarterly Meeting Book of Sufferings has been used as my main source for data relating to tithe prosecutions.[92]

In order to discover how Friends acted at the local level, particularly in relation to those aspects of their behaviour which brought them into contact or conflict with the authorities, I have also consulted the following local administrative material: the minutes of Lancaster Monthly Meeting, Lancaster Women's Monthly Meeting, Lancaster Particular Meeting and Lancaster Women's Particular Meeting.[93]

Minute books relating to the Monthly and Particular Meetings at Swarthmore (housed at the Library of the Society of Friends in London) have also been used.[94] The archive at Lancaster also contains various manuscript volumes containing copies of official epistles sent from London, legal advices etc., and numerous bundles of business papers and letters of which I have also made use.[95]

In addition to providing an almost intimidating volume of manuscript material, seventeenth and eighteenth century Quakers were also prolific authors. By 1700 Friends had produced some 3,853 printed broadsides, pamphlets and books, and there is no evidence to suggest that their literary prowess diminished noticeably in the eighteenth century.[96] The type of material published varied enormously, and included autobiographical tracts and posthumously published journals, editions of collected works, doctrinal works, edited collections of sufferings, and appeals to the King or Houses of Parliament.[97] Much of this material is held in the Library of the Society of Friends in London, but I have also been fortunate to have had access to the Quaker Collection of printed books in Lancaster University Library, and a small number of printed works held in the archive at Lancaster Friends Meeting House.[98] In general I have consulted those works which either relate directly to issues which brought Friends' and the authorities into conflict, notably tithes and oaths, or otherwise which have some relationship, either by subject or author, with Lancashire and the North-West.

The book begins by drawing heavily on the collected writings of the Lancashire Quaker, Richard Hubberthorn, in an attempt to define Quaker attitudes towards the Establishment.[99] Hubberthorn, a member of the Valiant Sixty, is one of those early Friends whose life, work, and early death has passed into Quaker mythology.[100] The majority of Friends have remained largely ignored by Quaker historians who have concentrated instead on those who were either prolific authors, or who occupied the centre stage in London by virtue of their political or ministering activities.[101] The views and opinions of other less public Friends have generally gone by default, the assumption being that the unknown majority shared the views of the known minority. However, it is frequently the experiences and attitudes of the Friends in the counties, who refused to swear when called to by officials, or who refused to allow the tithe farmer into his or her fields, which reveal the true nature of the Quaker relationship with the authorities. I hope that if I have achieved nothing else in writing this work, that I have at least enabled some of these unknown Friends in Lancashire to speak for themselves, in the process allowing them to correct a number of misconceptions which have arisen because of a concentration by historians on the known few.

REFERENCES

1. I shall use the descriptions Quaker and Friend interchangeably throughout this book. Although the main emphasis of this study is on the period 1660–1730, evidence will be drawn from the period c.1647–1745 in order to allow both for thematic continuity and a continuity of argument.

2. For this relationship see, for example, I.M. Green, *The Re-Establishment of the Church of England 1660–1663* (Oxford, 1978), *passim.*; R.A. Beddard, 'The Restoration Church', in J.R. Jones (ed.), *The Restored Monarchy 1660–1688* (London, 1979), pp.155–175; Norman Sykes, *Church and State in England in the XVIIIth Century* (Cambridge, 1934), *passim.*

3. The title of Richard Clark's thesis is 'The Quakers and the Church of England, 1675–1718: a study in intellectual and ecclesiastical history'; he has published some initial findings in '"The Gangreen of Quakerism": An Anti-Quaker Anglican Offensive in England after the Glorious Revolution', *Journal of Religious History*, 11 (1981), pp.404–29

4. See, for example, John Bossy, *The English Catholic Community 1570–1850* (London, 1975), pp.91–95; Christopher Haigh, *Reformation and Resistance in Tudor Lancashire* (Cambridge, 1975), *passim.*; B. Nightingale, *Lancashire Nonconformity; or sketches, historical and descriptive of the Congregational and Old Presbyterian Churches in the County* (6 vols., Manchester, 1890–93), *passim.*; B. Nightingale, *Early Stages of the Quaker Movement in Lancashire* (London, 1921), *passim.*; A.B. Anderson, 'Lancashire Quakers and Persecution' (University of Lancaster, MA thesis, 1971), *passim.*; R.C. Richardson, *Puritanism in north-west England. A regional study of the diocese of Chester to 1642* (Manchester, 1972), *passim.*

5. See, for example, William Farrer and J. Brownbill (eds.), *The Victoria History of the County of Lancaster* (8 vols., London, 1906–11), *passim.*; Thomas Baines, *Lancashire and Cheshire, past and present: a history and a Description … from the earliest ages to the present time* (2 vols., London, 1867), *passim.*; J.D. Marshall, *Lancashire* (Newton Abbott, 1974), *passim.*; and C.M.L. Bouch, *Prelates and People of the Lake Counties. A History of the Diocese of Carlisle* (Kendal, 1948), *passim.* For the economic history of the area in the early modern period see Alfred Fell, *The Early Iron Industry of Furness and District: an historical account from the earliest times to the end of the eighteenth century* (Ulverston, 1908), *passim.*; A.P. Wadsworth and J. de Lacey Mann, *The Cotton Trade and Industrial Lancashire* (Manchester, 1931), *passim.*; and F. Walker, *Historical Geography of Southwest Lancashire before the Industrial Revolution* (Chetham Soc., n.s. 103, 1939), *passim.* The following unpublished theses provide much information on the economic and social history of the North-West during the period under discussion: J.V. Beckett, 'Landownership in Cumbria, c.1680–1750' (University of Lancaster, Ph.D. thesis, 1975); B.G. Blackwood, 'Social and Religious Aspects of the History of Lancashire, 1635–1655' (University of Oxford, B.Litt. thesis, 1956); W. King, 'The Economic and

Demographic Development of Rossendale' (University of Leicester, Ph.D. thesis, 1979); C.B. Phillips, 'The Gentry in Cumberland and Westmorland 1600–65' (University of Lancaster, Ph.D. thesis, 1974)

6. For this view see Christopher Hill, *Change and Continuity in Seventeenth Century England* (London, 1974), pp.3–47; Hugh Barbour, *The Quakers in Puritan England* (London, 1964), pp.72–84; Richardson, *op.cit.* pp.1–17

7. This commonly used phrase was first coined by Dr Thomas Hodgkin: see, Ernest E. Taylor, *The Valiant Sixty* (London, 1947), p.10. For a short guide to early Quaker belief see W.C. Braithwaite, *Spiritual Guidance in the Experience of the Society of Friends* (London, 1909), *passim*. Howard H. Brinton's *The Religious Philosophy of Quakerism. The Beliefs of Fox, Barclay, and Penn as Based on the Gospel of John* (Wallingford, Penn., 1973) is a thoughtful and stimulating guide to early Quaker thought. The best source for Quaker belief and practice in the late seventeenth and early eighteenth centuries remains Barclay's *Apology, passim*.

8. Quoted in Barbour, *The Quakers in Puritan England*, p.72

9. Hugh Barbour and Arthur Roberts (eds.), *Early Quaker Writings* (Grand Rapids, Michigan, 1973), p.93

10. Richard Hubberthorn, *The Cause of Stumbling Removed from all that will receive the Truth* (1657), in *A Collection*, p.172

11. *Journal*, p.174

12. A.R. Barclay (ed.), *Letters to Early Friends* (London, 1841), p.5

13. Barbour and Roberts (eds.), *Early Quaker Writings*, pp.65, 71

14. Taylor, *op.cit.* p.44

15. Their history is told in *ibid.* and Elfrida Vipont, *George Fox and the Valiant Sixty* (London, 1975), *passim*. For accounts of the earliest Friends see also Norman Penney (ed.) *The First Publishers of Truth* (London, 1907), *passim,*; for Lancashire see also Henry J. Cadbury, 'First Publishers of Truth in Lancashire', *JFHS*, 31 (1934), pp.3–19

16. Taylor, *op.cit.* pp.42–43; for Quaker links with Seeker congregations, see *Beginnings*, pp.78–97

17. Taylor, *op.cit.* pp.42–43

18. Barbour, *The Quakers in Puritan England*, pp.83–84

19. *Beginnings*, p.135

20. Barclay, *op.cit.* p.312

21. *Journal*, p.373

22. *Beginnings*, pp.327–38

23. Barclay, *op.cit.* pp.312–13

24. *Journal*, p.114–16; *Beginnings*, pp.98–104. Accounts of Margaret Fell's life can be found in the following: Maria Webb, *The Fells of Swarthmoor Hall and their Friends, with an account of their ancestor Anne Askew, the Martyr* (London, 1865) *passim.*; Helen Crossfield, *Margaret Fox of Swarthmoor Hall* (London, 1913), *passim.*; Isabel Ross, *Margaret Fell Mother of Quakerism* (London, 1949), *passim*. Margaret Fell's first husband, Judge Thomas Fell, died in 1658; although in 1669 she married George Fox – "in part the marriage was intended to end rumours of an illicit relationship between the two, but more probably it was intended as a symbolic union of men and women Friends..." I have, in order to avoid confusion, referred to her throughout the book as Margaret Fell. For the above view of her marriage, see the entry by Craig Horle in Richard Greaves and Robert Zaller (eds.),

Biographical Dictionary of British Radicals in the Seventeenth Century (London, 1982), vol.1, p.274

25. B.G. Blackwood, *The Lancashire Gentry and the Great Rebellion, 1640–60* (Chetham Soc., 3rd series, 25, 1978), pp.89, 94; Ross, *op.cit.* pp.3–4, 115– 24
26. *Beginnings*, p.134
27. *Second Period*, pp.9–15
28. Some of the motives for persecution are discussed in more detail below in chapters 2 and 6
29. B.S. Capp, *The Fifth Monarchy Men* (London, 1972), pp.199–200
30. *Second Period*, p.7
31. Among the victims were James Nayler, Thomas Aldam, George Fox the Younger, Edward Burrough, Richard Hubberthorn, Samuel Fisher, Richard Farnsworth and Francis Howgill: Christopher Hill, *The Experience of Defeat* (London, 1984), p.166. Fox described part of the prison at Launceston, Cornwall, where Quakers were kept, thus: "a nasty stinking place where they said few people came out alive; where they used to put witches and murderers before their execution; where the prisoners excrements had not been carried out for scores of years, as it was said. It was all like mire, and in some places at the top of the shoes in water and piss, and never a house of office in the place, nor chimney!" *Journal*, p.252
32. Hill, *The Experience of Defeat*, p.166
33. For an account of this, see *Second Period*, pp.251–89
34. For the Wilkinson-Story separation see *Second Period*, pp.290–323
35. *Second Period*, p.309
36. Thomas O'Malley, "'Defying the Powers and Tempering the Spirit", A Review of Quaker Control over their publications 1672–1689', *Journal of Ecclesiastical History*, 33 (1982), p.75
37. *ibid.* p.76
38. *ibid.* pp.72–88
39. *Second Period*, pp.279–81; Arnold Lloyd, *Quaker Social History 1669–1738* (London, 1950), pp.150–53
40. Eric Evans, "'Our Faithful Testimony" – The Society of Friends and Tithe Payments, 1690–1730', *JFHS*, 52 (1969), p.115; *Political Associations*, pp.2–112. For a summary of the functions of the Meeting for Sufferings, see, Lloyd, *op.cit.* pp.84–93
41. *Epistles from the Yearly Meeting of Friends, Held in London, to the Quarterly and Monthly Meetings in Great Britain, Ireland, and Elsewhere, from 1681 to 1817* (London, 1818), p.v. For the Yearly Meeting, see Lloyd, *op.cit.* pp.134–46
42. The development of the Monthly Meetings is discussed in *Second Period*, pp.251–60. I base my remarks on the functions of Quarterly, Monthly and Particular Meetings on L. Hugh Doncaster, *Quaker Organisation and Business Meetings* (London, 1958), pp.13–17
43. Although, when citing material drawn from LQMM, I have not distinguished between the Quarterly Meeting and Quarterly Meeting for Sufferings, the latter of which was a sub–committee reporting to and advising the former. Its membership was drawn from that of the Quarterly Meeting
44. For the regional history of Quakerism in the county see: Elisabeth Brockbank, 'The Story of Quakerism in the Lancaster District', *JFHS*, 36 (1939), pp.3–20; Robert Muschamp, 'The Society of Friends in the

Lancaster District in the Seventeenth Century', *TLCAS*, 42 (1926), pp.21–41; Michael Mullett (ed.), *Early Lancaster Friends* (Lancaster, Centre for North-West Regional Studies Occasional Paper no. 5, 1978), *passim*.; Harper Gaythorpe, 'Swarthmoor Meeting-house, Ulverston; A Quaker Stronghold', *TC&WA&AS*, n.s. 6 (1906), pp.237– 83; Ross, *Margaret Fell Mother of Quakerism*, pp.67–88; Robert Muschamp, 'Historical Notes on the Society of Friends or Quakers in Manchester in the Seventeenth Century', *TLCAS*, 31 (1913), pp.45–62; Robert Muschamp, 'The Society of Friends in the Bolton District', *TLCAS*, 45 (1928), pp.32–43; Robert Muschamp, 'The Society of Friends, Bury District in the 17th Century' (reprinted from the *Bury Guardian*, October 21st, 28th, November 4th, 1933), *passim*.; W.E. Axon, 'The Pemburtons of Aspull and Philadelphia, and some Passages in the Early History of Quakerism in Lancashire', *TLCAS*, 30 (1912), pp.153–63; Robert Muschamp, 'The Society of Friends in the Seventeenth Century with a few Later Notes', *TLCAS*, 46 (1929), pp.78–92; James Murphy, 'The Old Quaker Meeting House in Hackins Hey, Liverpool', *THSLC*, 106 (1954), pp.79–98; M. Muriel Shearer, *Quakers in Liverpool* (Liverpool, 1982), *passim*.; W.S. Weeks, *Clitheroe in the Seventeenth Century* (Clitheroe, 1923), *passim*.

45. For Quakerism in Preston, see, Dilworth Abbatt, *Quaker Annals of Preston and the Fylde, 1653–1900* (London, 1931), *passim*.

46. Brockbank, 'The Story of Quakerism in the Lancaster District', pp.7–14

47. These Meetings have been identified from the data presented in Appendices 3 & 4

48. Michael Watts, *The Dissenters* (Oxford, 1978), p.509

49. These were Bickerstaffe; Blackrod; Bradley Hall (Near Chipping); Briercliffe; Collingfield (near Cartmel); Colthouse; Coppull; Duckinshaw; Flookburgh; Freckleton; Great Singleton; Grimsargh; Haigh; Hardshaw; Haslingden; Heaton Norris; Kellet; Knowsley; Lancaster; Liverpool; Manchester; Marsden; Mitton (near Clitheroe); Neatby (Out-Rawcliffe); Newton-in-Cartmel; Oldham; Penketh; Preston; Radcliffe; Rossendale; Samlesbury; Spooner Close (Hawkshead); Stangend (Hawkshead); Swarthmore; Waddicar; Winstanley; Yealand. HMC *Kenyon*, pp.230–31; Nightingale, *Early Stages of the Quaker Movement in Lancashire*, pp.182–89. For Quaker Meetings for Worship, see Lloyd, *op.cit.* pp.121–33; Richard Bauman, *Let Your Words be Few. Symbolism of Speaking and Silence among Seventeenth Century Quakers* (Cambridge, 1983) pp.120–36

50. Nightingale, *Early Stages of the Quaker Movement in Lancashire*, pp.189–97. These places for worship were at: Alston; Ashton in Makerfield; Brindle; Butterworth; Clitheroe; Coniston Crompton; Dalton; Gaite (near Tunstall); Garstang; Goosnargh; Haighton; Hawkshead; Hothersall; Kirkham; Langtree; Lanshaw (near Colne); Little Eccleston; Padiham; Pendle; Penington; Poulton; Ramsgreave; Thornley (with Wheatley); Ulverston; Wavertree; Wray

51. See Appendix 4

52. The assumption that tithe sufferers were likely to be heads of households (male or female) is my own; for family/household size, see Peter Laslett, 'Size and Structure of the Household in England over Three Centuries', *Population Studies*, 23 (1969), p.211; E.A. Wrigley and R.S. Schofield, 'English Population History from Family Reconstitution: Summary Results

1600–1799', *Population Studies*, 37 (1983), p.176, table 12

53. Some indication of the number of Friends not liable to pay tithes in the county is given in Appendix 3

54. See Appendix 3

55. J.S. Rowntree, *Quakerism Past and Present* (London, 1859), pp.68–88

56. These figures are arrived at using data presented in *ibid*. p.81, n.6

57. Watts, *The Dissenters*, p.509. For a detailed discussion of his sources, see *ibid*. pp.490–508. For a further confirmation of this decline in numbers, see John Burgess, 'The Quakers, the Brethren and the Religious Census in Cumbria', *TC&WA&AS*, n.s. 80 (1980), pp.103–111

58. Watts, *The Dissenters*, p.509

59. *ibid*.

60. *ibid*. p.285

61. A.B. Anderson, 'Lancashire Quakers and Persecution' (University of Lancaster, MA thesis, 1978), pp.72–79; Alan Cole, 'The Social Origins of the Early Friends', *JFHS*, 48 (1956–58), pp.99–118

62. *ibid*. p.116

63. *ibid*. p.117

64. Anderson, *op.cit.* pp.76–77

65. *ibid*. p.77; for Cole's occupational data for Lancashire see Watts, *op.cit.* p.350

66. Richard T. Vann, 'Quakerism and the Social Structure in the Interregnum', *Past and Present*, 43 (1969), p.72

67. Richard T. Vann, *The Social Development of English Quakerism* (Cambridge, Mass., 1969), pp.78–79

68. *ibid*. p.164

69. Judith Jones Hurwich, 'The Social Origins of the Early Quakers', *Past and Present*, 48 (1970), pp.159, 162; see also Vann's reply, 'Rejoinder to Judith Jones Hurwich', *Past and Present*, 48 (1970), pp.162–64

70. Barry Reay, 'The Social Origins of Early Quakerism', *Journal of Interdisciplinary History*, 11 (1980), p.67; William Wayne Spurrier, 'The Persecution of the Quakers in England, 1650–1714' (University of North Carolina, Chapel Hill, Ph.D. thesis, 1976), p.301

71. Margaret Spufford, 'Status of some Seventeenth Century Rural Dissenters', in Derek Baker (ed.), *Studies in Church History*, vol.8 (Oxford, 1972), pp.203–11

72. This is an impression drawn from a wide reading of Quaker suffering records, and also two published collections of Quakers wills from the North-West; J. Somervell, *Some Westmorland Wills 1686–1738* (Kendal, 1928), *passim.*; W.G. Collingwood, 'A Book of Old Quaker Wills', *TC&WA&AS*, 29 (1929), pp.1–38. The gradual accumulation of wealth is also reflected in the pages of William Stout's autobiography, see *Stout, passim.*

73. Perhaps surprisingly there is no comprehensive guide to Quaker records. However, some information may be gleaned from Edward H. Milligan and Malcolm J. Thomas, *My Ancestors were Quakers, How can I find out more about them?* (London, The Society of Genealogists, 1983), *passim.*

74. See, for the keeping of minute books during a separation at Reading in the 1670s, *Second Period*, pp.470–71

75. These printed epistles are published in *Epistles from the Yearly meeting of Friends, op.cit. passim*. For the Yearly Meeting see also Lloyd, *op.cit.* pp.134–46

76. LSF, Book of Cases, vol.1, 1661–1695, vol.2, 1695–1738, vol.3, 1739–1806, vol.4, 1802–1818

77. So Lancashire Friends were advised to "bring a true account of all such corn as was taken from them, the value as near they can and when and by whom taken". (LQMM, vol.1, 5/11/1686). They were to "bring up a full value thereof as near as they can with the day of the month and year and the persons names that do take it with what witnesses they can get. And that this account be brought up by the Particular Meeting to the Monthly Meeting and be transcribed and brought up to the Meeting here for Sufferings". (LQMM, vol.1, 6/2/1687). It was emphasised that "the Monthly Meeting, after the same be brought before them, take care to see the same sufferings be carefully perfected and digested before the bringing up the same to the Meeting of Sufferings". (LQMM, vol.1, 6/2/1693). For the extent to which suffering accounts sent to London were subsequently checked before any publication, see the case of Robert Hubberstey below, chapter 2; and *Besse*, vol.1, p.lv

78. Between 1650 and 1699 Friends published some 252 petitions or appeals to Parliament or other authorities; in addition they published 248 pamphlets or broadsides which contained abstracts or listings of sufferings. Barbour and Roberts (eds.), *op.cit.* pp.567–73

79. Port 16.34, George Fox and others to Friends, London, 8/5/1680

80. *Political Associations*, pp.64–72

81. Edward Beekham, Henry Meriton and Lancaster Topcliffe, *A Brief Discovery of some of the Blasphemous and Seditious Principles and Practises of the People called Quakers; Taken out of their Most Noted and Approved Authors* (London, 1699), p.25. When the authorities seized a Quaker "register book" from Friends in York in 1670 it was remarked that they contained "a very methodical record of their sufferings": CSPD, 1670, p.542

82. *Besse*, p.lii

83. *Besse*, p.liii

84. *Besse*, p.liv

85. *Besse*, p.liv; see also Barbour, *The Quakers in Puritan England*, p.189

86. *Besse*, p.liv

87. LYMM, vols.1–9, 1672–1747; GBS, vols.1, 3, 5, 7, 8, 11, 14, 16–21, 1650–1750

88. The series comprises 42 volumes

89. The Swarthmore Manuscripts held in the Library of the Society of Friends comprise seven volumes of letters and papers, the majority of which concern the early years of the Society. Nineteenth century transcripts to the MSS are housed at LSF. See also, G.F. Nuttall, *Early Quaker Letters: A Calendar of the Swarthmore Manuscripts, vols.1, 2 and 4, 1652–1660* (unpublished typescript, available at LSF and other major libraries), *passim*. A typescript listing of vol.7, prepared by Craig Horle, is available at LSF. Other associated collections in LSF are Abraham MSS, Audland Letters 1653, Spence MSS, A.R. Barclay MSS (this forms the core of the material printed in Barclay (ed.), *Letters of Early Friends*), Caton MSS, and the Spence MSS. Typescript listings and indexes to all of these collections, prepared by Craig Horle, are available at LSF. Most of the material contained in these collections relates to the first thirty years of Quakerism only

90. Michael Mullett and Ralph Randles, *An inventory of the documents and muniments kept in the Friends Meeting House in Lancaster* (unpublished typescript available in LFMH, The Library of the University of Lancaster

etc., 1976); for a brief description of this collection, see Michael Mullett, 'Historical Documents at Friends Meeting House Lancaster', *JFHS*, 54 (1976), pp.33–34

91. LQMM, vols.1–2, 1669–1776; LWQMM, vol.1, 1675–1777
92. LQMS, vols.1–3, 1654–1743
93. LMMM, vols.1–2, 1675–1767; LWMMM, vol.1, 1676–1749; LPMM, vols.1–2, 1698–1795; LWPMM, vol.1, 1737–1799
94. SMMM, vols.1–4, 1668–1762; (vol.2, 1674–1691, *wanting*); SWMMM, vols.1–4, 1671–1771; (vol.3, 1717–1731, *wanting*); SPMM, vols.1–2, 1699–1756; SWPMM, vol.1, 1712–1755
95. It should be noted that some of the business papers and documents originally preserved in the Lancaster Meeting House were destroyed by fire in 1851. When the fire was discovered police gained entry to the Meeting House and "found that the fire arose from some burning documents in the old iron chest in which they were deposited, and which had been forced open. Water was procured as soon as possible, and the flames extinguished, but not before a great portion of the papers were irretrievably destroyed". The fire was started by vandals. *Lancaster Guardian*, 10th May 1851, quoted in Robert Muschamp, 'The Society of Friends in the Lancaster District in the Seventeenth Century', p.24
96. Barbour and Roberts (ed.), *op.cit.* pp.567–73; for a bibliography of Quaker writings see Joseph Smith, *A Descriptive Catalogue of Friends' Books ... From their First Rise to the Present Time* (2 vols., London, 1867), *passim.*; and his *Bibliotheca Anti-Quakeriana; or a Catalogue of Books Adverse to the Society of Friends* (London, 1873), *passim*. Early Quaker writings relating to Lancashire are described in Henry Fishwick's 'Quaker Lancashire Literature of the Seventeenth Century', *TLCAS*, 5 (1887), pp.105–16
97. Barbour and Roberts (eds.), *op.cit.* pp.567–73
98. For the Quaker Collection, see John S. Andrews, 'Some Early Quaker Material in the University of Lancaster Library', *Gutenberg-Jahrbuch*, 1976, pp.333–39; for printed material at LFMH, see Michael Mullett, 'Historical Records and Early Printed Books at Lancaster Quaker Meeting House', *Gutenberg-Jahrbuch*, 1978, pp.358–62
99. See *A Collection, passim.*
100. For his life, as told by a Quaker historian, see Elisabeth Brockbank, *Richard Hubberthorne of Yealand, Yeoman-Soldier-Quaker, 1628–1662* (London, 1929), *passim.*
101. This generalisation can be sustained by a rapid survey of the available Quaker biographies, which concentrate mainly on Fells, Foxes, Frys, Penn and Woolman, or by a scan through the indexes of histories such as *Second Period*

1

The Quakers and
the Establishment

The Quaker attitude to civil government was fashioned by two sets of obligations. These were clearly defined in a petition addressed to the Quarter Sessions at Lancaster in January 1661, written by Quakers imprisoned during the clampdown on Dissent which followed the abortive Fifth Monarchist rising that had taken place some twelve months earlier. In the petition Friends demanded "that as becometh Saints we may serve our God, and as Subjects we may serve our King and Country in all just Requirings".[1] Many of the tensions and strains that existed both within the Society, and between it and the government arose because of the difficulty that Friends, both as individuals and as geographically united groups, encountered in trying to reconcile these two forms of service. Friends faced a further problem in attempting to arrive at a definition of the "just Requirings" of government that both satisfied the state and maintained Truth's testimonies. Two areas in which unsatisfactory definitions led to conflict both between Quakers and the state and between Friends themselves, namely oaths and tithes, will be discussed in detail in later chapters.[2]

It is my intention here to examine, first, how Friends viewed government, and what roles they felt it should undertake. This will be done mainly with reference to the written works of Lancashire Quakers. Secondly some consideration will be made of the practical, and often pragmatic, definition of the government's "just Requirings" that Friends arrived at, and of the problems that Friends encountered in trying to meet such requirements. The nature of the evidence for this second section is such that reference will be made to the activities and views of Friends throughout England and Wales, though wherever possible a North-West "flavour" will be retained. The general purpose of this chapter is to lay the groundwork for the more detailed discussion of North-West, and more particularly, Lancashire, Quakerism that follows.

The attitude of early Friends towards civil government can be seen clearly in the writings of the Lancashire Quaker, Richard Hubberthorn. Born at Yealand in 1628, Hubberthorn was the son of a farmer who held land under customary tenure from Sir George Middleton, the Catholic-

royalist lord of the manor of Yealand. Hubberthorn was educated at the
Free Grammar School at Warton and worked for a time with his father on
the land. In 1648 he joined the army, was rapidly promoted to the rank of
captain, and served in the cavalry under Fairfax, and under Cromwell at
the battles of Dunbar and Worcester. In 1651 he returned to Yealand, and
following his father's death in the mid-1650s he took over the tenancy of
the family farm.[3] As a tenant of Sir George Middleton he was to be
involved in a bitter dispute between tenant and landlord on the Yealand
manor which involved the imposition by the lord of the manor of allegedly
excessive and arbitrary fines and entry fees. This dispute was under way in
1649, and was not resolved fully until 1659.[4] By that time Hubberthorn
was active as a Quaker minister, having been convinced following a
meeting with George Fox in 1652. He travelled widely throughout the
country but in 1662 became one of the many prominent young Friends to
die in the post-Restoration repression of dissenting groups, leaving the
unchallenged leadership of the movement to George Fox. Although
apparently of slight constitution, Hubberthorn possessed many of the
virtues traditionally associated with the northern yeoman, "he was very
wise, and knew his season when to speak and when to be silent; and when
he spoke, it was with much discretion and deliberation".[5]

Hubberthorn, like virtually every other Friend who put pen to paper,
was certainly discreet in his remarks concerning civil power. He wrote
shortly after the Restoration that Friends were, and always had been

> obedient subjects under every Power ordained of God, and to every
> ordinance of man (set up by him) for the Lord's sake, whether unto
> King as Supream, or unto Governours or any set up in authority by
> him, who are for the punishment of evil-doers, and for the praise of
> them that do well, ...[6]

Spiritual legitimacy, however, although the mark of a government to
be obeyed, did not guarantee in itself a government that was good. Laws
might be unjust, but as Hubberthorn had written three years earlier,
"Magistrates are to be honoured by subjection to their just commands,
Requests and Laws; and by patient sufferings under their corrupt Laws
and evil Commands, and not resisting evil ...." Governments appointed by
God were to be obeyed, no matter how oppressive, and Friends could not
act "by outward opposition, as rebellion, by insurrection, plots or carnal
weapons", for, as Hubberthorn wrote, "that is contrary to our life".[7]

This Quaker statement of non-resistance or at the most passive
resistance, was in accord with protestant views of the citizen's obligations to
the magistrate which had developed since the Reformation. According to
Luther, God had commanded obedience to magistrates, good or bad.[8] This
doctrine was enshrined in English political thought during the sixteenth
century. Theorists allowed that where a tyrant gave commands which were
contrary to God's, then the tyrant could be disobeyed. However, any

subsequent punishment imposed by the tyrant had to be endured by the transgressor without either complaint or resistance. Active resistance to the magistrate could not be justified, and would without question lead to anarchy.[9] Even the most hardened sceptic would have agreed to the truth of this proposition following the disruptions of the Civil-War period and its aftermath. Royalist sympathisers had continued to write of the unlawfulness of active resistance, and its inevitable dire consequences, throughout the 1640s and 1650s. Late in the reign of Charles II Tory political propagandists revived the theory of passive obedience; its durability was reflected in the difficulties faced by the members of the Convention Parliament in explaining the events of 1688. Their eventual solution, that James II deserted his throne, thereby breaking his contract with the nation, left the theory of non-resistance intact.[10]

This philosophy of passive obedience did not totally prevent Friends from voicing political opposition under the rule of an identified tyrant or oppressor. Hubberthorn explained in *A short Relation of the twelve changes of Government that hath been in England within these 8 years*, published in 1660, that each of these alleged twelve governments had "had a word of Wisdom and Counsel administered unto them, what they should do that they might be established". This wisdom, although "from the Lord", was delivered "through his Servants". Thus the way was open for Quaker petitioning and pamphleteering in order to encourage the magistrate to act on behalf of Truth. Moreover, whilst Friends could not work against government, God could: the "twelve" governments of 1652–60 had all "been raised up and cast down again by one Hand and Power" and, as the Restoration establishment was clearly reminded

> it is by that immediate power of God (which hath broken them) that you must stand (if you do stand) for God is the same; and will be to you as he hath been to others, as you answer or not answer his requirings: For it is not Persons that God accepts, but he that fears God and works righteousness, is accepted of him.[11]

Hubberthorn saw the civil magistrate as the means through which a reformation of manners might be achieved in God's outward world. He frequently berated justices for their failure to apprehend brawlers, drunkards, common thieves and fraudsters whilst they prosecuted Friends for holding meetings or refusing to remove their hats to superiors. Such a justice, he said, was "no minister of God, but an encourager of evil doers, and discourager of those that do well, who declare justice from God against those who thou should act justice upon". This preponderance of evil and lewd behaviour, unpunished and sometimes encouraged by justices of the peace and magistrates was frequently alluded to by Hubberthorn and other Quaker writers. It was almost offered as a justification of their attitudes that Friends were acting in the place of a deficient and corrupt law-enforcing system.[12]

When Friends were prosecuted for their actions, the magistrate walked the narrow path between laws relating to civil affairs, and laws relating to conscience. The "Magistrates Law reaches but to the outward man to keep that in peace and good order, and not to the inward man to binde or limit that".[13] If a magistrate could be construed as acting against a Quaker simply on the grounds of his religious belief, and these were grounds to which Friends themselves gave a wide interpretation, then he had moved from the 'outward' to the 'inward'. There could be no legislation to govern this inward man: the Inner Light, as Hubberthorn told a justice at Norwich in 1654 "hath set me free from being bound to the will of any man".[14] It was according to this Light, "the light of Christ in the Conscience", that all laws were to be made, and further there would be "no law to limit to or from this or that matter of Religion". Friends thus claimed an absolute freedom of worship for all. Hubberthorn did not envisage a limited toleration guaranteed by law, such as Friends and other Dissenters were offered in 1689; "we do not mean that we would have a law according to Religion", there would simply be no law against it.[15] Freedom of worship was a natural right, independent of positive law and which no valid law could violate.

Other Friends claimed toleration on more pragmatic grounds. John Crook, a justice of the peace prior to his conversion to Quakerism in 1655 argued that by allowing Friends freedom of worship the state would boost its economy. "The denying of liberty of Conscience unto Quakers and others", he wrote, "is one cause why Trade is so decayed, and Discontent encreased …"[16] The duty of the magistrate, according to John Locke, was "that provision may be made for the security of each man's private possessions; for the peace, riches and public commodities of the whole people"; each of these was threatened by the tumults which followed on from intolerance and persecution.[17] So the Quaker Crook, like John Locke, "was content to ask for liberty in the name of trade".[18] As we shall see this was not the only occasion upon which Quakers anticipated the view of the philosopher whose theories were to underpin the political thought of the eighteenth century.[19] However, Crook, like Locke, was not writing in the eighteenth century, and the society to which he appealed apparently had little taste for his views on civil and religious polity.

It has been suggested that "in 1660 the mass of men in England … had conceded the case for religious toleration with very few reservations".[20] However, the men who governed England following the Restoration were less inclined to concede the need for religious liberty. On the contrary 1660, and more particularly 1662, saw the Church of England regain its official spiritual monopoly in England. This reflected a consensus among the governing classes, both at Westminster and in the counties, that future political and social stability rested upon religious unity. For those who wished to turn the clock back to the certainties of pre-Revolutionary society, "the Church of England had taken on its celebrated role as the vehicle for social and political conservation in the life of the nation".[21]

This reactionary vehicle tolerated no passengers. The state from which Quakers like Hubberthorn and Crook sought toleration was far in advance, both in terms of organisation and chronology, of the primitive early modern English state, "which lacked adequate natural legitimation and relied on Christian sanctions to keep subjects in order".[22] It was ironic that whilst Quakers were moving towards a purely secular view of society the religious legislation of the post-Restoration period was "making communicant membership of the established church the test of political acceptability, and, in time, social respectability". The divisions created by this intolerance of Dissent were to persist well beyond 1689.[23]

How far, if at all, did these general Quaker views of the moral scope of the state change during the period under discussion? Hubberthorn's views were echoed as early as 1661 in the petition from Friends imprisoned in Lancaster Castle already referred to: there Friends claimed they had acted no evil towards "any Person or Power appointed of God for the punishing of evil Doers, and for the Praise of them that do well", reiterating the principle of passive obedience.[24] Passive obedience was a subject touched on by Thomas Atkinson of Cartmel in his *Exhortation to all People*, published in 1684. Friends were against plotting and carnal warfare, and wished to live peaceably with the magistrate, whose "Sword was and ought to be for the punishment of Evil-doers, and for the praise of them that do well".[25] Making a rare Quaker comment on the events of 1688 George Whitehead wrote that James II

> thought himself safe both with Dissenters in allowing them their Liberties, and with the Church of England, by their Professed Doctrine of Passive Obedience and Non-Resistance; And especially Safe with the Quakers, by their Passiveness and Non Resistance …

The King, he concluded, had abdicated his throne, not through the abrogation of these principles, but rather through the actings of "Divine Providence".[26] In her controversial address to William III in 1698, Margaret Fox repeated the, by then, oft-heard denial of conspiracy against governments (as will be seen below this was most often publicly stated after periods of intense political activity, or even conspiracy, by and amongst Friends). She also added praise for the toleration granted by William and assured him of forthcoming rewards from a higher authority.[27] With the laws against Quaker Meetings conditionally suspended, the call for freedom of worship receded from Friends' writings, and official campaigning concentrated on the tithe question. Friends continued in their regular and increasingly high-pitched denials of opposition towards any government established by God, but they also found themselves frequently called upon to add thanks for favours granted by the authorities. As these favours increased, so Friends found themselves forced to change, or at least define, their views of reciprocal obligations towards government rather more clearly than they had done previously.

The question of Friends' obligation to government, beyond that of inert obedience, was not dealt with at any length by Hubberthorn. He confined himself to the observation, made during his famous discourse with Charles II in 1660, that Friends would be both obedient to, and assist in, a godly government, "in righteousness and civil things, both by body and Estate".[28] He offered no definition of the likely extent of this assistance, and his lack of clarity on this point reflects a general hesitancy among Friends over their participation in and with civil government, which was to continue throughout the seventeenth and eighteenth centuries. As general millenialistic hopes faded with the Restoration, so for Quakers the question of co-existing with a government that was not going to be overturned (in the immediate future) became pressing. Certainly in London, and especially in the Meeting for Sufferings, Friends seem quickly to have discarded Hubberthorn's demand, typical of the tolerationism of the 1650s, for an absolute freedom of worship for all, coming instead to expect through the passing of a number of specially constructed bills or clauses to bills, a specially protected, not to say constricted, sectarian place in the world, with a set of unique obligations to the government.[29] Outwith the obligations contained in this legislation, however, it is difficult to construct a clear Quaker "theory of service" towards the government.

Hubberthorn's offer to Charles II that Friends would actively assist government raised the issue of their direct participation in state service. The earliest development of a code concerning Friends' involvement in government activity seems to have come from a Meeting of Elders held at Balby, Yorkshire, in November 1656. The Meeting agreed that "if any be called to serve the Commonwealth in any public service which is for the public wealth and good" they should do so not least in order to set an example of righteous behaviour.[30] There are in fact numerous examples of Friends holding office before the Restoration; many of course, like Richard Hubberthorn, were involved in the army before their convincement. Others, for example the two northern Friends Gervase Benson and Anthony Pearson, had held and continued to hold, offices of justices of the peace.[31] By 1659, however, such service was less common. Edward Burrough, perhaps the most radical of early Quaker writers, complained that Friends had been deprived of their "Birthright Privelledge", that, "we have been cast out, and Rejected, cast out of places of all trust in the Nation, as if we deserved noe Place of Fidelity amongst you, noe Not to have any office, ..."[32] The willingness to serve did not, however, abate even after 1660, when the supersession of the Interregnum regime, whose godly ethos Friends tended to support, might have been expected to terminate their readiness for public duties. Margaret Fell made it clear to Charles II during one of their many interviews in 1660 that there were many Friends who were prepared to serve the new regime, but who would be prevented from doing so by the barrier of an oath.[33]

The Quaker refusal to swear, based on the scriptural imperatives "swear not at all" (Matthew 6, 34) and "let your yea be yea; and your nay,

nay" (James 5, 12) may in practice have prevented many Friends from holding office, but it did not diminish the intention or desire to serve. This point was made in a pamphlet written by George Whitehead in 1677, but not published until 1691: he wrote "when we ... offer our service to the Commonwealth; its their fault in refusing our just offer, not ours in refusing their unjust one". Whitehead was saying that Friends were acting justly, and carrying out their duties towards the state, in offering to serve. The state, on the other hand, was being unjust in demanding an oath from its would-be loyal servants. In a pamphlet addressed to Parliament in 1694, seeking legislation to ease Quakers from the burden of swearing, Friends did indeed offer to forego any form of service in government if it would ease the passage of such legislation.[34] At other times, however, Friends were at pains to establish that an oath should be no barrier to their serving even the most minor office. In 1677 the Meeting for Sufferings sought counsel's advice as to whether a Friend, if elected, could serve in the office of constable without swearing. The reply was that "it is the election which makes him an officer, and not the oath, which is but a more strict obligation upon him for the due execution of his office."[35] When, in 1723, London Friends, elected to serve as constables within the city, were refused entry to office on Affirmation, counsel was again consulted. Opinion then was that "it is true his Affirmation is not to qualify him to bear any office or place of profitt in the government, but this is neither office or place of profitt, but an office of burthen and charge".[36] In 1702, when the Occasional Conformity bill was under discussion in Parliament, Friends anxiously sought from counsel, and received, assurance that the offices of questmen, constables, church wardens, tax collectors and assessors did not require the taking of the sacraments, and would thus be outside the scope of the Act.[37]

In Lancashire 13 Friends between 1660 and 1740 were prosecuted for not swearing when summoned or elected to serve in civil offices. Of these, nine were to serve as jurymen, one as a constable, one as a church warden and two at unspecified posts. None of these Friends refused office, and in at least one case a year was served before any action was taken.[38] Clearly in other cases Friends served office willingly without any obstacles being placed in their way. Sir Roger Bradshaigh may have been thinking of Quakers when he complained in 1666 that conventicles in Warrington went unmolested, "the Constables of this Towne beinge Generally Ellected of the same stampe".[39] In 1678 a number of Friends from Swarthmore meeting were distrained for refusing to pay fines imposed under the terms of the Conventicle Act. However, a number escaped the attention of the bailiffs "upon a Friend being constable where they live, the warrant rests in his hands".[40] Richard Cawson, a Friend from Caton, served as a constable in his village and only encountered difficulties when it came to enforcing a warrant for distress against a fellow Quaker.[41] The office of constable was troublesome, unprofitable and unpopular; the constable, often reluctant to disrupt local harmony, was one of the "wretched village officers" who was "ensnared at the point where national legislative prescriptions and local customary norms intersected". The difficulty in attracting candidates for these posts may have led to a communal blind-eye being turned to Quakers who would serve only without swearing. On the other hand Friends clearly wished to be seen to be accepting their communal responsibilities in serving such offices.[42]

The short reign of James II pushed Quaker principles of service, and those of Dissenters in general, into the limelight. From 1686 the King had introduced a large number of his fellow Catholics into governmental service and in April 1687 the Declaration of Indulgence granted Dissenters freedom to worship. In an attempt to gain a firm basis of support and tie down a future Parliament to the repeal of the Penal Laws and Test, James, through his agents in the counties, set about replacing intractable county officers and corporation personnel with those of a more sympathetic nature.[43] Lancaster was one of the Corporations that was extensively reshaped: John Greenwood, a Presbyterian, was elected mayor, and seven of the ten aldermen were replaced. William Stout, the Quaker grocer, noted that in the county as a whole "Even Quakers were encouraged to undertake to be justices of the peace and magistrates in corporations, but generally declined".[44] One of those who did not decline was the Lancaster Friend, Joshua Lawson, a member of one of the town's most successful entrepreneurial families, who was appointed to the town's common council.[45] At Preston, the "regulator" of the corporation, John Scansfield, was a Quaker.[46] Elsewhere in the North, at York, Friends were considering recommending Catholics to be appointed as justices, and wondered "whether two or three Friends might not be taken into the commission with the rest".[47] In the traditional puritan regions of the South-West and East of the country, however, Friends did not fare so well; at Norwich the corporation refused to give thirty-eight Quakers their freedom without the taking of an oath, despite a letter from the sovereign ordering the suspension of the oaths. At Bristol Friends elected to the common council were fined when the oath prevented them from taking up office.[48]

This new liberty also affected the lesser office of constable following the 1687 case involving three Friends in London, who were refused office because they would not swear, although they claimed they were exempted from the oath by the King's Declaration. Friends petitioned the monarch who commanded that all "Quakers should now and for the future either be allowed to serve the said office without taking any oath, or else that they be not fined or otherwise molested upon that account".[49] This order was circulated throughout the counties in order to relieve Quaker office-holders of any difficulty they might encounter, but in June of the following year the Meeting for Sufferings in London received a letter from James Fell, a member of Swarthmore Meeting "concerning his being urged to swear to execute the office of a constable. That he showed the King's order for Friends to take the office of constableship ... to one Justice Fleming, who flighted it saying he did not matter it, without he had it under the King's broad seal". The letter was passed to William Penn in order to gain further assistance from the King but no outcome was reported in the weeks before the Revolution of 1688.[50]

The 1689 Toleration Act gave Dissenters some relief from the burden of unacceptable oaths required upon election or appointment to office. Those scrupling the oaths were allowed to act in office by deputy; in 1713 the Meeting for Sufferings drew this clause to the attention of Friends in Graythwaite, Cumberland, who had sought advice on this matter, pointing out that "Friends generally complys withall".[51] On the other hand, successive Affirmation Acts of 1696, 1714 and 1722 contained clauses that prevented Quakers from using a form of words other than the required oaths to qualify themselves to serve on juries or to hold any government office. These Acts carefully enshrined the principle that religious freedom was bought at the price of civil exclusion. In 1736 Friends from York, who had experienced some difficulty in this matter, attempted to include a clause in the proposed bill for relief from tithe prosecutions that would give "an explanation of the Affirmation Act respecting the serving of offices of sheriffs, aldermen and on juries". The Meeting for Sufferings, ever sensitive to the mood of the moment, decreed that "nothing of that nature shall be solicited for" and circulated their opinion to MPs already approached by the Yorkshiremen.[52]

However, despite on the one hand a legal embargo against Quakers participating in government, and on the other an apparent reluctance by the Meeting for Sufferings to acknowledge that Friends ever did so participate, there is considerable evidence to show that in the eighteenth century many Friends continued either to wish to serve or actually did serve in official positions.

It may be that the exceptional social, economic and numerical prominence of Lancaster Friends inclined them in an atypical way to serve their local community. It is certainly clear that in Lancaster Quakers played an important role in the local community by filling various minor official posts. Between 1709 and 1736 the Quakers Elijah Salthouse, Samuel Satterthwaite, William Stout, Edward Wallbank, Joshua Townson, John Dillworth and Thomas Tomlinson all acted as assessors of the land-tax at least once. In 1712, 1713 and 1715, Edward Wallbank, Rowland Atkinson and Joshua Townson acted as collectors of this tax, whilst in 1716 Joshua Townson and John Tomlinson acted as collectors of the window tax.[53] These posts were burdensome and unglamorous, and honesty and integrity was not always an essential qualification for appointment.[54] Friends in Lancaster, however, were clearly anxious to carry out the fiscal obligations expected from prosperous members of the community, even to the extent of overcoming the difficulties of oaths and Affirmation, scrupled by most Lancashire Friends until 1722. Such difficulties, moreover, were not always avoided; in 1703 a Westmorland Friend, Thomas Braithwaite, "was returned as an assessor of the land tax and refusing to take the affirmation was fined ten pounds".[55] Some seven years earlier, in 1696, Sir Daniel Fleming was able to write to Viscount Lonsdale that "All our Assessors have taken the Oaths except some Quakers, who were rejected by the Commissioners".[56]

Lancaster Quakers also acted as administrators of the Poor Law, this despite the existence of the Society's own system of poor relief. In 1711 Samuel Satterthwaite was elected as assessor of the poor, and also served as an overseer in 1712, as did John Dillworth in 1714.[57]

These Friends were prominent both in local Meetings (John Dillworth succeeded William Stout as clerk of the Monthly Meeting in 1734) and in business, and thus can be seen to have been fulfilling dual obligations imposed upon them by their religious beliefs to their co-religionists, and by their social status, to their fellow citizens. Despite the Corporation Act of 1661, which forbade Dissenters from holding office in municipal corporations, several of Lancaster's most eminent Quakers served as burgesses for the commonalty (common-councilmen). Robert Lawson served in 1727 and 1741, when John Lawson was also a burgess. In 1746 Abraham Rawlinson, Robert Lawson the younger, Thomas Hutton Rawlinson, Miles Birket and James Backhouse all acted as common council men.[58] Such service by Friends was recognised by William Penn, writing in 1711 before the passing of the Occasional Conformity Act, designed to keep Dissenters generally out of corporate office. Penn wrote "As we are Free-men of Corporations, and Members of Companies, by the Terms of Admission, we are bound to do in our Course the several Duties thereof, which by this Bill, we are not only rendered incapable of (viz. by the imposition of an oath of conformity, and a requirement to take the sacrament at least thrice yearly), but also subject to Fines and Penalties for not doing them".[59]

All this, however, should not be taken to imply that Friends were always welcome to participate in local government.

In York Friends were elected to serve the office of sheriff in successive years between 1717 and 1720. The taking of the sacrament, however, was rigorously enforced by the corporation, and the inevitable Quaker refusal resulted in fines of £70 for each person. Thomas Hammond wrote to the Meeting for Sufferings in 1720, complaining "that the magistrates intend for the future, as long as there are any of our Friends of tolerable ability in that city, to make choice of one every year ... if there be no prevention it will tend to the impoverishment of many families". Friends appear to have had difficulty in resolving this problem, and similar elections took place in 1726 and 1733, leading to the attempt by the Yorkshire Quarterly Meeting to clarify the legal position of Quakers elected to public office.[60] Such cases of malicious prosecution were, however, comparatively rare. It has been possible to trace only one such occurrence in Lancashire which centred on Robert Abbatt's difficulty in being made a freeman of Preston. This case dragged on for three years between 1725 and 1728, before what was described as an "accommodation" was reached between Abbatt and the town magistrates. A more serious outcome was the disillusionment that the affair provoked amongst leading members of the Quarterly Meeting for the methods of relief commonly adopted by the Meeting of Sufferings.[61]

Whatever the case with other Dissenting communities, it is clear that with the Friends "malicious" action, such as those instances above, were designed to exploit not the refusal but the statutory incapacity of Friends fully to qualify themselves for office in local government. Nonetheless, Friends were willing to assist the government by "body". They had never, as Penn pointed out "fought after any Place of Profit or Trust in the Government", but when office did come their way, most Friends were willing to oblige by serving. Writing in 1696 Thomas Ellwood stated clearly the position adopted by most Quakers when he pleaded that others should not "exclude their Fellow subjects from a share in the Care, Support and Preservation" of the "Government of England" which Friends "have as much reason as they (with respect to our Estates, Liberties, and Lives) to wish and see the Welfare and Safety of".[62] If Friends could serve with such ease, how then did they regard the question of paying taxes, particularly when they held such a clear testimony against the payment of tithes, and any other form of Church fee or rate?

Anthony Pearson in his *Great Case of Tithes*, first published in 1657, clearly defined the distinction between the obligation to meet civil demands and the demands of church or priest,

> But that I may not be mistaken, as if I went about to take away the Magistrates Power to raise Taxes, Assessments, or other charges, for the service and Defence of the Nation, it is needful to distinguish between those Things that are called Civil, and such as are called Spiritual: for civil Ends and Uses, the People may give Power to their Representatives to raise moneys, or any other civil Thing.

Such demands, made with the sanction of civil authority, were "to be paid because commanded by the State".[63] Friends found support for the payment of civil taxes in the scriptures, as with the case of oaths they were able to produce a simple maxim to state their case, "Render unto Caesar the things that are Caesar's, and unto God the things that are God's".

Friends went to great lengths to stress how willingly they wore this particular badge of citizenship, and no doubt one reason for this was a desire to distance themselves from the radicals of the 1650s, most notably the Fifth Monarchy Men, who had called for a reduction, and not infrequently an abolition, of all taxes.[64] In addition Friends were no doubt anxious to deflect some of the animus which descended upon them from the propertied classes whose tithes and impropriations they refused to pay. Their payment of "lawful" taxes proved their integrity, and served to stress the iniquity of "unlawful" tithes. George Fox, in a paper published in 1670 to convince the authorities of the peaceableness of Quaker Meetings, emphasised the extent of Quaker compliance with civil demands: "And as for the word, Disloyal to the King, We have alwayes paid our Taxes, and Assessments, and other Dues, more than any People according to our abilities". In a paper written in 1694 calling for relief in the case of oaths, Friends again stressed their importance in the maintenance of the state; they "cheerfully pay to the support of the Government; and by their Trades, and Industry (according to their Capacities) advance the National Stock".[65] This almost unrivalled zeal to fill the coffers of the Treasury was only occasionally tempered by leading Friends. In 1662, in a letter to King Charles, Margaret Fell put forward what was in effect a plea for reciprocity when she complained that "we must pay Taxes, and Assessments, Poll Money, and Chimney-Money, and Benevolence-Money to pay soldiers to fall thus violently upon us in our Houses".[66] Such complaints, however, were rare. It was only when the demands of the state were seen to invade some areas of the Quaker conscience of Friends that problems arose. Moreover, in an apparent attempt to maintain good relations with the civil governments, Quaker leaders defined this conscience so as to exclude contentious areas of Quaker thought which might have led to a refusal to pay taxes.

The new regime of William of Orange faced the considerable financial burden of overseas war. Amongst a variety of methods used to raise revenue was the poll tax which was levied on five separate occasions between 1689 and 1694.[67] The first tax, to be collected annually, set a rate of one shilling per head with specific assessments for particular ranks of persons and office holders. Among these were clergymen in receipt of an annual income of £50 or more, "and every Preacher or Teacher in any Meeting House whatsoever". This group was assessed at 20 shillings per annum, increased to 20 shillings per quarter in the Act of the following year which increased the general assessment to 4 shillings.[68] It soon became apparent that some Friends were being taxed under this legislation as maintained ministers and were in consequence refusing to pay their assessments. Friends' belief in a free ministry, the backbone of their testimony against tithes, would clearly have been compromised by the payment of the tax; this, and the fact that those public Friends who could be deemed to exercise a kind of ministry received no payment for their gift, was the basis of their refusal. The Poll Acts contained two other clauses which presented Friends with some difficulties. The first stated that anyone in possession of two houses could be taxed twice, and laid open those Friends whose names were entered in the deeds to Meeting Houses to double taxation. The second, that anyone who had not taken the Oath of Allegiance and Supremacy (meaning chiefly Catholic recusants and Non-Jurors) should be taxed twice, was in fact dealt with in the legislation by a clause which specifically excluded Friends from double taxation if they had subscribed to the Declaration of Fidelity set out in the 1689 Toleration Act. This particular clause was included in all subsequent Acts dealing with taxation passed during the reign of William III. Friends, however, remained open to distraint for refusing to pay the assessment of a minister until the Poll Act of 1693 removed the ambiguity in the clause relating to Dissenting ministers, by stating explicitly that they too should be in receipt of an annual income, in this case in excess of £40 per annum.[69]

The interpretation of the Poll Act legislation varied from county to county. In Cheshire, following a declaration at the Quarter Sessions by Sir Thomas Mannering that Quakers were not to be assessed as preachers, "Friends were all cleared upon it".[70] Further north, however, the authorities seem to have placed a more malicious interpretation on the Act. In June 1690 it was reported to the Meeting for Sufferings from Westmorland "that Justice Fleming in open court gave instructions that all, both men and women that preach among the Quakers are to be assessed 20 shillings a person (as preachers)". John Blaiking, one of the Friends so taxed, was able to reverse distraint procedure by convincing the tax commissioners, to whom all appeals were to be addressed, that such an assessment was a "penal imposition".[71] Elsewhere Friends were less fortunate. In Lancashire in June 1690 Margaret Fox was distrained to the value of £2 9s., having been assessed as a preacher and refusing payment. She also had goods taken to the value of 20 shillings "for not subscribing as a widow". This last imposition seems particularly curious, as although her first husband was dead, she was still married to her second, George Fox, who did not die until January 1691.[72]

The assessment and collection of the 1692 Poll Act again saw some Friends in difficulties. Armed with hindsight the Meeting for Sufferings was able to advise

> that Friends be industrious with the assessors that they may not assess them double, nor as preachers, nothing being received. But where any Friends are doubly taxed that they may appeal to the commissioners within the time limited for appeals and reason the matter with them about it.[73]

Such advice, although well meant, was not always practicable. When Roger Haydock of Penketh attempted to appeal against his assessment as a preacher he was called upon to verify his status on oath. Needless to say, his testimony against swearing prevented the appeal from going any further, and Haydock had wheat taken from him to the value of 26 shillings and sixpence.[74] Other Friends in Lancashire also suffered, but none found themselves in the position of William Atkinson of Hawkshead Monthly Meeting. Atkinson, assessed as a preacher, also found himself appointed to serve as collector of the tax in his division. "He collected and paid into the receiver all that he had received in his division" excepting his own assessment of 40 shillings for two quarters. This deficit in his accounts caused the tax commissioners to obtain a warrant of distress against Atkinson, taking goods worth in all £12.[75]

The Meeting for Sufferings was active in soliciting relief for Friends so affected. Legal opinions were obtained from the Attorney-General and

Solicitor-General supporting the Quaker position and circulated to the Quarterly Meetings in the counties. Members of Parliament were approached, as in the case of the 1692 land tax, in order to ensure that the clause relating to Friends not being double taxed for refusing to take the Oath of Allegiance would be included in forthcoming tax legislation.[76] The Quarterly Meeting for Sufferings in Lancashire urged that cases illustrating the hardship that Friends were under with respect to the tax should be presented to Parliament. Unusually, it also declared that individual sufferers should send their own accounts, unchecked, to London.[77] The result of this agitation was the cessation of discriminative taxing when future polls were assessed and collected. In this case Quaker leaders had readily accepted that the refusal to pay a tax, assessed both incorrectly and unjustly, was consistent with the Truth. They had argued that it was unjust to exempt clergymen who earned less than £60 per annum from the tax, whilst including all Dissenting preachers, regardless of earnings. Friends in particular were discriminated against because they received no payment as ministers. This however was not a

> design to withdraw our Shoulders from bearing our part of the common charge for support of the Government; to which we are thankful for the liberty and peace we enjoy ....[78]

It was in order to maintain these civil enjoyments that Friends refused to accept that a tax should not be paid because the ends to which it was put were inconsistent with Truth. This matter arose in 1695 following the passing of an Act for Granting to his Majesty "certaine rates and duties upon Marriages Births and Burials ... for the terme of Five Yeares for carrying on the Warr against France with vigour".[79] Such an objection was clearly seen to jeopardise the fragile relationship that had been established between the Quakers and the state since 1660. Moreover, a refusal to pay towards war would have led to a refusal to pay all taxes; every money-raising bill passed in the early years of William III stated explicitly that its purpose was either to support the army or the wars in Ireland and France.[80]

On the 2nd of the fifth month (July) 1695 it was brought to the attention of the Morning Meeting that Elizabeth Redford, a woman Friend from London, had spoken in a public meeting at Wandsworth to the effect "that Friends should not pay towards the late Act relating to births, marriages and burials, being to carry on war etc." This was not the first time that Redford had come to the Meeting's attention. As an author in 1694 she had submitted to the Morning Meeting a paper for vetting which it had been unable to approve. Earlier in 1695 the Meeting had expressed unease about a paper published by Redford "beyond the seas". Interviewed at the July Meeting she refused to accept the rebuke of the leading Friends who comprised its membership, and instead owned that she did warn Friends not to pay to death, neither to pay birth, nor to join in pollution with the lord's sacred works in uniting and joining his people in marriage, and pretended she was moved of the lord thereunto

In response to her public pronouncement the Meeting judged

that tribute is to be paid by Christians persuant to Christ example, direction and the practise of true Christians for above this 1600 years, without disputing or questioning the use they put it to for they must be accountable for that"

and continued that Elizabeth Redford should be exhorted to recognise that her views were mistaken, in order to prevent the Meeting having to testify against her publicly.[81] The matter also came to the attention of the Meeting for Sufferings, which ordered that Friends belonging to Westminster Monthly Meeting should "reprove her for her said action and if she shall persist therein to disown her". This Meeting was also clear that her views were "contrary to Friends constant sense and practise under all governments since we were a people".[82]

Beyond their general import it is not clear what Redford's words were at Wandsworth. She has, however, left enough printed material for it to be possible to piece together what was a coherent philosophy which denied both the payment of taxes to support war, and also the increase of materialism and "worldly ways" within the Society. In *The Love of God, is to Gather the Seasons of the Earth and their Multitudes into Peace*, published in the late 1690s or early 1700s, Redford stated her position on taxation: "and as to Tribute to Caesar, true Tribute is to be paid to Caesar in Obedience, and for the uniting of the Christian Faith, and Tranquillity of their People and Nations, that hath not a sting, and a point of a sword at the End". The payment of such taxes was but a temptation to Friends, as was the lure of wealth and possessions. Friends were exhorted "not to lay up for yourselves, Treasures upon Earth, where Moth and Rust doth corrupt, and where Thieves break through, and Steal", preferring instead the secure and incorruptible "Treasures in Heaven".[83] This theme was repeated in *A Warning from the Lord to the City and Nation in Mercy to the People*, which was published in December 1695. In particular, however, she criticised those engaged in warfare, warning them to "fear God, give glory to his Name, for the hour of his Judgement is come". "I hear some say", she wrote,

who do you call Israel? To that I answer with my souls satisfaction, all they that fear God and work Righteousness shall be excepted and are willing to cleanse their Hands from shedding of Blood and keep themselves unspotted from the World, for the Blood that is shed in the Earth is displeasing the Lord .... [84]

In *A Warning, a Warning from the Lord*, published in 1696, Friends, and the population in general, were again warned to shun material pleasures, and that they should not let their "Happiness be upon Money; for that hath been the great Magna Charta of the World ..."[85]

Elizabeth Redford was active in propagating her views, and she came into frequent conflict with the Meeting for Sufferings after the 1695 incident. In December 1700 Westminster Monthly Meeting produced a certificate of denial against Elizabeth Redford, who had apparently sent some of her papers to the King. The papers were criticised for "meddling with the government and forbidding Friends paying the taxes". The Monthly Meeting's paper to the King was "to acquaint him that she is and has been denied by us for many years". Redford continued to cause problems, and in February it was reported to the Monthly Meeting "that several women Friends do meet in the evenings with Elizabeth Redford who is not in unity with Friends, neither is this Meeting satisfied with their so Meeting". Men Friends were instructed to act quickly to prevent a separation.[86] Daniel Quare, a member of the Meeting for Sufferings, who through his position as royal watchmaker had some access to the throne, presented the paper to the King the following week.[87] In June 1701 the Meeting for Sufferings was informed that Redford had delivered a paper to both Houses of Parliament "as if she was a Quaker". The response to this was a printed paper drawn up by the Meetings, "importing that she is and hath been for several years past disowned by the people called Quakers"; this notice of disownment was delivered both to Members of Parliament and Monthly Meetings in and about London. It was also directed that the printed paper should be "delivered to the Yearly Meeting in order for the Quarterly Meetings in the Counties to have them", apparently to prevent Redford's views gaining some support within the Society outside of London.[88]

As we shall see, Redford's criticisms of the worldly ways which typified London Quakerism at the end of the seventeenth century, and the striking eschatological tone to her writings, reflected views which were widespread among the Friends of the North-West. It is, however, only in relatively recent years that views on taxation similar to those held by Elizabeth Redford have become dominant within the Society.[89] However, Quaker leaders in the early eighteenth century were aware that both in England, and perhaps more especially in America, similar ideas did exist amongst Friends, and they were equally aware of the dangers these views could pose to the movement's relationship with the state. In an interview with Peter the Great, Thomas Story stated clearly that Friends paid "taxes to Caesar, who of right hath the direction and application of them ... to peace or to war".[90] But in 1711 Story actually found himself under severe criticism in Pennsylvania for urging colonialists to pay towards a tax designed to support a military expedition to the French colonies. Back in London, writing at least four years after the event, Story vigorously defended his (and the official) view on taxation, citing in his support the fact that both

English and Dutch Quakers willingly paid taxes to support a war between their respective countries in the reign of Charles II. Perhaps his strongest and most realistic argument, however, was that Friends had not wanted to "offend the Queen and Government of Great Britain".[91]

Redford's appeals coincided with an abortive attempt at the Yearly Meeting of 1701 to convey the status of a "suffering" to the refusal to pay the tax on births, burials and marriages. A minute was made that "this Meeting does not judge it meet that what any suffers by omitting their giving notice of births, burials and marriages should be recorded as a suffering for conscience sake, and that Benjamin Bealing do take notice thereof that he may not enter any such".[92] In the autumn of the same year the Meeting for Sufferings was urging Friends "to take care persuant to former advice to answer what the law directs relating to births, burials and marriages by paying the tax ..."[93] It would be wrong to see this, however, as a groundswell of opinion amongst Friends supporting the views of Elizabeth Redford. There are two reasons for this; firstly, the law relating to the tax suffered from considerable maladministration and general evasion, to the extent that two further pieces of legislation were passed by Parliament to strengthen it.[94] For example, in Cumberland and Westmorland Friends who had paid the tax found themselves prosecuted in 1703 for non-payment.[95] There was a second difficulty that had little to do with the peace testimony. The original legislation demanded that ministers of the Established Church should keep registers of all births, marriages and burials, and that such registers were to be open to inspection by tax officers. Although Friends were not obliged to keep registers for the purpose of the tax, officers did demand to see what records they had. There seems to have been a reluctance among some Friends, however, to allow their registers to be seen by government officers, and this view had some support in the Meeting for Sufferings where it was feared that such an inspection might lay many open to prosecution who had failed to pay their taxes through ignorance of the law.[96] Such a reluctance may also have been due to the poor level of recording births etc. apparently prevalent in many Meetings.[97] This perhaps surprising ignorance and maladministration among Friends, as well as government officials, led to many members of the Society being liable to distraint for non-payment of the tax. Finally, it seems likely that among some Friends there was simply a reluctance to declare to the world the births etc. of those of the Truth.

The pragmatic approach displayed by Friends to the payment of direct taxes in support of war was also applied to the payment of duties imposed by customs and excise, the proceeds of which could be directed towards the cost of military adventures. Friends encountered problems at the customs house over the imposition of oaths on goods imported or exported, and also faced similar difficulties with the excise; this matter is discussed in more detail below.[98] It can be noted here, however, that from 1698 onwards the Yearly Meeting became increasingly concerned with the fact that Friends were apparently evading payments on goods. Noting that

> this Meeting [understands] that some in the government have reported that some persons who are called Quakers have used secret and indirect ways to take up their goods without paying the customs and duties which the law hath laid upon them, whereby the King is defrauded of this right ...

the Yearly Meeting stated that any so doing were "out of Truth".[99] Clearly there was a great temptation for Friends to act in such a way, especially those in a merchant community such as Lancaster where fraud and corruption were apparently tolerated at the highest levels.[100] Two Friends within the compass of Swarthmore Monthly Meeting were discovered to have been guilty of frauds. In 1703 the Particular Meeting ordered Friends "to deal with John Cowell concerning his late offence in defrauding the government". Cowell was a contrite offender, and four weeks later the Monthly Meeting noted the receipt of his paper of condemnation "for making malt privately". In 1723 the same meeting demanded a paper from Isaac Fell who had been "concerned in running goods whereby as appeared to us the government is defrauded of its due ... being so disagreeable to our principles and repeated advice..."[101] William Stout suggested that merchants of all religious persuasions were prepared to take advantage of the laxity in Lancaster. Quakers may or may not have shared in this relaxed outlook in practice, but the point is that their treatment of indirect taxation had to do with the immorality of fiscal avoidance rather than with the ethical question of the purpose to which the sums levied were put.

It can be seen from the above that Friends in general went to considerable lengths to meet Richard Hubberthorn's two criteria of service to the government, by body and estate. There was however, a third form of service which should be discussed here, namely "by Voice", or simply participating in elections. As will be seen below, Friends claimed an "interest" in their respective Members of Parliament, an interest that was reflected in their extensive lobbying campaigns both nationally and locally. This interest was created or obtained through Quaker involvement in elections, which was widespread from as early as 1656. In that year Gervase Benson and Thomas Aldam, a Friend from Warmsworth in Yorkshire, wrote to Friends in the vicinity of the City of York urging them to attend the poll for knights of the shire in order "to bear witness to the truth before men".[102] Quakers appear to have voted both in county and borough elections. Their influence in the outcome of elections was sometimes considerable, though their critics were exaggerating wildly when they claimed that in 1708 it was sufficient "to hold the balance of England, and to be counted by each Party, as they shall think will sute most for their Advantage; for they boast already, that they have among them Forty thousand Freeholders".[103]

As with so many aspects of public life, Friends found a problem with respect to the oath required of electors. In the absence of registers of freeholders, would-be electors were required to swear that they possessed sufficient estate to enable them to vote. This restriction was re-stated explicitly in An Act for the Further regulating Elections of Members to serve in Parliament, passed in 1695.[104] The sheriffs supervising shire elections were instructed "to poll noe Freeholder whoe is not sworne if soe required by the Candidates or any of them". Writing in 1712 the Quaker reformer John Bellers criticised this system, suggesting in its place a system of parish registers of freeholders "By which means any County Poll may be capable of a scrutiny", pointing out that the registers could also be used to enforce more accurate land tax returns.[105] By 1707, however, Friends who were prepared to use the Affirmation granted in 1696 were officially allowed to vote. This did not prevent the Meeting for Sufferings continuing to ensure that any legislation affecting elections contained clauses excusing Quakers from taking an oath. In Lancashire, where a majority of Friends declined the Affirmation, there was unease over some of the moves being made in London which could, it was thought endanger the ability of Quakers refusing the oath on Affirmation to vote in that county. In 1708 the Quarterly Meeting expressed dissatisfaction with the form of words to be used instead of an oath abjuring the Stuarts; a letter was sent to London "to signify the dissatisfaction of this Meeting as to what they recommended to the counties to offer to the government for Friends to declare instead of the Abjuration Act upon elections for Members of Parliament or otherwise".[107] Six years later in the first year of the reign of George I, Parliament passed an Act to perpetuate the affirmation of 1696.[108] William Stout felt that this perpetual Act would have been obtained sooner but for the fact that towards the end of Queen Anne's reign Friends "had generally appeared and voated on all occasions for the succession to the Crown in the House of the Elector of Hanover".[109]

The ability of Friends in Lancashire and elsewhere to vote, whilst declining to swear or affirm, rested on the fact that the oath or Affirmation was to be required of electors only if insisted upon by the candidates. Thus at the election held for Members for the county of Brecon in 1695, the candidates Sir Roland Gwyn and Edward Jones met before the poll when "The Qualification of the Electors were settled, and among the rest, it was agreed, "That those that had Leases for Lives and Quakers that could make out their Estates, should vote".[110] In Hertfordshire, in the same year, the defeated candidate Robert Cecil complained that his opponent had been elected by, amongst other things, refusing to accept the vote of Quakers who were freeholders "on account that they would not swear".[111] In 1710, Charles Cholmondeley, one of the Tory candidates for the county of Cheshire was advised by Harley to solicit for Quaker votes, apparently with some amount of success.[112] In the same year, Quaker freeholders were apparently responsible for returning the High Church Tories Sir Thomas Hanmer and Sir Robert Davers in the county of Suffolk.[113] In Cumberland in 1722, Gilfred Lawson, a Tory candidate for the county, openly sought the votes of Friends despite the fact that he had voted against the Toleration Act in 1689.[114] In the same year, George Lucy, a Whig candidate in Warwickshire, wrote to a Mr Sute, the Earl of Sunderland's agent in London, that he had approached Friends in that county, who were "doubtfull in concerning themselves in Elections". Lucy asked that he might be forwarded "something that was lately writt to encourage them to intereste themselves".[115] In 1727 the votes of Hertfordshire Quakers were accepted in an election when they supported the Jacobite candidate Charles Cesar. This was apparently done at the bidding of Walpole, who favoured the return of Cesar rather than his opponent, a Hanoverian Tory.[116]

Friends also appear to have been involved in borough elections throughout the country. In 1690 Thomas Speed voted at Bristol "having not appeared but once before", in order to show his "sober dissent from those who declared themselves to be spirited for Persecution".[117]

At Clitheroe in 1693 Richard Coulbourn, a Quaker flaxmonger, voted in the borough election; his vote was eventually rejected, not because he had failed to swear when voting but for his failure to take the required oaths in order to qualify himself as a burgess.[118] At Cockermouth in 1695 and 1701 Quaker votes were actively sought after to secure victory for the Whig candidate in the borough election.[119] At Pontefract in 1714 Sir William Lowther complained that the mayor of the corporation had deliberately refused to accept the legal votes of Quakers.[120] Tobias Jenkins, mayor of York in 1720 and Member of Parliament for the city, wrote that his support came from "the grave People, that are very steady, of the Quakers which I believe I have to a man ..." This was despite the dispute, then at its height, between Quakers and the corporation of York, over the malicious appointment of Friends to civic office.[121]

In Lancaster Friends who were qualified as freemen would have been able to participate in election: in Liverpool Dissenters including Quakers were recognised as having an important voice in determining the outcome of elections.[122]

It is difficult to ascertain how far the Quaker vote may have been organised in the light of evidence which shows Friends voting for High Church Tories, Jacobites and Whigs. Members of the Meeting for Sufferings certainly involved themselves in what was sometimes an abortive attempt to influence votes in the election for the Oxford Parliament of 1681. Friends were urged to support "sober, discreet and moderate men", who were "against persecution and Popery" and who "deport themselves tenderly towards our Friends". In all this, however, they were to "be very cautious of giving any just occasion of offence".[123] A similar circular letter had been sent to the Quarterly Meetings by the Morning Meeting in 1675.[124]

In 1681, however, the endeavours of Friends were thwarted by events beyond their control, with the Parliament in which they had placed much hope being dissolved after a session lasting only seven days.[125] The response to this was a circular letter to Friends urging them to refrain from public political activity, and "not to use those reflecting disgustfull terms of distinction of (Whig and Tory)". In the same month of September an epistle from George Fox was published calling upon Friends to "keep out of the Restless, Discontented, Disquieted Spirit of the World about the Government".[126] A similar turn of events followed Friends' increasing involvement in local government under James II and an uneasy debate at Yearly Meeting in 1688 concerning the choosing of Members of Parliament and Quakers holding office. Fox's opinion then was that it was "not safe to conclude such things in a Yearly Meeting". In October, with a Dutch fleet ready to bring William III to England, Fox was again advising Friends to withdraw from public life and concentrate on "those things which are above where Christ sits, and not those things which are below, which will change and pass away".[127] By 1695, however, Friends were yet again prepared to involve themselves in earthly affairs. Writing from London Benjamin Bealing, clerk of the Meeting for Sufferings, advised Friends in boroughs and corporations to vote in the forthcoming election "for such as are prudent and for liberty of conscience ... and will vote for our relief in case of oaths". Friends, he wrote, should be "circumspect and unanimous for the matter of the moment".[128]

By the early eighteenth century as William Stout showed, Friends were again prepared to identify themselves with particular factions or parties at elections. In 1708 it was argued by their critics that the Affirmation should not be accepted in place of an oath at the poll, because "so lately, at the Election of this present Parliament" they had united in their votes to "oppose the church".[129] Sir Thomas Hanmer, a High Church Tory, wrote in 1710 of "a great many Quakers" in Suffolk, who "promise nobody and preserve themselves indifferent, by which I conclude they have received no instructions from their leaders".[130] Some Friends viewed the vote as a powerful weapon. In 1713, at the height of the Affirmation controversy, the Quakers who were seeking a modification of the form of words granted in 1696, obstructed a campaign by the Meeting for Sufferings for a renewal of that Act. One of their methods was to approach MPs with the promise "do not pass this bill for the renewing the solemn Affirmation this session, it is yet time enough, see how we shall behave ourselves at the next election of Members of Parliament".[131] This, incidentally, was the same group who in a paper intended for delivery to Parliament offered to "forgo and be debarred from our natural right of voting in elections", noting that it was not

> agreeable to the simplicity and abstractedness of our testimony and profession to intermeddle less or more with the governments of this world, and that it hath visibly proved a snare to such of our Friends as have meddled that way.[132]

By 1736, when Friends were agitating for relief from tithes, critics of their campaign frequently asserted that they were likely to receive favour from Parliament, and justices of the peace, through their large and organised electoral influence. One of Walpole's biographers claimed that his prime motivation in presenting the tithe-bill of 1736 to Parliament was the desire to acknowledge long-standing electoral support from Friends in Norfolk, and particularly Norwich.[133]

Throughout the late seventeenth and early eighteenth centuries Quakers were able to enjoy many of the rights of citizenship enjoyed by others. Friends were, moreover, anxious to be seen to enjoy these rights, whether it be serving a minor or arduous office, voting at an election or "cheerfully" paying taxes to support war. Friends were concerned to claim these rights even before 1689, when so many were the victims of legislation specifically designed to exclude them from normal society, by fines, imprisonment or transportation. After many penalties were removed or suspended by the 1689 Toleration Act, Friends everywhere sought to exercise what they considered to be their natural rights, and perform their civil duties. Both in Lancaster and London, Friends had in common some shared perceptions of the state and the reciprocal responsibilities of state and subject. As will be seen, however, there was within this shared perception sufficient diversity to engender serious disputes between Friends within the Quarterly Meeting for Lancashire and the Meeting for Sufferings in London. First, however, there should be some discussion of the state's perception of Friends.

REFERENCES

1. *Besse*, vol.1, p.310
2. For the case of Elizabeth Redford, and Friends refusing to pay civil taxes, see below, this chapter. For tithes and oaths see chapters 3, 5 and 6
3. Elisabeth Brockbank, *Richard Hubberthorne of Yealand, Yeoman-Soldier-Quaker 1628–1662* (London, 1929), pp.21–23, 32–33, 44. The optional 'e' at the end of Hubberthorn, adopted by Elisabeth Brockbank, is not used here. Despite Friends' later associations with pacifism, a number of early Quakers, perhaps most notably Hubberthorn and James Nayler, served in the parliamentary army. Pacifism, in the words of Alan Cole, "was not a characteristic of the early Quakers; it was forced upon them by the hostility of the outside world". Alan Cole, 'The Quakers and the English Revolution', in T. Aston (ed.), *Crisis in Europe 1560–1660* (London, 1965), p.344. For Nayler see *Beginnings*, pp.61–62. See also Hugh Barbour, *The Quakers in Puritan England* (London, 1964), pp.221–22
4. J. Rawlinson Ford, 'The Customary Tenant-right of the Manors of Yealand', *TC&WA&AS*, n.s. 9 (1909), pp.147–60; Brockbank, *Richard Hubberthorne of Yealand*, p.22
5. *Second Period*, pp.25–37, 218–19; see the testimony of Edward Burrough in *A Collection*, p.9
6. Richard Hubberthorn and George Fox the younger, *An Answer to the Oath of Allegiance and Supremacie, from the People called Quakers* (1660), in *A Collection*, pp.240–41. The scriptural source for this reference is 1 Peter, 2,

13–14 "submit yourselves to every ordinance of man for the Lord's sake; whether it be to the King, as supreme; or unto governors, as unto them that are sent by him for the punishment of evildoers and for the praise of them that do well".

7. Richard Hubberthorn, *The Rebukes of a Reviler fallen upon his own Head* (1657), in *A Collection*, p.135; Richard Hubberthorn and George Fox the younger, *An Answer*, p.241; see also Barbour, *The Quakers in Puritan England*, p.197

8. J.W. Allen, *A History of Political Thought in the Sixteenth Century* (London, 1928), pp.15–30

9. *ibid.* pp.125–133; this view of passive resistance is repeated almost word for word by John Locke in his letter on Toleration, see John Locke, *The Second Treatise of Government* (ed. J.W. Gough, Oxford, 1956), p.155

10. J.W. Allen, *English Political Thought 1603–1660* (London, 1938), vol.1, pp.514–19; H.T. Dickenson, *Liberty and Property. Political Ideology in Eighteenth-Century Britain* (London, 1977) p.20; J.P. Kenyon, *Revolution Principles. The Politics of Party 1689–1720* (Cambridge, 1977), pp.5–20; for later attempts by theorists to legitimise the events of 1688 see *ibid.*, pp.21–34; see also Gerald Straka, 'The final phase of Divine Right Theory in England 1688–1702', *English Historical Review*, 77 (1962), pp.638–58

11. Richard Hubberthorn, *A short Relation* (1660), in *A Collection*, pp.276, 282

12. Richard Hubberthorne, *The distance between Flesh and the Spirit, etc.* (1656) in Hubberthorn, *A Collection*, pp.68–69. In the opinion of John Crook, the law was like a spider's web, "which catches flys, but lets wasps go free", John Crook, *An Apology for the Quakers ...* (London, 1662), p.4 Both these writers were looking to the magistrates to enforce the sort of reformation of manners that had taken place in Lancashire during the Interregnum: see Keith Wrightson, 'The Puritan Reformation of Manners, with specific reference to the Counties of Lancashire and Essex, 1640–1660' (University of Cambridge, Ph.D. thesis, 1974), p.171 and *passim*. For Hubberthorn's view of the legal system see *The real Cause of the Nation's Bondage* (1654) in *A Collection*, pp.217–24

13. Richard Hubberthorn, *The Rebukes of a Reviler*, p.148; Fifteen years later his opinion was restated by the Quaker apologist Robert Barclay; "since God hath assumed to himself the Power and Dominion of the Conscience, who alone can mightily instruct and govern it, therefore it is not lawful for any whatsoever, by virtue of any Authority or Principality they bear in the Government of this World, to force the Consciences of others ....", *Apology*, p.13

14. Richard Hubberthorn, *The Mittimus Answered by which R H was sent Prisoner to Norwich Castle by Ralph Woolmer, Justice of the Peace, October 9, 1654* (1654), in *A Collection*, p.38

15. Richard Hubberthorn, *The Rebukes of a Reviler*, p.148

16. *Beginnings*, p.175; John Crook, *An Apology for the Quakers*, p.4

17. John Locke, *The Second Treatise of Government* (ed. J.W. Gough, Oxford, 1956), p.154–55

18. Maurice Cranston, *John Locke* (London, 1957), p.387; for the link between Locke's views on toleration and trade and those of his patron, Lord Ashley, see *ibid.* pp.110–12

19. Crook's *Apology* was published in 1662; although published in 1689 Locke's views on toleration were first drafted in 1667. See Cranston, *John Locke*,

p.111. For the correlation between Quakers' and Locke's views on property, see below, chapter 5. "Locke, beyond any other writer was to be the moving spirit of the eighteenth century", Gerald Cragg, *Reason and Authority in the Eighteenth Century* (Cambridge, 1964), pp.5–6

20. W.K. Jordan *The Development of Religious Toleration in England* (London, 1940), vol.4, p.467. One of these reservations was the Quakers, for whom "orthodox opinion" decreed "a fresh and severe wave of persecution" in the 1660s, *ibid*. p.246

21. R.A. Beddard, 'The Restoration Church', in J.R. Jones (ed.) *The Restored Monarchy 1660–1688* (London, 1979), pp.155–57; for the provenance of these ideas of unity see Conrad Russell, 'Arguments for Religious Unity in England, 1530–1650', *Journal of Ecclesiastical History*, 18 (1967), pp.201–26; see also, Dickenson, *Liberty and Property*, p.21

22. Michael Mullett, *Radical Religious Movements in Early Modern Europe* (London, 1980), p.80

23. Beddard, *op.cit.* p.160; Mullett, *Radical Religious Movements*, p.83

24. *Besse*, vol.1, p.310

25. Thomas Atkinson, *An Exhortation to all People* (n.p., 1684), pp.4–5

26. George Whitehead, *The Christian Progress of ... George Whitehead* (London, 1725), p.630; during the events of the autumn of 1688 Friends had been advised to "let your dwelling and walking be in Christ Jesus, who is called the word of God, and His Power, which is over all. And set your affections on things that are above, where Christ sits at the right hand of God ... and not those things which are below, which will change and pass away". George Fox, *A General Epistle to Friends* 17/8/1688 (London, 1688), p.1

27. LSF, Port. 41.84, Margaret Fox to King William, 24/4/1698: this is printed in *A Brief Collection*, pp.531–32

28. Richard Hubberthorn, *Something that lately passed in Discourse between the King and R H* (1660), in *A Collection*. p.271

29. See Richard T. Vann, *The Social Development of English Quakerism 1655–1755* (Cambridge, Mass., 1969), pp.156–57, who argues that the consequence of this process combined with the growth of the "idea of membership" was that Friends became only "the most picturesque of His Majesty's Protestant Dissenters". This however was a long-term development which lay well beyond the intermediate, though formidable, barrier of the Clarendon Code, for which see below

30. Quoted in *Beginnings*, p.313, where there is a full account of the Balby Meeting, pp.310–14

31. For Anthony Pearson and Gervase Benson see below, chapters 3 and 5

32. Edward Burrough, *To the Parliament and Army (in general) of the Commonwealth of England etc* (1659), quoted in Barry Reay 'The Quakers and 1659; two newly discovered broadsides by Edward Burrough', *JFHS* 54 (1977), p.110

33. LSF, Port, 23. 37, Margaret Fell to George Fox, 31/5/1660: "I spoke to him [i.e, Charles II] concerning the oath that Friends could not take and told him that there would be exaction [?] at the assizes for it would be offered to Friends who were to do service for their country ..." See also Isabel Ross, *Margaret Fell, Mother of Quakerism* (London, 1949), p.131

34. George Whitehead, *Christ's Lambs Defended from Satan's Rage, In a Just Vindication of the People Called Quakers ...* (London, 1691), p.41; *A Brief*

Representation of the Quakers Case of Not Swearing; and why they might have been, and yet may be Relieved therein, by Parliament (London, 1694), pp.6–7

35. LSF, Book of Cases, vol.1, p.35; for the oaths required of constables and petty-constables see *The Book of Oaths* (London, 1715), pp.207–08, appendix pp.5–6. I owe this reference to Dr J. William Frost of Swarthmore College, Pennsylvania

36. LSF, Book of Cases, *ibid.* vol.2, p.257

37. *ibid.* vol.2, pp.95–99

38. Nicholas J. Morgan 'Lancashire Quakers and the Oath, 1660–1722', *JFHS*, 54 (1980), p.242; see below, chapter 3

39. 'Sir Roger Bradshaigh's Letter-Book', *THSLC*, 63, n.s. 27 (1912), p.157

40. LQMS, vol.1, 1678, p.62

41. LMMM, vol.1, tithe-testimonies, 28/12/1707

42. S.A. Peyton (ed.), *Minutes of Proceedings in Quarter Sessions held for the Parts of Kesteven in the County of Lincoln 1674–1695* (Lincoln, Lincoln Record Society, vol.25 (1928)), p.cxxvii; Keith Wrightson, 'Two Concepts of Order: justices, constables and jurymen in seventeenth century England', in John Brewer and John Styles (eds.), *An Ungovernable People* (London, 1980), pp.21–22. Richard Milner, a Friend from Chester, wrote that constables involved in enforcing the Conventicle Act "all up and down the Country cry out, what a trouble it is to them ... so that as several of them say, they can neither eat nor sleep ....", *A Few Words to the King and both Houses of Parliament* .... (np., 1675), p.1

43. J.R. Western, *Monarchy and Revolution* (London, 1972), pp.203–23; John Miller, *Popery and Politics in England, 1660–1688* (Cambridge, 1973), pp.218–26

44. Michael Mullett, 'Conflict, Politics and Elections in Lancaster, 1660–1688', *Northern History*, 19 (1983), pp.80–82, (I am grateful to the author for lending me an earlier typescript version of this article); Stout, p.92

45. J. Brownbill, *A Calendar of Charters and Records belonging to the Corporation of Lancaster* (Lancaster, 1929), p.67

46. Michael Mullett, 'To Dwell Together in Unity: The Search for Agreement in Preston Politics, 1660–1690', *THSLC*, 125 (1974), pp.77

47. MMS, vol.6, 30/1/1688

48. John T. Evans, *17th Century Norwich, Politics, Religion, and Government 1620–1690* (Oxford, 1979), p.315; Russell Mortimer, 'Bristol Quakers and the Oath', *JFHS*, 43 (1951), pp.75–77

49. LSF, Port. 41.17; MMS, vol.6, 11/9/1687

50. MMS, vol.6, 1/4/1688; for a study of the relationship between Penn and James II see Vincent Buranelli, *The King and the Quaker. A Study of William Penn and James II* (Philadelphia, 1966), *passim.*

51. 1 Will. & Mar. c. 18; MMS, vol.21, 10/5/1713

52. MMS, vol.26, 17/1/1736

53. LPL, MS. 108, pp.20–113

54. For some comments on the social status and honesty of land tax officers see W.R. Ward, *English Land Tax in the Eighteenth Century* (Oxford, 1963), pp.5, 42

55. MMS, vol.16, 6/6/1703

56. MMC, *Le Fleming*, p.343, Sir Daniel Fleming to Viscount Lonsdale, 20 May, 1696

57. LPL, MS. 108, pp.20–113

58. LPL, Election Returns, MSS. 5009, 5012, 5013
59. William Penn, *Considerations on the Bill Depending for Preventing Occasional Conformity* (n.p., 1703?), p.1
60. MM.S, vol.23, 13/3/1720, 17/4/1720; W. Pearson Thistlethwaite, *Yorkshire Quarterly Meeting (of the Society of Friends) 1665–1966* (Harrogate, 1979), p.372; see above, Introduction, n.52
61. MMS, vol.24, 14/3/1725, 13/6/1725, 22/8/1725, 10/4/1726, 23/12/1727, 2/6/1728; LQMM, vol.2, 7/8/1725, 6/11/1725, 6/2/1726, 5/8/1726. The Quarterly Meeting noted on 6/2/1726 "that all the methods made use of there, [i.e. London] are not effectual for his relief" and appointed a separate committee of Friends for the "future consideration" of the matter.
62. William Penn, *Considerations on the Bill Depending ...*, p.1; Thomas Ellwood, *A Sober Reply on behalf of the People, Called Quakers ... etc.* (London, 1699), p.9, quoted in Beatrice Saxon-Snell, 'The Making of Thomas Ellwood', *JFHS*, 36 (1939), p.33
63. Anthony Pearson, *The Great Case of Tithes* (6th ed., London, 1732), pp.27, 40
64. B.S. Capp, *The Fifth Monarchy Men* (London, 1972), pp.148–50
65. George Fox, *A Declaration from the People of God, Called quakers, against all Seditious Conventicles ....* (n.p., 1670), p.l; see also *Journal*, p.558; *A Brief Representation of the Quakers Case of Not-Swearing* (London, 1694), p.3
66. Abstract of a Letter given by M.F. to the King at Hampton-Court, 1662, after the passing of the Quaker Act, in *A Brief Collection*, p.37
67. Henry Horwitz, *Parliament, Policy and Politics in the reign of William III* (Manchester, 1977), pp.71–75, 93–94; Jennifer Carter, 'The Revolution and the Constitution', in Geoffrey Holmes (ed.), *Britain after the Glorious Revolution 1689–1714* (London, 1969), pp.47–49
68. 2 Will. & Mar. c. 11; 3 Will. & Mar. c. 6
69. 5 & 6 Will. & Mar. c. 14; see Whitehead, *The Christian Progress*, pp.666–69
70. MMS, vol.7, 11/5/1690; an abstract of Friends' sufferings in England for refusing to pay the tax is contained in *The Suffering Case and Complaint of some of the People Called Quakers* (n.p., 1692?), *passim.*
71. MMS, vol.7, 6/4/1690, 11/5/1690; George Fox wrote to the Meeting for Sufferings that he "received another letter out of the North concerning the Sufferings of Friends there, how that the magistrates distrained of Friends 20s. for preaching though some of their estates are hardly worth 20s a year ...", LSF, Port. 36.61, G.F. to the Meeting for Sufferings, Edmonton, 29/9/1690
72. GBS, vol.5, pt. 1, p.261: the Act for 1689 stated that "Every widow respectively according to her Husband's Degree shall pay the Third Part Rated by this Act on that Degree of which the Husband of such wife was in his life time", 2 Will. & Mar. c. 2, v.
73. MMS, vol.8, 8/2/1692
74. GBS, vol.7, pt. 1, p.303; John Haydock, *A Brief Account of the Life, Travels, Sufferings and Death of Roger Haydock*, in *A Collection of the Christian Writings ... of ... Roger Haydock* (London, 1700), p.212
75. MMS, vol.8, 20/11/1692
76. *Political Associations*, p.28; MMS, vol.8, 23/10/1692
77. LQMM, vol.1, 4/11/1692
78. *Some Reasons offered with submission on behalf of the Preachers among the People called Quakers, for their Exemption from being Taxed as such in the Poll Bill* (n.p., 1692?), p.1

79. 6 & 7 Will. & Mar. c. 6

80. i.e. 2 Will. & Mar c. 11: An Act for Raising Money by a Poll and otherwise towards the Reduceing of Ireland and Prosecuting the Warr against France; 4 Will. & Mar. c. 1: An Act for granting to their Majesties an Aid of Foure Shilling in the Pound for One yeare for carrying on a vigorous War against France.

81. LSF, Morning Meeting Minutes, vol.2, 10/10/1694, 6/3/1695 2/5/1695

82. MMS, vol.10, 5/5/1695; Redford dealt contemptuously with the men who were sent to read her the Monthly Meeting's minute of disunity. They reported "that she said she would neither hear it read nor receive it, upon which the Friends went up stairs to her lodging and put it into her room, but she brought it again and threw it back amongst the Friends who were appointed ... to deliver it to her", LSF, Westminster Monthly Meeting Minutes vol.2, 4/10/1695

83. Elizabeth Redford, *The Love of God is to Gather the Seasons of the Earth and their Multitudes into Peace* (n.p., c.1690), pp.5, 7; although the date of this work is given as c.1690, it should be noted that the text contains the following: "and Jesus was raised an Example of the Christian Faith, and the Lord sent forth a Great manifestation of Peace through him, that it should be obeyed, and yet the whole world is in War, after so great a manifestation of Peace; and 1711 Year since, and a light is now again sent forth to the Cesars of the Earth ...", pp.4–5

84. Elizabeth Redford, *A Warning from the Lord to the City and Nation in Mercy to the People, to see if they will yet seek Him* (n.p., 1695), p.1

85. Elizabeth Redford, *A Warning, a Warning from the Lord, in Mercy to the People, to see if they will yet Seek Him* (n.p., 10/4/1696), p.1

86. LSF, Westminster Monthly Meeting Minutes, vol.2, 1/11/1700, 5/12/1700, 5/1/1701

87. MMS, vol.14, 27/10/1700; for Daniel Quare, the Quaker inventor of the repeating watch, see *DNB*

88. IMS, vol.15, 23/3/1701, 30/3/1701, 6/4/1701

89. See below, chapter 7; many current Friends support the campaign for a "peace tax", which demands the right for pacifists and conscientious objectors to divert that part of their taxation which would normally contribute towards military expenditure to a "peace fund", to be used for non-military purposes; see for example *The Guardian*, 31/5/1983

90. Thomas Story, *A Journal of the Life of Thomas Story* (Newcastle, 1747), p.124, quoted in *Second Period*, pp.601–02

91. Emily E. Moore, *Travelling with Thomas Story* (Letchworth, 1947), pp.123–27; the manuscript of Story's defence can be found at LSF

92. LYMM, vol.2, 1701, p.341

93. MMS, vol.15, 10/8/1701, 17/8/1701

94. 7 & 8 Will. III, c. 35, 8 & 9 Will. III, c. 20

95. MMS, vol.16, 25/2/1703; vol.17, 10/1/1704, 17/1/1704, 7/2/1704, 21/2/1704

96. MMS, vol.16, 28/3/1703, when Friends in Bristol were advised "not to expose their Registers, being not impowered by Law to keep any, least by that, it should amount to an information against such of our Friends as have neglected through ignorance and not designedly" to enter their births etc.

97. For deficiencies in the maintenance of registers see Vann, *op.cit.*, pp.160–61;

for Friends registering births with the local minister for the purpose of taxation see Ellen K. Goodwin, 'Caldbeck Parish Registers', *C&WA&AS*, 9 (1888), p.5

98. See below, chapter 3
99. LYM, vol.2, 1698, p.229
100. Writing in 1704 William Stout recalls that while John Hodgson, the foremost Lancaster merchant in the seventeenth century, was at the peak of his prosperity "it was not accounted of us a crime to bribe the officers of the custom(s) or defraud the King of his customs". *Stout*, p.147; Hodgson is incorrectly identified as a Quaker in M.M. Schofield, *Outlines of an Economic History of Lancaster* (2 parts, Lancaster, 1946), part 1, p.10
101. SPMM, vol.1, 1/6/1703, 5/7/1703; SMMM, vol.3, 7/7/1703, vol.4, 7/3/1723, 4/4/1723
102. Thomas Aldam and Gervase Benson to Friends in general, 5/6/1656, in *The Friend*, May 1880, p.110
103. *Some Reasons Humbly offered ... why the Quakers Affirmation should not pass instead of an Oath at Future Elections of Parliament* (London, 1708?), p.1
104. 7 & 8 Will. III, c. 25
105. John Bellers *An Essay Toward the Ease of Elections of Members of Parliament* (London, 1712), p.4
106. 6 Anne. c. 18, clause 18: "That every Person who shall refuse to take the Oath last herein before recited or being a Quaker shall refuse to declare the Effect thereof upon his Solemn Affirmation ... shall not be capable of giving any vote for the Election of any such Member ..."
107. LQMM, vol.1, 7/8/1708, 6/11/1708, 7/5/1709; MMS, vol.20, 17/12/1709
108. 1 Geo. I, c. 26
109. *Stout*, p.173: this passage is slightly confused, for Stout seems to assert that the right to prove freeholds at elections upon the Affirmation was first granted in 1714, though as we have seen above (n.106) this was in fact provided for in 1707. It is interesting to speculate what difference this would have made to Stout and his fellow Lancastrians who, although scrupling the Affirmation until 1722, apparently voted at elections well before that date.
110. *Journal of the House of Commons*, vol.11, p.463
111. *ibid*. p.393
112. Edward Hughes, *Studies in Administration and Finance* (Manchester, 1934), p.260
113. Mary Ransome, 'Church and Dissent in the Election of 1710', *English Historical Review*, 56 (1941), p.86
114. R. Hopkinson, 'Parliamentary Elections in Westmorland and Cumberland, 1695–1723' (University of Newcastle, Ph.D. thesis, 1973), p.118
115. British Library, Add. Ms. 61,496, Fos. 84–7, quoted in J.D. Alsop, 'Manuscript Evidence of the Quakers Bill of 1722', *JFHS*, 54 (1980), p.255
116. J.H. Plumb, *Sir Robert Walpole, the King's Minister* (London, 1960), p.99
117. Thomas Speed, *Reason against Rage: Being some Animadversions upon a late Scurrilous Libel Prefixed to a Sermon Preached Nine and thirty Years ago* (London, 1691), pp.15–16: I owe this reference to Russell Mortimer
118. W.S. Weeks, *Clitheroe in the Seventeenth Century* (Clitheroe, 1923), pp.184, 293; for Coulborn see also, *The Cry of Oppression in a few Instances of the Late Distresses Made upon some of the peaceable People, called Quakers, in the Counties of York and Lancaster* (London, 1683), p.1

119. Hopkinson, *op.cit.* pp.126–29
120. 'Pontefract Quakers and the 1714 General Election', *JFHS*, 48 (1956–58), p.233
121. Quoted in J.D. Alsop, *op.cit.* p.255
122. Romney Sedgewick, *The Commons 1715–1754* (3 vols., London, 1970), vol.1, p.270; J.M. Wahlstrand, 'The Elections to Parliament in the County of Lancashire 1685–1714' (University of Manchester, MA thesis, 1956), p.177
123. LSF, Book of Cases, vol.1, pp.82–83; LSF, Gibson MSS, vol.3, 95
124. Arnold Lloyd, *Quaker Social History 1669–1738* (London, 1948), p.90; Douglas R. Lacey, *Dissent and Parliamentary Politics in England 1661–1689* (New Jersey, 1969), p.109
125. David Ogg, *England in the Reign of Charles II* (2nd ed., 2 vols, Oxford, 1956), vol.2, pp.614–19
126. LSF, Book of Cases, vol.1, p.98, "The advice of some ancient faithful Friends" 3/9/1681: at least one of these "ancient" Friends, George Whitehead, had signed the earlier letters to electors, and it is difficult to see clear evidence to support the view of Arnold Lloyd that this change in emphasis was precipitated by a struggle for "control" of the Meeting for Sufferings between William Penn and the "older Quakers", with the turn of events being to Penn's disadvantage. See Lloyd, *op.cit.* p.91; George Fox, *To the Flock of Christ, Everywhere to be Read in their Assemblies* (London, 1681), p.1
127. LYMM, vol.1, 1688, pp.199–200; George Fox, *A General Epistle to Friends* (London, 1688), p.1
128. LFMH, 2Bxxv, Benjamin Bealing to Friends, London, 19/8/1695; this document is printed in Mullett, *Radical Religious Movements*, p 139
129. *Some Reasons Humbly offered ....*, p.1
130. HMC, *Calendar of the Manuscripts of the Marquis of Bath preserved at Longleat, Wiltshire* (London, 1908), vol.3, p.442
131. MMS, vol.21, 29/11/1713, 5/12/1713
132. LSF, Gibson MSS. vol.3, 131, "The case of the people called Quakers in North Britain who conscientiously refuse to swear", c.1720
133. *Political Associations*, pp.98, 103

2

The Quakers' Relations with Crown and Parliament

Whatever their theoretical views of the state, its legitimacy to make and enforce laws and impose and collect taxes, and the religious implications of accepting office under it, Quakers (like many of their contemporaries) had a shrewd appreciation of the mechanics by which government operated at all levels. They understood the processes by which legislation was initiated and passed into the statute book; they knew how it could be modified in practice, and further knew how its effects could be vitiated by a hint from the highest authority. At the level of the county, Friends familiarised themselves with the procedures by which laws were put into effect, and were able to identify the officials through whom the effects of policies could be altered in their own favour. In order to examine further the relations of the Quakers with the state, this chapter will concentrate on the relationships Friends maintained with the monarch and Parliament in London, and the local county establishments of gentry and justices.

The sources for such a study are patchy: at the highest level Friends were meticulous in recording every word that passed at meetings with the monarch,[1] whilst in the county conversations with local MPs, assize judges or justices were less often recorded. Despite the importance which Friends might have attributed to particular encounters, members of the ruling elite often viewed them in a different light; Quakers are rarely mentioned in the diaries of contemporaries,[2] and outside of the immediate post-Restoration years they feature but modestly in official sources such as the State Papers or Cobbett's *Parliamentary History*. Nonetheless, enough data have survived to outline the relationships between Friends and the monarch in London, and Friends and the county establishments, particularly in the North. Before moving to this however, it is necessary to consider why Friends found it so vital to construct these links with government at any level.

Following the Restoration, Quakers found themselves victims of a number of legislative Acts directed either specifically against them, or against Dissent in general. The passing of these Acts, known collectively as the Clarendon Code, reflected the deep suspicion and hostility frequently displayed towards Dissenters, and particularly Quakers, by Parliament in the 1660s.[3] Upholding the established religion through the Act of Uniformity was, in the eyes of the Commons

> the most probable Means to produce a settled Peace and Obedience through the Kingdom[4]

Consequently the Cavalier Parliament took vigorous action to block Charles II's efforts in 1662 and 1672 to give relief to the Dissenters, passed statutes in 1664 and 1670 to prevent Dissenters meeting and frequently called upon the King to ensure that all the penal laws were put into execution.[5] Nonetheless there was within the Commons, with its minority of MPs sympathetic to Nonconformity, a variety of opinion on the matter of Dissent; the extent of this tolerance is sometimes obscured by the emphasis placed by historians on the repressive attitudes underlying the Clarendon Code. On the occasion of the passing of both Conventicle Acts at least a third of those members who voted did so in the negative.[6] In 1672, having opposed the freedom granted to Dissenters by Charles II in his Indulgence of that year, the Commons went on to consider a Bill for granting ease to the same body of people.[7] Such legislation was not passed, but the attitude of the Commons towards Dissent was mollified, "even in that angry parliament that had been formerly so severe upon them".[8] The apparently growing threat from popery and from France deflected hostility away from Dissenters while the panicky Cavalier attitudes that had given rise to penal legislation in the wake of the radical puritan insurrections, such as Venner's rising in the early 1660s, were assuaged in the 1670s.

All the same, Dissenters in general and Quakers in particular had to face up to the realities of the Clarendon Code. In addition to these measures of deliberate religious discrimination, Friends also came into conflict with the state through their refusal to swear oaths of any kind and their refusal to pay tithes. These refusals also brought Friends within the sphere of ecclesiastical jurisdiction: non-attendance at church on Sundays, however, was an offence punishable by the civil authorities which often led to Friends being prosecuted under statutes originally aimed at Roman Catholics.[9] Quakers, furthermore, found themselves suspected of involvement in most of the post-Restoration plots, notably the Fifth-Monarchists uprising, the Farnley Wood Rising and the Kaber Rigg plot.[10]

The years of intense persecution of Friends between 1660 and 1689 have been the subject of considerable study by both Quaker and non-Quaker scholars, often with Lancashire as a particular focus.[11] Anderson's work, from which the table following is taken, is particularly valuable in showing the variable incidence of persecution of Friends in post-Restoration Lancashire.[12] Sufferings were concentrated at the start and end of the period, and the Conventicle Act was at its height of application in the years of the Tory Reaction,[13] years which also saw a massive increase in the incidence of prosecutions for the non-payment of tithe, thereby strengthening the view that such prosecutions were as much motivated by religious as by financial factors. This intensification of prosecution was followed by an abrupt halt during the reign of James II when Friends achieved a degree of toleration that was only confirmed, and not introduced, by the Act of 1689.[14] However, under James, prosecutions and seizure of goods for non-payment of tithes increased, perhaps a reflection of the frustrations of Anglican gentry who were prevented from enforcing the purely penal laws against Dissent by the actions of a Catholic monarch.

Table 1   Quaker Sufferings in Lancashire 1660–1690

	1660 –64	1665 –69	1670 –74	1675 –79	1680 –84	1685 –90
Gaoled for non-payment of tithes	8	7	9	6	5	
Goods seized for same	3	6	21	124	134	197
Goods seized for absence from public worship	2	6	9	37	114	4
Goods seized for attending meetings	2	3	4	53	124	12
Gaoled for attending same	196	22	13	17	12	3
Other	1	1	2	–	–	–

Although action against conventicles was at its height in the period of intense reaction against religious dissent following the Exclusion Crisis, the nature of suffering had changed. In the period 1660-64 imprisonment outweighed distraint, whereas in the years 1680-84 distraint outweighed imprisonment; the difference reflects the fact that whereas the 1664 Conventicle Act gave alternative penalties of fines or imprisonment for those attending or holding conventicles, the second Act of 1670 imposed only fines, which were directed against preachers and those owning the houses where meetings were held.[15] The main aim of this legislation was, therefore, enticement to conform through the threat of financial or material loss, rather than any crude desire to impose physical sufferings.[16] Sir Daniel Fleming, one of the chief instigators of anti-Quaker prosecutions in Lancashire and Westmorland, clearly stated this when he wrote to Joseph Williamson in London in August 1670:

> Wee have convicted many Quakers and are levvying of their fines which make some of them come to church and in time will, I hope make many more conform .... After we have routed all conventicles, the levvying of 12d for every Sunday will, I hope, bring them back to Church. It is as clear as day that nothing will convince them of their errors so soon as the drawing of money from them: for a greater part of their religion – not withstanding their great zeal and pretences – is tyed to their purs-Strings.[17]

The intensity of prosecutions suggested by Fleming (who is describing activities in both Westmorland and Lancashire) is not reflected in the data for Lancashire. It should also be noted that the maintenance in the 1670s of the policy envisaged by Fleming at the time of the second Conventicle Act was interrupted by Charles II's Declaration of Indulgence of 1672. Moreover, the view that the beneficial effect of the indulgence extended beyond its withdrawal in 1673 is reflected both in Anderson's data and contemporary opinion. The Yorkshire born courtier Sir John Reresby described the Indulgence as "the greatest blowe that ever was given, since the King's restoration, to the Church of England". Its consequence was that "all the lawes and care of their execution against the separetists afterwards could never bring them back to due conformity".[19] Fleming himself wished "that all Nonconformists may be content with it, and that the Kings giving them an inch may not encourage them hereafter to demand an ell".[20] Clearly, despite its enforced withdrawal the Indulgence, and the spirit of toleration it breathed, did not vanish after 1673: Robert Barclay wrote in 1674 that "a kind of Negative Liberty has been obtained, so that at present for the most part we meet together without disturbance from Magistrate".[21]

Nonetheless, Friends in Lancashire, in common with Dissenters elsewhere, found themselves under particularly severe persecution in the early 1680s. If the ethos of the 1672 royal declaration to some extent prevailed for the remainder of the 1670s it was submerged during the Tory Reaction. For Lancashire Friends the years 1680–84 accounted for 33% of all sufferings recorded between the years 1660 and 1690. It was, wrote Margaret Fell, "a time of great Persecution by informers", when "the Justices in our country were very severe...." Their aim, she concluded, was "to ruine us, and to weary us out, and to enrich themselves".[22] William Stout graphically described the extent of financial and other material losses suffered by Friends during this period: he saw the results as being first, that the number of Friends emigrating to Pennsylvania increased, but secondly, and somewhat contradictorily, that "the sevir persecution rather increased the Protestant dissenters in England".[23]

Following the accession of James II in 1685 prosecutions under the Conventicle Act quickly declined.[24] For that year, Besse lists only three Friends imprisoned for meeting, and two for absenting themselves from public worship.[25] Anderson found twelve Lancashire Friends who suffered distraints between 1685 and 1690 for attending Meetings, but beyond these cases conflict between Quakers and the courts were confined to matters concerning tithe: 38% of all cases in this category between 1660 and 1690 were recorded in these years.[26] With the suspension of the laws against Dissenters in 1689 this was to be the established pattern for the rest of the period under discussion, with the exception of the spate of distraints made upon Friends in 1714 following the passing of the Leather Act in 1711, and occasional "malicious" prosecutions under the Conventicle Act in the 1690s.[27] The experience of Lancashire Quakers between

1660 and 1689 was shared by Friends throughout the country, and this illustrates a common background against which relations with the government and Parliament on a national level can be viewed.

Given his relationship with the Stuart family, and the encouragement which Friends had received at court since 1660, it is perhaps not surprising that Robert Barclay chose to dedicate his *Apology* to Charles II.[28] In this definitive statement of Quaker belief and practice Barclay set out to establish the nature of the relationship between King and Quaker. Friends, he wrote, "have not spared to Admonish, Exhort and Reprove Thee"; such behaviour was the fulfilment of an historic task, for Friends were acting "as ever the true Prophets in Ancient Times used to do to those Kings and Princes, under whose Power, Violence and Oppression was acted".[29] The brusque manner of the Quaker approach to the monarch, like their message, was determined by the dictates of Christian simplicity. It was "not lawful to give Men such flattering Titles as Your Holiness, Your Majesty, Your Eminence, Your Grace, Your Lordship, Your Honour, etc ...", neither was it allowed to "kneel, or prostrate themselves to any Man, or to bow the Body, or to uncover the Head to them".[30] Thus in any encounter between a Quaker and royalty, the Friend, by his outward appearance and speech, could be seen to be bearing a "plain testimony" against the vanity and worldliness of the court.

Early Friends, it has been suggested, displayed a "total lack of regard for the pretensions of monarchy", both in terms of the material splendour which was generally associated with royal courts, and also with the concept of divine status which surrounded the institution of kingship itself.[30] Nonetheless, Friends were political opportunists, and despite the evident commitment of some to the 'Good Old Cause', in 1659[32] they joined in the welcome given to the return of the Stuarts. This was not only because the Restoration marked an end of the prosecutions Quakers had been under in the later years of the Commonwealth; Charles II's conception of a powerful sovereign able to temper Parliament's penal laws found a ready response amongst Quakers.[33] It is true that some Quakers were contemptuous of the supposed divine nature of kingship – a view nicely expressed in William Stout's sceptical comment regarding the medicinal power of the royal touch: "how farr a conceit may agrivate or cure a distemper is doubtful to detirmine".[34] Yet Friends steadily showered the King with requests for succour, sharing to some extent traditional popular fantasies about the King as a righter of all wrongs. When Friends thanked James II for his first Declaration of Indulgence they even alluded to the belief, which James encouraged, in the therapeutic powers of the royal touch: the King had removed persecution, "such a sore Evil, as could only be cured by your Majestie's Royal Hand".[35]

During the years immediately following the Restoration, and before the rise of the Meeting for Sufferings in London, the Society appears to have allowed its members to approach the King freely. Such ease of access was encouraged by the affability of Charles II, at least earlier in his reign, and his court's "air of summer relaxation".[36] The case of Adam Barfoote, from Staffordshire, is apparently typical. A "very plain and honest man", he went to London in October 1666 with "a great weight upon him". In the metropolis he came upon the monarch and the following encounter ensued:

> he met the King in his coach (as it were supposed) going a hunting. And he stepped to the coach side, and laid his hand upon it and said: "King Charles, my message is this day unto thee, in the behalf of God's poor, afflicted suffering people"; and gave him his pay [paper], (which indeed were weighty words), and pressed him on to read it. The King said, "How dost thou think I can read it now?"

The result of the interview during which the King remained "mild and moderate" was, like many others, inconclusive.[37] For all that, the incident seems to support the view that Friends were allowed to approach the throne freely, as the spirit guided them, with restraint from neither their fellow Quakers, nor from the King's servants. However, whilst Friends did enjoy an astonishing ease of access to the throne, it will be demonstrated that for the most part personal petitioners to the sovereign were being carefully chosen by Friends from as early as 1660. In addition it will become apparent that Friends, like all other royal petitioners, were subject to the fluctuating whims of the King, were dependent on the goodwill and influence of others at court to gain access, and were never sure of a positive or practical response.

Clarendon wrote in his memoirs that "the King had always admitted the quakers for his divertisement and Mirth", believing them to be the least harmful of all the Dissenting "factions".[38] The reception they received in a notoriously dissolute court often reflected this view. Pepys described one encounter between the King and "a pretty Quaker woman" thus:

> The King showed her Sir J Minnes as a man the fittest for her quaking religion, saying that his beard was the stiffest thing about him. And again merrily said, looking upon the length of her paper, that if all she desired was of that length, she might lose her desires. She modestly saying nothing till he begun to seriously discourse with her, arguing the truth of his spirit against hers.[39]

For all this coarseness, in tolerating the presence of the Quakers and other Dissenters during times of persecution, Charles II was able publicly to dissociate himself from the rigours of his Parliament's laws, and also prevent the total alienation of a small but vociferous group of his subjects.

The King's attitude towards Dissenters, and Quakers in particular, was nothing, however, if not variable. This is amply illustrated in the events surrounding the passing of the first Conventicle Act in 1663. According to the most recent account the Act was passed only with the connivance of

the monarch who felt that the Quakers and other nonconformists had
betrayed his earlier leniency by their alleged involvement in anti-
government plots in the North.[40] At least one contemporary opinion
partly contradicts this view; Gilbert Burnet, rehearsing views which he was
later to attribute to James II, was of the opinion that

> the king was much for having it passed; not that he intended to execute
> it, but he was glad to have that body of men at mercy, and to force them
> to concur in the design for a general toleration [41]

Whatever the dynamic behind the Act's passing, its impact was short-
lived;[42] the Conventicle Act, argues Ronald Hutton, "was dying naturally
long before it formally expired in 1668", partly due to a rapid return to
favour by Friends and other Dissenters after 1664.[43]

The fluctuations in and impenetrable motives underlying royal
attitudes to Quakers must have made the task of those of them entrusted
with approaching court difficult and uncertain. It certainly frustrated the
King's officials both in London and the country, who despaired at the
effect that royal favour had on Dissent.[44] Despair combined with suspicion
to lead some to doubt the sincerity of the King in his endeavours to secure
the Church against the Quakers, who hoped that "the Lord will put it into
the King's heart to prevent their wicked designs in time".[45] Anglican
zealots feared rather than hoped that the King would interpose himself to
soften the blows of repression. Daniel Fleming, for example, writing of the
first Conventicle Act hoped "this will stop their meetings, etc. unless they
obtain favour at Whitehall, which would much encourage them",[46] and
after George Fox was released from imprisonment in 1666 following the
intervention of the King on his behalf Fleming was in despair because the
Quakers "hope great things from him [Fox] on his arrival in London. His
release will much discourage justices from acting against Quakers".[47] The
discharge of Margaret Fell from her sentence of *praemunire* in 1668
provoked similar sentiments: it did "not a little encourage the rabble of
fanatics and discourage all magistrates acting against them".[48] Justices in
the North, or some parts of it, would act only in accordance with the
prevailing royal sentiments: "till accounts are received of what is done in
London, nobody will prosecute the rigour of the law".[49]

"A friend at Court", wrote one aspirant, "can do wonders".[50] The
Quakers, despite the apparent spontaneity of their royal interviews, were
as dependent on the good offices of such friends, and their own ability to
make an interest with the King, as was any other royal petitioner. Within.
the royal family the Friends could count on the support of Prince Rupert[51]
and Princes Elizabeth, a cousin of and regular correspondent with Robert
Barclay.[52] Perhaps the most influential supporter of Dissent in the Court
was George Villiers, Duke of Buckingham, "who heads the fanatics", and
from whom "the fanatics expect a day of redemption".[53] His actual links
with Dissenters may not have keen as close as was supposed by contem-

poraries, but it was noted that four leading Friends visited him during his imprisonment in the Tower in 1677.[54] Friends were also able to enlist the support of the Marquis of Halifax, whilst George Fox, a notable absentee from the royal petitioning of this period, maintained a fruitful relationship with the courtier Richard Marche.[55]

Once access was assured, Friends carefully selected those to attend the King with an eye to any possible claim they might have on his largesse. When Margaret Fell visited Charles II in July 1660 to petition on behalf of Fox, she took with her Ann Curtis, daughter of Robert Yeamans, the royalist sheriff of Bristol who had been hanged for his loyalty to the crown in 1643.[56] The King "showed much love to her", although not enough to prevent her from writing to him later reminding him of his unfulfilled promise to intervene in Fox's imprisonment.[57] Similarly fruitless was the visit of an un-named Friend who, according to his story, had an even greater claim on the royal gratitude: he had carried Charles ashore on his flight to France following the Battle of Worcester and "now desired nothing of him, but that he would set Friends at liberty". Like those many non-Quakers who claimed favour for similar acts during the Civil War the Friend's reward was little; although he conveniently carried a list of the names of 110 Friends who were imprisoned under sentence of *praemunire* the King would promise only that six Friends would be released.[58]

The courtier Sir John Reresby regretted that

> It was a great fault in our princes, that though upon request made to them they would grant and give orders for the thing desired, but took little care how they were obayed therein, which proved of ill effect to them.[59]

In the giving of promises, said Burnet, Charles II was "liberal to excess, because he intended nothing by them, but to get rid of importunities, and to silence all further pressing upon him".[60] Transforming these promises into action entailed persistent and expensive attendance at court; this, and the variety of channels that a single supplicant might be directed through before achieving success, militated against the type of spontaneous approach which Friends at least liked to think they were making to the sovereign.[61] When Friends obtained a royal order for the release of imprisoned Quakers in 1661 it was only after "the Truth, with *great labour, travail and care, came over* all, for Margaret [Fell] and Thomas Moore went often to the King ...".[62] When in 1670 George Fox sought to effect his wife's release from one of the periodic imprisonments she suffered under the sentence of *praemunire* which had been passed against her in 1663, he engaged the assistance of her two daughters, Mary Lower and Sarah Fell. It was only by "*diligent* attendance on it [that] they at *length* got an order from the King that their mother should not be molested", an order which proved to be short-lived, requiring a further delegation to attend court the next year.[63]

"Movings of the Lord" were clearly not sufficient when it came to working through the earthly corridors of the court, and so the majority of the 85 petitions, personal letters or printed papers which were delivered to Charles II by Friends (which accounted, of course, for only a fraction of the petitions delivered to Charles during his reign) were subject to strict supervision.[64] The two prime movers of regular and planned visits to the King in the immediate post-Restoration years were Margaret Fell and Thomas Moore:[65] later George Whitehead and Ellis Hookes (who was to be first clerk to the Meeting for Sufferings) also played a prominent part in planning and sustaining these approaches.[66] Fell's personal record as a petitioner was prodigious. She began her career of solicitation in 1660 when she travelled from Swarthmore to the capital, having been "Mov'd of the Lord to go to London, to speak to the King concerning the Truth, and the Sufferers for it ...."[67] Her work in the capital was vigorous and systematic: she wrote and circulated papers to all the royal family, "to the King, to the Duke of York, to the Duke of Gloucester, and to the Queen Mother, to the Prince of Orange, and to the Queen of Bohemia ...."[68] In all she was to spend eighteen months in London between 1660 and 1662 petitioning the King: in 1685 she visited the dying Charles and a few weeks later his brother, the new King. Her final address to the throne was in 1698, only two years before her death.[69]

In the later years of Charles II's reign Margaret Fell continued to play a leading role in the presentation of Quaker petitions at court. Under the guidance of the Meeting for Sufferings, founded in 1675, such approaches developed into co-ordinated visits to the King by one or a few outstanding individuals. However, in his tacit alliance with the Tory Anglicans in the last five years of his reign – a pact that allowed his reign to close in belated tranquillity – Charles showed himself much less receptive to such approaches than he had been in the early 1660s. To his mind Dissenters of all persuasions had forfeited his good will by their support of the opposition during the Exclusion Crisis.[70] In 1681 the King, both personally and through his council, ordered that the laws against Dissenters "vermin which swarm the land" – should be vigorously enforced,[71] an order whose effect is clearly shown in the data presented in Table 1. Despite the continued presence of Dissenters at court it was widely reported that the King had declared that he would "stick to his old friends, the old Cavaliers, and the Church of England party".[72] Burnet's observation concerning Charles – "in the end of his life he became cruel"[73] – is confirmed by the events of Margaret Fell's last visit to him in 1685. In marked contrast to earlier meetings with the King, which had been notable for their casual intimacy, Charles was "so Rough and Angry" that he refused to receive the paper she had prepared for him.[74] Fell's attempt to resurrect the informality of the 1660s with the new King was equally fruitless: James was still in the first 'Anglican' phase of his reign, and his response to her plea for relief from persecutors was simply "Go home, go home".[75]

The system of royal visitations pioneered by Fell, Moore and White-head, whereby leading individuals spoke to the sovereign on behalf of the Society, was to reach its apogee during the reign of James II when William Penn was to become the leading spokesman for Friends at court.[76] Among Friends Penn, said Burnet, "had the greatest credit, as he had free access at court".[77] Though James' accession had seen a dramatic change in the atmosphere of the court, with a revival of almost Caroline formality and morals, James was "still more accessible than most monarchs";[78] Penn, although a Quaker, was a trained courtier who clearly moved easily in such an atmosphere. His close relationship with James was cemented simply by a shared belief in the desirability of religious toleration, although not particularly (in Penn's case) in the removal of the political disabilities placed on Recusants.[79] This relationship, through which Penn came to act not only as an ambassador for James, but also as an ambassador to James on behalf of his co-religionists, was exploited by Friends in the same way they had earlier exploited the affability of Charles II.[80]

If the presence of Quakers at his court had been first an amusement for Charles, and later an irritation, then for James they served a far more important function. Their support, and that of other Dissenters, was an essential part of the King's religious strategy:

> the papists not being numerous enough by much to contest with the Church of England, he thought to make that party stronger by gaining to it the dissenters, whom he bated with liberty of concience.[81]

The visible sign of this support was the presentation to the King of petitions thanking him for his two Declarations of Indulgence of 1687 and 1688.[82] Burnet criticised those "who had so long reproached the Church of England, as too courtly in their submissions and flatteries, [and] now seemed to vie with them in those abject strains".[83] Halifax, in his *Letter to a Dissenter* warned against such petitioning: "these bespoken thanks are little less improper than love letters that were solicited by the lady to whom they are directed".[84]

Friends, encouraged by Penn, were at the fore of those who wished to thank the King.[85] In April 1687 for instance, an address of thanks from London Quakers was presented to the King for his first Indulgence. "The King looked very pleasant and smilingly upon Friends and seemed very much contented with it", whilst Friends had "a satisfaction in their proceedings".[86] For Friends any subsequent embarrassment caused by these encounters – which were generally recorded only in documents for private Quaker consumption[87] – could be got round; what became of concern was the lasting reflections made upon the Society owing to Penn's continued personal loyalty to the ex-monarch after 1688.[88] It should be stressed though, that in his positive approaches to James II, Penn reflected the views of the Society's leadership and that subsequent Quaker attempts to vilify Penn for misrepresenting Friends' views have little basis in the record of the Society's official conduct in 1687–88.[89]

Because of the persistent taint of Jacobitism, Penn, not to put too fine a point on it, became a scapegoat to the Williamite regime after 1688 for the Quaker leadership's enthusiastic collaboration with James.[90] However, to censure Penn may have implied an inhibition on personal approaches to the throne, and after 1688 we see a gradual retreat from the earlier emphasis placed on individuals going informally to court (something that was no doubt encouraged by the personalities of both Charles and James)[91] towards a position where all addresses and petitions were presented by delegate groups collectively representing the views of the Society, or, more typically the views of the Meeting for Sufferings. Attempts had been made to do this as early as 1675,[92] but it was not until after the Penn debacle, and particularly in the 1690s, that success was achieved. In 1698, with the force of 23 years practice behind it, the Meeting was able to state its position explicitly, "that when any Friend or Friends are inclined to make application to the King in matters relating to this Meeting, that they first acquaint this Meeting, and take their advice and direction therein".[93] It was ironic, especially given the fact that her son-in-law William Meade had led the attack on Penn from within the Society, that Margaret Fell was to be the first victim of this new regulation.[94]

In 1698, at the age of 83, Margaret Fell paid her last visit to London, apparently unaware of changes that had taken place both within the Society and at court. Some at the Yearly Meeting were concerned at her presence in the capital; there was, it was reported "some exercise, perticularly by the means of M.F. whose extreme age some few did impose upon to her dishonor ...."[95] Fell however once more took upon herself the heroic mantle of the early 1660s, delivering (by the hand of her daughter) a letter to William III written in tones entirely redolent of 1660 and 1661.[96] She first strove to link the Restoration and the Glorious Revolution – "I was exercised in this manner the first year King Charles the second came to the crown ... And now I am to acquaint King William" – and went on to reiterate the sufferings and loyalty of Friends since that date.[97] The letter, with its nostalgia for the 1660s, has inspired the many biographers of Margaret Fell,[98] but it resulted in a wounding response from the Meeting for Sufferings. In July a minute was approved that

> Whereas on the 24/5 past a paper was delivered to the King by one possibly not acquainted with a minute and order of this Meeting relating to public concern of Friends bearing date 18/1/1698 last past, for the prevention of the like for the future the said former minute is here again repeated verbatim and the Quarterly Meetings severally to be acquainted therewith.[99]

The minute, along with a letter explaining the desire of the Meeting for Sufferings "to prevent any inconveniency of any ones presenting anything to the government on behalf of Friends before its presented to this Meeting" was duly circulated, not least to Lancashire Quarterly, and Swarthmore Monthly, Meetings.[100]

Under the care of the Meeting for Sufferings the petitions, addresses and approaches to the throne can be seen to have been of two distinct varieties. First there were petitions and approaches on behalf of specific individual sufferers; secondly there were addresses of thanks from the whole Society for particular items of legislation, and also regular loyal addresses, as if the Society were a corporation or borough, upon occasions of national danger or the coronation of a new monarch. In contrast with Friends' earlier contacts with the crown, all such addresses were governed by a new impersonality and formality of approach, which was to increase as the eighteenth century progressed.

The matter of relief for individual sufferers was a workmanlike affair, with Friends being obliged to approach the throne either directly or via high-ranking officials (perhaps with a local interest), generally on several occasions in any one case. The mechanics of a royal solicitation, and the stage at which it would be considered a worthwhile course to take, are illustrated by the case of Margaret Coulborn from Freckleton. In July 1692 she was found guilty at the Preston assize of blasphemy, having claimed that "I have seen Christ with my eyes, and felt him with my hands".[101] Margaret Coulborn was also accused of denying the Resurrection – a reflection, perhaps, of aspects of traditional Quaker christology – and of adultery.[102] Her defence, rejected by the court at Preston, was that her words, intended as an explanation of the source of her authority for preaching, had been deliberately misinterpreted.[103] What is clear is that she was an active and successful Quaker preacher in an area where the vigilant Anglican incumbent Richard Clegg of Kirkham, who had instigated the trial, rightly feared losses of parishioners to the Friends.[104]

Refusing to pay a fine of ten pounds, Coulborn was imprisoned at Lancaster Castle, and remained confined despite Quaker approaches to Lord Willoughby, vice-chancellor of the Duchy of Lancaster, "to stop proceedings and get this poor woman discharged", to the Barons of the Exchequer, and to the assize at Preston.[105] At this stage it was also decided to utilise royal influence. Hester Beedle presented a petition to Queen Mary on the prisoner's behalf, and received the promise "that she would take care in the Friends case by speaking to the judges that goes that circuit".[106] This was followed with an approach by Thomas Lower to a Lord Chief Justice, informing him of Margaret Coulborn's case, and "that the Queen had particularly spoken to him to get her discharge". This move was a success, and it was reported in September 1694 that "Margaret Coulborn was discharged by the Judges at the latter end of the assizes".[107]

The release of the imprisoned Quakeress did not bring to an end the interest of the Meeting for Sufferings in the matter. Thomas Lower, one of the Lancashire correspondents at the Meeting for Sufferings, wrote asking her "to send a few lines of acknowledgement to the Queen for her kindness". The desired paper was sent first to the Meeting for approval, and before being presented it was edited and a clean copy returned to Lancashire for Coulborn's signature. Eventually in December 1694, nearly four years after the case had begun, the case came to a close with a note that "the paper of thanks of Margaret Coulborn is delivered to the Countess of Derby for the Queen".[108]

It is clear from the Coulborn case that Friends were still able, even after the embarrassments of the late 1680s, to utilise the personal influence of the throne in order to make lesser officials look more kindly upon the Quakers they faced in the courts. As we have seen, King William III was less accessible than James had been.[109] However, he was able to delegate the more public aspects of his duties, and the special prerogative of mercy that traditionally belonged to Queens, to Queen Mary, who, as we have seen, was quite capable of intervening in the process of law to assist a single Quaker.[110] In order to maintain their influence at court, however, Friends found it desirable to remind the sovereign and his family continually of Quaker loyalty, and also of the traditional access granted to, and favour given from, the throne, which by the early eighteenth century they were claiming as an age old Quaker privilege.

The addresses of the whole Society were normally prepared and delivered by small sub-committees of the Meeting for Sufferings comprising eminent metropolitan and perhaps some provincial Friends.[111] The group – no longer the outstanding individual as with Fell and Penn – presenting the address might nevertheless include a Quaker with some existing entree at court such as Daniel Quare, the Quaker clockmaker under William and Mary[112] or, under Anne, Nicholas Gates, "whose daughter had been nurse to the Duke of Gloucester her beloved only child", and who was able to speak "a few words of acknowledgement of favour to his family".[113]

The royal response to the increasingly formal Quaker addresses were also marked by stereotyping: the addresses would be "kindly accepted" and Friends would receive an assurance from the monarch that "he would protect Friends".[114] After initial disagreement in 1687 – prompted by objections from the rigorist Aberdeen Quakers – about the inclusion of the word 'humble' in such addresses, the word and its derivatives became standard.[115] When a delegation of Friends led by George Whitehead greeted George I in 1714 they approached "the royal presence" in "great humility".[116] George II was met by Friends in a similar fashion; Joseph Wyeth, who had replaced George Whitehead as the leading Quaker courtier following the latter's death in 1723, led a group with a "humble" address, which they "humbly" begged they might present to the sovereign, asking at the same time permission that they might "with great deference humbly approach thy royal presence on the same solemn occasions, which we do now".[117]

Some Friends were not unaware of the departure which such courtly and ritualistic approaches to the throne marked from the behaviour expected of Quakers, for example as described by Barclay in his *Apology*;[118] nor was there an absence of protest against the suggestion that delegations should adopt more courtly postures, such as the kissing of hands. Henry

Gouldney penned the following sardonic account of the Quaker interview
with George I following the 1715 rebellion. George Whitehead, he wrote,

> had the usual honour to present it [the address] with an introductery
> discourse. Though not very long, yet considering it was not lively, was
> too long in the occasions. Upon presenting it, it was returned by the
> King to him for reading, and he, by a previous agrecment, delivered it
> to B. Coole who read it with an aier usual to his eloquence, and made
> humble Corsees at the end of every Paragraffe. At the end, he
> concluded with Amen saith the Reader and G.W. as wittily added: so
> say we all – the King seemed pleased with our appearance, and I
> suppose might have been favour'd to kiss his hand, wch some seemed
> willing enough of, had we not before declared our dissatisfaction in
> introduceing a Novility, and if they wd., we wd. either not goe, or at
> least signifie to him our straight[ness] in the case.[119]

As we shall see later, Gouldney, like the majority of Lancashire
Quakers, was one of those Friends who refused to take the Affirmation
granted to them in 1696. These Friends tended to be opposed also to the
urbane lifestyles adopted by London Quakers (and by Friends elsewhere
in the South), which to Gouldney were typified by Quaker behaviour at
court.[120]

Nonetheless such audiences, despite their increasing (and to some,
objectionable) conformity to worldly ways, served a number of valuable
functions for the Friends. Firstly, in bringing together urban and rural
Quakers from the North and South, and even in the early 1700s
rehabilitating William Penn within the structure of collective approaches,
they publicly reasserted unity within the Society.[121] More importantly these
meetings reassured Friends that they could rely on the continued favour of
the monarch and also served a function in sustaining a public image of
Quaker loyalty. After Penn's deputation had visited Queen Anne in 1702,
he and John Vaughton were instructed to "take care to get the Queen's
answer to said address inserted in the *Gazette*".[122] Thus, by publicising the
reception they found at court, and the assurance of protection they received
from the monarch, Friends were doing their utmost to inform the world
they were the sovereign's most loyal Dissenters.[123]

Friends were also anxious in their addresses to establish a reputation
for supporting the throne during difficult times. They had been at pains to
deny any involvement in the Monmouth Rebellion; in Somerset, with 3
Quakers implicated in the disturbances, Friends obtained and presented to
James II, along with an assurance of their loyalty, certificates from their
Anglican neighbours of their innocence and good behaviour.[124] As we have
seen, their commitment to James thereby attested was followed by equally
firm support for William and Mary – and for Anne. Then, on his accession
they told George I that it was their "known principle to live peacably
under governments". His arrival had "dissipated the just apprehensions"

which they were under, "of losing those religious and civil liberties which
were granted ... by law in the reign of King William III".[125] Following the
"late Unjust and Unnatural Rebellion" of 1715, they claimed

> we can do no less than assure the King, That as it is our Duty to
> demean Our Selves towards the King's Person and Government, with
> all Faithful Obedience, so we are determined, by Divine Assistance,
> devoutly and heartily to Pray the God and Father of all Our Mercies,
> To vouchsafe unto the King a Long, Peaceable and Prosperous
> Reign...[126]

In their ever-intensifying commitment to the Hanoverian succession
Friends were even tempted in 1745 to dilute their peace testimony and had
to be warned by the Meeting for Sufferings against being concerned "in
the public Associations for providing men, horses, arms, or promoting any
other warlike preparations". The Meeting was confident that such a
refusal would in no way detract from Friends' well known "fidelity and
cheerful submission" to the "mild and just government" of George II.[127]
Earlier, they had been urged to "excite" neighbours, friends and "all under
our influence, to the most steady adherance to the present government, as
an effectual evidence ..." of their loyalty.[128] Despite the warning by the
Meeting for Sufferings, some Friends drew an exceedingly fine dividing
line between non-belligerence and active support for the Protestant
Succession; at Darlington for instance Quakers allegedly provided 10,000
woollen waistcoats for the Duke of Cumberland's army as it marched
towards a Scottish winter.[129] Elsewhere Friends provided intelligence and
eager hospitality for the Duke and his troops.[130] In the light of such
support, risking if not breaching the Quaker peace testimony, it is not
surprising that the Quaker post-Culloden address was particularly
welcome to George II: "he had not received any one which had give him
so much real satisfaction".[131]

As Friends' loyalty to the political establishment deepened, so, as we
have seen, the style of their addresses became more courtly and more
emphatic. As we have also seen, Friends received the assuring words they
sought; "I am always pleased to do you service", "you may be assured of my
protection", or other such intimations of goodwill and favour. Such
phrases, although bland and part of courtly ritual, reflected the genuine
commitment of Quakers nationwide to the Hanoverians. William Stout
for instance, a barometer surely of the feelings of the average Quaker in
the provinces, carefully noted the results of these interviews in his diary.
He wrote that it "gave great satisfaction to all well wishers of the nation's
true interest" when the new King George declared his support for the
1689 Toleration Act. In 1727 a similar declaration from George II "gave
great satisfaction to all people ... of all ranks and persuasions".[132]

Access to the court, and to the King's person, remained fairly easy
for Friends during the period under discussion. However, the relaxed

spontaneity of the interviews with Charles II, depending in part on the King's tolerance of the Quaker supplicants as unwitting entertainers, was replaced by an increasing formalism in those with William, Anne and the Georges. At the same time, although the sovereign continued to play an important role in government there was no longer sufficient latitude for a monarch to issue an Indulgence suspending the laws as Charles II had done in 1672;[133] nor, after the Toleration Act was there much need for a King to exert himself in defence of any of his Protestant subject's right at least to worship. Royalty could still usefully intercede on behalf of particular Quakers embroiled in the process of the law, but on general issues, and particularly matters involving legislation, with the political initiative shifting elsewhere all the sovereign could do was recommend the Quaker case to his supporters in Parliament. So in 1695, in response to a petition seeking relief from statutory oaths, King William told George Whitehead that "he would do what he could for us ... and speak to some of the Members in the said case". A year later he told Daniel Quare that he would approach the Speaker on Friend's behalf in the same matter "if he had opportunity".[134] By the 1720s although Friends had become an ever present feature of the court, their presentation of addresses and petitions had become little more than ritual protestations of loyalty, designed mainly for public consumption. In order to bring about changes in the law, Friends chose instead to rely increasingly on the good offices of "divers persons of distinction", "persons of the highest station", "persons in power", and "principal persons in authority" at Westminster.[135]

The scale of Quaker petitioning of the monarch was matched, if not exceeded, by their petitioning of Parliament. After 1689 Friends concentrated their parliamentary lobbying, if not to change the law, then in order to gain exemptions for themselves in respect of those parts of their "Quakerly" behaviour which set them apart from the world, and often put them outside the law. The matters of oaths,[136] tithes,[137] taxation,[138] and the tacit recognition of the Quaker mode of marriage,[139] all became the subjects of major campaigns. The history of this particular aspect of the Quaker's relationship with the state has been written by N.C. Hunt, who examined Quaker parliamentary activity in the context of the origins of political pressure groups, presenting Friends as a prototype of, say, the Anti-Corn Law League.[140]

Hunt stressed the response of the Society to outside pressure and adversity, its concentration on Parliament, its marshalling of data so as to persuade the legislature to change the law, and the co-ordinating activities of a central committee, in this case the Meeting for Sufferings. By doing so he confined himself to discussing the organisation of lobbying, and with the exception of the Tithe Bill campaigns of the 1730s, he avoided discussing any of the broader issues behind the Quaker campaigns, for example the Affirmation controversy of the eighteenth century.[141] Consequently Hunt provided only a partial picture of the Meeting for Sufferings, whose archive made up the bulk of his source material. Hunt argued that the Meeting "was from the outset intended to be the spear-head and galvanising force of as strong a political pressure group as could be created",[142] but it is clear that it was in fact only at best a secondary co-ordinator for these pressure group activities. The Meeting for Sufferings was primarily concerned with providing legal and other advice for Friends either undergoing or under threat of prosecution: it was preoccupied with seeking relief for imprisoned Friends at home and overseas: and it was central to the maintenance of discipline and the day-to-day administration of the Society.[143]

It was part of Hunt's view of the Friends as a prototype of a nineteenth and twentieth century pressure group that they compiled information so as to get parliament to change the law; this overlooks the fact, as we have seen, that they showed themselves anxious before 1689 to get the monarch to give dispensations *from* the law. Nonetheless Friends did, as Hunt shows so clearly, use the Meeting for Sufferings as a means to bring pressure to bear on Members of Parliament. Having admitted as much we must beware of writing the history of the pressure group before its advent. Any attempts – notably by James II in 1687–88 – to pin Parliament down, to bring pressure to bear on Parliament from the outside, were deeply resented by those who subscribed to the pure doctrine, proclaimed in answer to James II s notorious "Three Questions", that members should vote only on the basis of debates in the House.[144] In the face of such parliamentarianism, extraneous attempts to sway members were likely to be regarded as species of "tumultuous petitioning", and thus all approaches to Parliament needed to be cautious, discreet, and well supervised.

In organising approaches to Parliament, the Meeting for Sufferings adopted the same powers of central control that it had claimed for approaches to the monarch. When Quarterly Meetings wrote to county representatives at Westminster on a particular matter their letters were directed to be first sent "unsealed" to the Meeting in London.[145] If we return to Hunt's analysis of the similarities of the Meeting for Sufferings to a political association, we may say the Meeting for Sufferings was not a pressure group, but it was in *some* ways like the spearhead of a pressure group. It is perhaps a common fault of interest groups to fall in more with those to whom they are supposed to represent their constituents' interests and less with the views of the constituents themselves. If this happened to the Meeting for Sufferings, it may cast a different light on the Meeting's wish to have sight of all letters directed to Westminster which claimed to contain the Quaker viewpoint. Indeed it is possible to suggest that in its guise as an "early political association", the Meeting for Sufferings (as opposed to the Society in general) came to regard particular Bills or clauses as not a means to an end (the end in question being some sort of relief for Friends) but as an end in themselves, the end being the maintenance of the Meetings *raison d'être*. It was the growth of this attitude in London which led to an increased sense of alienation in both the more remote counties such as Lancashire and Yorkshire, and also in

Scotland and Ireland. As will be seen later this was never shown more clearly than in the struggle for a modified Affirmation.[146]

Hunt showed that in order to obtain favours from the government, the members of the Meeting for Sufferings became increasingly quiescent to government wishes. Campaigns were embarked upon, for instance, only with the concurrence of a "Person in Power", (whom Hunt identifies as Walpole), and who advised Friends when they might expect to receive a sympathetic hearing.[147] For its part, the Meeting for Sufferings was alert to incidents involving Friends that might cast the Society in a bad, or extremist light, for example the refusal of Lancashire Friends to pay fee-farm rents in the late 1690s.[148] This, like other cases, was prompted to some degree by an acceptance by the Friends involved that the demands of Truth were greater than any civil impositions.[149] Increasingly as the eighteenth century wore on, the administrators of the Society in London tempered their view of Truth to accord with the political realities which they had to face in order to achieve the concessions which they felt Friends needed.[150] Needless to say, this opened up a schism between provincial Friends and the Meeting for Sufferings, who wished to see discretion in the place of zeal, and an acceptance of the expedient in the place of "unprofitable and tedious debates".[151]

As we have seen, the attitude of Parliament towards Friends prior to 1689 can be gauged in some degree from the nature of the anti-Dissenter laws passed during the period, and from Parliament's frequent calls for these laws to be enforced. However, Parliament was rarely unanimous in these actions and a persistent undercurrent of tolerationist sentiment was evident at Westminster.[152] The extremities of religious policy presented by James II (combined with a practical recognition that the liberty granted to Dissenters by him could never easily be recalled) were enough to convince many parliamentarians that the time had arrived for some official recognition to be given to Dissenters.[153] Between the passing of the Toleration Act in 1689 and the failure of the Quaker Tithe Bill campaign of 1736 Friends gained successive concessions from Parliament in matters relating to their behaviour and testimonies. In recognition of the influence they had apparently gained in Parliament, much of the popular opposition to Friends was directed at MPs in the form of petitions and appeals from the localities, questioning Quaker loyalty and calling for the suppression of their meetings.[154] The success of such moves, "looked upon by many in authority as a confronting and opposing the Act of Toleration", was limited;[155] nonetheless there remained within Parliament a rump of anti-Quaker sentiment which rarely failed to take advantage of any opportunity to express their opinions.

Friends were decried during the debates on the Bill of Indulgence in 1689 as disloyal crypto-Catholics.[156] In the course of the many debates which led to the passing of the Occasional Conformity Act of 1711, they were branded, along with other Dissenters, as being "against the church and government".[157] During the reign of Queen Anne a political alliance between country Tories and a disillusioned and demoralised clergy united under the slogan of the "Church in Danger" to mount an effective campaign against Dissent.[158] The 1711 Act (passed at the fifth attempt) prevented Dissenters from holding public or corporate office by outlawing the common practice of occasional conformity.[159] In 1714 a second measure, the Schism Act, designed "to extirpate nonconformity ... in every part of the nation" forbade teaching in any schools not in receipt of a Bishop's license.[160] Ultimately neither of these Acts was effective.[161] But taken together they reveal a strong and persistent parliamentary opposition to the Toleration granted in 1689.

Neither did the Quaker parliamentary triumphs, such as the Affirmation Act of 1722, pass without the presence of determined opposition. In the debate in the House of Lords the Bishop of Rochester objected to such a concession being "allowed to a set of people who were hardly Christian"; deriding the Toleration of 1689 he added "that the calling the Quakers, Christians by act of parliament, was a sort of side-wind reflection upon Christianity itself".[162] In a later debate on the bill the same Bishop, supported by the Archbishop of York, and also the Earl of Stafford, Earl Coningsby and Lord North and Grey, "endeavoured to prove, that the Quakers were not Christian".[163] Such views were not repeated during the debates on the Tithe Bill of 1736, which failed to enter the statute book due as much to a dispute between Walpole and Bishop Gibson of London, and also to the fact that the Bill was ill-prepared, than to the presence of any anti-Quaker sentiment in the House.[164] Nonetheless the Quaker refusal to pay tithe was condemned in the Lords as being a pretence of seditious consequences, whilst in the Commons the Jacobite Sir John St. Aubin, in tones reminiscent of the early 1660s, argued that Friends stood for "wild excesses, which under the false colour of religion would invade the order and discipline of civil society.[165]

Thus although Friends did, as Hunt shows, increasingly win the support of both Houses of Parliament, there remained a considerable bulk of opposition towards legislation designed to favour Quakers, both amongst the prelates in the Lords and the Tory supporters of the Established Church in the Commons. What remains to be seen now is how far those supporters and opponents of Dissent in Parliament put their views on Quakerism into practice in the country. In Lancashire, as elsewhere, the men elected to serve in Parliament were also prominent and active members of the county bench, and thus to a large extent their views and actions can be taken as being representative of the establishment in the country. What follows is a general discussion of the parliamentary representation of the county drawn from secondary sources, and then a more detailed discussion of particular Members of Parliament, designed to examine and illustrate the various factors outwith considerations of political or religious loyalty that might determine an MP's behaviour. This will be supported by evidence drawn from secondary material and printed and manuscript Quaker sources. Finally I will contrast the difficulties which the Establishment faced in coming to terms with Quakerism with some of the difficulties which Friends faced in coming to terms with the Establishment, for it is with these difficulties that the subject matter for the bulk of this book is concerned.

A total of fourteen Members of Parliament sat for Lancashire in the Commons; the county freeholders returned two knights of the shire, whilst the boroughs of Lancaster, Preston, Wigan, Liverpool, Clitheroe and Newton returned two Members each.[166] The representation of the county was dominated by two major considerations, family influence and family continuity, and both tended to militate against the influence which Quakers might wish to exert on particular MPs.[167] The Stanley family, despite periods of occasional governmental displeasure, were probably the most influential in the county; as head of the family, the Earl of Derby could wield considerable influence over both the nominations to particular constituencies and also the behaviour of substantial parts of the electorate. The family could count amongst its members six who sat in Parliament between 1660 and 1740, whilst other relatives, for example, Thomas Patten, MP for Preston in the Convention Parliament and father-in-law of Sir Thomas Stanley who sat for the borough between 1695 and 1698, also held seats.[168] The Derby family held particular influence in Preston although their main rival for parliamentary influence, Charles Lord Brandon, could be reasonably confident of support in Lancaster, and to a lesser extent Liverpool.[169] It was surely unfortunate for Lancashire Quakers that one of their most famous martyrs died whilst imprisoned for non-payment of tithes at the suit of the Countess of Derby in 1663. The Stanleys, described as the family which "never forgot", can hardly have relished the reflections made by Quakers against the Countess following the death of Oliver Atherton, and more particularly the judgement that was noted to have befallen her, that "On that Day three Weeks when Oliver Atherton's Body was carried through Ormskirk to be buried, the Countess died", an illustration, wrote George Fox, of how "the Lord pursued the hard-hearted persecutor".[170] Although the Stanleys were allegedly uninterested in the prosecution of Dissent, there is certainly no evidence to suggest that they had any inclination to promote the interests of Friends before the Glorious Revolution or for that matter after.[171] In addition their main agent in the country, Roger Kenyon, was a keen proponent of the full execution of the laws against Dissent.[172]

The Stanleys and the Brandons were not the only families to exert local influence in parliamentary elections. The Legh family dominated proceedings in the borough of Newton, whilst the Bradshaighs effectively controlled the borough of Wigan. Five members of the Legh family, all Tories, sat in Parliament between 1660 and 1740, whilst four members of the Bradshaigh family gave it continuous representation in Parliament for all but seven years in the same period.[173] Family links among the parliamentary representatives of the North-Western counties were ubiquitous.[174] Of the 139 individuals who represented the county and its boroughs in Parliament between 1660 and 1740, at least 84, or sixty per cent, were related to at least one other Member sitting for Lancashire during the years 1640–1740. Thirty-one of these had fathers who sat for seats in the county during this period, 25 had brothers and 22 had sons. Fifty MPs had other close relatives who sat for the county.[175] It need hardly be added that those MPs without any strong ties of kinship to their fellow-Members for the county did find equally natural bonds with them in terms of a shared outlook on the world, stemming from the possession of identical positions in society, shared levels of wealth etc.[176] This strong element of family continuity in the county's parliamentary representation was also to be found in Cumberland and Westmorland, where there was similarly a strong rivalry between two leading families (the Musgraves and the Lowthers) for the possession of political influence.[177] It will be shown below that the continued presence in Parliament of families with long-standing traditions of conflict and hostility towards Quakers and Quakerism almost guaranteed that Lancashire Friends gained little sympathy from their representatives at Westminster. The support they did find came either from staunch Whigs, or, in the post-Revolution era, from men not drawn from traditional gentry stock, as much motivated by commercial as religious precepts. This lack of direct political influence, combined with an apparent inability to influence the conduct of the Society in London, accounted in great part for the distinctive nature of Friends in the county.

Amongst the foremost instigators of prosecutions against Lancashire Quakers in the post-Restoration period there were several Members of Parliament. Richard Kirkby, MP for the borough of Lancaster between 1661 and 1681, Thomas Preston of Holker Hall, MP for the borough of Lancaster between 1664 and his death in January 1679, and Sir Roger Bradshaigh, MP for the County between 1660 and 1678, were but three of a number of parliamentarians who clashed with Friends either through their position as justice of the peace, owners or impropriators of tithe, or both.[178] Whatever the reason for the conflict, this particular group of MPs were unlikely to transmogrify their hostility to Quakers in the country into support for them at Westminster. Moreover the continued presence of members of their families in Parliament into the late seventeenth century, and in the case of the Bradshaighs, mid-eighteenth century, ensured that ancient hostilities remained alive.[179] A brief examination of these three particular families will reveal just how intense the anti-Quaker feeling was amongst them.

Richard Kirkby, sometimes known as Colonel Kirkby, was the Member of Parliament for the borough of Lancaster between 1661 and 1680. His father, Roger Kirkby, had sat for the borough in 1640 until he was disabled as a royalist in 1642; Richard Kirkby's son, Roger, was the Member for Lancaster between 1685 and 1687, and from 1689 to 1702.[180] The family estate was at Kirkby Ireleth in Furness, some four and a half miles to the North-West of Ulverston on the Duddon estuary, and Kirkby was a

neighbour of Margaret Fell's Swarthmore estate. Much of the later
hostility shown by Kirkby to the Quakers arose due to the contrasting
fortunes of his and the Fell family during the Civil War and Interregnum
period.[181] During this time the career of Margaret Fell's first husband,
Judge Thomas Fell, blossomed; a barrister by training he became a justice
of the peace for Lancashire in 1641 and a Member of the Long Parliament
for Lancaster, replacing Roger Kirkby in 1645. In 1649 he was appointed
vice-chancellor of the Duchy of Lancaster and attorney for the County
Palatine; two years later he became an assize judge for the Chester and
North Wales circuit.[182] Fell's estate of Swarthmore was also considerably
expanded during this period by his purchase of fee-farm rents and
confiscated land, assisted, it was alleged, by an abuse of his position in
Parliament and the use of forged debentures.[183]

In contrast to this good, if questionable fortune, the experiences of the
Kirkbys were gloomy. Roger Kirkby had been discharged from the
commission of the peace in 1641. The loss of local influence implied by
disablement was compounded by sequestration, and between the outbreak
of Civil War and the Restoration the income of the family fell by over fifty
per cent. The return of the monarch in 1660, moreover, brought little
reward except a position in the Coldstream Guards for Richard Kirkby,
then head of the family, and his son Roger.[184] In 1668 Richard Kirkby was
forced to ask the House of Commons for protection against his creditors;
five years later he petitioned the sovereign for office, claiming he was
without bread, clothes, money and credit,[185] a claim he repeated in 1680,
the year before his death. In view of these facts it is not entirely surprising
that Colonel Richard Kirkby did his utmost when the opportunity arose to
encourage the prosecution of Quakers in the Swarthmore area, to whom
Judge Fell had afforded some measure of protection; in particular Kirkby
encouraged the financial disablement of Fell's widow, Margaret. After all,
there can have been nothing more irksome to Kirkby than to see his rival's
widow not only reaping the fruits of his misfortune, but also distributing
them amongst heretics.

Kirkby was an active parliamentarian; he chaired seven and sat on 285
committees in the Cavalier Parliament, including the committee which
drew up the first Conventicle Act. In 1670 he spoke in the House against
toleration.[186] As a justice of the peace he was responsible for breaking up
Quaker meetings and instigating prosecutions under the Conventicle Act,
both in Lancashire and in London, where he fulfilled his military duties.[187]
The reason for his particular notoriety, however, was the leading role he
played in the prosecution of Margaret Fell and George Fox at the
Lancaster assizes in March 1663/64. Kirkby, along with his cousin Sir
Daniel Fleming, had instigated the initial proceedings against the two
Friends at the Sessions, and during Margaret Fell's trial it was Kirkby who
urged the presiding Judge Twisden to pass the sentence of *praemunire*
against her.[188] Fleming, as has already been seen, was keen to attack the
Quakers' economic resources, and Kirkby probably shared this view; in

1685 Kirkby's brother, William, similarly a justice of the peace in the county ordered Daniel Abraham to tell his mother-in-law (Margaret Fell) that "we will not take your lives, but whilst you have anything, we will take it".[189] The *praemunire* of 1664, however, no doubt also fulfilled Kirkby's not unreasonable desire to turn the tables on his neighbour. There was even possibly a more positive side to this vindictiveness, for it could be claimed in Kirkby's defence that he sought stability in his own locality. Thus he supported the attempts by Margaret Fell's son, George Fell, an opponent of Quakerism, to obtain his mother's forfeit estate in 1664.[190]

Although unsuccessful, Kirkby and George Fell attempted the same course in 1669, when Margaret Fell was again imprisoned under the sentence of 1664.[191] What is important to remember is that Kirkby also carried this local campaign against Quakers into Parliament, moving in 1668 that the laws of 1662 and 1663 against Dissenters be more rigorously enforced.[192] In the view of George Fox, Kirkby, like so many other members of the post-Restoration Lancashire establishment, came to a sad end through his activities against Friends: "Colonel Kirkby wasted away all his estate and buried three wives".[193] This judgement notwithstanding, Kirkby's son continued to live at the estate of Kirkby Ireleth until shortly before his death in 1708, when it was sold. Although he had favoured the repeal of the Penal Laws and Tests, and despite his close association with Lord Brandon, Roger Kirkby maintained his father's animus against Friends.[194]

He was partly motivated by economic considerations, and was one of the many Lancashire landowners who took advantage of legislation passed in 1696 in order to obtain judgement by means of a justices' warrant against Quakers refusing to pay tithes.[195] The frequent prosecutions which he brought guaranteed a continuation of the conflict between his family and Friends which his father had begun.[196]

If one Member of Parliament might harbour strong personal grievances against the Quakers because of rancour at the fortunes of Puritan and then Quaker neighbours, then others could have equally personal reasons for not favouring them. Thomas Preston of Holker Hall falls into this category; he was knight of the shire from 1664 to his death in January 1678. His eldest son, by his marriage to a daughter of Sir Gilbert Houghton (whose family were prominent in the representation of the borough of Preston), also named Thomas, sat for Lancaster from 1689 until his death in January 1696. Although he died without a male heir, the family tradition in Parliament was continued by his daughter's husband, Sir William Lowther of Marske, who obtained the Holker estate by this marriage, and by his son, Thomas, who sat for Lancaster between 1722 and 1745.[197] The Holker estate lay some two miles to the South-West of Cartmel, which like Swarthmore was an early centre of Quakerism in Lancashire. Thomas Preston was lord of the manor of Cartmel and lay impropriator of all the tithes within Cartmel parish.[198] Local office holding in Furness had profited Preston and allowed him to expand his estates before 1640. However, as with Kirkby, the Civil War, and his staunch loyalty to the royalist cause, brought an end to Preston's prosperity, and a composition fine of some £1,592, levied in 1649, left the Holker estate in a perilous financial condition.[199] Thomas Preston's solution to such hardship was to increase the level of customary fines payable by his tenants, and to maximise the yield of tithes due from his impropriations in and around Cartmel. Like other landlords he experienced severe opposition, led in this instance by Thomas Atkinson, who was converted to Quakerism three years later when George Fox first visited the village.[200] This dispute, which in the first instance involved the generality of the inhabitants of Cartmel, was to continue after 1660 in a heightened form, specifically between Preston and his Quaker tenants. Moreover, as will be shown below, his son, Thomas, also experienced the same need to receive tithe payments, and experienced the same difficulty with Quakers. Both were prepared to use the threat of the laws directed against Dissenters, and in particular Quakers, in order to expedite the payment of their tithes.[201]

The hostility of the Preston family towards Friends was illustrated in 1660 when Fox was imprisoned in Lancaster Castle. There he received a visit from "old Preston's wife, of Holker, and a great company with her and she used many abusive words to me and told me my tongue should be cut out and I should be hanged".[202] Thomas Preston himself, like Richard Kirkby, was involved in the trial of George Fox and Margaret Fell in 1663 that led to Margaret Fell's *praemunire;* Holker Hall was used as a private meeting place for Lancashire justices to plan their strategy against Quakers, and Preston took an active part in the examination of Fox and Fell.[203] Thomas Preston's son clashed with Quakers over his claims for tithe, and also in his capacity as justice and deputy lieutenant.[204]

As late as 1686, when Friends in London were beginning to view their persecutors with more tolerant eyes, Thomas Lower, Margaret Fell's son-in-law, described with relish an accident that had befallen Preston, apparently as a judgement for his proceedings against Friends.[205] George Fox drily noted that Preston and his children had suffered premature deaths, whilst his wife "died in a miserable condition".[206]

If the attitude of Members of Parliament towards Quakers could be determined at least in part by personal and financial considerations, as in the case of the Kirkbys and Prestons (and later the Lowthers of Marske), then it could also be governed by considerations of duty. Both Preston and Kirkby were active members of the bench in Lancashire, and as the local enforcers of the penal laws against Dissenters and recusants they were placed in the front line of the conflict between Quakers and the state.[207] As has been shown above, their particular attitudes to Quakers could not be expected to lead them to dispense an impartial justice towards Friends, and certainly neither could they, or their successors, be expected to further the Quaker cause in Parliament. Other MPs who were also active on the bench, clashed with Quakers only when attempting to fulfil their sworn duty as magistrates. One such was Sir Roger Bradshaigh of Haigh Hall, Wigan, who was a magistrate, sheriff of the county and, between 1660 and 1678, knight of the shire for the county. After being created a Baronet in 1679, Bradshaigh was succeeded by his son in Parliament, who sat for Wigan in 1679, and for the county in 1685. He in turn was followed by his son, Roger, who sat in Parliament for a period of over fifty years from 1695 to 1746.[208]

The first Sir Roger Bradshaigh, who was a minor at the outbreak of the Civil War, saw his estates remain relatively unmolested throughout the duration of the conflict. On attaining his majority he was able to assist the royalist cause by joining with others in order to employ a variety of legal devices which eased the burden of sequestrations passed upon less fortunate neighbours.[209] As an entrepreneur who employed the majority of his capital exploiting the vast mineral resources that lay beneath his estates at Haigh, Sir Roger seems to have had little dependence on income from tithe or other forms of rents which might bring about conflict with Quakers.[210] That such conflicts did arise was due mainly to the fact that Sir Roger was a conscientious and dutiful local administrator. Bradshaigh had been uprooted from a Catholic home, and despite his Protestantism remained tolerant of neighbouring Roman Catholics, amongst whom he could number the Blundells of Crosby.[211] He was convinced, however, that the "Phanaticks", were a threat to the stability of local and national government.[212] As sheriff, and a prominent justice, Bradshaigh was no doubt responsible for the resolution which came from the Lancashire justices of the peace in August 1664 that "the Acts for suppressing unlaw- ful Conventicles upon pretence of Religion by what sort of dissenters soever, presbiterian or other, be put in due and impartial execucion".[213] It is also possible to see Bradshaigh's hand behind the address from the Lancashire justices which was sent to the Lords of the Council following Charles II's Declaration of Indulgence in 1672. The protesting justices received the reply that the Privy Council "would not wish [the statutes against the Dissenters] executed according to the rigour and letter of the lawe", which was precisely what Bradshaigh and some of the other prominent magistrates sought. In Parliament Sir Roger was equally active in maintaining the rigour of the law against the Protestant Dissenters, being involved in the drafting of the Conventicle Acts of 1664 and 1670.[214]

The Bradshaighs were connected with numerous other Members of Parliament, and justices of the peace through a tangled web of marriages. Sir Roger senior, through his marriage with Katherine, daughter of William Pennington of Muncaster, became a brother-in-law of Geoffrey Shakerley, who had married another of Pennington's daughters.[215] Shakerley, who had been a colonel in the royalist army during the Civil War, was rewarded for his loyalty after the Restoration with the position of governor of Chester Castle, which he held until his death in 1696. Described by Fox as "a cruel persecutor of Friends" he sat in Parliament as a Member for Wigan between the years 1661 and 1679.[216] Shakerley's

eldest son, Peter, succeeded his father to the position of governor of
Chester Castle in 1696, whilst he also sat in Parliament as a Member for
the borough of Wigan between 1689 and 1698, and for Chester between
1698 and 1714. A die-hard Tory, Peter Shakerley was one of those
Members who spoke against the Bill for a Quakers' Affirmation read in
Parliament in April 1692 on the grounds "that they are a people not well
affected to this government".[217] Sir Roger Bradshaigh was also a kinsman
and close associate of Richard Kirkby, and supported him as a fellow-
justice, a relative, and a social peer, in his actions against Quakerism.[218]
Through his kinship with Kirkby, Bradshaigh also came into the orbit of
the *bête noire* of the North-West Quakers, Sir Daniel Fleming of Rydal
Hall. Fleming was also, of course, a justice of the peace and a regular
informant of government officials in London. Like Bradshaigh he was a
dedicated official, but unlike Bradshaigh equally determined to see all laws
against Catholic recusants and Dissenters put into effect according to the
wording of the statute.[219]

It would be misleading, however, to suggest that Friends received no
help or encouragement from Lancashire parliamentarians, either before,
or after, the passing of the Toleration Act of 1689. Not all the family
groupings that were established amongst the representatives of the county
were as hostile as the Kirkbys, Prestons and Bradshaighs, and there were
certain dynasties, such as the Ashtons of Whalley, whose religious leanings
might have suggested if not wholehearted support for Friends, then at least
some reservations regarding the general enforcement of pre-1689 religious
legislation.[220] Moreover, as the seventeenth century drew to a close and the
eighteenth century progressed the changing character of the representatives of some of the county's boroughs suggests that Lancashire Friends
could reasonably expect at least a hearing from some of their MPs.[221]

Finally it should be noted that in practice some of those who by
reputation and apparently action were most hostile to Dissent in general
and Quakers in particular could sometimes act on behalf of Friends,
motivated by a network of local ties as complex as those which might lead
them to act against them.

A notable example of a Member of Parliament with an anti-Quaker
reputation who yet acted on behalf of Friends comes not from Lancashire, but from the adjoining county of Westmorland, and involves Sir
Christopher Musgrave of Edenhall and Hartley. Sir Christopher sat as MP
for Carlisle, Westmorland, Appleby and the University of Oxford between
1661 and his death in 1704, and like his father, Sir Philip Musgrave, who
had sat as an MP for Westmorland, Sir Christopher held strong views
against any sort of Dissent, seeing in it a gathering point for anti-
government sentiment.[222] Both were active within their own county
against Quakers; Sir Philip, "a violent man", was prominent in the trial of
the Quaker leader Francis Howgill at Appleby in 1663. He viewed Friends
as "brainsick discontented men" with rebellious designs; in 1670 his son
wrote to London that the Quakers were very brisk, and looking for a

sudden alteration in government.[223] In Parliament both supported any measures designed to strengthen the church and extirpate Dissent, particularly when represented by Quakers, described by Sir Christopher as "a sort of people who will subvert the very foundation of government".[224] Sir Christopher came to particular prominence in the Parliaments following the Glorious Revolution, where along with such MPs as Sir Thomas Clarges he represented the interest of staunch Anglican Tories, and showed a particular mistrust of Quakers, opposing their plea for an Affirmation on the basis of their questionable loyalty.[225] Quaker sources, however, show that Musgrave adopted attitudes in Westmorland different from those he showed in Parliament. Local Quakers claimed some experience of his moderation towards individual Friends, and this reputation for tolerance towards them was confirmed in 1695 by his support for George Whitehead's efforts to relieve Friends being taxed as preachers.[226]

Of course it is possible that the Westmorland Quakers were being naive if they believed that Musgrave would show the same kindness to them in London as he had in his native locality, although Whitehead had expected, and received, a sympathetic hearing. Other MPs, however, were prepared to speak up for Friends despite possible damage to their parliamentary reputations. Sir Thomas Clarges, Musgrave's companion and confidant at Westminster, a leading Anglican Tory, acted on behalf of Friends in March 1679 when he presented a Bill in Parliament designed to prevent Quakers from suffering malicious prosecutions as recusants.[227] Friends had had detailed dealings with Clarges over the contents of the Bill and were (unjustifiably) confident of its passing through the Commons.[228] Clarges was later to make a name for himself through his attempts to limit the term of the Toleration Act to seven years lest the granting of religious liberty to Dissenters should prove too great a danger to the security of the state and church.[229] That two such well known opponents of Dissent should favour Friends seems remarkable. Perhaps at least in Musgrave's case it can be argued that the power of local contacts and loyalties (Whitehead was also a son of Westmorland) was sufficient to overcome political positions based on national considerations and parliamentary connections.[230] After all, a Quaker as neighbour was no doubt far less fearsome than the spectre of the subversive fanatic which was occasionally conjured up during parliamentary debates.

In Lancashire, Quakers were apparently able to depend on the goodwill of a small number of MPs in order to gain a favourable voice in Parliament or influence to exert against persecutors and prosecutors. Given the nature of the sources used in this discussion, it is easier to identify those parliamentarians who were in conflict with Friends, such as the Kirkbys, Prestons and Bradshaighs, rather than those who were acting in conjunction with them. However, it is possible to name a few Members for the county constituencies who were prepared to act on behalf of Friends, and at the end of our period to make some generalisations as to which MPs might have been liable to support Quakers.

In November 1680 Friends from the South of Lancashire petitioned the two Members of Parliament for the county, Charles Gerrard, Lord Brandon and Sir Charles Houghton of Houghton Tower, for relief from the prosecutions they were then experiencing, especially under statutes which were originally designed to prevent the growth of recusancy.[231]

Such applications to MPs or to Parliament in general were not, as has been shown above, unusual from Quakers who continued the petitioning tradition established by numerous religious and political groups during the Civil War period. In this case, however, Friends could justifiably hold out hopes of a successful response, as they were approaching two of the Nonconformists' main sources of political support in the county. Nor was the petition from the Lancashire Friends a spontaneous act, for the authorship of such a paper had been discussed during the previous month in a correspondence between George Fox and Thomas Lower. Writing to Fox, then in London, from Swarthmore on 17th October, Lower mentioned a conversation he had had with Sir Charles Houghton

> who hath promised he will do what lies in his power to relieve us in our grievances and sufferings upon application of some of our Friends in London to him. I found him very loving and respectful and he promised fair whatever he will perform. However if some Friend or Friends did address themselves to the Lord Charles Gerrard and this Sir Charles Houghton, unto both of whom I have spoken and they have promised fair, and it might do well to remind them therof and keep them loving and friendly and active in this session for Friends good.[232]

Sir Charles Houghton was one of a small number of Lancashire parliamentarians with strong Dissenting connections; his father was the Presbyterian Sir Richard Houghton "an irreconcilable opponent of the Republic" who had sat as an MP for the county in the Long Parliament.[233] Sir Charles, who sat as a knight of the shire during the two Exclusion Parliaments between 1679 and 1681, and again in 1689, had close links with some of Lancashire's most eminent Nonconformist ministers, notably Thomas Jolly and Henry Newcome, but he was apparently not averse to hearing the petitions of Friends, despite the mutual hostility which they and individuals such as Jolly displayed towards each other.[234]

In purely political terms Houghton's interest lay in favouring the Dissenters, who formed an important part of his electoral following, but his apparent kindness to Friends no doubt also resulted from his staunch Whig principles, displayed during the Exclusion crisis.[235] Possibly another factor influencing Houghton was the desire to remain on good terms with the increasingly powerful Brandon, who until his death in November 1701 was probably the Lancashire Quakers most powerful, although not always effective, ally in the county.

Charles Gerrard, Viscount Brandon, was the son of the first Earl of Macclesfield, a distinguished royalist commander during the Civil Wars who had become an influential courtier under Charles II following the Restoration. In 1661 Macclesfield (or Viscount Brandon as he then was), was responsible for effecting the release of George Fox from custody imposed during the alarm which followed on the abortive Fifth Monarchy rising.[236] The first Earl's Whiggish sentiments and political activities led to his disfavour at the Stuart court: he was a noted Exclusionist and with his son was implicated in the Rye House Plot. The Earl fled to Holland to escape trial in 1685, from whence he returned three years later with William of Orange.[237] Lord Brandon, reprieved of a death sentence imposed on him for his part in the plot, was reconciled with James II and became "a violent asserter of that King's dispensing power" in Lancashire. In particular, according to Roger Kenyon

> He was one that pressingly moved the people to promise to chose men for the Parliament that would take away our penall lawes and testes.[238]

As part of this campaign, he wrote to "the Lancashire Nonconformists, it being his post to introduce that party to complement that King", with apparently mixed results. In Lancaster and Liverpool, towns where he exerted considerable influence, there were some favourable answers to the King's "Three Questions", though for the most part the county answered against the proposal, with Quakers from the countryside and Lancashire "north of the sands" answering strongly in the negative.[239]

Lord Brandon had first been elected to sit for the county in 1679, and with the exception of the election of 1685 he was returned to every Parliament until he succeeded his father in 1694.[240] Brandon was clearly identified with the Dissenting cause and was generally supported, as in the 1685 election, by the established freemen and by Nonconformists and Quakers, or as William Stout described them "all sober people".[241] Following the Revolution of 1688 he regained and exerted considerable influence over the town's electorate, one of his successful candidates being Roger Kirkby who nonetheless, as we have seen, held strong anti-Quaker sentiments. By 1698 one commentator characterised the election held in Lancaster in that year as a pitched battle between the Church and the Meeting House (or Anglicanism versus Nonconformity), with Brandon's candidate being firmly placed in the latter.[242]

Not only did Brandon recover his position in Lancaster borough, but after 1689, by successfully distancing himself from James II he regained and extended his influence in the county, was appointed lord lieutenant in 1689 in place of Lord Stanley and was in addition appointed *custos rotolorum*, a post which he also held in Cheshire.[243] Brandon was thus able to exert considerable influence on the composition of the Lancashire bench, an institution that had not been noted for its consistency in the application of the penal laws against Dissenters even at the best of times.[244] Critics such as Roger Kenyon were dismayed at the number of Dissenters or their supporters who were finding their way onto the bench in place of established Tories through the influence of Brandon, whose associates were described as papists and arch-fanatiques.[245] For Friends, such changes would in theory have eased the introduction of their newly-won toleration, especially given the animus which some of the long-serving justices showed both to it and the Quakers.[246] Brandon's support, albeit somewhat passive, for the Quakers, however, can be deduced from more than the cumulative effect of his actions and sentiments: if anyone in the county was "a person of power" to whom Friends felt they could turn it was he, although Kenyon alleged that "the countrey generally speaking, neither loves him nor feares him".[247] Minute books are reticent to reveal such instances, but one, concerning the case of Robert Hubberstey, may suffice to show Brandon's involvement with, and support for, Friends.

In April 1699 Robert Hubberstey, a Friend from Yealand, was imprisoned at Lancaster for non-payment of three years' tithes with a total value of £6 10s at the suit of the Dean and Chapter of Worcester, impropriators of tithe at Yealand and Warton.[248] Friends in London, acting for the Meeting for Sufferings, investigated Hubberstey's case and eventually included it with a number of others in a pamphlet that was presented to Parliament calling for an end to the "ruinous ways" and "unnecessary severity" that Quakers could encounter in tithe proceedings.[249]

None of this, however, did anything to secure Hubberstey's release, and by the time of the summer Assizes in 1700 Hubberstey, "having not been out the gates of the prison this seventeen months", made personal application to Lord Brandon (by then Earl of Macclesfield) seeking his discharge. The response of the lord lieutenant to this request was immediate, for "the Earl said he would discharge him". Clearly, however, words required some action to support them, and so Friends in London were requested to "apply themselves to the said Earl when he comes to London to put him in mind of his promise".[250] The Earl's promises were kind and his good will towards Quakers considerable. However, as Hubberstey's case shows, the actual effectiveness of even Brandon's intercession on behalf of the Quakers was limited. Friends sought, without success, to arrange a meeting with him when he was known to be in London and for a crucial period Brandon was out of the country acting as an extraordinary envoy to the court of Hanover. He returned in October 1701 but died in the following month, leaving Friends to seek relief elsewhere.[251] Hubberstey's release, and that of James Waithman, who had joined him as a prisoner for tithes in the time that had elapsed since 1699, was finally secured on 20th January 1701. Ironically, after trying to get relief from a pro-Nonconformist Whig, the Friends were finally delivered through the intervention of the Bishop or Oxford.[252] In Brandon Friends believed they had found a supporter who held out the prospect of influence both in court, at Parliament and in the county. In many ways Brandon was less able than Friends thought to produce the results they wanted, although after his death they began to find wider support among the county's parliamentarians, more, particularly as the influence of some of the older families declined to be replaced by new dynasties of men motivated as much by the dictates of commerce as by the dictates of conscience.

Among this group of new men the one most closely associated with the Quakers was Robert Heysham of Lancaster and London. Heysham, a native of Lancaster, was MP for the borough between 1691 and 1715, and subsequently sat as a London Member between 1715 and 1722.[253] He was appointed a justice of the peace for the county in 1702, and, though rarely in attendance, he apparently held this post until his death in 1722.[254] A merchant active in both London and Lancaster, as such he was associated with prominent Quaker businessmen, notably Robert Lawson of Lancaster, who before his ill-fated speculation in South Sea stock in 1721 was probably the wealthiest Quaker merchant in the town. Heysham was a joint owner with Lawson of the ship *Robert*, and through Lawson would have come into contact with many of the town's Quakers.[255] Heysham was a Tory, but this does not seem to have prevented him from advancing the Quaker cause in Parliament. Indeed his support of the 1722 Affirmation Act was notable, although perhaps stemming from the great pecuniary advantage it offered to those merchants who were involved in trade with Friends.[256] In December 1721 he was one of a committee of six ordered by the House of Commons to prepare a Bill modifying the Affirmation first granted to Friends in 1696 (a matter of much concern to Lancashire Quakers); he had previously spoken in favour of the Quakers petition in the House.[257] Shortly after the successful passage of this Bill through the House Heysham died, earning in the process a glowing tribute from William Stout, who described him "as a very great benifactor to the town in generall and to many [in] particular, and genearus to all without partialety in respect to religious profession".[258]

However, in contrast with Robert Heysham, his brother William and his nephew William Heysham junior, both of whom also sat as MPs for the borough of Lancaster, were Tories, but of a more traditional stripe; what little is known about their political careers should undermine any naive belief that all "monied men" were necessarily sympathetic towards Friends. Both were active in the Lancaster merchant community and would have had business links with Quakers. William Heysham junior, who succeeded his father as MP in 1716 and sat until his death in 1727, was a close, but from Stout's point of view, unsatisfactory, business associate.[259] Though he is recorded as having voted against the Whig government in every recorded division during his parliamentary service, Heysham's business relations with Quakers make it unlikely that he objected to the 1722 Affirmation Act which was supported by his uncle.[260]

The other constituency where Quakers were likely to attract the sympathy of its commercially minded MPs was Liverpool. From the turn of the century merchant interests dominated the representation of this borough. Men such as the Whigs John Cleveland, Sir Thomas Johnson, Richard Gildart, the four Norris brothers and the Tory William Clayton were all to a greater or lesser degree involved in trade, and though the importance of Quakers in the Liverpool commercial community was far less than it was in Lancaster they still benefited from important connections.[261] Men such as Robert Lawson had contacts throughout the county, and William Stout had business links with two of the most important Liverpool MPs, Sir Thomas Johnson, who sat between 1701 and 1722, and his son-in-law Richard Gildart, MP between 1735 and 1754.[262] Johnson, "the founder of modern Liverpool", was extensively involved in the tobacco trade until his failure in the early 1720s when he gave up his seat in Parliament and apparently moved to London.[263] Stout had a variety of contacts with Johnson before this which suggest how closely the merchant communities of the two towns were intertwined.[264] Johnson was a staunch Anglican who held a pragmatic view of Dissent based on the premises of the Toleration Act; he believed that Dissenters should be free to worship but banned from serving in public office: "Toleration allowed to dissenters, I doe often say, is all our dissenters desire".[265] Such views allowed merchants like Johnson and his son-in-law Gildart, for whom Stout was acting as a commission agent in 1729, to offend neither their friends nor their religion.[266]

As in Lancaster, however, one must suggest a degree of caution in making the assertion that all non-landed or merchant MPs, or indeed all Whigs, supported Friends.[267] Although Liverpool tended to return Whigs to Parliament, its internal politics "lay less in nonconformity than in an assertion of municipal self-sufficiency against the predominantly tory gentry".[268] Seen against this background, the views of men such as Johnson towards Friends and Dissenters in general are easily explained, as are those of the Norris family. Four sons of Thomas Norris of Speke Hall, Thomas, William, Richard and Edward, sat in Parliament for the borough between 1688 and 1722; two of the brothers, Thomas and Richard, served in the office of sheriff of Lancaster in 1696 and 1718, whilst Richard was also mayor of Liverpool in 1700.[269] This powerful family, whose Catholic origins lay only in the recent past, were staunch Protestants. Certainly Thomas Norris was sufficiently concerned for his religion to move an amendment to the Bill for the Preservation of Game debated in Parliament in February 1692/93, "to enable every Protestant to keep a musket in his house for his defence".[270] Such militancy did not, however, extend to the family's support of Dissent. In 1696 a "Mr Norres", most likely William Norris (later Sir William), acted as one of the tellers for the noes in a parliamentary vote to engross the Bill for the More Easy Recovery of Tithes, which first gave Quakers the Affirmation. His younger brother, the physician and Fellow of the Royal Society, Edward Norris, similarly voted against the repeal of the Occasional Conformity and Schism Acts in 1715, and there is no evidence that either he or his three brothers held any strong affection for, or possessed close links with Quakers.[271]

It is clear from the cases cited above that personal inclination, family ties, community and neighbourhood obligations, and business and other economic associations and considerations were as important in shaping the varying attitudes of Lancashire Members of Parliament to Quakers, and in influencing them to act on behalf of Friends either in London or in the counties, as were religious or political principles. Moreover, it seems evident that whilst one set of factors might act in order to govern an individual's behaviour in London, another set, leading to totally different behaviour, might well act in the country. As shown earlier, Quakers identified a set of clear mutual obligations both between citizen and government and electorate and elected.[272] From these observations Friends were led to expect a certain degree of responsiveness from their representatives in Parliament to their petitions and addresses, and particularly so from the MPs whom they had supported. In practice, however, some MPs remained either implacably hostile to Quakerism or stolidly indifferent to it. Neither would Quakers in a county such as Lancashire be naive enough to expect a favourable hearing from those Members who came into these two categories, although in the case of men such as Colonel Kirkby this did not prevent them from entering into a lengthy dialogue with them. Matters were probably made more difficult in the North-West by its predominantly Tory character and by the large numbers of Jacobite or crypto-Jacobite MPs representing the various constituencies in Parliament.[273] Their presence could not have helped Friends, for despite the fact that some of the Lancashire Quakers may have supported James II there is no evidence to suggest anything other than that the Lancashire Friends continued to be aggressively hostile towards Jacobitism and Catholicism throughout the period under discussion.[274] The close links with the court of St. Germain were confined for the most part to Friends in London, and Friends in Lancashire were denied access to the county's Jacobite circle.[275]

The nature of the Quakers' relations with crown and Parliament should not obscure the question of principle as to whether it was in order for Christians to act with men of the world in order to reduce or alleviate sufferings which by their very nature, and to some extent in proportion to their severity, were a mark or badge of a Quaker's subservience to, and unity with, the Truth. Persecution, wrote Isaac Pennington, was a mark of those who had rejected the world, for "that which comes into the life of Christ, comes presently into a proportion of suffering from that which is contrary to his life ..."[276] So the

> disciple of Christ, who is persecuted for conscience sake, who suffers from men and their laws for the uprightness of his heart towards, and for his obedience unto Christ, that man is precious in the eye of Christ and hath his blessing with Him: yea, the more men disteem and hate him upon this account, the greater is his blessedness ....[277]

According to Barclay, Friends, in order to "know ... perfection" were

> to partake of the Fellowship of Christ's Sufferings, and be made

conformable unto his Death, that thou may'st feel thy self Crucified with him to the World, by the Power of his Cross in thee.[278]

Hubberthorn wrote that Friends should bear "patient suffering" under the world's "corrupt Laws and evil Commands".[279]

In 1672 Robert Barclay had claimed that

what Liberty we now enjoy, it is by His Mercy, and not by any outward Working or Procuring of our own, but 'tis He has wrought upon the Hearts of our Superiours ...[280]

Barclay may have been unaware of the dubiety of this statement, but by 1675, with the inception of the Meeting for Sufferings, it was recognised that there were difficulties in determining how far any particular Friend might feel able to use the law or persons of influence in order to relieve suffering. The Meeting's members decided in the end on an appeal to the individual conscience:

a freedom is left to those sufferers to use such means as consists with the unity of Friends and their own peace and satisfaction in the Truth, and the bearing a faithful testimony in the Truth.[281]

However, as has already been seen, the Meeting for Sufferings became increasingly concerned with objectives which, although originally intended as an aid or service to Truth, gradually became almost ends in themselves, leading to the substitution of actions guided by the Truth to actions guided by expediency. This was almost inevitable given the parcel of contradictions which underlay the founding articles of the Meeting, and which were also common in Quaker attitudes to the law.

These contradictions arose from the fact that whilst Friends were prepared to suffer "patiently" within the law, they were not prepared to do so when the power of the law had been exceeded.[282] Although Friends on the one hand displayed contempt for lawyers, judges and other appurtenances of the legal system they nonetheless retained a respect for, and belief in, "the fundamental laws of England".[283] Who, wrote William Penn,

can truly esteem himself a Free Man, when all pleas for Liberty are esteemed Sedition, and the Laws that give and maintain them, so many insignificant pieces of Formality.[284]

It was these laws which supported "the good Old English Government", of which none were greater lovers than Friends.[285] Thus on the one hand the Meeting for Sufferings advised sufferers "not to let out their minds into too much expectation of outward reliefs by Friends ... in point of law". They were to "patiently and principally depend upon the Lord and his power to plead their case".[286] On the other hand the Meeting noted it is convenient that Friends who suffer beyond the limits and severity of the law have an understanding thereof, for divers causes, and especially to be capable of laying it on the heads of those persecutors for exceeding their own laws in severity, and that they may know in what cases relief may be had ....

Friends were able "to endeavour a relief by the law of the land, to stop the destroyers", providing such was not "prejudicial to Truth's testimony".[287]

Although, as shown above, Quakers in Lancashire were ready to exploit persons of influence and those Members of Parliament or officials who were predisposed to favour them, their general attitude to sufferings retained much of the flavour of the movement's early period. The boundaries they drew up for Truth's testimony did not allow them to accept the expediencies so eagerly sought after by the Meeting for Sufferings. It will become apparent later that Friends in the North-West counties, and elsewhere, were in fact reluctant to gain parliamentary dispensations allowing them either to affirm or to be relieved either from paying tithes or from the full severity of the law for not paying tithes. This is not to say that they rejected use of the law or influence in cases when sufferings were due to "unjust" prosecutions, such as those under statutes designed only to penalise Roman Catholics, or when legislation was intended to protect functional parts of the Quaker lifestyle, such as marriage. In general, however, Friends accepted sufferings as a part of their witness and, although relief was sometimes sought in cases of great severity, the large majority of Quakers in the county underwent without protest imprisonments for attending conventicles, distraints and fines for non-payment of tithe and the disabilities caused by not swearing, regarding this all as a distinctive mark of a peculiar people.

When Thomas Dockray wrote to George Fox from Lancaster in April 1681 he could give a fair account of the prisoners then in the castle for attending conventicles, adding "all is well, George, for Friends are freely given up and many take not much thought what shall come ..."[288] Amongst these prisoners was Roger Haydock from Coppull, a ministering Friend who was closely associated with the administration of the Lancashire Quarterly Meeting. Following his death in 1697, Hardshaw Monthly Meeting which covered the south-west part of the county gave a testimony giving account of his life, pointing out that

all his sufferings he underwent with great simplicity, as well as patience, the Lord's hand alone without Carnal Contrivance being truly regarded eyed and depended on for his Enlargement, so that he was made to Triumph in the Lord for his Deliverance.[289]

Haydock was no exception, but was rather typical of the Friends who "rather inclined to submit to prison if providence so order their lot" as opposed to accepting genuine, but possibly compromising favours.[290]

Thus a further factor has to be considered when attempting to outline the relationship which existed between Quakers and the Establishment, as represented by monarch, law and Parliament. It is impossible to generalise about the attitudes to Quakers of Members of Parliament (frequently also representing the county administration) because of the complex web of factors which governed their behaviour both in London and Lancashire. It is equally difficult to generalise about the view which Friends held of this Establishment. To some extent it was far easier for a Quaker to face hostility than measured toleration and indulgence. Whilst most Friends appear to have accepted a view of the monarch which enabled them to accept any favour from his hand as one from God's appointed magistrate on earth, they were less sure, particularly outside of London, as to how they should regard Parliament and its Members. In their approaches to the monarch the plain and forthright Quaker had been replaced by the rehearsed delegation striking courtly attitudes and employing extravagant but empty courtly language. In their approaches to Parliament Friends had become the tools of Walpole's ministry, waiting upon his word to approach the Commons for favours, as opposed to the word of another.[291] Nonetheless, whilst Friends possessed a sophisticated appreciation of how the legislature and executive, and the actors within it, functioned they retained a deep suspicion as to how far it might be prompted to function on their behalf. It was this feeling, deeply held in Lancashire, and no doubt frustrating to the highly politicised mandarins of the Meeting for Sufferings, which ensured that conflict between Quakers and the Establishment continued well into the eighteenth century, no matter how accommodating the latter might promise to be.

REFERENCES

1. Such meetings are generally recorded in the minutes of the Meeting for Sufferings, and also in the Book of Cases.
2. Typical are the *Memoirs of Sir John Reresby*, a barometer of Tory gentry sentiment during the period, where, although Sir John was a prominent justice in a county with a large and active Quaker population, the Friends are only mentioned on three occasions: see Andrew Browning (ed.), *The Memoirs of Sir John Reresby* (Glasgow, 1936), pp.452, 538, 552
3. These Acts were: The Corporation Act, 13 Car. II, c.l; The Act of Uniformity, 14 Car. II, c.l; The Conventicle Act, 16 Car. II, c.4: and the Five Mile Act, 17 Car. II, c.2. Friends were also liable for prosecution under the specifically designed Quaker Act of 1662 (14 Car. II, c.l) for which see below pp.191, 206–07
4. *Journal of the House of Commons*, vol.8, p.13
5. *ibid.* vol.8, p.443, vol.9, p.60; *Parliamentary History*, vol.4, p.527
6. *Journal of the House of Commons*, vol.8, p.90, vol.9, p.131. A biographical index of Nonconformist MPs can be found in Douglas Lacey, *Dissent and Parliamentary Politics in England 1661–1689* (New Brunswick, NJ, 1969), appendix II, pp.373–475

7. *Journal of the House of Commons*, vol.9, pp.252, 258–59, 281: Lacey, *Dissent and Parliamentary Politics*, pp.67– 68

8. Bishop Burnet, *History of His Own Time from the Restoration of King Charles II to the conclusion of the Treaty of Peace at Utrecht* (4 vols., London 1815), vol.1, p.449

9. These were 23 Eliz. c. 1, 29 Eliz. c.6; and 3 Jac. I, c.4. They are summarised in *Second Period*, p.1. In order to prevent prosecutions under these laws, and to temper their indignation at being prosecuted as Roman Catholics, Friends successfully endeavoured in 1678 to obtain certificates from "justices of the peace, constables, or other persons that are esteemed greatly known to men", confirming them to be "neither papists nor reputed papists": LQMM, vol.1, 27/10/1678. A large number of these certificates for the Lancashire Quaker communities can be found in GBS, vol.3, pt. 2, 1678, pp.794–97. The popular support which these suggest shows a dramatic change from the picture of popular hostility towards Quakers which Barry Reay has identified as existing towards Friends in the late 1650s: see Barry Reay, 'Popular hostility towards Quakers in mid-seventeenth century England', *Social History*, 5 (1980), pp.387–407

10. B.S. Capp, *The Fifth Monarchy Men* (London, 1972), pp.199–200; Michael Watts, *The Dissenters* (Oxford, 197), p.225; *Second Period*, pp.29–30. At least three Friends appear to have been involved in the events at Kaber Rigg *ibid.* p.30. For some indication of official suspicion of Quakers see CSPD, 1661–62 p.596; 1663–64, pp.216, 346–76, 540, 571, 592

11. See B. Nightingale, *Early Stages of the Quaker Movement in Lancashire* (London, 1921), *passim.*; and A.B. Anderson, 'Lancashire Quakers and Persecution', (University of Lancaster MA thesis, 1971), *passim.*; some of Anderson's findings may also be found in his article 'A Study in the Sociology of Religious Persecution: The First Quakers', *Journal of Religious History*, 9 (1977), pp.247–62. For more general works see *Second Period*, pp.21–150, and William Wayne Spurrier, 'The persecution of the Quakers in England, 1650–1714', (University of North Carolina, Ph.D. thesis, 1976), *passim.*

12. Anderson, 'Lancashire Quakers and Persecution', p.55

13. For the Tory Reaction see David Ogg, *England in the Reign of Charles II* (2nd. ed., 2 vols., Oxford, 1956), vol.2, pp.620–50; J.R. Western, *Monarchy and Revolution: the English State in the 1680s* (London, 1972), pp.46–81

14. 1 Will. & Mar. c. 18

15. 22 Car. II, c. 1

16. See Anderson, 'Study in the Sociology of Religious Persecution', p.253

17. HMC *Fleming*, p.71

18. Although Friends sought relief under the terms of the Declaration they did not license their meeting houses as it directed: see *Second Period*, pp.81–84; for the Declaration of Indulgence see Frank Bate, *The Declaration of Indulgence 1672. A Study in the Rise of Organised Dissent* (London, 1908). *passim.*

19. Browning (ed.), *Memoirs*, p.85

20. CSPD, 1671–72, p.311, Fleming to Williamson, Rydal, 12th April 1672. He wrote privately a few days earlier that "the Judges were not free to discourse of the Toleration Declaration, nor I find any pleased therewith", HMC *Fleming*, p.90

21. *Apology*, p.509

22. *A Relation of Margaret Fell* in *A Brief Collection*, p.10; as early as 1658 a Quaker from Suffolk, Anthony Kettle, had been told by two justices of the peace that they "hoped to have a new Law, whereby they shoul[d] curb the Quakers", who would have "Punishment by the Bushel": *Besse*, vol.1, p.666

23. *Stout*, pp.77–78; Michael Watts writes of the "survival, invigoration, and, in many respects strengthening of Dissent during the period of persecution": *The Dissenters*, p.244. For Quaker emigration from Lancashire, see Anderson, 'Study in the Sociology of Religious Persecution', p.262; W.E.A. Axon, 'The Pemburtons of Aspull and Philadelphia, and some Passages in the early history of Quakerism in Lancashire', *TLCAS*, 30 (1912), pp.153–63

24. Writing of 1686 Burnet observed that "intimations were every where given, that the King would not have them [Dissenters], or their meetings, to be disturbed": *History of His Own Time*, vol.2, p.345. James issued two formal Indulgences in April 1687 and April 1688: *Second Period*, pp.130, 143

25. *Besse*, pp.329–30

26. See Table 1

27. See below, n.246

28. Barclay was a cousin of Charles II by virtue of his father's marriage to a daughter of Sir Robert Gordon of Gordonstoun: John Barclay, *Diary of Alexander Jaffray ... with Memoirs of the Rise, Progress, and Persecutions, of the People Called Quakers, in the North of Scotland* (2nd. ed., London, 1834), p.261

29. *Apology*, p.ix

30. *ibid.* p.515

31. Michael Mullett, *Radical Religious Movements in Early Modern Europe* (London, 1980), p.9. In view of what follows it is harder to sustain the suggestion that Quakers, due to the "innate characteristics of fundamental Christianity" were "critical of national monarchism", *ibid.*

32. Alan Cole, 'The Quakers and the English Revolution', in T.H. Aston, *Crisis in Europe 1560–1660* (London, 1965), pp.350–53

33. For the extent of prosecutions in pre-Restoration Lancashire, see Anderson, 'Study in the Sociology of Religious Persecution', p.251. Charles's view of the extent of his powers may well have been tempered by the events of the 1670s; in an interview with Friends in 1677 Charles answered their request for relief thus: "that it was not proper for the King to and council to relieve but [for] the Parliament who were capable of giving relief ... if the King in council may save estates, he may in council take estates": MMS, vol.1, 17/11/1677

34. *Stout*, p.69

35. *London Gazette*, no. 2273, 1 September 1687, quoted in Helen Farquhar, 'Royal Charities, Touchpieces for the King's Evil', *British Numismatic Journal*, 14 (1918), p.100. See also Keith Thomas, *Religion and the Decline of Magic* (London, 1973), pp.228–35, 243–44

36. J.H. Plumb, *The Growth of Political Stability in England 1675–1725* (London, 1967), p.27

37. A.R. Barclay (ed.), *Letters of Early Friends* (London, 1841), pp.158–59. Barfoote may have come from Worcestershire, see *Besse*, vol.2, p.60

38. Quoted in Robert Latham and William Mathews (eds.), *The Diary of Samuel Pepys* (11 vols., London, 1970–83), vol.5, p.13, n. 1

39. *ibid.* pp.12–13. The interview took place in January 1663

40.　Ronald Hutton, *The Restoration: a political and religious history of England and Wales 1658–1667* (Oxford, 1985), p.208

41.　Bishop Burnet, *History of His Own Time*, vol.1, p.351

42.　See Table 1

43.　Hutton, *The Restoration*, p.263

44.　For the view of Secretary Williamson in 1671 see CSPD, Addenda, 1660–1685, pp.341–42

45.　CSPD, 1663–64, p.66

46.　CSPD, 1663–64, p.444: see also p.457 for Fleming's opinion of the bench's attitude to Friends

47.　CSPD, 1666–67, p.128

48.　CSPD, 1667–68, p.546

49.　CSPD, 1670, p.267, Charles Whittington to Williamson, 10 June 1670

50.　CSPD, 1667–68, p.472, R. Manley to Rob. Francis, Jersey, 4 July 1668

51.　For an example of his sympathetic and helpful attitude towards Friends see A.R. Barclay (ed.), *op.cit.* p.130

52.　*Second Period*, pp.350, 446

53.　CSPD, 1667–68, p.259, Viscount Conway to Sir John Finch, February 1668

54.　Lacey, *Dissent and Parliamentary Politics*, pp.43–44; CSPD, 1676–77, p.564. The Friends were William Penn, William Meade, Thomas Rudyard and Benjamin Bealing.

55.　MMS, vol.2, 6/2/1683; *Journal*, pp.395–96, 501–02, 531–32

56.　Isabel Ross, *Margaret Fell, Mother of Quakerism* (London, 1949), pp.129–30. Ann Curtis was later prominent in a separation among Friends in Reading following the Wilkinson-Story controversy of 1677; *Second Period*, pp.470–72

57 .　CCPD, 1660–61, p.455

58.　A.R. Barclay (ed.), *op.cit.* pp.170–73, Ellis Hookes to Margaret Fox, London, 16/11/1669. The Friend's name is given as Richard Carver. For some of the many other claims made on Charles II for acts of loyalty performed after the Battle of Worcester – see CSPD, 1661–62, pp.262, 393, 395, 397, 623, 624

59.　Browning (ed.), *Memoirs*, p.140

60.　Burnet, *History of his own Time*, vol.1, p.114, who also thought that "he had been obliged to so many, who had been faithful to him, and careful of him, that he seemed afterwards to resolve to make an equal return to them all: and finding it not easy to reward them all as they deserved, he forgot them all alike", vol.2, p.270

61.　See for example the case of Ann Woodcock, described in her letter to Lord Arlington, that "he bade her give him another paper, but knows not what to give; sent Sir Wm. Walters letter and the Quaker's petition to the Dean of Westminster and he sent word he had given them to the Duke [of York] who would give them to his Lordship, and desire him to take charge of the business. His Highness would not have done so, had he not intended good". CSPD, 1665–66, p.174. For some indication of the expense of petitioning see MMS, vol.4, 6/12/1685, 12/12/1685, where Friends experienced some difficulty in raising the 100 guineas required to "defray the charges" of a successful approach to James II

62.　*Journal*, p.404 (my emphasis)

63.　*Journal*, pp.557–79 (my emphasis); see also Ross, *op.cit.* pp.235, 253

64.　LSF, Edward H. Milligan, background paper presented to the Meeting for

Sufferings, January 1977, p.1, where the totals for Quaker petitions can be found

65. Moore, from Harlswood in Surrey, paid his first of many visits to the court in December 1660 – his vivid description of his meeting with the King is in A.R. Barclay (ed.), *op.cit.* p.93. Shortly afterwards he was granted the privilege of remaining "free from all molestation about the Oath of Allegiance, so long as he remains faithful to the Government", CSPD, 1660–61, p.506. Moore was one of an influential number of ex-justices of the peace among early Friends; see *Beginnings*, p.456. For other JPs, see Hugh Barbour, *The Quakers in Puritan England* (London, 1964), p.91

66. For Hookes see *Second Period*, pp.288–89. For an early example of Whitehead's organisational prowess see A.R. Barclay (ed.), *op.cit.* pp.126–29, George Whitehead to George Fox, London, 4/3/1664

67. Margaret Fox, *A Relation of Margaret Fell*, in *A Brief Collection*, p.4

68. *ibid.*

69. See below, this chapter

70. Watts, *The Dissenters*, p.253

71. CSPD, 1680–81, pp.440, 610

72. CSPD, 1682, Secretary Jenkins to the Marquis of Worcester, 29th August 1682, p.356

73. Burnet, *History of His Own Time*, vol.2, p.271; see also Kenyon, *The Stuarts*, p.153

74. Margaret Fox, *A Relation of Margaret Fell*, in *A Brief Collection*, pp.10–11

75. *ibid.* pp.11–12. Reresby wrote of this period that "all things seemed now to look very auspicious, the King not giveing the least token to change the religion, but much the contrary": Browning (ed.), *Memoirs*, p.367

76. Penn's complex relationship with James II is dealt with fully in Vincent Buranelli, *The King and the Quaker. A Study of William Penn and James II* (Philadelphia, 1962), *passim.*; see also *Second Period*, pp.128–48

77. Burnet, *History of his Own Time*, p.383. For Burnet's harsh opinion of Penn and his abilities see, *ibid.* p.371 78. Kenyon, *The Stuarts*, pp.160–61; John Miller, *James II a Study in Kingship* (London, 1978), pp.121–22. "It was...", wrote Burnet, "said that now we should have a reign of action and business, and not of sloth and luxury, as the last was", *History of His Own Time*, vol.2, p.285

79. Watts, *The Dissenters*, p.258; *Second Period*, p.148

80. For Penn's missions on behalf of the sovereign see, for example Western, *Monarchy and Revolution*, p.205, who describes his trip to Holland. In 1688 the Meeting for Sufferings compiled a paper concerning Friends being forced to swear in ecclesiastical courts, deciding "that William Penn be desired to lay it before the King", MMS, vol.6, 4/3/1688

81. Browning (ed.), *Memoirs*, pp.469–70

82. Public declarations of support had been equally important for Charles II in 1672, when "great endeavours were used by the court to persuade the nonconformists to make addresses and compliments upon it": Burnet, *History of His Own Time*, vol.1, p.398

83. *ibid.* p.400

84. George, Marquis of Halifax, *A Letter to a Dissenter, upon Occasion of His Majesty, James the Second's, late gracious Declaration of Indulgence, of the 4th April 1687* (London, 1687), in *Parliamentary History*, vol.4, p.cxciii

85. But for other approaches to the throne see, for example R.A. Beddard, 'Vincent Alsop and the Emancipation of Restoration Dissent', *Journal of Ecclesiastical History* 24 (1973), pp.161–84

86. MMS, vol.6, 29/2/1687; for their address following the second Indulgence see *Second Period*, p.145

87. Although for the publicity given to the 1687 address see above

88. For the attitude of the new government to Penn, see *Second Period*, pp.161–68

89. For an indication of the views of Friends on James' policy see *Second Period*, p.144–45. Penn was not alone in his meetings with James: for the activities of Robert Barclay, author of the *Apology*, see *ibid.* p.149, and John Barclay (ed.), *Diary of Alexander Jaffray ... with Memoirs of the Rise, Progress, and Persecutions, of the People Called Quakers in the North of Scotland* (2nd ed., London, 1834), p.441

90. For the attack on Penn from within the Society, see *Second Period*, pp.173–74

91. The personality of the new King – "he hated talking, ... he could not bring himself to comply enough with the temper of the English, his coldness and slowness being very contrary to the genius of the nation" – equally discouraged such approaches: Burnet, *History of His Own Time*, vol.2, p.366

92. MMS, vol.1, 18/8/1675

93. MMS, vol.12, 18/1/1698

91. Some of the personal hostility between Meade, the Fell family and William Penn is discussed in Norman Penney, 'George Fox's Writings and the Morning Meeting', *Friends Quarterly Examiner*, 36 (1902), pp.63–72

95. S. Locker Lampson, *A Quaker Post-Bag* (London, 1910), p.140, John Tomkins to Sir John Rhodes, London, 18/5/1698. Earlier Tomkins had written to Rhodes that "She will be lead by her son Wm into something or other, which may not be of the best consequence to Truth", *ibid.* p.134

96. LSF, Port. 41.84, Margaret Fox to King William, London, 24/4/1698; this is printed in *A Brief Collection*, pp.531–32

97. *ibid.*

98. Isabel Ross concluded the the letter "was different, informal and personal", apparently setting it above the official approaches to the King, see *Mother of Quakerism*, p.377

99. MMS. vol.12, 15/5/1698

100. LFMH, 2Ai:5, LMMM, vol.1, 7/9/1698; SMMM. vol.3, 8/9/1698

101. MMS, vol, 8, 14/8/1692; LSF, *Book of Cases*, vol.1, p.225

102. R. Cunliffe-Shaw, *Kirkham in Amounderness, the Story of a Lancashire Community* (Preston, 1949), p.651

103. GBS, vol.7, pt. 1, p.293

104. Cunliffe-Shaw, *Kirkham in Amounderness*, p.651. For Clegg's other attempts to prevent the growth of Quaker Meetings at this time of heightened missionary activity by Lancashire Friends, see below chapters 6 and 7

105. MMS, vol.8, 14/8/1692, 16/9/1692, 2/10/1692, 23/4/1693, vol.9, 7/5/1693, 3/9/1693 18/3/1694, 15/4/1694

106. MMS, vol.9, 6/5/1694, 13/5/1694

107. MMS, vol.9, 27/6/1694

108. MMS, vol.9, 21/7/1694, 26/8/1694, 2/9/1694, 21/10/1694

109. For King William's refusal to touch for the King's Evil, for example, see Stephen B. Baxter, *William III* (London, 1966), p.278; for his lack of

sociability see above, n.91

110. Baxter, *William III*, p.279

111. In 1697 the Meeting decided that "none but members of this Meeting" were to be present when the content of an address to William III was under discussion; by 1728, such was the pressure from London Quakers to be present on such occasions, the Meeting ruled that "no other Friend go up but the 12 appointed, and that they take a copy hereof to show any Friend that would invade himself": MMS, vol.12, 24/10/1697; vol.24, 20/10/1728

112. See, for example, MMS, vol.12, 30/10/1697, 7/11/1697, 11/12/1697

113. MMS, vol.16, 4/5/1702

114. This was the response of William to the delegation of February 1697 led by Quare and Whitehead: MMS, vol.12, 11/12/1697

115. *Second Period*, p.134: for an account of the history of Friends in North East Scotland see Barclay (ed.), *Diary of Alexander Jaffray*, pp.225–542

116. MMS, vol.21, 29/7/1714

117. *Second Period*, p.178; MMS, vol.24, 21/5/1727; this minute is transcribed in full in Appendix 1

118. See above, this chapter

119. Locker Lampson, *A Quaker Post-Bag*, pp.101–02, Henry Gouldney to Sir John Rhodes, London, 31/3/1716. See also MMS, vol.22, 8/4/1716

120. See below, chapter 4

121. For example the address of the Yearly Meeting to Queen Anne, led by William Penn, and including "country Friends that were nominated by the Yearly Meeting", MMS, vol.16, 29/3/1702

122. MMS, vol.16, 4/5/1702. For an example of the care taken by Friends in publicising such events see MMS, vol.15, 17/2/1702

123. Richard Vann uses the description "the most picturesque of His Majesty's Protestant Dissenters": *The Social Development of English Quakerism* (Cambridge, Mass., 1969), p.157

124. MMS, vol.4, 17/5/1685, 24/5/1685, 7/6/1685, 28/6/1685. Stephen C. Morland (ed.), *The Somersetshire Quarterly Meeting of the Society of Friends 1668–1699* (Somerset Record Society, vol.75, 1978), p.171, 24/7/1685; 'Two West-Country Friends and the Monmouth Rebellion', *JFHS*, vol.12 (1915), pp.35–36. For a general account of the rebellion see P. Earle, *Monmouth's Rebels* (London, 1977), *passim*.

125. MMS vol.21, 29/7/1714

126. Locker Lampson, *A Quaker Post-Bag*, p.100

127. MMS, vol.28, 15/8/1745, 18/8/1745

128. MMS, vol.28, 20/7/1745

129. "Woollen waistcoats for Troops', *JFHS* 12 (1915), p.48; 'The Acts of the Rebels', *JFHS*, 19 (1921), pp.33–34; A. Speck, *The Butcher, the Duke of Cumberland and the Suppression of the '45* (Oxford, 1981), p.210, n. 67

130. Chancellor Ferguson, 'The Retreat of the Highlanders through Westmorland in 1745', *TC&WA&AS*, 10 (1889), pp.219–22; 'On Behalf of the King, 1745', *JFHS*, 19 (1922), pp.83–87

131. This message was conveyed to Friends at the end of the royal interview by the Duke of Grafton, who added "they might acquaint their Friends thereof": MMS, vol.28, 6/4/1746; for the names of the 186 Friends who signed the Address see LSF, Book of Cases, vol.3, pp.19–23. The Address is printed in full in John Gough, *A History of the People called Quakers, from their*

first Rise to the Present Time (4 vols., Dublin, 1739–90), vol. 4, p 336

132.   *Stout*, p.172, 197

133.   For the continued involvement of the monarch in government see Plumb, *The Growth of Political Stability*, pp.108–14, who concludes, however, that the "basic stability of politics … no longer rested on the Court": *ibid.* p.179

134.   MMS, vol.10, 5/10/1695, 20/10/1696

135.   MMS, vol.26, 14/11/1736, 28/11/1736; vol.27, 14/1/1743, 20/11/1743

136.   Of course, even before the Toleration Act Friends were lobbying to protect their "peculiarities", their religious testimonies that set them apart not only from other subjects, but also from all or most other Dissenters. In 1680 they met to consider "the endeavours of Friends with the Parliament to gain relief against the illegal proceedings of the ecclesiastical court in imposing oaths". Following an earlier general application for relief from oaths in 1689 Friends petitioned Parliament in January 1691/92 for a "short Bill for Friends' words to be taken instead of an oath in Chancery, Exchequer and Customs Houses". MMS, vol.2, 14/11/1680; vol.7, 27/10/1689; vol.8, 11/10/1691, 1/11/1691, 11/11/1691, 12/12/1691–2. Subsequent to the passing of the first Affirmation Act in 1696 (7 & 8 Will. III, c.34), Friends endeavoured to have inserted in any Bills that specifically imposed an oath clauses enabling Quakers to utilise their Affirmation. See, for example, MMS, vol.15, 14/12/1701, where Friends began an attempt to exempt themselves from the proposed Abjuration Oath.

137.   See, for example, the attempt of the Meeting for Sufferings to amend the contents of the Bill for Small Tythes considered in Parliament in May 1690: MMS, vol.7, 11/2/1690

138.   For Quaker agitation on the Poll taxes of the 1690s see above, chapter 1

139.   In 1694, for example, Friends succeeded in having the following clause inserted in the Act for Taxing Marriages, Births and Burials (6 & 7 ill. & Mar. c. 6): "all persons comonly called Quakers or reputed as such … who shall cohabitt and live together as man and wife shall and are hereby made lyable to pay the several and respective duties and sums or money payable upon marriages": this is typical of the *ad hoc* way in which they sought to gain institutional protection for their form of marriage. (Quaker marriages were not recognised fully by the law until 1753, and not "confirmed as good in law" until 1837: Rufus Jones, *The Later Periods of Quakerism* (2 vols., London, 1921), vol.1, p.190). Friends also sought protection from Parliament in other (often opportunist) ways, as in 1697 when "The Meeting being acquainted of a Bill ordered to be brought in to prevent mischief by squibs and other fireworks by Sir Henry Colt – its desired that provision may be made therin against tumults, riots, assaulting houses and breaking windows", a form of disturbance often directed against Quakers MMS, vol.12 17/10/1697

140.   *Political Associations*, pp.1–112

141.   *ibid.* pp.49–61. For the Affirmation controversy see below, chapter 4, *passim.*

142.   *Political Associations*, p.3

143.   MMS, vol.1, 18/8/1675; *Second Period*, pp.281–86; Arnold Lloyd, *Quaker Social History* (London, 1950), pp.150–53. A less secular view than Hunt's describes the functions of the Meeting for Sufferings as follows: "to help Friends in prison while persecution lasted and thereafter to supervise books, travelling ministry and other national needs": Hugh Barbour, *The Quakers in Puritan England*, pp.248–49

144. Reresby commented that "either he was to be a parliament man, or he was not; if he was, noe man could honestly say how he would voat til he came ther .... ": Browning (ed.), *Memoirs*, p.497

145. *Political Associations*, pp.37, 45

146. See below, chapter 4, *passim*.

147. Originally the "Person in Power" was a general term used by Friends to represent the administration, but gradually, as he grew more powerful, the "Person" became Walpole; *Political Associations*, pp.55, 57, 74. For a succinct view of Walpole's attitude to Friends see J.H. Plumb, *Sir Robert Walpole, The King's Minister* (London, 1960), pp.97–98; for Friends view of Walpole see *Stout*, pp.212, 234

148. See below, chapter 6

149. See, for example, the Elizabeth Redford affair, above chapter 1, and the prosecutions of Northern Quakers who refused either to swear or affirm at the customs, below, chapter 3

150. One example of Friends' adjustments to these realities was the highly stylised language they employed in their approaches to the crown; see below, Appendix 1

151. The phrase was used by the Meeting for Sufferings to describe the controversy which surrounded the Affirmation: LFMH, 2Ai:23, Epistle from the Meeting for Sufferings, 16/11/1712

152. See above, chapter 1

153. Reresby, for example, believed in 1698 that "most men were now convinced that liberty of concience was a thing of advantage to the nation", Browning (ed.), *Memoirs*, p.497. The Marquis of Halifax wrote to Dissenters in general in 1687 that "Things tend naturally to what you would have ...", the "Church of England convinced of its error in being severe to you; the parliament whenever it meeteth, sure to be gentle to you ....", *A Letter to a Dissenter*, p.cxcviii

154. George Whitehead, *The Christian Progress of ... George Whitehead* (London, 1725), pp.675–77. For examples of this type of anti-Quaker literature, see Edward Beekham, Henry Meriton and Lancaster Topcliffe, *A Brief Discovery of some of the Blasphemous and Seditious Principles and Practises of the People, Called Quakers* (London, 1699), and *Some Few of the Quakers Many Horrid Blasphemies, Heresies And Their Bloody Treasonable Principles Destructive to Government Delivered to the Members of Both Houses of the Lords and Commons* (London, 1699)

155. LFMH, 2Ai.6, Letter from the Meeting for Sufferings, 17/12/1699

156. *Parliamentary History*, vol.5, p.264–5

157. *ibid.* pp.153–54

158. G.V. Bennet, 'Conflict in the Church', in G. Holmes (ed.), *Britain after the Glorious Revolution* (London, 1969), p.165; G. Holmes, *The Trial of Doctor Sacheverell* (London, 1973), pp.43–44

159. An Act for Preserving the Protestant Religion by Better Securing the Church of England as by Law Established and for Confirming the Toleration granted to Protestant Dissenters: 10 Anne c. 6. For the earlier attempts to pass similar Bills, see Watts, *The Dissenters*, pp.265–67

160. An Act to Prevent the Growth of Schism and for the further security of the Churches of England and Ireland as by Law Established: 13 Anne c. 7. G. Clark, *The Later Stuarts* (2nd. ed., Oxford, 1956), p.236

161. Both Acts were repealed in 1719. The Occasional Conformity Act proved to be ineffective, whilst the Schism Act was never enforced as it was due to come in to effect on the day Queen Anne died: Watts, *The Dissenters*, 266–67. However in Lancashire Quaker schoolteachers had suffered a spate of prosecutions since 1689 for teaching without a licence from the Bishop of Chester: see LSF, Book of Cases, vol.2, pp.39–40, 135–36, and LQMM, vol.1, 4/8/1705. For a summary of Quaker educational provision in the county see Ralph Randles, "'Faithful Friends and well qualified", The Early Years of the Friends' School at Lancaster', in Michael Mullett (ed.), *Early Lancaster Friends* (Lancaster, Centre for North-West Regional Studies, Occasional Paper No. 5, 1978), pp.33–42

162. *Parliamentary History*, vol.7, pp.937–38

163. *ibid.* vol.7, p.942. Of these opponents of Quakerism, two, Francis Atterbury, the Bishop of Rochester and Lord North and Grey were arrested later in the year for their involvement in the Jacobite conspiracy known as the Atterbury Plot; see Bruce Lenman, *The Jacobite Risings in Britain 1689–1746* (London, 1980), pp.196–202

164. *Political Associations*, pp.92–99. According to the Earl of Scarborough, who voted against the Bill, "it is acknowledged of all sides, that the Bill now under consideration is a very imperfect and incorrect Bill", whilst according to Lord Bathurst, who nonetheless voted in its favour, there was "scarcely one clause in the Bill which can stand unamended"; *Parliamentary History*, vol.9, pp.1214–15. In the debate, apparently with an eye to 1722, Viscount Harrington commented that "I have seen a noble lord of this House taken down in very harsh terms by a prelate, for calling Quakers Christians. I hope I may now call them so, without incurring any such reprimand ...", *ibid.* vol.9, p.1213

165. *Parliamentary History*, vol.9, p.1162. St Aubyn, knight of the shire for Cornwall, was an "extreme Tory" with close Jacobite associations: Romney Sedgewick, *The House of Commons 1715–1754* (3 vols., London, 1970), vol.2, pp.401–02

166. W. Pink and A. Beavan, *The Parliamentary Representation of Lancashire (County and Borough) 1258–1885* (London, 1889), pp.5–10; for a more detailed account of the parliamentary structure of the Lancashire, see J.M. Wahlstrand, 'The Elections to Parliament in the County of Lancashire 1685–1714', (University of Manchester, MA thesis, 1956), pp.1–20

167. For the extent and importance of the family, see P. Hurst, 'Family Continuity in the Parliamentary Representation of the North West Counties in the Seventeenth Century' (University of Lancaster, M.Litt. thesis, 1980), *passim.*

168. William, ninth Earl of Derby lost considerable political influence in the county following the Glorious Revolution: Lionel Glassey, *Politics and the Appointment of Justices of the Peace 1675–1720* (Oxford, 1979), pp.277–78. The Stanley MPs were Charles Stanley (Preston 1702–05, Lancashire 1705–13), Edward Stanley (Lancashire 1661–65), Sir Edward Stanley (Lancashire 1727–36), James Stanley, later tenth Earl of Derby (Clitheroe 1685–87, Preston 1689, Lancashire 1689–1702), Sir Thomas Stanley (Preston 1695–98) and William Stanley (Liverpool 1660–70) Pink and Beavan, *op.cit.* pp.78, 80, 82, 84, 156, 158, 190. For their early history see Barry Coward, *The Stanleys Lords Stanley and Earls of Derby, 1385–1672* (Chetham Soc., 3rd series, 30, 1983), *passim.*

169. Wahlstrand, *op.cit.* pp.vi–vii: for Brandon see below
170. *Besse*, vol.1, p.311; Michael Mullett 'To Dwell Together in Unity : The Search for Agreement in Preston Politics, 1660–1690', *THSLC*, 125 (1974), p.64; *Journal*, pp.464–66
171. For Lord Derby's indifference to Dissent see 'Sir Roger Bradshaigh's Letter Book' *THSLC*, 63 (1912), p.160. According to Barry Coward, however, the eighth Earl "aligned himself with Anglican royalists against anyone tainted with a history of collaboration with the parliamentary and republican regimes of the recent past. All Dissenters, Protestants and Catholics alike, were smeared as regicides and subversives": Coward, *op.cit.* p.141. Roger Haydock described the ninth Earl Derby as being "moderate" towards Friends, *A Collection of the Christian Writings ... of Roger Haydock* (London, 1700), p.209
172. For Kenyon, see HMC *Kenyon, passim.*
173. The Legh MPs were Peter Legh (Newton 1685), Richard Legh (Chester 1656, 1658, Newton 1660–78), Thomas Legh (Liverpool 1685–87), Thomas Legh (Newton 1698–1702) and Thomas Legh (Newton, 1701–13): Pink & Beavan, *op.cit.* pp.192, 281, 282, 185–86; see also Lady Newton, *Lyme Letters 1660–1760* (London, 1925), *passim*. For the Bradshaigh family, see below
174. The "pattern of old county families maintaining or even extending their positions within both the county and Parliament in the seventeenth century emerges in Lancashire and Cheshire": P. Hurst, *op.cit.* p.43
175. This analysis is based on the genealogical data provided in Pink and Beavan, *op.cit. passim*. Although there is some reason to suspect a degree of inaccuracy in this source, it is likely that this has led to an under-recording of family ties as opposed to an over-recording. Thus, if anything, the linkages amongst the Lancashire MPs during this period were more extensive than those indicated here.
176. For the social cohesion of the gentry, see G.L. Mingay, *The Gentry, the Rise and Fall of a Ruling Class* (London, 1976), pp.16–17
177. R. Hopkinson, 'Parliamentary Elections in Westmorland and Cumberland 1695–1723' (University of Newcastle, Ph.D. thesis, 1973), pp.1–2; P. Hurst, *op.cit.* p.29
178. Pink and Beavan, *op.cit.* pp.77–78, 120
179. The last direct representative of these families to sit in Parliament was Sir Roger Bradshaigh, 3rd Baronet of Haigh Hall, who sat for the borough of Wigan between 1695 and February 1747. He maintained the family's local influence by serving as mayor of Wigan in 1698, 1705, 1724 and 1729 and was also a justice of the peace. Originally a Tory he identified himself with the Whigs from 1714 onwards, significantly absenting himself from the vote to repeal the Test and Occasional Conformity Acts. Within the county his reputation as a "violent Tory" persisted after his political conversion. Pink & Beavan, *op.cit.* p.231; A.J. Hawkes, 'Sir Roger Bradshaigh', *Chetham Miscellanies* vol.VIII (Chetham Soc., n.s. 109, 1945), Pedigree of Bradshaigh of Haigh, facing p.1; Romney Sedgewick, *op.cit.* vol.1, pp.481–82; Glassey, *op.cit.* p.192
180. Pink & Beavan, *op.cit.* pp.120–21
181. This point of interpretation is a matter of dispute between two of the biographers of Margaret Fell of Swarthmore: see Helen Crossfield, *Margaret Fox of Swarthmoor Hall* (London, 1913), pp.104–05; and Isabel Ross, *Margaret Fell Mother of Quakerism* (London, 1949), p.68. Margaret Fell's

letter to Colonel Kirkby, dated 1663, in which she denies any "cause given by me or any that ever belonged to me, to thee, or any of thy family" is in LSF Spence MSS, III, 134, and is incorrectly cited by Ross, *op.cit.* p.168, n.1, as Spence MSS, III, 34. See also *CSPD*, 1663–64, p.448

182. Ross, *op.cit.* pp.3–5

183. B.G. Blackwood, 'Social and Religious Aspects of the History of Lancashire 1635–55' (Oxford University, B. Litt. thesis, 1956), p.150, and *The Lancashire Gentry and the Great Rebellion* (Chetham Society, 3rd. series, 25, 1978) pp.89, 94

184. H.S. Cowper 'The Kirkbys of Kirkby in Furness in the Seventeenth Century', *TC&WA&AS*, n.s. 6 (1906), p.109; Blackwood, *The Lancashire Gentry and the Great Rebellion,* pp.113–14, 142, 149, n.20

185 Basil Duke Henning, *The House of Commons 1660–1690* (3 vols., London, 1983), vol.2, pp.688–89. CSPD, 1673 75, p.355, 1676–77, pp.484–85, 1680–81, p.697

186. Henning, op.cit. vol.2, p.688; *Journal of the House of Commons*, vol.8, p.473

187. *CSPD*, 1664–65: Daniel Fleming to Williamson, Rydal October 1st, 1664: "There have been some sharp encounters lately between Col. Kirkby and some Quakers, who conventicled at Mrs Fell's house ..." Fox wrote that whilst he was in London in 1670 "Colonel Kirkby came to several meetings to break them up with a company of foot ... ", *Journal*, p . 572

188. 'The Examination of Margaret Fell, before Judge Twisden, at the Assizes held at Lancaster, the 14th Day of the 1st Month, 1663/4', in *A Brief Collection*, pp.276–93; *Journal*, pp.466–69, 474–84; CSPD, 1663–64, p.448. The writ *praemunire* had the effect of putting the accused out of the King's protection; real property was forfeited for life, personal property absolutely: David M. Walker, *The Oxford Companion to Law* (Oxford, 1980), p.975

189. For Fleming see below; *A Relation of Margaret Fell* in *A Brief Collection*, p.12. For confirmation that William Kirkby shared his brother's dislike and suspicion of Quakers see MMS, vol.5, 9/2/1686

190. *CSPD*, 1664–65, p.161, Petition of George Fell of Swarthmore, Co. Lancaster, to the King; for a particularly unfavourable portrait of George Fell and his relationship with his mother at this time see Ross, *op.cit.* pp.178–81

191. For Margaret Fell's second imprisonment, and the actions of George Fell see Ross, *op.cit.* pp.220–25; Fox wrote to his wife from Enfield that "Now I hear that he [George Fell] hath been with Kirkby and Monck and such like, and I understand his intent is to have Swarthmore", LSF, Thirnbeck MSS. 8, 23/10/1669, quoted in Henry J. Cadbury, *Narrative Papers of George Fox* (Richmond, Indiana, 1972), pp.104–05

192. P. Hurst, *op.cit.* p.90

193. *Journal*, p.504

194. Pink & Beavan, *op.cit.* p.121; Henning, *The House of Commons*, vol.2, pp.689–90, where it is suggested that his support of James II's policies were mainly inspired by his need to gain the King's pardon for killing a fellow officer in a duel. He had mortgaged Kirkby Ireleth to a London banker, and was never able to redeem the estate, *ibid.* p.690

195. LQMS, vol.1, Hawkshead Meeting 28, 29 & 30/4/1697, where Roger Kirkby is recorded as having taken out twelve warrants for tithe against Quakers from Hawkshead Meeting.

196. See LQMS, vol.1, Hawkshead Meeting, 18/4/1698, 10/6/1699, vol.2, 18/6/1701

197. Pink & Beavan, *op.cit.* pp.76, 78–79, 121–24, 161

198. In addition the estate included property around the town of Dalton, in Ulverston and Lancaster: J.V. Beckett, 'Landownership in Cumbria c.1675–1750' (University of Lancaster, Ph.D. thesis, 1975), pp.274–75

199. B.G. Blackwood, 'The Economic State of the Lancashire Gentry on the Eve of the Civil War', *Northern History*, 12 (1976), p.71 and *The Lancashire Gentry and the Great Rebellion*, p.145

200. B.G. Blackwood, 'Agrarian Unrest and the Early Lancashire Quakers', *JFHC*, 51 (1966–67), p.73; another landlord with similar difficulties was Sir George Middleton of Leighton, a justice of the peace who was later to be deeply involved in the trial of Fox and Margaret Fell at Lancaster in 1663–64: *Journal*, pp.456–60; Blackwood, 'The Economic State of the Lancashire Gentry', p.62 and 'Agrarian Unrest', p.75

201. For a detailed account of the two Prestons' clashes with their Quaker tenants in Cartmel over tithes and the jurisdiction of local courts, see below, chapter 6. In addition to increased tithe payments, the second Sir Thomas Preston sought to increase his income by claiming a right to the estate of his cousin, Sir Thomas Preston of Furness, a Jesuit. The latter had granted the potentially valuable iron-ore mines on his estate to the Society of Jesus as a charitable bequest and it was these his cousin sought: Michael J. Galgano, 'Iron Mining in Restoration Furness, the case of Sir Thomas Preston', *Recusant History*, 12 (1975–76), pp.215–16; *CSPD*, 1682, pp.218, 293

202. *Journal*, p.378

203. *Journal*, p.457. During the trial Margaret Fell complained that "I had not been here, but by my Neighbours"; 'An Examination of Margaret Fell', in *A Brief Collection*, p.283

204. *CSPD*, 1683, p.187

205. MMS vol.5, 31/10/1686

206. *Journal*, p.504; judgements such as this, and those that befell Richard Kirkby were a favourite Quaker (and Dissenting) genre. In 1678 Friends had been encouraged "to send up lists and particulars of all examples of God's judgements upon persecutors and oppressors of the Truth", but by 1701 such manifestations of conflict with the world were deemed superfluous. So the Yearly Meeting ordered the previous direction to be "suspended, seeing through the good providence of God and favour of government we have our liberties ...": MMS, vol.1, 23/3/1678; LYM, vol.2, p.340, 1701. Lancashire Friends were recording judgements as late as at least 1699, see LQMS, vol.1, p.266, Knowsley Meeting, 1699. For Quakers and judgements generally see also Cadbury, *Narrative Papers of George Fox*, pp.209–32 Friends were not alone in recording such instances of divine retribution on persecutors. For some non-Quaker examples see, Henry Fishwick (ed.), *The Note Book of the Rev. Thomas Jolly, A.D. 1671–1693* (Chetham Society, n.s. 33, 1895), pp.31, 51, 56, 60, 66. See also Keith Thomas, *op.cit.* pp.108–12

207. Richard Kirkby appears to have remained a justice until his death in 1681, as does his son Roger who died in 1708. Thomas Preston was also a long serving justice, and was appointed a deputy lieutenant in 1660; his son, Thomas, was also a deputy lieutenant for the county. Pink & Beavan, *op.cit.* pp.78, 120–21; Glassey, *op.cit.* p.285 n.1; A.J. Hawkes, *op.cit.* p.24 n.1.

Spurrier concludes that "some J.P.s enforced the Penal laws against dissent from a sense of duty rather than from persecuting zeal" *op.cit.* p.179

208. A younger brother of the third Sir Roger Bradshaigh sat as MP for the borough of Wigan between 1708 and 1713 : Pink & Beavan, *op.cit.* pp.77–79, 231–32

209. Blackwood, *The Lancashire Gentry and the Great Rebellion*, pp.115, 124; Hawkes, *op.cit.* pp.9–13

210. For Sir Roger Bradshaigh's mining activities, see Hawkes, *op.cit.* pp.14–20; the Bradshaighs do not appear in Quaker Suffering records as prosecutors for tithes.

211. Henning, *op.cit.* vol.1, p.705; Michael Mullett, 'A Receptacle for Papists and an Assilum'; Catholicism and disorder in late seventeenth century Wigan', (unpublished typescript lent by the author), p.4, where Bradshaigh is described as "at least a 'church papist'". One of the royalists that Bradshaigh had assisted during the Civil War was his cousin, the Catholic William Blundell of Crosby: Blackwood, *The Lancashire Gentry and the Great Rebellion*, p.124

212. Hawkes, *op.cit.* pp.38–41

213. B. Quintrell (ed.), *Proceedings of the Lancashire Justices of the Peace at the Sheriff's Table* (Record Society of Lancashire and Cheshire, vol.121, 1981), p.139

214. HMC *Kenyon*, pp.84, 95; *Journal of the House of Commons*, vol.8, p.473, vol.9, p.231

215. 'Sir Roger Bradshaigh's Letter Book' *op.cit.* p.144, n.2

216. Pink & Beavan, *op.cit.* p.228; Fox described a violent encounter between a young Friend and a drunken Shakerley, *Journal*, pp.534–36; for Shakerley's enforcement of the law against Dissenters in post Restoration Chester, see P.J. Challinor, 'Restoration and Exclusion in the County of Cheshire', *Bulletin of the John Rylands Library*, 64 (1981–82), pp.362–63

217. Pink & Beavan, *op.cit.* p.230; H. Horowitz, *The Parliamentary Diary of Narcissus Luttrell 1691–1693* (Oxford, 1972), p.198

218. *CSPD* 1664–65, p.161; The second Thomas Preston of Holker married Elizabeth Bradshaigh, daughter of Sir Roger Bradshaigh (1st Baronet): Hawkes, *op.cit.* Pedigree of the Bradshaigh family, facing p.i and p.24 n.1

219. H.S. Cowper, 'The Kirkbys of Kirkby in Furness'. Pedigree of the Kirkbys of Kirkby Hall, facing p.97 for Fleming see HMC *Le Fleming, passim*. Fleming, from Rydal Hall in Westmorland, was continually aware of the dangers from "the Quakers of whom we have too many, this part of the county joining upon that part of Lancashire where George Fox and most of his cubs are and have been for a long time kennelled": *CSPD*, 1663–64, p.340

220. Sir Ralph Ashton of Whalley, a Member of the Long Parliament and a Presbyterian, sat as a Member for Clitheroe between 1661 and 1662, and 1679 and his death in January 1680. Sir Ralph had voted against the Corporation Act, but he apparently gravitated back to the Anglican Church before his death. His attitude to Quakerism was probably governed in part by his need to recover tithes for the parish of Whalley, the impropriation of which formed part of the Whalley estate. There is evidence of long-standing conflict between the Ashtons of Whalley and Friends from Marsden and Rossendale Meetings over tithe payments. After 1697 when the Whalley estate was passed on to the Ashtons of Middleton, descendants of the

parliamentary commander Colonel Ralph Ashton the tithe disputes were continued by Sir Ralph Ashton of Middleton and Whalley who had sat as a Whig MP for Liverpool between 1676 and 1679, and for Lancashire between 1695 and 1698: Pink & Beavan, *op.cit.* pp.80–81, 253–56; *VCH Lancashire*, vol.6, p.383; D.R. Lacey, *Dissent and Parliamentary Politics in England*, p.374; for examples of sufferings see LQMS, vol.1, Marsden Meeting, 24/4/1658, 13/10/1676, 9/9/1700, vol.2, Marsden Meeting, 16/8/1710; *Besse*, vol.1, pp.329–30, and below chapter 6. Of the alternative spellings Ashton, and Assheton, used for the name of these families, Ashton will be used throughout this book

221. These new MPs referred to included for example, the Heyshams at Lancaster, the Norris family and Thomas Johnson at Liverpool, see below
222. P. Hurst, *op.cit.* pp.89, 143; for this Sir Christopher Musgrave see also J.A. Downie, 'The Disenfranchisement of Christopher Musgrave, MP., by Carlisle Corporation in 1692', *TC&WA&AS*, n.s. 75 (1975), pp.174–87
223. *Besse*, vol.2, pp.11–12; C. Horle, 'Judicial Encounters with Quakers 1660–1688', *JFHS*, 54, (1977), pp.89–90; *CSPD*, 1666–67, p.54; 1670, p.318
224. C. Robbins, *The Diary of Roger Milward* (Cambridge, 1938), p.217, quoted in P. Hurst, *op.cit.* p.143
225. Horowitz, *Parliament. Policy and Politics*, p.22; and *The Parliamentary Diary of Narcissus Luttrell*, p.294
226. MMS, vol.5, 5/9/1686; LSF, Port 36.63, Thomas Camm to Sir Christopher Musgrave, 19/10/1692; Whitehead, *Christian Progress*, p.608
227. MMS, vol.1, 6/1/1679; for Clarges, a zealous Churchman, acting with Musgrave see, for example, Horowitz, *Parliament, Policy and Politics*, pp.69–72
228. *Political Associations*, pp.7–8
229. *Parliamentary History*, vol.5, p.265
230. For Whitehead's origins in Westmorland see *Beginnings,* pp.162 63. For some comments on the gentry's sense of responsibility towards their localities, tenants and neighbours, see Mingay, *op.cit.* pp.121–24
231. GBS vol.3, pt.2, p.808, "To Charles Gerrard and Charles Houghton", "From us so-called Quakers in the South part of Lancashire", 1/9/1680
232. LSF, Port 36.55, Thomas Lower to George Fox, Swarthmore, 17/8/1680
233. Pink & Beavan, *op.cit.* p.79; Lacey, *op.cit.* pp.412–14
234. Lacey, *op.cit.* pp.412–14; in 1654 Newcome had considered "the dangers we may soon be in from these Quakers; what a woful plague God may make them". By 1691 he still thought them "a people raised up to ridicule the excellent religion". Richard Parkinson (ed.), *The Autobiography of Henry Newcome M.A.* (Chetham Soc., vols 26 & 27,1852), pp.52, 274
235. For the Dissenters electoral support of Houghton see Lacey, *op.cit.* p.224
236. *DNB*; *Journal*, p.396
237. *DNB*; for details of the Rye House Plot see David Ogg, *England in the Reign of Charles II*, pp.645–48
238. Western, *op. cit.* p.223; HMC *Kenyon*, pp.234–35
239. HMC *Kenyon*, p.212; HMC *Le Fleming*, pp.205–07
240. Pink & Beavan, *op.cit.* p.78
241. *Stout*, pp.100–02; see also Michael Mullett, Conflict, Politics and Elections in Lancaster, 1660–1638, *Northern History*, 19 (1983), pp.76–78
242. Mullett, Conflict, Politics and Elections, p.81; Horowitz, *Parliament. Policy and Politics*, p.238; Wahlstrand, *op.cit.* p.165

243. Glassey, *op.cit.* pp.277–78
244. There were several complaints that the magistrates of Lancashire were sometimes reluctant to enforce the penal laws against Dissenters and recusants, see HMC *Kenyon*, pp.114, 118–22; B. Quintrell, *op.cit.* p.188 n.132. Sir Philip Musgrave complained to his son Christopher in 1675 that "if a strict account be given of Justices whose zeal for the Church has made them proceed to put in execution the laws against the enemies of it, the number in this county [Westmorland] would be small": *CSPD*, 1675–76, p.573. J.S. Cockburn shows that the attitude of circuit judges to the enforcement of the pre-1689 laws against Dissent could also vary considerably: *A History of English Assizes 1558–1714* (Cambridge, 1972), pp.247–48
245. HMC *Kenyon*, p.233; see also *CSPD*, 1690–91, p.502
246. Some justices in Lancashire, Cheshire and Westmorland seem to have been more aware of the conditional nature of the 1689 Toleration Act than its subsequent historians; for post-1689 Conventicles see GBS, vol.7, pt.1, pp.282, 293–95; MMS, vol.19, 27/12/1707, 11/9/1709
247. HMC *Kenyon*, p.234
248. LSF, Port 13.38, Testimony of Robert Hubberstey, 1707
249. LFMH, 2.A.xxxvi:2, John Tomkins to William Stout, London, 15/5/1699; LFMH, 2.Ai:9, Benjamin Bealing to Lancaster Meeting, London 13/11/1699; the case was printed in *To the Lords and Commons in Parliament Assembled. An Account of some late and present sufferings, of some of the People called Quakers* (London, 1700), p.2
250. MMS, vol.1, 6/7/1700
251. LMH 2.A.xxxvi:3, John Tomkins to William Stout, London 2/9/1700; MMS, vol.14, 25/8/1700, 29/9/1700, 27/10/1700; *DNB*
252. MMS 16/11/1701
253. Pink & Beavan, *op.cit.* p.122
254. Glassey, *op.cit.* pp.285, 293
255. *Stout*, pp.55–56, 180–81
256. One of the arguments most frequently used by the Quakers to support their case for relief from oaths was that the requirement to swear was inhibiting them from advancing the wealth of the nation as merchants and manufacturers. See *A Brief Representation of the Quaker's Case of Not Swearing* (London, 1694), p.3
257. Romney Sedgewick, *op.cit.* vol.2, p.136
258. *Stout*, p.188
259. Pink & Beavan, *op.cit.* pp.123–24: *Stout*, pp.129, 131, 136, 196, 283–84
260. Romney Sedgewick, *op.cit.* vol.2, pp.136–37
261. For the importance of Friends in the Lancaster merchant community see *Stout*, pp.52–63. The foothold of Quakerism in Liverpool in the seventeenth and early eighteenth century was never as strong as in Lancaster. See James Murphy, 'The Old Quaker Meeting House in Hackins Hey, Liverpool', *THSLC*, 106 (1954), pp.79–98; Robert Muschamp.'The Society of Friends in the Seventeenth Century with a few later notes', *TLCAS*, 46 (1929), pp.78–92. For a brief history of Quakers in Liverpool see M. Muriel Shearer, *Quakers in Liverpool* (Liverpool, 1982), *passim.*
262. Pink & Beavan, *op.cit.* pp.194–95, 198–99
263. A.C. Wardle, 'Sir Thomas Johnson. His Impecuniosity and Death', *THSLC*, 90 (1938), pp.181–95; *DNB*

264. *Stout*, pp.148–49, 164

265. E.M. Platt, 'Sir Thomas Johnson', *THSLC*, 52 (1902) pp.158–59

266. *Stout*, p.204; for Gildart see, Wardle, *op.cit.* pp.181–95

267. As we have seen, whilst Brandon and one of his Whig coterie were "loving" to Friends, others, and notably Roger Kirkby, were not. See above and Michael Mullett, 'The Politics of Liverpool, 1660–88', *THSLC*, 124 (1972), pp.31–32

269. Pink & Beavan, *op.cit.* pp.192–96; for Thomas and William Norris see *DNB*; for the Norris family see Thomas Heywood (ed.), *The Norris Papers* (Chetham Soc., 9, 1846), *passim*.

270. Blackwood, *The Lancashire Gentry and the Great Rebellion*, p.120; Horowitz, *The Parliamentary Diary of Narcissus Luttrell*, p.444

271. *Journal of the House of Commons*, 11, p.502; Romney Sedgewick, *op.cit.* vol.2, p.297

272. See above, chapter 1

273. For example, Richard Shuttleworth, who sat for the county between 1705 and 1749, reputed "One of the strongest Jacobites in England". Edward Harvey, member for Clitheroe between 1705 and 1722 and arrested several times for his involvement in Jacobite conspiracy; Henry Fleetwood, who sat for Preston between 1708 and 1722, amongst many others. Romney Sedgewick, *op.cit.* vol.1, p.424, vol.2, pp.39, 114–15

274. See *Second Period*, p.189, where it is suggested that the fundamentalism of the Lancashire Quakers was linked to their alleged Jacobite sympathies. Friends' continued hostility towards Catholicism can be seen in the contents of many of the tithe testimonies presented to Monthly Meetings in Lancashire for which, see below. A hostility towards Catholicism should not, of course, be taken as implying a hostility towards Catholics

275. For the role of London Quakers in supplying the exiled court at St. Germain see R.A. Hopkins, 'Aspects of Jacobite Conspiracy in England in the Reign of William III' (University of Cambridge Ph.D. thesis, 1981) pp.135–36, who concludes that there was "genuine popular support" for James II amongst Quakers, p.494. See also Pierre Burger, 'Spymaster to Louis XIV: A Study of the Papers of the Abbe Eusebe Renaudot', in Eveline Cruickshanks (ed.), *Ideology and Conspiracy: Aspects of Jacobitism, 1669–1759* (Edinburgh, 1982), pp.114–15

276. Isaac Pennington, *Concerning Persecution* (1661), in Hugh Barbour and Arthur Roberts, (eds.), *Early Quaker Writings* (Grand Rapids, Michigan, 1973), p.373

277. *ibid.* pp.377–78

278. *Apology*, p.254

279. Richard Hubberthorn, *The Rebukes of a Reviler fallen upon his own Head* (1657), in *A Collection*, p.135

280. *Apology*, p.511

281. MMS, vol.1, 18/8/1675

282. The Yearly Meeting advised in 1676 "That Friends be careful of entangling themselves in the law because of some small irregularities in proceedings but if the law be materially transgressed and the severity of it exceeded by our persecutors that Friends in God's wisdom use their liberty upon serious and good advice amongst themselves so as Truth and its testimony may be kept clear over all". LFMH, Yearly Meeting Minutes and Epistles, vol.1, p.34

283. See, for example, Richard Hubberthorn, *The Real Cause of the Nation's Bondage* (1659), in *A Collection*, pp.222–23. For a general survey of Restoration Quakers and the legal system see Alfred W. Braithwaite, 'Thomas Rudyard, Early Friends' "Oracle of Law"', *JFHS*, supp.27. (London, 1956) *passim*.

284. William Penn and William Mead, *The People's Ancient and Just Liberties Asserted* ... (London, 1670), preface, and *passim*.

285. William Penn, *The Proposed Comprehension, Soberly and not Unreasonably Considered* (London, 1672), p.1

286. MMS, vol.1, 18/8/1675 .

287. *ibid.*

288. LSF, Port 16.35, George Fox to Roger and John Haydock, 3/2/1684, containing extracts of letters written by Thomas Dockray

289. *A Collection of the Christian Writings ... of Roger Haydock, op.cit.* sig. C1

290. MMS, vol.11, 4/7/1696

291. See Appendix 1

3

The Quakers and the Oath

The Quaker refusal to swear oaths was one of the testimonies which frequently brought Friends into conflict with the established authorities of Church and state, leading to personal and financial suffering. What follows is an attempt to quantify the extent of Quaker prosecutions for not swearing, in order to compare the results with the claims made by Friends of the difficulties which not swearing imposed upon them. This quantification will be set against the background of the legislative framework which required Friends (and others) to swear oaths in a variety of circumstances. In addition, evidence will be presented to show some of the means by which it was possible for Lancashire Quakers to avoid the burden of oaths imposed by the state whilst remaining loyal to their witness against swearing. It will be argued that such means were available to Friends principally because they generally enjoyed the support and confidence of the local communities in which they lived and worked. First, however, there is a need to examine the importance of the oath in seventeenth and eighteenth century society, and the reasons which Quakers offered for not swearing.

   One of the few scholars to have studied the place of the oath in society is Christopher Hill, in a short and perceptive essay in his *Society and Puritanism*.[1] Hill explains that the oath served two distinct functions; firstly, it was a "means of ensuring obedience" as an "oath of loyalty", and secondly, in judicial and other proceedings it was "an oath to tell the truth".[2] The force of the oath was contained in the supernatural sanction which was inherent to it, and as is shown below it impinged upon virtually every aspect of day-to-day life. Hill argues that, as such, the oath was a feature of "pre-contract society"; its general importance and the awe in which it was held were deleteriously affected by the "sixteenth century economic changes" which "shook the theoretical standards as well as the economic and political foundations of the old order".[3] The result of this, says Hill, was that "supernatural sanctions became less necessary in a society in which honesty was manifestly the best policy", and that "it paid a man to make his word his bond because of the rise in social importance of credit, reputation, respectability".[4]

Commerce, however, was not the only factor undermining the sanctity of swearing. Common lawyers, anxious as ever to secure their markets, attacked the use of the oath *ex officio* in ecclesiastical and other courts.[5] Conscientious Puritans preferred to reject outward collective observances, stressing instead the importance of the "inner intention" of the individual.[6] To free men, aware that the oath was used discriminately against the lower orders of society, "refusal of oaths became a proclamation of human equality".[7] As if this was not enough, the background to these developments was one of broken covenants during the Civil War and Commonwealth period and outrageous false-swearing in the Popish Plot of 1678.[8] The consequence of this, says Hill, was simply that "the use of oaths was declining".[9]

Although I agree with the majority of his argument, I will argue here that in one respect Christopher Hill is fundamentally wrong in his analysis of the place and importance of the oath in seventeenth-century England. Quite simply, far from declining in use, the oath was increasingly becoming the last (and to be sure, ineffective) resort of an Establishment whose methods of policing and administration were inadequate to deal with the social changes and sophisticated commercial developments that were taking place around it. Thus, at the very time that, as Hill shows, the oath was being held in least regard by a large proportion of the population, the state was attempting to use it to regulate even more areas of social, political and commercial life. It is doubly ironic that the Quakers, who scrupled swearing, should suffer because they held the oath in higher regard than did the majority of swearers.

Objections to the oath certainly abounded. Not only did it recede in the face of the stress laid upon the individual conscience by a number of Protestant groups, but it also became a casualty of the growing rejection of superstition and magic.[10] Moreover, lawyers did not restrict their attack on swearing to the illegality of the *ex officio* oath used in Church courts. Barbara Shapiro has argued that during the seventeenth century a number of enlightened but nonetheless influential members of the legal profession were attempting to improve "the scientific certainty of judicial fact finding".[11] The consequence of this was that the oath, which after all merely represented the procedural legality of a witness, was viewed as less important than the witnesses' credibility. Thus juries were increasingly called upon to judge not only the fact, but also the credibility of witnesses, and "testimony under oath was no longer assumed to be truthful".[12] Among the groups who argued against swearing, besides the Quakers, the Levellers were probably the most prominent. In *The Case of the Army Truly Stated* (1647), they complained of "burthensome Oaths" and demanded that "all statutes enforcing the taking of oaths, as in towns corporate, the oath of supremacy, etc ... may be repealed and nulled".[13] This plea against the use of oaths in matters commercial and material was repeated for spiritual affairs, John Lilburne arguing in *An Agreement of the Free People of England* (1649), that there should be no

Lawes, Oaths or Covenants, whereby to compell by penalties or otherwise any person to any thing in or about matters of faith, Religion, or God's worship.[14]

The Ranter argument against oaths took the form of encouraging false-swearing and cursing, whilst the Fifth Monarchy Men, like the Quakers, adopted a practical objection by refusing all oaths.[15] At the other end of the political spectrum was Thomas Hobbes, who argued that:

the Oath addes nothing to the obligation. For a Covenant, if lawfull, binds in the sight of God, without the Oath, as much as with it.[16]

Despite these growing objections to the oath, and the increasing scepticism with which many viewed the supernatural sanctions backing it, Restoration government continued to rely on the sworn word of men. The returned regime hoped to secure itself by the Oaths of Supremacy and Allegiance, opponents being rooted out by such means as the Corporation Act, which required all borough officials to take these oaths. Refusal meant not only loss of office, but according to the statute, that "to all intents and purposes ... the said respective persons so refuseing were naturally dead".[17] Groups such as the Quakers who "maintained sundry dangerous Opinions and Tenants as amongst others that the taking of an oath in any case whatsoever although before a lawfull Magistrate is altogether unlawfull and contrary to the word of God ..." were to be punished under the terms of the so-called Quaker Act of 1661.[18] The Act, which enforced fines for the first two offences and transportation for the third, was clearly designed to prevent the spread of any opinions that called the oath into question, and thus threatened the prop upon which society rested.[19]

To the state the importance of the oath in securing loyalty and guaranteeing the honest performance of promises, clearly overcame any public or private doubts as to its efficacy. That is not to say that the state was unaware that scepticism was being made manifest by widespread perjury. It has been suggested, for example, that the multiplicity of oaths required from court and other officials as early as the reign of Charles I were imposed as a response to oath breaking and that "the less effective they were, the more were devised".[20] In many respects this seems to have been the case throughout the later seventeenth and early eighteenth centuries; oaths may have been declining in terms of their power to dictate action, but they were not declining in use.

In order to justify the proliferation of oaths official propagandists, particularly leading divines, produced defences of lawful swearing. Isaac Barrow, Master of Trinity College Cambridge preached a sermon 'Against rash and vain Swearing' in which he first of all, and significantly, agreed that their value would be diminished by casual use:

human society will be extremely wronged and damnified by the dissolving or slackening these most sacred bonds of conscience: and consequently by their common and careless use; which soon will breed a contempt of them, and render them insignificant, either to bind the swearers, or to ground a trust on their oaths.[21]

The danger of this was that oaths were "the great prop of society", maintaining:

the safety, peace and welfare thereof, in observing laws, dispensing justice, discharging trusts, keeping contracts and holding good correspondence mutually.[22]

Perhaps the most forthright statement by the Establishment in support of swearing came from John Tillotson (later Archbishop of Canterbury) in a sermon preached in 1681 on 'The lawfulness and obligation of oaths'.[23] This, as Tillotson explained, was a subject close to his heart "as men have run into the wildest extremities … particularly in the matter of oaths: some making conscience of taking any oaths at all, and too many none at all of breaking them".[24] For Tillotson the oath was

the utmost security that one man can give to another of the truth of what he says; the strongest tie of fidelity; the surest ground of judicial proceedings; and the most firm and sacred bond that can be laid upon all that are concerned in the administration of public justice, upon judge and jury, and witness.[25]

In an important sentence Tillotson conceded that an oath was not "always a certain and infallible decision of things according to truth and right", but he returned to his central point, that if "an oath will not oblige men to speak truth, nothing will".[26] Much of the sermon was devoted to a detailed refutation of the Quaker objection to swearing, suggesting the degree of alarm with which Friends' opinions were viewed. However, in this, as in the rest of the sermon, Tillotson was at pains to stress the necessity of legal swearing for the good ordering of society, for, as he wrote,

it is not possible to find any security equal to that of an oath, because the obligation of that reacheth to the most secret and hidden practises of men, and takes hold of them in many cases where the penalty of no human law can have any awe or force upon them.[27]

Nor did this opinion fade noticeably following the Toleration Act of 1689 or the establishment of the Hanoverian succession. As late as 1722, when a modified form of Affirmation for Quakers was passing through the House of Lords, members of the Church could complain that it "might weaken the security of all governments, an oath".[28]

This theorising to support swearing can be paralleled in the extent of legislation passed through Parliament explicitly demanding an oath in some form or other. In the parliamentary session 1695–1696, during which the first Quaker Affirmation Act was passed, some forty public Acts passed onto the statute book. Of these, twenty, exactly one half of the total, contained an explicit reference to the use of an oath.[29] The assessors of the land tax were to swear to enter office, and appeals against their assessments were to be entered on oath.[30] Poor prisoners were to swear upon obtaining their discharge from prison; seamen who absented themselves from their duties through illness were to swear (with sworn witnesses) as to the nature of their sickness.[31] Shippers of silver and bullion were to swear as to its foreign origin, and lawyers were to take the oaths and declaration in order to practise.[32] Freeholders were to swear to their qualification before they could vote in elections, and distillers of "low wines" were to testify on oath to the quality of their spirits.[33] Salt weighers could only be employed after they were sworn.[34] In addition, a number of the twenty Acts which did not explicitly refer to swearing did in fact depend on the oath for their administration. Amongst these were excise Acts depending on the *ad valorem* method of assessing duties, a method which in turn depended on swearing.[35]

Thus, despite the cynicism towards swearing that was increasing throughout the seventeenth century, often manifesting itself in widespread perjury, the oath increased, rather than declined in use.[36] For the state, the oath remained ostensibly the only means of ensuring loyalty and conformity amongst its subjects and officers at the highest and lowest levels.[37] In the increasingly complex world of commerce, the oath seemed the only means in the possession of the state to ensure that it collected its legal dues from imports, and exports, and the only means by which the judiciary could impose honesty in business dealings. The impartiality and accuracy of all legal proceedings depended on the oaths of court officials, plaintiffs and defendants, although sworn jurymen were now being told to judge more closely the circumstantial credibility of the evidence of the sworn witness. The oath, as Tillotson was prepared to concede, did not guarantee truthfulness, but it seemed to be all the state had. And so statute by statute, year by year, the number of oaths required increased, as did the opportunities for evasion and perjury. In the midst of this were the Quakers, already in some respects an anomaly, a group of people who spoke the Truth in all their actions and words, and who despite their contempt for the oath and its worldly connotations were still outraged when informers perjured themselves on oaths or when neighbours falsely swore at the customs-house.[38]

The Quakers' testimony against oaths was based initially on two pieces of scripture which forbade swearing. In chapter five of the Gospel of Matthew the matter was clearly stated:

> Again, ye have heard that it hath been said by them of old time, Thou shalt not forswear thyself, but shalt perform unto the Lord thine oaths: But I say unto you, Swear not at all, neither by heaven, for it is God's throne, nor by earth, for it is his footstool ...

But let your communication be Yea, yea; Nay, nay: for whatsoever
is more than these cometh of evil.[39]

The second passage opposing the use of oaths and underlining Matthew
5, 33–7, came from the Epistle of James, where readers were urged to
"swear not but let your yea be yea; and your nay, nay".[40] Friends interpreted
these two scriptures as an abrogation of any Old Testament command to
swear, for like tithes, oaths were abolished under the new covenant of
Christ.[41] Christ's command was clear, "Swear not at all, neither by that oath
which David and the Jews swore by, nor any other oath".[42]

Robert Barclay built on these scriptural bases and summed up the
developed Quaker attitude towards oaths in the following manner in 1672:

It is no ways lawful for a Christian to swear, whom Christ hath called
for his Essential Truth, which was before all Oaths, forbidding him to
swear; and on the contrary, commanding him to speak the Truth in all
things, to the Honour of Christ who called him; that it may appear,
that the words of his Disciples may be as truly believed, as the Oaths of
all the worldly Men.[43]

Thus the unworldly Quakers spoke "the Truth in all things", which,
they argued, was a rare event amongst worldly oath-takers. Richard
Hubberthorn pointed out to the newly restored Charles II that "it is so
common amongst men to swear and engage either for or against things,
that there is no regard taken to them, nor fear of an Oath".[44] Three years
later, in 1663, at Chester, Hubberthorn complained that

all those who will not lye and swear, and use deceit, but yea and nay,
such a one cannot have trading in your Markets; for none can buy nor
sell who have not the Mark of the Beast upon him; but he who loveth
and telleth a lye, hath the most priviledge and advantage among you.[45]

William Penn, in *One Project for the Good of England*, written in 1679,
proposed a form of declaration (which he claimed would be acceptable to
Friends) to replace the Oaths of Allegiance and Supremacy, for, he argued,
governments were secured not by oaths "but by all having agreed to the
laws, by which they are to be governed". Oaths were ineffective, "For
neither in private cases, nor yet in public transactions have men adhered to
their oaths, but their interest".[46] As we have seen, this secular conception
of obligation based on interest, as opposed to spiritual sanction, underlay
the Quaker attitude to government.[47]

This double-pronged attack on swearing, supported on the one hand
by the weight of scripture, and on the other by the widely acknowledged
abuse of oaths in society, was supported by a third contention. The Quaker
truth, it was suggested, was better than the truth of the ordinary man,
whether or not it was supported by oaths. George Fox, for example, was

able to recount the case of Thomas Hammersley, a Quaker who served as a foreman of a jury in 1665 without being sworn. When the jury had returned its verdict the judge commented that he had "never heard such an upright verdict as that Quaker brought in".[48] Richard Hubberthorn stated that "that therefore which we speak of in the truth of our hearts, is more than what they swear".[49] In 1683, in a letter to Roger Haydock which is discussed more fully below, William Shewen suggested (on behalf of the Meeting for Sufferings) that when confronted with a Quaker making a plain declaration as to the truthfulness of what he said, a magistrate might well "commend it above their common oaths".[50] Friends not only spoke the truth, but by any objective measure they could think of they spoke more truth, word for word, than non-Friends.[51]

In many respects the Quaker refusal to swear was backed by more powerful and cogent arguments than any of their other testimonies. John Tillotson in his defence of swearing, having already acknowledged the growing abuse of oaths, turned to the Quaker's case. "I will grant", he wrote,

> that there is scarce any error whatsoever that hath a more plausible colour from scripture than this, which makes the case of those who are seduced into it the more pitiable.[52]

His interpretation of Jesus' pronouncement on oaths in Matthew, was, not surprisingly, that it was a prohibition of "oaths in ordinary conversation", a view shared by Isaac Barrow. Tillotson also put forward more practical arguments against the Quaker refusal to swear: it was "very prejudicial to them that hold it", rendering "those who refuse oaths in all cases almost intolerable to human society".[53] Furthermore, it encouraged others to refuse oaths, and thus further undermine the basis of social stability. Tillotson's arguments, however, were not directed at Friends, and in the final analysis the only means at the disposal of the Establishment for combating Quaker non-swearing was to employ the coercive measures contained in statute-law against those who refused oaths, and to ensure that Quakers did not gain the protection from the law that ordinary men swore to obtain. An Essex Quaker, Robert Lovet, who had complained at the assizes of robbery, was told by Judge Street that "he would take no notice of it no matter if all Quakers were robbed, till they swore".[54] This, at least in theory, was the Establishment response to the Quaker's testimony against oaths until the introduction of the first Affirmation Act in 1696. In practice, however, this response was modified in two important ways. Firstly, the principle of exempting Quakers and other Dissenters from some statutory oaths was in fact conceded in a limited number of specific cases prior to the passing of the first Affirmation Act in 1696. The Toleration Act, for example, allowed Quakers to make a Declaration of Fidelity and Christian belief in place of the Oaths of Allegiance in order to benefit from its provisions.[55] The Poll Act of 1690 (and a number of subsequent Poll Acts) maintained this concession to Friends. Whereas Anglicans or other Dissenters who failed to take the Oaths of Allegiance were to be double taxed, Quakers would only suffer the penalty if they neglected to make their Declaration.[56] Secondly, however, there appears to have been a considerable laxity by officials in the enforcement of those laws and regulations that might impose oaths upon Friends. It is to the actual experience of Quakers in Lancashire with regards to the oath that we now turn.[57]

The laws which required oaths to be used were of two distinct varieties. First, there were those directed against the post-Restoration Dissenters, some of which laws were suspended by the Toleration Act of 1689.[58] For Friends the most important of these, in theory, was the Quaker Act of 1662, the purpose of which was to prevent any person from refusing to take an oath, and the Conventicle Act of 1664 which laid down that the refusal to take an oath in court was punishable by fines and transportation.[59] Earlier legislation, notably 7. Jac. I. c. 6., which required any person over the age of eighteen to take the Oath of Allegiance when demanded by two justices (often in practice a single justice) was used both before and after the implementation of the Clarendon Code. The punishment for this refusal was imprisonment and the threat of *praemunire*.[60] The Quaker Act, the second Conventicle Act (the first had expired in 1667) and the Act of Uniformity and Five Mile Act were conditionally repealed in 1689.[61] The Corporation Act, which required all persons holding corporate office to take the Oath of Allegiance, and also demanded that they should receive holy communion according to the rites of the Anglican Church, and the Test Act (which required the same of all government servants) were not repealed.[62]

Secondly, Friends were open to sufferings through the operation of a variety of laws, more incidental than penal, concerning matters of trade and property which demanded the sanction of an oath. Foremost in this category was the requirement of oaths in order to import and export goods, prove wills, enter copyholds and gain freedoms. Furthermore, Friends might be called upon to swear in order to serve a number of offices from alderman to constable.[63] There was little doubt that the purpose of this restrictive net went beyond the mere discovery and punishment of religious Dissenters to underpinning the security of the state. This was made clear to George Fox at the Lancaster Assizes of March 1664 when he was told by the presiding Justice that "the King was sworn, the Parliament was sworn, and he and the justices were sworn, and the law was preserved by oaths".[64]

In Lancashire as in many other counties, Friends rigorously maintained their testimony against swearing whenever it was seen to be brought into question. In 1676 Lancaster Monthly Meeting ordered that

John Townson and Henry Wilson do go and exhort and admonish William Eccleston and see if he will condemn the evil action of swearing or making oaths, contrary to the practise of truth.[65]

and when some four years later Emy Hodgson, a Friend from Swarthmore Meeting, swore in front of a justice on the Act for Burying in Woollens, she was ordered to write a paper denying her actions and present the same to the court at which she had sworn.[66] In 1693, following enquiries from the Meeting for Sufferings in London as to what form of words, if any, Friends might accept from Parliament in place of an oath, the Quarterly Meeting for the county decided

> that yea yea and nay nay ought to be stood by and to and that nothing more be offered or accepted to or from the government to ease the burthen of oaths but what truly is commanded with Christ's command.[67]

This decision prepared the way for a repudiation in Lancashire of the ease which was granted to Friends over the matter of swearing in the Affirmation Act of 1696. This repudiation embraced both "test" oaths and routine declaratory oaths. The wording of the Affirmation, which included the phrase "in the presence of Almighty God", had been accepted only as an expedient by the Friends lobbying Parliament, who faced severe opposition from the supporters of the Established Church.[68] However, to many Friends in both the North and South this practical and politic expedient was little more than another oath, invoking as it did the presence of God to give sanction to the words of the speaker.[69] It was not until 1722, when a perpetual Affirmation omitting reference to God was granted, that Lancashire Quarterly Meeting decided that it could accept the form of words offered in place of an oath. Thus, with the exception of a small number of specific instances, Friends were open to prosecution for refusing to swear or affirm in the circumstances outlined above for a period of some sixty years following the Restoration.[70] It is the purpose of the following study to examine in detail the recorded sufferings of Lancashire Quakers for refusing to swear, and to suggest some reasons for the results that emerge.

The figures shown in Table 2 overleaf are drawn from two sources. Those in parentheses are from Joseph Besse's *Collection of the Sufferings of the People called Quakers* (1753), ostensibly drawn from the same annual accounts that were used to compile the Great Book of Sufferings, and covering the period 1660–1689. The main set of figures, covering the period 1660–1722, comes from the sections of the Great Book of Sufferings containing the returns sent to London from Lancashire. Material from the Lancashire Quarterly Meeting Book of Sufferings has not been included in the main sequence, for samplings showed it to be particularly inaccurate for the period 1660 to 1670, when little systematic recording seems to have taken place at a local level.[71]

I have divided the cases in which Friends refused to swear into six sections. In the first place, and most markedly just after the Restoration, Quakers were penalised for refusing the Oaths of Allegiance and

Table 2   Sufferings of Lancashire Quakers for Refusing to Swear,
1660–1722

	1660 -69	1670 -79	1680 -89	1690 -99	1700 -09	1710 -19	1720 -22
Refusing the Oath of Allegiance and "For not Swearing"	252 (196)	11	1				
Refusing to Swear in Tithe Cases	13	15 (1)	12 (13)	41			
Refusing to Swear in Chancery and Exchequer		3					
Refusing to Swear for Manufactured Goods						14	
Refusing to Swear for Office	8 (2)	2	2		1		
Other			3 (2)	·2			

(Source: GBS, vols.1–16; *Besse*, vol. 1, pp.300–330)

Supremacy. Many entries in Besse and the Great Book of Sufferings give no clear indication of the exact type of prosecution that Friends were under in this respect. This was the case, for example, with the 41 Bickerstaff Friends "sent ... to the common jail at Lancaster" early in 1661 after justice Nathaniel West had asked them "if any would take the oath"; their refusal led to committal, as did that of the eight Quakers taken at Thomas Patefield's and imprisoned "for refusing the oaths" before two justices.[72] We may safely assume that in those cases the phrase "the oaths" is shorthand for the Oaths of Allegiance and Supremacy commonly built into post-Restoration discriminative measures such as the 1661 Corporation Act. So we may group these "sufferings" together with a large number of cases in which Friends' refusal to swear Allegiance and Supremacy was specified in the record.

A second category of non-swearing compounded the offence that Quakers committed in law when they refused to pay their tithes. Thus it was with the 33 Friends "who came to jail on the 28th day of the 2nd month last (1691) upon attachment for not answering upon oath to their adversaries bill for tithe ..."[73] Thirdly, I have grouped together a number of cases in which Friends felt themselves to be penalised by "great sufferings, and extreme hardships in our persons and estates, ... being not admitted by law, to answer in the Court of Chancery and Exchequer without oath" in civil suits over matters of debt and land-titles.[74]

Next comes a class of sufferings stemming from Friends' refusal to comply with the government-imposed sworn attestations accompanying the manufacture or import of such goods as "candles or leather (which require the taking of an oath, or the present affirmation)" – refusals which, it was claimed in 1721, "have already ruined some, and apparently tend to the ruin of many more".[75] Fifthly, some Quakers were called upon to swear oaths when they were drafted or elected, perhaps maliciously, for local government office. Finally, there were miscellaneous actions ("other" in the table) under the Burial in Woollens Act and for refusal to swear in other cases.[76] In all the cases in the table, Friends fell foul of the law, for refusal of oaths, either as subjects (Allegiance and Supremacy), as Quakers (Quaker Act), parishioners (tithe and other dues), litigants (title and debt), merchants and manufacturers (leather, etc), or citizens (local office).

Out of a total of 380 individual sufferings recorded for refusing to swear in the Great Book of Sufferings, 322 occurred between 1660 and 1689. Nearly 70 of these were confined to the two years following the Restoration of Charles II. In 1660 the number given for refusing to swear was 58, whilst 105 Friends refused the Oath of Allegiance; the following year the figures were 35 and 13 respectively. These figures, and the method in which oaths were tendered to Friends at this time, are consistent with the interpretation of persecution in these early years as representing a purge by an insecure regime of the politically suspect.[77] Friends in all parts of the county were arrested and imprisoned for refusing to swear: at Yealand "the constable of the town with several soldiers with swords and pistols entered the house and seized the whole meeting", sending 26 Friends to Lancaster Castle; the following day the armed soldiers returned and took the remaining twelve to the same destination.[78] Seven days later twelve Friends were taken at Bickerstaff "by soldiers, who said they came by order of the Earl of Derby", and having refused the Oaths of Allegiance at Wigan, were taken to the county gaol.[79] The thirteen Friends who were taken at a meeting in Manchester in June 1661 were met by troops of a more nervous disposition, for

> the meeting being ended there stood armed men with halberks [halberds] and pikes threatening to slay them if they came upon them, and immediately came the men called justices and apprehended them and tendered them the oath of obedience as they called it, but Friends in the fear of the lord denied to swear …[80]

It is interesting to note that this highly organised operation against Friends did not always rely on their reluctance to swear in order to incarcerate them. In February 1660/61 "at Swarthmore, forty three persons were taken, some out of their houses, others from the market, and some from their labour and employments by a party of horsemen, and without any warrant, Mittimus, or examination before a magistrate, committed to Lancaster Castle".[81]

What is surprising about this exploitation of the Quaker refusal to swear is not its ferocity, but the fact that it ended as quickly as it did, especially as this was just at the time that national legislation, (in the form of the Quaker Act) capitalising on this refusal, was being introduced. After 1661 the number of prosecutions for refusing to swear or take the Oath of Allegiance exceeded ten on only one occasion, in 1668. For the most part the prosecutions and sufferings that involved the taking of an oath after this initial outburst were concerned with tithe prosecutions, and at the end of the period, customs.[82] Given the sudden decline in these prosecutions, and given the fact that Friends did not alter their position regarding oaths at this time, it can only be concluded that the use of an oath as a political weapon was superseded by the opportunities afforded to the authorities by the Conventicle Act of 1664 and other items in the Clarendon Code. This implies that the local authorities were not primarily interested in oath-swearing but merely used oaths to show up the presence of Quakers and to prosecute them for an "offence", being Quakers and attending conventicles, which before 1662 and 1664 was not clearly illegal in recent law. This view is reinforced by the experience of Margaret Fell, who in 1663 was twice offered the opportunity of not being asked to swear the Oaths of Allegiance, providing she agreed to desist from holding meetings at Swarthmore. At a private meeting of the north-Lancashire justices at Ulverston she was told that "if I would not keep a Meeting at my House, they would not tender me the Oath", whilst Judge Twisden told her at the Lancaster Assizes that "if you will give security that you will have no more Meetings, I will not tender the Oath to you".[83]

During the sixty-two years for which data have been gathered only 13 Friends are recorded as having suffered for refusing to qualify themselves for office on oath. Of these, nine were called to serve as jurymen either at local courts or the assizes at Wigan or Lancaster. Of these the most unfortunate was surely John Berley of Lancaster, who in 1663 was summoned to a court leet and court baron at Aldcliffe, a mile or so south-west of the town, by Robert Dalton of Thurnham. Chosen to serve on the jury Berley refused the oath which was offered to him and was fined eleven shillings and eightpence. Shortly afterwards Dalton's bailiff seized fifteen of Berley's sheep, worth in excess of three pounds, which were sold at Lancaster market to meet the fine. Shortly after this, Berley was chosen to serve on a jury at a court in Lancaster, and again refusing to swear he was fined six shillings and eightpence. On refusing to pay the fine he was sued by the town's bailiff for debt and imprisoned in the castle.[84] Of the remaining four Friends, two are simply recorded as having been called to serve an "office", one as a constable; the last, Miles Birket,

> was returned at the court baron held in the parish of Cartmel to serve the office of a massman, which said office he did accept of and serve, but it appearing at the next court held in the year 1709 that the said Miles had not been sworn to serve the said office, he was fined by the said court six shillings and eightpence;

eventually he had goods distrained to the value of nine shillings.[85]

The above incident illustrates what must have been a dilemma for many Friends, for although having no objection to holding such offices they were at least in theory prevented from doing so by the barrier of customary or statutory oaths. However, in Lancaster at least 14 Friends have been identified as having held minor offices of the corporation during this period, and a similar situation seems to have existed in Bolton.[86] The refusal of an oath required to qualify for office could lead to non-appointment, and a consequent loss of any of the benefits offered by the post in question: it did not, however, necessarily lead to prosecution or suffering. For example, in 1668 John Lawson, one of the first Quaker converts in Lancaster and a leading merchant within the town, was removed from the office of bailiff of the Customs for refusing to take the oaths.[87] He was not, apparently, fined or in any other way punished for this refusal, although later in the year he was subject to the discipline of the local Meeting for paying a fine in another matter in order to obtain a discharge from the town's prison.[88] In 1696 Sir Daniel Fleming wrote to Viscount Lonsdale from Rydal in connection with appointments of tax officials that "All our Assessors have taken the Oaths except some Quakers, who were rejected by the Commissioners"; rejected, but not apparently fined.[89] The Toleration Act of 1689 allowed Dissenters to act in office by deputy if they were elected or appointed to a post outside the scope of the 1673 Test Act, which required an oath of entry.[90] Friends, however, continued to serve in such burdensome offices as that of constable, where the appointee was legally required to swear "so help me God" that he would perform his duties. Furthermore, there was the added danger that, as constable, a Friend might be called upon to enforce the law against his coreligionists.[91]

In tithe actions personal inclination often determined the course that a prosecution for non-payment of tithe would follow, and the method of prosecution in turn determined the likelihood of Friends being called upon to swear.[92]

Whilst the use of the Oath of Allegiance in an open court was a convenient method to combat the danger perceived in the activities of Friends, the tender of an oath in an ecclesiastical court in a case of tithe merely prolonged the waiting of a cleric or lay impropriator for the payment of the claimed amount.[93] Out of the 80 prosecutions recorded for not-swearing in cases of tithe, 59 were clearly in suits brought in an ecclesiastical court, and of these 47 were sued by the same impropriator, Edmund Ashton of Whalley. Of these 47 Friends, 12 were involved in the same case in 1684, and 33 were sued together in 1691.[94] In the Exchequer there was more hope of taking advantage of Quaker principles in order to obtain an order of distress against Friends' goods, though the methods used, involving the process of contempt and outlawing, were both circuitous and probably illegal.[95] At least five Friends from Cartmel suffered in this way at the suit of Thomas Preston of Holker, and of the remaining sixteen prosecutions, eight were in the Exchequer, whilst the method of the others is not clear.[96] Imprisonment or distraints for refusing to answer on oath seem to have been the almost inevitable outcome of a tithe case brought in either ecclesiastical or Exchequer courts. The Act for the More Easy Recovery of Small Tithes (1696) and the Affirmation Act (1696) gave Friends at least technical relief from these sufferings by introducing a summary procedure for the recovery by the plaintiff of the tithe claimed with a set allowance for expenses.[97] The purpose of both these statutes with regard to tithe was to lessen the problems faced by the claimant during the proceedings; in Lancashire the number of Friends suffering for non-payment of tithe nearly doubled within two years of the Acts being passed.[98]

In comparison with the ecclesiastical and Exchequer courts, there are few cases of Friends suffering for refusing to swear or appear on oath in the Court of Chancery. Although it is difficult to estimate the number of cases in that court which involved Friends, it is clear from a variety of sources that the matters of debt and property dealt with were essential aspects in the day-to-day life of merchants and yeomen farmers. One only has to examine the Quaker complaints of the hardships they faced through not swearing to realise how important the proceedings of Chancery were to them.[99] In Lancashire there are only three cases of sufferings in Chancery recorded between 1660 and 1722, all of which occurred within two years of each other. The nature of the particular cases does show that the substance of Friends' complaints was realistic, but there is no evidence (at least in the case of Lancashire) to support the frequency with which they claimed prosecutions took place.

Henry Ashton, a distiller of Ormskirk, was sued in Chancery by David Poole, his debtor to the tune of £19, "he having no other way to defraud the said Henry Ashton of the aforesaid debt, knowing that for conscience sake he could not swear".[100] Thomas Gee of Preston sued Hamlet Percivall in the local Chancery Court for an account of seven years standing,

> and the said Hamlet gave in his answer, which the said Gee with many others did believe to be true, and Gee's attorney said the bill and answer did not differ a groat, and because the said Hamlet could not for conscience sake swear, it cost him seven or eight pounds.[101]

Thomas Crosby of Ormskirk, a grocer, was sued by a merchant from Liverpool for the sum of ten pounds, which Crosby claimed he had already paid,

> and the carrier being alive did and doth affirm the payment of the said ten pounds accordingly, but to prevent him bearing evidence he was joined defendant in the suit (and) the said Thomas Crosby called to answer, and because he could not swear to it for conscience sake, it cost him ten pounds or above.[102]

Friends in trade were also likely to face difficulties with regard to the customs and excise. It was widely felt that there were so many oaths expected of both ships-masters and merchants importing and exporting goods that the sanction of swearing was being devalued. One non-Quaker authority claimed that perjuries were "but too frequently committed at the Custom-House, viz. That it is but a Custom-House Oath; as if God who is omnipresent, did not see, and was not equally offended at profaning his Name there, as at any other Place whatsoever ... "[103] When, in 1832, many of the oaths connected with commercial declarations were abolished under the Act 1 & 2 Wm IV c. 4, it was explained that "From the frequent occasions on which such oaths and affirmations are required, ... the reverence and respect which should attach to such solemn obligations have been weakened".[104] The controller of the customs at Lancaster was warned in 1715 that there was some laxity in the procedure concerning the entry of oaths, and was reminded that "the oath be wrote on the original warrant being first signed by the merchant who makes the oath, and then yourselves or such of you before whom the same by law is to be administered ..."[105]

How then did Friends fare in this atmosphere of oathmaking and oath-breaking? It is clear from Table 2 that, even before the 1696 Affirmation Act, the oaths demanded at the customs were somehow avoided by Friends. In 1698 London Yearly Meeting warned Friends against using "secret and indirect ways to take up their goods without paying the customs and duties".[106] The county Quarterly Meeting did its best to ensure that Friends made a true entry of their goods at the customs-house, and later enquired of each Monthly and Particular Meeting "how Friends were clear from being concerned in defrauding the King of his duties and excise".[107] Furthermore, it is clear from a study of the commercial activities of William Stout and his fellow Quaker merchants in Lancaster that the official records contain numerous references to the type and quantity of goods which they were trading.[108] Given this seemingly large scale evasion of the official oaths, which must have involved some amount of complicity between customs-officers and Quakers, it is difficult to explain the outburst of prosecutions which took place on the passing of the Leather Act of 1711.[109] The duty, which was administered by the Tax Office as opposed to the Commissioners of Customs, (suggesting perhaps, a stricter administration) was required from all merchants importing leather, who were required to make an oath as to the value of their goods at the customs. Specially appointed officers, recruited mainly from the Board of Excise, were required to examine stocks of hides held by leather tanners and again verify the quantity of the same on oath, "which oath any Justice of the Peace or the collectors or supervisors that shall be appointed for the said duty in their respective districts are hereby impowered to administer".[110]

The result of the new legislation was almost immediate. Roderick Forbes, a Quaker from Aberdeen, wrote to his brother in February 1711 that a great many of our Friends are presently under suffering because they cannot verify their entries by Affirmation on the late Leather Act, so that as I came through Cumberland many Friends' goods were distrained to the value of twelve pounds ... although their entries were truly made and duties paid.[111]

A similar situation existed in Lancashire, where in 1711 nine Friends were "prosecuted by Edward Burghall of Wigan, head collector for the duty on hides and skins ... though the said collector acknowledged the receipt of the Queen's duty for the same".[112] Burghall had previously acted as surveyor of the excise for the county, and as such must have had some contact with Quaker merchants and distillers who would neither swear nor affirm.[113] In the north of the county five Friends were prosecuted, and in all nearly £175 was taken from the fourteen, out of a total seized from Friends in the county of £520.[114] A letter from Swarthmore Meeting to the Meeting for Sufferings complained that "except some relief can be had from London, divers of the tanners, etc, must give up their trades", and the following year the same Meeting decided to "collect the sufferings of Friends who have left their business or their trade because they did scruple the Affirmation".[115]

The Quaker response in London to the effect of the Leather Act was cool, with the representatives for Lancashire to the Yearly Meeting of 1712 reporting that it was "not without some difficulty" and "after an exercise of some meetings" that the prosecutions were accepted as *bona fide* sufferings.[116] The Meeting for Sufferings approached both the Attorney General and the Solicitor General for opinions on the situation of Friends who refused either to swear or affirm when making their declarations, concluding that they were "against the said Friends in their judgement". A further report to the Meeting on the Leather Act stated that "there is no relief (by the letter of the said Act) for any that shall refuse to make such entry as is therein required".[117] A petition was forwarded to the Lord Treasurer's Office stating the case of the northern Friends, but this apparently asked only that "they may have the privilege of Affirmation", something which by all accounts they had but in a form that was still unacceptable.[118] Indeed, the Meeting for Sufferings was at pains to stress that the suffering Friends were refusing to act as the law required, and in order to dissociate itself from these actions, it refused in May 1712 to consent to the printing of a paper to be delivered to Parliament giving account of the prosecutions. It was decided that it "being a new case – this Meeting thought meet not to consent thereto".[119] It finally attempted in the same month to approach Members of Parliament in order to obtain a clause "that Friends may be admitted to make their entries on a penalty in case of frauds" to be inserted in an Act for laying additional duties on hides; this method had been employed in the Hop Act of 1711.[120]

It seems clear that much of the apparent embarrassment of the Meeting for Sufferings at the activities of the Friends who were prosecuted for not swearing or affirming on the Leather Act was due to the fact that the Affirmation then in force was nearing the date of its expiry.[121] A paper printed early in 1712, which publicly stated the dissatisfaction of many Friends with an Affirmation that included the name of God, caused George Whitehead to write that

> The late bustle in public solicitation against the name of God in the solemn affirmation has rendered us very little as a people very weak and inconsistent in the eyes of the government; and opened the mouths of many against Friends. It has greatly offended our friends in the government and caused our adversaries to rejoice over us.[122]

Indeed, it is even possible to see the prosecutions under the Leather Act as the outcome of a concerted attempt by the "dissatisfied" Friends to apply pressure upon both the Meeting for Sufferings and the House of Commons, in order to obtain a modified Affirmation. Certainly it is otherwise difficult to explain the prosecutions of 1711 and 1712, which, given the unwritten accommodation between the officers of the customs and excise and the Friends of Lancashire and the other northern counties which "negative" evidence shows to have existed, need never have taken place.[123]

If, as it would appear from the foregoing, Friends were not being called upon to swear, it remains to be shown what collusive method, if any, was being used in order to avoid a breach of their testimony. It has been shown that Quakers in Derbyshire could be "relatively certain of a favourable Anglican attitude over oaths" when proving wills, that "there was a deliberate silence on the part of both Anglicans and Friends in many areas of the county about the technical compliance with the law" and that *Jurat* was entered against Friends names in probate cases.[124] In Westmorland, as a result of the influence of Gervase Benson on the officials of the court of the Archdeaconry of Richmond, Friends had "the privilege of proving wills and taking letters of administration without oaths". Thomas Camm, who gave account of this state of affairs in 1709 added that it had "continued to this day".[125] When Margaret Fox wrote an epistle criticising the Northern Friends who refused to use the Affirmation granted in 1696 she bitterly complained that "when they had occasion formerly to prove wills or put in answers, they were glad to see a clerk put in *Jurat* ... whereas now they may go plainly before the face of all to speak their solemn declaration".[126]

A correspondence between Roger Haydock and the Meeting for Sufferings reveals more than any other source about the arrangements that Friends came to with 'the world', and it is this that will be examined in the following pages.[127] Haydock, a Friend from Coppull, wrote to the Meeting for Sufferings in 1683, asking advice in the case of Friends who were summoned to appear in the Court of Chancery "by evil minded men, who having no right to such pretended interests as they claimed", were attempting to exploit the Quaker refusal to swear.[128] He explained that in fact Friends' answers had been accepted without an oath, "yet such answers ... were recorded as accepted upon oath, which to some Friends hath seemed a straight thing". The letter continued

> but a late chancellor made a rule of court, that no answer should be taken but in the presence of the plaintiff's attorney ... otherwise he to have 6 days notice before, of the place as well as time, where and when the commissioners sit to receive our Friends answer; this of late time hath made answers without oath more difficult to be accepted. But thus it sometimes falls when the defendants attorney knows whom the plaintiff hath joined in the commission ... then the Friends attorney lays out to inform himself if possible when the plaintiffs commissioner is either abroad or hath such earnest occasion elsewhere, that although 6 days notice be given him, he cannot meet the other commissioners, which if it take effect as several times it hath done, then the Friends answers is readily taken without oath, but still by the commissioners recorded as accepted upon oath ....

Was this, Haydock wanted to know, consistent with Friends' testimony regarding swearing?[129]

The Meeting for Sufferings clearly found it difficult to discuss such a candid account of Friends' activities, for the original minute recording the receipt and substance of Haydock's letter was scored out, only to be later prefixed, "This should stand".[130] Eventually William Shewen was nominated to write the reply to Haydock, and the Meeting's answer contained in the letter was typically cryptic.[131] It was agreed that

> Friends may have freedom in the spirit of God to offer or give their testimony in justice and truth as in the sight and presence of God, and solemnly to aver the truth of their answer in his fear, and if any court or magistrate is or shall be satisfied therewith, and account it equivalent with an oath, and record it accordingly ... we must not shun giving testimony in our right to prevent their misinterpretation.[132]

This phrase, a clear forerunner of the Affirmation granted in 1696, was to reach to "probates of wills, executorships, freedoms in corporations, entries at customs-houses and many other things". Avoiding comment on the method of entering answers described by Haydock, the letter continued

> seeing that in divers weighty cases Friends testimonies, depositions and answers have been accepted and recorded by officers in trust without an oath under the term *Jurat* in design only of doing them a kindness as knowing their answer would not otherwise be accepted in court. It would appear disingenuous, very imprudent and unfair ... to make a

[manuscript torn] discovery of this in court against the officer ... thereby causing such a one to be called in question and perhaps to lose his place, and not only so, but by such open discovery of such a nice scruple, cause the courts to be more inquisitive, strict and severe upon Friends ....

The letter concluded: "This is our present sense in the matter, if anyone otherwise minded, we may say as the apostle did in another case, the Lord will reveal it if they truly wait upon him".[133]

Two main conclusions can be drawn from the letter sent by the Meeting for Sufferings to Robert Haydock. Firstly, it is clear from its tone and contents that Haydock's account of Friends having *Jurat* entered on their behalf whilst not actually swearing was by no means exceptional, the main problem being seen in those who were uneasy about this procedure (the fact that no comment was made on the method employed by Lancashire Friends may indicate a desire on the part of the Meeting for Sufferings not to be informed of such technical details). Indeed, there was a note of pride in the suggestion that a magistrate, having accepted a Friend's word, might "it may be, commend it above their common oath", something that was doubtless also true for the acceptance of Friends' word by customs and excise officers, in preference to insincere oaths.[134] Secondly, the reply seems to have afforded the Meeting an opportunity to present to Friends in Lancashire the form of words it was seeking as an Affirmation. Haydock made no mention of any required phrase being used by Friends, and given their later position the use of the phrase "in the presence of God" by them would seem unlikely. The letter from London, however, stressed on several occasions that Friends were "clear against swearing" if they had only "in the fear of God solemnly promised or assented the truth as the case required".[135] Haydock had expressed concern only over the fact that Friends' plain answers were being called oaths, but perhaps in the answer of the Meeting for Sufferings we should see some anticipation of the problem which was to shake the Movement to its foundations at the turn of the century.[136]

What then can be said of the testimony of Lancashire Friends against swearing? Certainly the Quarterly, Monthly and Particular Meetings maintained a strong discipline with regard to all the outward aspects of Quaker life, exhorting and sometimes bullying Friends in order to prevent disorderly walking. Refusal to swear was seen as a basic testimony, and thus when it was brought into question, either on the rare occasions that a Friend was discovered to have sworn or when the introduction of the Affirmation in 1696 seemed to compromise Friends' testimony, the Meetings acted with all their strength and unity to reassert their position in the eyes of the world.[137] Friends were inevitably drawn into contact with their Anglican or Dissenting neighbours through their business and trade, and as sober and responsible citizens they were often called upon to serve, though not usually in exalted roles, the community in which they lived. In general, the Meeting for Sufferings advised Friends to take advantage of a clause in the Toleration Act of 1689 which allowed Dissenters who could not swear to act in office by deputy, but for the most part Lancashire Quakers and their fellow citizens were prepared to see the problem of oaths of entry overcome by accommodation in order to allow them to play their natural role in society.[138] Similarly, officers of court and customs saw little reason why these honest improvers of trade should have their right to property and profit threatened either by unscrupulous suits or strongly held scruples. Indeed, the length to which Friends' attorneys went in order to see an answer entered is some indication of the light in which Quakers were seen. It is interesting to note that only in the case of tithes, when Friends were considered to be threatening another's property rights, and the Leather Act, when a concerned group wanted to pressurise the Meeting for Sufferings, was there no obvious collusion with the world in order to avoid the problem of swearing.

REFERENCES

1. Christopher Hill, *Society and Puritanism in Pre–Revolutionary England* (revised edition, Harmondsworth, 1969), pp.370–406
2. *ibid.* p.371
3. *ibid.* p.384
4. *ibid.* pp.386, 405
5. *ibid.* pp.391–92
6. *ibid.* p.385
7. *ibid.* p.395
8. *ibid.* p.402
9. *ibid.* p.387
10. Keith Thomas, *Religion and the Decline of Magic* (London, 1973), pp.76–77
11. Barbara J. Shapiro, *Probability and Certainty in Seventeenth Century England* (Princeton N.J., 1983), p.187
12. *ibid.* pp.183–87; earlier debates in the legal profession had centred on the legality of the use of the oath *ex officio* by ecclesiastical and other courts, see Mary M. MacGuire, 'Attack of the Common Lawyers on the Oath ex officio', in *Essays in History and Political Theory in Honour of Charles Howard McIlwain* (Cambridge, Mass., 1936), pp.199–229
13. William Haller and Godfrey Davies (eds.), *The Leveller Tracts 1647–1653* (New York, 1944), pp.66, 82
14. *ibid.* p.323
15. A.L. Morton, *The World of the Ranters* (London, 1970), p.80; B.S. Capp, *The Fifth Monarchy Men* (London, 1972), p.180
16. Thomas Hobbes, *Leviathan* (Pelican Classics edition, London, 1968), p.201
17. An Act for the Well Governing and Regulating of Corporations, 13 Car. 11 Stat.2, c. 1
18. An Act for preventing the Mischiefs and Dangers that may arise by certaine Persons called Quakers and others refusing to take lawfull Oaths, 14 Car. II, c. 1

19. In practice the Quaker Act appears to have been little used: see, *Second Period*, pp.23–24, and below

20. G.E. Aylmer, *The King's Servants. The Civil Service of Charles I, 1625–1642* (London, 1961), pp.148–9

21. Rev A. Napier (ed.), *The Theological Works of Isaac Barrow* (Cambridge, 1859), vol 2, p.49. It has not been possible to date this sermon. To quote from the Reverend Napier, who edited this edition of Barrow's works, "it would be interesting to discover when and where these sermons were preached: but except in a few instances, neither the date nor the place of their delivery can positively be ascertained". It was first published in 1678, *ibid*. vol.1, p.xii. For the life and career of Isaac Barrow (1630–77), see *DNB*

22. *ibid*. p.44

23. The influence of Tillotson's sermons can be judged by the fact that they "were amongst the most favoured purchases of rural divines". His thoughts "found their echo in the pulpits of the country churches of the kingdom": Norman Sykes, *Church and State in England in the XVIIIth Century* (Cambridge, 1934), p.260. For Tillotson's life and career see *DNB*

24. *The Works of the Most Reverend Dr John Tillotson, Late Lord Archbishop of Canterbury* (Edinburgh, 1772), vol.2, p.1

25. *ibid*. p.2

26. *ibid*. p.3

27. *ibid*. p.4

28. *Parliamentary History of England*, vol., p.948

29. These statutes were 7 & 8 Will.III c. 3, 5, 6, 8, 10, 12, 14, 16, 18, 19, 21, 22, 24, 25, 27, 30, 31, 34, 35 and 39

30. 7 & 8 Will.III, c. 3

31. 7 & 8 Will.III, c. 12, c. 21

32. 7 & 8 Will.III, c. 19, c. 24

33. 7 & 8 Will.III, c. 25, c. 30

34. 7 & 8 Will.III, c. 31

35. See, for example, 7 & 8 Will.III, c. 20, An act for granting to His Majesty an additionall Duty upon all French Goods and Merchandize.

36. Although one critic suggested that in view "of the little sence the Generality of Men in Offices seem to have of the Obligation of their Oaths", legislators ought "either to lessen the number, or alter the Form of Oaths, or at least to take care that they were better discharged": *The Oath of a Constable, so far as it relates to his Apprehending NightWalkers and Idle Persons etc* (London, 1707), p.3

37. Although by the eighteenth century this view was being challenged, not least by Members of Parliament. In 1708 Henry Gouldney wrote to Robert Barclay giving account of Quaker attempts to lobby Parliament for a modified Affirmation to be inserted in a Bill to Prevent Bribery in Elections, which otherwise stipulated that an oath should be taken at the poll. "Several Members", wrote Gouldney, "said that oaths did not answer the end proposed because too many were less awed by them than by penalties and so they left out the oath and put in a penalty ..." In 1711 Roderick Forbes wrote to Barclay from London that in Parliament there "was a loud alarm against all manner of oaths, for many talked they wished oaths were quite abolished". Scottish Record Office, CH 10/3/55 (unnumbered bundle), Henry Gouldney and others to Robert Barclay, London, 2/1/1708, and Roderick Forbes to Robert Barclay, London, 15/12/1711

38. For an example of Quaker outrage see the case of Thomas Middleton, a Westmorland Friend, who was convicted for attending a conventicle ("though he was not there but was 60 miles off that day from the Meeting") on the false evidence of two informers. His attempts to prosecute the informers failed due to the obstruction of Daniel Fleming, who had been the justice responsible for Middleton's original prosecution. "The informers as they came home, confessed their fault to the Friend, and said they would do so no more, asking him forgiveness; but he told them he durst not, lest he should pervert the course of the law against perjury": MMS, vol 5, 5/9/1686, 10/10/1686. This example also serves to confute the argument of Alfred W. Braithwaite, that early Friends refrained from pursuing their grievances against informers in the courts. See his 'Early Friends and Informers', *JFHS*, 51 (1965–67), pp.107–15. For the customs see *Stout*, p.147

39. Matthew 5, 33–37

40. Epistle of James, 5, 12

41. For tithes, see below, chapter 5

42. Richard Hubberthorn, *Antichristianism reproved and the Doctrine of Christ and his Apostles justified against Swearing* (1660), in *A Collection*, pp.244–45

43. *Apology*, p.553

44. Richard Hubberthorn, *Somthing that lately passed in discourse between the King and RH*, (1660), in *A Collection*, p.269

45. Richard Hubberthorn, *A true Testimony of Obedience to the Heavenly Call ....* (1653), in *A Collection*, p.6

46. Hugh Barbour and Arthur Roberts,(eds.), *Early Quaker Writings* (Grand Rapids Michigan, 1973), pp.448–49

47. See above, chapter 1

48. *Journal*, p.182. Hammersley appears to have been a prominent Friend in Staffordshire, where his house at Basford, near Leek, was used for Meetings. See *Besse*, vol.1, p.652

49. Richard Hubberthorn, *Somthing that lately passed in discourse between the King and RH*, (1660), in *A Collection*, p.269

50. LSF, Port 16.32, *William Shewen's Answer to Roger Haydock*, London, 31/6/1683

51. This view of the Quaker's truth as being somehow superior to the truth spoken by non-Quakers explains in part the jealousy with which they guarded the Affirmation against use by non-Friends: see Richard T. Vann, *The Social Development of English Quakerism 1655–1755* (Cambridge, Mass., 1969), p.142

52. Tillotson, *Works*, vol.2, p.8

53. *ibid.* pp.8–9; Napier (ed.), *Theological Works of Isaac Barrow*, vol.2, p.63

54. MMS, vol.6, 19/8/1688

55. I Will. & Mar. c. 18; The view that Friends were being indulged was clearly shared by at least part of the population; John Airey wrote to George Whitehead in 1689 "of the clergy's and rabble's dissatisfaction that Friends have so much favour showed to them and liberty given them to worship the Lord as they have, they wanting to be at their old work of persecution again. And the clergy is much displeased to take it ill that Friend's words will be taken in matters where oaths are required from them", MMS, vol.7, 27/7/1689

56. 2 Will. & Mar. c. 11; see also 3 Will. & Mar. c. 6, 4 Will. & Mar. c. 1, 5 & 6 Will. & Mar. c. 14

57. The remainder of this chapter has appeared in a slightly modified form under the title 'Lancashire Quakers and the Oath 1660–1722' in *JFHS*, 54 (1980), pp.235–254. I am grateful to the editor(s) of that journal for their permission to reproduce it here

58. I Will. & Mar. c. 18, provided that a Dissenter taking the Oath of Allegiance, or a declaration to the same effect and a declaration of fidelity and Christian belief, would be exempt from penalties under the Conventicle Act, the Act of Uniformity, the Quaker Act and the Five Mile Act

59. 14 Car.II, c. 1, 16 Car.II, c. 4

60. *Second Period*, pp 14–15

61. The second Conventicle Act, 22 Car.II, c. 1, did not contain the clause directed specifically against Quakers refusing the Oaths of Allegiance which had been included in the Act of 1664. See 16 Car.II, c. 4, 18. For the Act of Uniformity and Five Mile Act see 14 Car.II, c. 4 and 17 Car.II., c2

62. 13 Car.II, c. 1; 25 Car.II, c. 2

63. For a general summary of the legal and civil disabilities caused by non-swearing see Arnold Lloyd, *Quaker Social History* (London, 1950), pp.80–83. For the use of oaths at the customs see E. Hoon, *The Organisation of the English Customs System 1696–1786* (Newton Abbot, 1968), pp.243–369. For the matter of Friends proving wills see H. Forde, "Friends and authority: a consideration of attitudes and expedients with particular reference to Derbyshire", *JFHS* 54 (1978), pp.115–125. As discussed above, oaths were also required of Friends if they wished to qualify themselves as electors. Many of the oaths put to Friends were originally designed to force recusants to deny the power and authority of Rome. For a list of oaths directed against Catholics see Ann M.C. Forster, 'The Oath tendered', *Recusant History*, 14 (1977), p.86

64. *Journal*, pp.483–484; Chief Justice John Kelying thought the refusal to swear would "subvert the Government, because without swearing we can have no justice done, no law executed, you may be robbed, your houses broken open, your goods taken away and be injured in your persons, and no justice or recompense had because the fact cannot be proved ...", quoted in Craig Horle, 'Judicial encounters with Quakers 1660–1688', *JFHS*, 54 (1977), p.98

65. LMMM, vol.1, 18/8/1676

66. SWMMM, vol.1, 11/12/1678, 11/1/1678–79, 6/3/1679; for Emy Hodgson's paper of denial see LSF, Dix MSS. F2

67. LQMM, vol.1, 3/11/1693, 1/8/1696

68. The Meeting for Sufferings had decided to accept these words on the advice of "the Members of Parliament appointed to prepare and carry in the Bill, and others, who do believe the bill will not pass if such solemn Affirmation was not in it. And rather than the Bill should not pass the Meeting was mostly satisfied that the Bill should go on ..." MMS, vol.10, 12/12/1695; and below, chapter 4

69. For this view see LSF, Port 20.101, John Haydock's letter to Friends of Hardshaw Meeting, Wigan, 10/1/1702, transcribed in full in Appendix 2; and below, chapter 4

70. 7 & 8 Will.III, c. 34, 8 Geo.II, c. 6; LQMM, vol.2, 13/2/1722

71. GBS, vols. 1–16; *Besse*, vol.1, pp.300–330; LQMS, vol.1, 1654–1700, *passim*.

72. GBS, vol.1, p.561, 13/11/1660; *Besse*, vol.1, p.309, 13/1/1661

73. GBS, vol.5, pt. 1 p.262, 28/2/1691

74. *The Case of the people commonly called Quakers, with some reasons humbly offered* ... (London, 1696), p.1; see also *A Brief representation of the Quaker case of not swearing* (London, 1694), *passim*. Not included here is "the business of Edward Harly concerning the acre of land taken from him because he could not swear", which was discussed once at the Quarterly Meeting, but does not appear as a suffering in any of the three sources used; LQMM, vol.1, 23/1/1674–75

75. *The Case of some Thousands of the People called Quakers in Great Britain who Conscientiously Scruple the present Affirmation* (London, 1721), p.1

76. GBS, vol.3, pt.2, p.851, 6th month 1683, p.881, 8/8/1684; vol.5, pt.1, p.262, 16/4/1690; vol.7, pt.1, p.303, 6th month 1693; *Besse*, vol.1, p.329, 1684

77. For these figures see Table 2. *Second Period*, pp.8–14; W.W. Spurrier, 'The persecution of the Quakers in England' (University of North Carolina, Ph.D. thesis, 1976), pp.119, 145–47

78. GBS, vol.1, p.561, 13/11/1660

79. GBS, vol.1, p.561, 20/11/1660

80. GBS, vol.1, p.563, 16/4/1661

81. *Besse*, vol.1, p.308, 24/11/1660

82. The largest number of Friends who suffered for not swearing in any of the given categories in Table 2 on any one occasion was 33, who were imprisoned "for not answering upon oath, to their adversaries bill for tithe", GBS, vol.5, pt.1, p.262, 28/2/1691

83. *A Relation of Margaret Fell*, and *The Examination of Margaret Fell before Judge Twisden*, (1663), in *A Brief Collection*, pp.7, 277. Clearly the use of the oath by local officials to discover Quakers, or the threat of its use to prevent Quakers from meeting, to an extent vitiates the official Establishment arguments for the retention of oaths.

84. GBS, vol.1, pp.567–68, 1663; versions of Berley's sufferings can also be found in *Besse*, vol.1, p.361, and B. Nightingale, *Early Stages of the Quaker Movement in Lancashire* (London, 1921), pp.122–23

85. GBS, vol.11, pt.2, p.448, 17/12/1709. A massman was probably a church-warden, elected annually in the local manor court or vestry. Although oaths could vary between parish and diocese, a warden would usually have to swear "you shall execute the Office of a Churchwarden in the Parish where you are chosen for this ensuing year, according to your skill and discretion in His Majesty's Laws, ecclesiastical now in force, so help you God". For the selection and duties of a churchwarden see S.A. Peyton (ed.), *Minutes of proceedings in Quarter Sessions held for the Parts of Kesteven in the County of Lincoln 1674–1695* (Lincoln, Lincoln Record Society, vol.25, 1931), pp.lv–lvi; L.M. Hill, 'County government in Caroline England 1625–1640', in Conrad Russell (ed.), *The Origins of the English Civil War* (London, 1973, p.76. For a variety of churchwardens' oaths see *The Book of Oaths* (London, 1715), pp.222–24, appendix, p.5. Although perhaps surprising, it seems that Quakers were prepared to serve the office of churchwarden. For a later case in which Quakers who had agreed to serve were refused office, see 'Bishop Ticolson's Diaries', part 4, *TC&WA&AS*, n.s. 4 (1904), p.57

86. Nicholas Morgan, 'The Social and political relations of the Lancaster Quaker community, 1688–1740', in Michael Mullett (ed.), *Early Lancaster Friends* (Lancaster Centre for North-West Regional Studies, Occasional Paper No. 5, 1978), p.25; W.E.A. Axon, 'The Pembertons of Aspull and

Philadelphia, and some passages of the early history of Quakerism in Lancashire', *TLCAS*, 12 (1912), p.161. This serving of minor offices was clearly not confined to Lancashire; see, for one example, Besse, *A Collection*, vol.1, p.667, for a Suffolk Quaker acting as a constable in 1658.

87. W.O. Roper, *Materials for the History of Lancaster* (Chetham Soc., n.s. 61, 1907), p.55

88. LMMM, vol.1, George Fox to John Lawson, 5/9/1669 (copied onto the final page in the minute book)

89. HMC, *Le Fleming*, p.343

90. "If any Person dissenting from the Church of England as aforesaid, shall herafter be chosen, or otherwise appointed, to bear the Office of High Constable, or Petty-Constable, Churchwarden, Overseer of the Poor, or any other Parochial of Ward-Office, and such Person shall scruple to take upon him any of the said Offices in regard of the Oath ... every such Person shall and may execute such Office or Employment by a sufficient Deputy, by him to be provided ..."; 1 Will. & Mar. c. 18, 7

91. For the selection and duties of a constable see Peyton, *op.cit.* pp.xlvi–liii. A variety of constables' oaths are in *The Book of Oaths*, pp.207–208, appendix pp.5–6. For the case of a Friend who as a constable carried out warrants of distraint against fellow-Quakers see LMMM, vol.1, testimonies, 28/12/1707

92. "When persecution did occur it was more often personality than principle that was at stake"; Eric Evans, "'Our Faithful Testimony' – the Society of Friends and Tithe Payments, 1690–1730', *JFHS*, 52 (1969), p.121

93. The ecclesiastical courts could only order payment to be made, and did not have the power or ability to enforce that order by granting or obtaining an order of distraint; see A.W. Braithwaite, 'Early Tithe Prosecutions, Friends as Outlaws', *JFHS*, 49 (1960), p.151

94. GBS, vol.3, pt.2, p.880, 17/7/1684, vol.5, pt.1, p.262, 28/2/1691

95. Friends had obtained a legal opinion that jurisdiction in matters of tithe lay only in the ecclesiastical courts. A.W. Braithwaite, 'Early Tithe Prosecutions', pp.150, 152–55

96. *Besse*, vol.1, p.329

97. 6 Will.III, c. 6 & 34

98. See below, chapter 6

99. *A Brief representation of the Quakers Case* (1694), pp.3–5 *The Case of the People called Quakers With Respect to many of their Friends in South Britain, and their Friends in general in North Britain, who conscientiously scruple the Taking of the present Affirmation* (London, 1720), *passim.; The Case of the People called Quakers, relating to Oathes and Swearing* (London, 1673), p.6

100. GBS, vol.3, pt.2, p.748, 1675. The result of the case that "the said Henry Ashton is under contempt for not answering ... and the said David Poole has got an injunction to stop him from recovering his said debt, so that he is likely to loose his just debt, and he [is] imprisoned besides"

101. GBS, vol.3, pt.2, p.769, 1674. This would be in the Lancashire Chancery Court at Preston. For its history and jurisdiction see Robert Somerville, 'The Palatinate Courts in Lancashire', in Alan Harding (ed.), *Law making and law makers in British History* (London, Royal Historical Society Studies in History Series, No. 22, 1980), pp.56–63

102. GBS, vol.3, pt.2, p.769, 1674. Such cases were not confined to Lancashire. In 1673, for example, Irish Quakers petitioned the lord lieutenant and council

complaining that they were frequently defrauded through their refusal to swear. They cited the example of Thomas Holme, (a native of Coniston and later surveyor general in Pennsylvania), who lost a debt of £200, and had goods seized besides, having been cited to appear in Chancery, in a manner similar to Thomas Crosby. H.S. Cowper, 'Captain Thomas Holme, William Penn's Surveyor General (1624–1695)', *TC&WA&AS*, n.s. 23 (1923), p.79

103.   Henry Crouch, *A Complete guide to the officers of His Majesty's Customs* (London, 1732), p.143, quoted in Hoon, *op.cit.* p.247

104.   Preamble to the Act; quoted in Henry Atton and Henry Holland, *The King's Customs* (2 vols., London, 1910), vol.2, p.161

105.   PRO, CUST 81/70, p.4

106.   LYMM, vol.2, p.229, 1698

107.   LQMM, vol.2, 1/8/1719

108.   *Stout*, Appendix A, pp.282–91

109.   9 Anne. c. 12 This duty on leather had been first introduced in 1697 by 8 & 9 Will.III, c. 21 for a period of three years. The Act had been allowed to expire in 1700 and was revived in 9 Anne., c.12: L.A. Clarkson 'The Leather Industry in the Seventeenth Century' (University of Nottingham, Ph.D. thesis, 1961), pp.396–98. For a counsel's opinion regarding the use of the oath in this Act see LFMH, 2Axxxvi:4, Legal opinions concerning oaths and leather tanners, 1711

110.   For the appointment of these officers see PRO, CUST 47/66, pp.35–43. The terms of the Act made no provision for Affirmation in lieu of oath; this may be an indication of the harsher political climate towards the end of the reign of Queen Anne, although in practice the Affirmation was generally available to Friends. For the case of a Friend (Thomas Dodgson) who swore to the value of his stocks of leather, deciding later that "he does not intend to take the oath any more but will rather choose to give off his trade", see SMMM, vol.3, 3/4/1712, 2/7/1712

111.   Scottish Record Office, CH 10/3/55 (unnumbered bundle), Roderick Forbes to George Forbes, London, 15/12/1711–12

112.   GBS, vol.14, pt.1, p.106, 24/4/1711. Friends were also prosecuted for refusing to swear under the terms of the Act in Westmorland, where "some Friends of Kendal having considerable quantities of leather which have lain drawn and dry ... and cannot dispose of it, by reason the officers refuse to stamp it according to law": MMS, vol.20, 22/2/1712. For sufferers in Sunderland and Durham, see MMS, vol.20, 28/10/1711, 25/11/1711

113.   PRO, CUST, 47/66, p.35

114.   LYMM, vol.4, p.247, 1712

115.   MMS, vol.20, 14/10/1711; SMMM, vol.4, 7/9/1712. For the importance of the leather industry to the North-West economy see, for example J.D. Marshall, 'Agrarian Wealth and Social Structure in Pre-Industrial Cumbria', *Economic History Review*, 33 (1980), p.515; Clarkson, *op.cit.* p.95. The distress caused to those Friends unable to sell their unstamped stocks of leather was no doubt due in part to the precarious structure of credit upon which the industry rested for its operation: *ibid.* pp.148–50

116.   LQMM, vol.2, 3/5/1712

117.   MMS, vol.20, 23/9/1711, 30/9/1711. The Quakers were clearly not prosecuted in this matter without considerable forethought on the part of the authorities. On October 4th, 1711, Bishop Nicolson of Carlisle noted in

his diary that during the days work at Penrith sessions "The cause of ye Quakers, refuseing to swear to yir Stocks of leather, long debated; and at last ye Judgemt given against them confirmed, Mr Agl. alone dissenting". 'Bishop Nicolson's Diaries, part 4', *TC&WA&AS*, n.s. 4 (1904), p.54

118. MMS., vol.20, 21/10/1711; PRO, T 4/9, p.34, 19th December 1711
119. MSS, vol.20, 17/3/1712. London Yearly Meeting, on "consideration of this new case being very weighty on Friends, not to reject or take no notice of the sufferers, have agreed that the said sufferings be now entered under this title, viz. for that they declare they could not verify their entries as the law directs", LYMM, vol.4, p.257, 1712
120. MMS, vol.20, 26/3/1712; 9 Anne c. 13
121. The first Affirmation Act had been renewed in 1702, and was due to expire in 1715. See *Political Associations*, p.49
122. George Whitehead to Robert Barclay, 4th March 1712, quoted in *Second Period*, p.192; for an account of the proceedings of the Meeting for Sufferings in relation to renewing the Affirmation see *Political Associations*, pp.50–54
123. There was a spate of prosecutions of Friends in 1716 and 1717 who refused to affirm or swear to the value of their stocks of leather according to the Act, in both Lancashire and Yorkshire. See MMS, vol.22, 3/6/1716, 29/1/1717, 21/4/1717, 29/9/1717, 13/10/1717, 20/10/1717
124. Forde, 'Friends and Authority: a consideration of attitudes and expedients, with particular reference to Derbyshire', *JFHS*, 54 (1978), pp.124–25. Dr Forde shows that of the twelve Quaker wills which she was able to trace proved prior to 1696, four had executors who were non-Friends, three executors (all widows) used vicars or curates to swear as substitutes, one executrix renounced administration in favour of a non-Friend, whilst the four remaining (Quaker) executors are recorded as having sworn. After 1696 thirty-three executors affirmed, whilst twenty-one are recorded as having sworn; *ibid.* pp.117–18
125. LSF, Port 7.75, pp.9–10; this is printed in N. Penney (ed.), *The First Publishers of Truth* (London, 1907), p.251. Benson, a former mayor of Kendal, justice of the peace and a proctor at civil law was commissary of the Archdeaconry of Richmond prior to the Civil War. His own position on the oath was somewhat ambiguous, maintaining that "the calling of God to witness, or saying, God is my witness, etc. without adding of somewhat more, is neither Oath nor Swearing ...", and that this "true witness-bearing, as it was before swearing was, is not received in Judicial proceedings for want of an Oath ...". In practice, he was open "unto their (men's) punishment (which hitherto, blessed be God, I and some others have found, not according to the rigour of the Law, but with some moderation)"; *Beginnings*, pp.91–92; Gervase Benson, *A True testimony concerning oaths and swearing* (London, 1669), pp.30, 39, 47
126. LSF, Miller MSS, Trans 13, Margaret Fox to Friends, 19/11/1697–98
127. For Roger Haydock see *A Collection of the Christian Writings ... of ... Roger Haydock* (London, 1700), *passim*. and T.C. Porteus, 'Roger Haydock of Coppull – A Brief Biography and Ten Original Letters', *TLCAS* 52 (1937), pp.1–66, and below, chapter 7
128. GBS, vol.2, pt.2, p.830, Roger Haydock to the Meeting for Sufferings, 11/6/1683

129. *ibid.*
130. MMS, vol.3, 17/6/1683
131. MMS, vol.3, 21/7/1683, 28/7/1683; there is some suggestion that Friends
      wished to take advantage of this liberty in order to take action against their
      adversaries, which the Meeting for Sufferings advised against, "Friends
      desiring to follow peace with all men."
132. LSF, Port. 16.32, endorsed "Wm. Shewens answer to Roger Haydock to be
      presented to the Meeting for Sufferings, about recording *Jurat*", 31st 6th
      month 1683. Friends clearly saw a distinction between this method and that
      of employing a substitute to make an oath in court. When a Quaker from
      Kent was convicted for this offence in 1678 the Meeting for Sufferings
      asserted "that we do utterly detest and abominate in our very souls the
      thought and much more the actions of employing or permitting any man to
      personate us in giving in any answer on oath as if we were the very person
      and the act ours", and further, "that we do esteem it a far greater crime to
      suborn than swear ....", LSF, Book of Case, vol.1, pp.42–43
133. LSF, Port 16.32
134 . *ibid.*; see also above
135. *ibid.*; the first bill for an Affirmation presented to Parliament in 1690 used
      the phrase, "I call God to witness, and appeal to him as judge of the truth of
      what I shall say" *Second Period*, pp.181–83
136. The best account of a dispute that has in general been underestimated by
      Quaker historians is to be found in *Second Period*, pp.181–204. See Chapter 4
137. The discipline against oaths was maintained both by chastising offenders, as
      in 1676 when Lancaster Monthly Meeting "ordered that John Townson and
      Henry Wilson do go and Exhort and Admonish William Eccleston and see if
      he will condemn the evil action of swearing or making oaths", and also by
      ensuring that sufferers did not compromise their testimony. Thus in 1685
      the Quarterly Meeting for Sufferings answered a query from a suffering
      Friend in the following manner, "A prisoner for the Truth refusing to take an
      oath cannot release himself of imprisonment by giving bond to transport
      himself [overseas] but dishonour the Truth". LMMM, vol.1, 18/8/1676;
      LQMM, vol.1, 30/7/1685
138. MMS, vol.21, 10/5/1713

4

The Affirmation
Controversy

In order to relieve themselves from the hardships, whether actual or perceived, which the refusal to swear could lead them into, the Quakers launched a sophisticated campaign of petitioning and lobbying, aimed at both the court and Parliament.[1] The outcome of this was the 1696 Affirmation Act, which allowed Quakers to make a declaration in a set form of words in place of an oath. The Act was to remain in force in the first instance for seven years.[2] However, far from heralding an era of peace and tranquillity for Friends, the 1696 Act rather inaugurated or intensified a period of dissent and dissatisfaction within the Society which was to last at least until 1722. The basis of the dispute which arose was the wording of the declaration contained in the 1696 Act. However, as the internal dispute continued, the issues at stake broadened to take in a comprehensive critique of the state of post-Revolution Quakerism. This critique was offered generally by Friends from those counties, both North and South, farthest from London, and from Friends in Scotland and Ireland, although the dissidents did have important supporters in the capital.[3] Fundamentally then it was a critique of the "established" London, and certainly urban, Quakerism which dominated the administration of the Society and determined the face which it presented to the Establishment in London. At the heart of this critique was a desire by these dissatisfied Friends to reassert the principles, as they saw them, of the earliest Quakers.

The Affirmation sanctioned by Act of Parliament in 1696, "I, A B, do declare in the presence of God the truth of what I say", was accepted by the Meeting for Sufferings as a necessary expedient.[4] Advised that "the Members [of Parliament] appointed to prepare and carry in the Bill, and others, do believe the Bill will not pass if such solemn Affirmation was not in it", the Meeting for Sufferings concluded that "rather than the Bill should not pass the Meeting was mostly satisfied that the Bill should go on being persuaded it will be for the general ease of Friends".[5] This collective act of self-deception was prompted, in part, firstly by the knowledge that Friends were not likely to be offered anything more acceptable by the government. Secondly, leading Friends were no doubt aware that to refuse the offer of "ease", supported as it was by the King himself, could wreck the relationship that they had carefully cultivated with the court and leading politicians since 1689.[6] They were caught in a cleft-stick partly of their own making.

Nor should it be thought that the Meeting for Sufferings was not aware of the potential difficulties they might encounter through choosing a form of words deemed unacceptable by a large body of Friends. As early as November 1690 the lines were being drawn for the dispute which was to follow the passing of the 1696 Act. In that month the Meeting for Sufferings gave consideration to a "form of solemn declaration for Friends" to be included in a Bill, under discussion in the House of Lords.[7] The meeting discussed two alternatives:

> I, A B, do sincerely and solemnly declare in the presence of God that I will true answers make to all such questions as shall be asked me in the case now depending and that I will speak the truth, the whole truth, and nothing but the truth and God is my witness of the truth of what I shall say

and

> I, A B, do sincerely and solemnly declare in the presence of God that I will true answers make to all such questions as shall be asked me – and that I will speak the truth, the whole truth and nothing but the truth – and I call God to witness and appeal to him as Judge of the Truth of what I shall say

Of these, the former, in which the deity assumed only a passive role as guarantor, had much less the character of an invocatory oath and was the Meeting's preferred choice.[8] But, sensing that this first declaration might be too far from an oath to receive decisive support in Parliament, the Meeting concluded that it would accept the second "with the words (in the case now depending) rather than the Bill should be lost by refusing it." In the event the second was chosen.[9]

Some weeks later, following the successful passage of the Bill through the House of Lords (it eventually failed in the Commons through lack of time),[10] Henry Gouldney described its reception amongst Friends:

> some ffrds are dissatisfied wth. the manner of wording of our Declaration, that we may not be desceived that by the pretence of excusing us from the Common forme, we may go into a new one, more invocating and impricating, wch. many concludes amounts to an Oath, or however, beyond the Command of Christ that says: What is more than yea yea or nay nay comes of evill in Temporall Concernes ... and the title of the Act runs: that Whereas we scruple the forme of swearing now used wch. implyes that they account this but another

forme for the same thing, many stumbles at it and none hartily likes it, yet some is for accepting of it so ... for my part, I am affraide the world will repraoch us if we should comply of swearings, and so lessen our testimony against it; but to have our words simply taken, wth. an equall punishment for the fallsiefieing our words wth. perjury, would be a great advantage to our bussieness in trade and I should be glad of it.

Gouldney added as a postscript:

some learned of the world hearing it already, say tis an oath. I am apt to think ffrds. will be troubled to answer the many oppositions we may meet wth. by Professors upon it ....[11]

Gouldney, a London linen merchant, was an influential Friend who was later to be prominent amongst the "dissatisfied Friends", working within the Meeting for Sufferings for an amendment to the 1696 Affirmation Act.[12] His letter of 1690 clearly sets out the three points upon which the debate amongst Friends over oaths and the Affirmation centred. These were firstly, whether Friends might accept any form of relief from the authorities over oaths. Secondly, if relief were given, were Friends prepared to accept a prescribed form of words to be used rather than the simple freedom to speak without swearing. Thirdly, if relief were accepted, and if it comprised a set form of words, then what were those words to be?

As a preliminary to all other discussion, assuming that they maintained their testimony against all oath swearing, Friends first needed to determine whether or not it was necessary to accept any form of relief over oaths from the government. Gouldney, like the majority of Friends, felt that it was. As a Quaker businessman, one whose business dealings theoretically involved him, more than might be the case with a rural Friend, in all sorts of contractual statements and statutory declarations normally made on oath, he felt he "would be glad" of some concession to Quaker scruples, but generally such concessions as treated Quaker practices and Affirmations as if they were oaths, rather than requiring oaths from Quakers.[13] In this Gouldney echoed much of the propaganda issued by Friends in support of their campaigns against swearing. The various barriers erected by oaths prevented Quakers, or so their spokesmen claimed, from fully contributing to the wealth of the nation through their trading activities.[14] However, although generally accepted by Quaker historians, this view that oaths were a real obstacle to trade is in need of some modification in view of the detailed evidence presented above in relation to Lancashire.[15] Moreover, it is abundantly clear that Friends elsewhere, particularly in London, were successfully active in commerce both before and after the Affirmation Act of 1696. A cursory reading of suffering records for counties other than Lancashire suggests a lack of prosecutions for not-swearing in fields of economic activity where oaths were required.[16] It must therefore be concluded that many businessmen found established methods of trading which allowed them, either with or without the collusion of officials, to operate despite the difficulty posed by oaths. For them some form of Affirmation was a convenience, but a necessity only in view of the scrupulous Quaker conscience which frowned upon evasion and informal collusion: the Quaker insistence on a *bona fide* Affirmation was in a double sense an outcome of Friends pre-occupation with Truth. In addition, Friends agitating for an agreed Affirmation may also have been motivated to obtain the apparent permanence of an official and legal Affirmation in case a change in the political climate prevented previous loose, unwritten informal agreements, based on fluctuating good-will, from operating. The Affirmation campaign can be interpreted in the light of an already developed Quaker group psychology: perhaps they had already emerged as a rather precise people who liked to know in writing exactly where they stood.[17]

Whatever the complex motives in pursuing an Affirmation, there was agreement that Friends should seek exemption from the requirement to swear.[18] This consensus immediately led to the second point in the debate. Henry Gouldney thought Friends should seek to "have our words simply taken". More explicitly the Lancashire Quarterly Meeting concluded in 1693, after consulting its constituent parts, that

> yea yea and nay nay ought to be stood by and to and that nothing more be offered or accepted to or from the Government,

a view which was duly transmitted to the Yearly Meeting in London.[19] Support for this view faded following the passing of the first Affirmation Act, when the majority of Friends ceased debating the rights and wrongs of using a prepared declaration or form of words, preferring instead to make the existing form of words more palatable. This reflected a realistic assessment on the part of the dissatisfied Friends of the limits of govern-mental indulgence of Quakerism. The Lancashire Quakers who but months after the passing of the first Act asked the Meeting for Sufferings "to make further application to the government as the Lord shall open a way for further relief" were soon to be found asking specifically

> that further application be made to the Parliament if the Act be renewed that it may be so worded as it may be to the general satisfaction of Friends.[20]

However, the acceptance by Friends in Lancashire and elsewhere that some form of declaration was the only likely means of gaining relief did not by any means mark a total capitulation to the views of the Meeting for Sufferings. The declaration, as they pointed out, had to "be to the general satisfaction of Friends", and if not then no relief should be accepted from the government, and the Affirmation Act, which was renewable every seven years, should be allowed to expire.[21]

Not all Friends accepted the apparent inevitability of an Affirmation being required in place of an oath, for to some the use of any unspontaneous or elaborated declaration was no different to swearing. Prominent amongst the dissatisfied Friends propagating this view was Joseph Skidmore, who in 1713 published his *Essay upon the Vth of Matthew*.[22] Skidmore argued that the use of any extrinsic form of words to sanction the truth of a particular statement was contrary to the teachings of Christ, and probably tantamount to an oath. Thus the detailed wording of an Affirmation was irrelevant for it was the Affirmation itself which breached Christ's commands.[23] The Meeting for Sufferings judged that Skidmore's work

> Lays stumbling blocks in the way of the weak, renders both satisfied and dissatisfied friends guilty of swearing, tends to sow discord amongst brethren and to bring a reproach upon our Yearly Meetings.[24]

Underlying their objection to this and other similar works by Skidmore, and determining the Meeting's attitude to all attempts to oppose or change the Affirmation granted in 1696, was a fear that in conceding to demands for change the Meeting would lose both face and authority, within and without the Society. It was typical then that they viewed Skidmore's writings as tending to

> widen that difference already too much formented, and to invalidate the authority of such meetings where all the members may not happen to be of one mind, by which role the conclusions of all meetings of business may be rendered ineffectual, and the discipline of the church laid waste.[25]

In order to preserve its position, the Meeting therefore characterised all those Friends who opposed an Affirmation as being ultimately opposed to the good order of the church.[26] It was the adoption of this view by the majority of the Meeting for Sufferings, as much as any difference over political beliefs or allegiances, that was at the root of the bitter dispute over the Affirmation.[27]

Lancashire Friends also tended to reject the extreme views of writers such as Skidmore, inasmuch as they "rather tended to widen differences than to reconcile and unite us in that true love which is the sure bond of lasting fellowship".[28] For these Friends, however, reconciliation depended simply on obtaining "an Affirmation in such terms and form as may be easy and satisfactory to all".[29] This, the actual form of the words to be used, was the third and most contentious point in the debate amongst Friends over the Affirmation.

Having conceded that some form of declaration was the only means of obtaining relief from swearing, the dissatisfied Friends needed to ensure that the actual words themselves did not breach the Quaker testimony against oaths. Ultimately the debate centred on the inclusion in the 1696

Affirmation Act of the phrase "In the presence of almighty God" and it was not until 1722 that a suitable form of words, "I, A B, do solemnly, sincerely and truly declare and affirm", was accepted by both groups of Friends and the government.[30] The concern of Friends was expressed by Henry Gouldney, "that we may not be desceived that by the pretence of excusing us from the Common forme, we may go into a new one, more invocating and impricating, wch. many concludes amounts to an oath".[31] The assertion that the first Affirmation was little more than an oath, and the consequent implication that many Friends were guilty of swearing only served to heighten the bad feeling that existed between the opposing groups. In 1713, following a number of "undue reflections", the Yearly Meeting resolved that

> some in breach of the good order of this meeting have reflected on Friends by asserting the present Affirmation to be an oath, which hath had very ill consequences and may yet have greater by creating jealousies and misunderstandings to the breach of unity, which practise this meeting doth testify against.[32]

The concern of the dissatisfied Friends, however, was less the good order of Meetings and more the common reputation of Quakerism and the face it presented to the world, to ordinary people in the provinces, some of whom, according to Gouldney, in 1690, "say tis an oath".[33]

This opinion, perhaps crude but obviously current, that the Affirmation contained in the 1696 Act was tantamount to an oath, clearly gained strength in some quarters during the years leading up to 1722. In that year, in the debates in the House of Lords concerning the modified Affirmation Act, it became clear that those wings of the political establishment least sympathetic towards Friends equated the 1696 Affirmation with an oath.[34] Moreover, the Act of 1696, rather than being seen as an indulgence or relief, was rather viewed officially as a mild palliative, designed to encourage the Quakers back into the swearing fold.[35] A petition to the Lords from the "London clergy" argued that "the continued use of the said solemn affirmation would by degrees have entirely cured that people of all those unseasonable prejudices against an oath".[36] In objecting to the modified affirmation it was stated that

> they have been hitherto under the real obligation of an oath, though dispensed with as to some formalities, with respect to the manner of wording and taking it.[37]

More explicitly the "solemn affirmation" was "equivalent to an oath", and that if continued it "will probably extinguish those scruples" of the Quakers against swearing.[38] Thus, perhaps ironically, in their dispute with the Quaker establishment the dissatisfied Friends were at one with those groups most hostile to Quakers and Dissent in general.

As suggested above, it was in the actions taken by the Meeting for Sufferings to stifle the opponents of the 1696 Affirmation Act that the root cause of the bitterness in the dispute lay. As much as a doctrinal matter, the Affirmation controversy became a debate over the nature and exercise of authority within the developing Society of Friends. It has been portrayed by some historians, notably W.C. Braithwaite as also representing a political debate amongst Friends.[39] Those in favour of the Affirmation were "mostly Whig in their sympathies", whilst those dissatisfied with the Affirmation were by implication Jacobites or of Jacobite leanings.[40] The evidence for this suggestion is threefold. Firstly, there is the undeniable fact that those Friends who sought the Affirmation were deeply involved with Whig politicians in the negotiations leading up to the passing of the 1696 Act. Subsequently they were to become even more enmeshed with Whig power-brokers in their attempts to gain further relief from oaths and tithes, a process documented by Norman Hunt in *Two Early Political Associations*.[41] Secondly, there is the identification of William Penn, presumed a Jacobite, with the dissatisfied Friends.[42] Thirdly, there is the cryptic remark made in a letter written by Margaret Fell in 1698 and cited as evidence to support his view by Braithwaite, that

> The rise and beginning of all this contest and difference was that Friends might not seek to this power and government for anything.[43]

However, I will argue below that for a variety of reasons those last two points, the views of Penn and Fell, cannot be adduced as conclusive evidence to prove Jacobitism amongst the dissatisfied Friends. Further I will show briefly that in Lancashire those Friends most anxious for a reform in the Affirmation were also those most implacably hostile to Jacobitism.

In fact, Quaker struggles for power, especially William Meade's rivalry with Penn, largely explain the allegation that Penn and those who shared his views on the Affirmation were Jacobites, anti-Whigs, and anti-Williamites.[44] It is against this same background that Margaret Fell's letter which, cryptically enough, suggests Jacobite motivation for dissatisfaction with the Quakers' Affirmation, should be read. For in much of her writings in the 1690s she was greatly influenced, if not totally dominated, by William Meade who had played a major part in the negotiations at Parliament which led to the Affirmation Act of 1696.[45] What little information survives relating to Meade shows him as a determined, strong-willed individual. There is little to dispute the suggestion that he was seeking at least partially to inherit his father-in-law's place amongst Friends, and his eventual failure to do so no doubt caused his withdrawal from the Quaker business Meetings in the early eighteenth century.[46] However, in the last decade of the seventeenth century he was prepared to exploit the considerable reputation of his mother-in-law, gained during the early years of the Society, to expound his views amongst Friends.[47]

Given these considerations, little or no authority should be given to the much quoted statement of Margaret Fell, concerning the political view-points of the two parties involved, in the Affirmation dispute.[48]

As we have seen, Quakers shared few of the Tory/High Church theories of the divine nature of kingship and indefeasible hereditary right upon which much of the post-Revolution loyalty to the Stuarts rested.[49] Nor were they likely to agree with English, Welsh, and Scottish Jacobites that the accession of William III had marked the start of an era of depression and social dislocation.[50] Indeed, if we take these opinions to be symptomatic of post-1688 Jacobite thought, then there is little evidence to associate Friends with them. As far as Lancashire Quakers are concerned, it has already been shown how dependent they generally were on Whig parliamentarians for relief both on a local and national scale.[51] In general, they shared a mutual dislike and distrust of those amongst the political establishment who were Jacobites or held Jacobite sympathies after the Revolution and who tended in outlook to be unsympathetic to Quaker-ism.[52] These men were High Church (sometimes Catholic) traditionalist, opposed to toleration, preferring land to trade; the treatment the Quakers received from the likes of the Bradshaighs of Haigh typified the hostility with which they were viewed by the High Tory and Jacobite squirearchy, especially with Catholic leanings.[53]

To William Stout, typical of the Lancashire Quakers who sought an amendment to the Affirmation Act of 1696, King William III "was a prince of much clemancie and charety to his subjects of all religious professions".[54] His allegiance to the post-Revolution political establishment was absolute. Jacobites and Papists (collectively) on the other hand, he regarded with a mixture of fear and contempt, not least because they breached his own standards of commercial behaviour by carrying out "indirect and illegal practises in the custom[s]".[55] Quaker loyalty to the principles of 1688 was such that they were at times penalised because "they had generally appeared and voated on all ocations for the succession to the Crown in the House of the Elector of Hanover".[56] Moreover, as Stout astutely observed, the parliamentary opposition to those allegedly Jacobite Quakers who sought an easier Affirmation came in 1722 precisely from the Jacobite conspirators whom they might have been expected to support.[57] In short, the "Jacobite" anti-Affirmation Act Quakers are insubstantial figures. Nor should it surprise us to find that, insofar as they held political attitudes, Quakers aligned with the rest of the Dissenting community behind the Revolution principles, especially that of toleration, which the Whigs made their own.[58] If Quakers were not Whigs, then the increasing retrospective regrets of High Tories after 1689 about the toleration, regrets culminating in the ferocious post-Sacheverell measures of 1710–14, ensured that Quakers could never be counted, despite the appearance of a populist Toryism after 1689, in the political spectrum that ranged from Tory to Jacobite.[59]

If the view that a dispute over the Affirmation was a dispute over political allegiance can thus be discounted, it remains to consider in more detail the suggestion that it was rather a dispute over the nature and exercise of authority amongst Friends. This can be done by examining in more detail some of the actions of the Meeting for Sufferings in defending the use of the Affirmation. In addition, the response to these actions, both on the part of Friends collectively in Meetings and as individuals can also be studied. In this way it will become apparent that the dispute over the Affirmation did not rest solely on the three initial points outlined and discussed above. Nor was its underlying cause only a concern over authority within the church. For in addition to these the dispute was also related to a continuing tradition of missionary zeal within those counties or Quarterly Meetings which opposed the initial Affirmation.[60] Foremost amongst these was Lancashire, but equally prominent were Ireland, Scotland, Westmorland and Yorkshire.

In defending the Affirmation contained in the Act of 1696 the Meeting for Sufferings claimed that the use of the form of words granted by the government was consistent with the previous practice of "antient faithful friends".[61] A printed epistle from the Meeting which was distributed throughout the Quarterly Meetings set out to show "what now is Friends most general practice in that case and what vindication they have made against opposers therein".[62] In particular such influential Friends as George Fox, Richard Hubberthorn, Edward Burrough, Isaac Pennington, Robert Barclay and William Penn were shown to have used or offered to use a form of words in place of an oath that closely resembled the Affirmation, most importantly in the inclusion of words similar to, "In the presence of God".[63] Hubberthorn, for example, was quoted from his interview with Charles II in 1660 as saying "What we do affirm, we can promise before the Lord, and take him to our witness in it".[64] The *Epistle* concluded that "it was consistent with our Testimony to speak in the Fear, in the Sight, or in the Presence of God, who is Witness, or before God ..." Friends were warned not "to count or call this a subjecting our Testimony to the Will of Man, seeing God hath so far subjected Man's Will to our Christian Desire".[65] Lest any Friends should consider opposing the Affirmation, the *Epistle* ended

> And seeing tis now granted by the Government, we hope none will distrust the Lord's Alliance therein, now, any more than formerly, or any more than in waiting upon him in Meetings, since it has been permitted by Men so to do.[66]

The Meeting for Suffering's attempt to claim precedent in support of the form of the 1696 Affirmation was a disingenuous move designed to outflank Northern Friends who had already based their rigorist position on the declarations of early Quakers. As early as 1693 Swarthmore Monthly Meeting noted:

> as to the request of the Quarterly Meeting concerning the sense of this Meeting, what they can say instead of an oath, it is the sense of this

Meeting that Christ's own words of yea and nay be kept to and that this Meeting hath good unity with the printed paper formerly read in that case first printed and put forth in the year 1666 under several Friends' hands ....[67]

Lancaster Monthly Meeting ordered that "the Declaration made in '66 concerning what could be offered instead of an oath to Parliament etc." was to be distributed to its Particular Meetings, who responded the following month that "Friends have good unity with the same".[68] The paper to which they referred was 'A Declaration from the People, called Quakers, what they can say instead of an Oath', which was contained in a printed pamphlet *To the King and both Houses of Parliament Now sitting at Westminster*, first published in 1666.[69] The pamphlet, which in addition to the 'Declaration' contained accounts of Quaker sufferings for not swearing, and an address to the parliamentary Committee for Grievances, was authored by a number of prominent Friends "on behalf of all the Suffering People of God".[70] Among them was George Whitehead, who by 1696 was probably the Quaker most closely associated with the passing of the Affirmation Act.[71]

These Friends based their arguments on the Quakers' literal interpretation of the scriptures, and a view of history which placed Friends as direct descendants of the early Church, and the early Protestant martyrs.[72] "We cannot", they stated,

> give forth a better Form of Words to testify the truth, than that which Christ hath laid down, which is Yea, yea and Nay, nay, which the Apostle, and the Fathers, and the Martyrs Preached, and Practised, and Suffered for ....[73]

So Friends claimed as authorities not only Matthew 5 and James 5, but also primitive Christians such as Policarpus, Bishop of Smyrna, who, "when he was required by the Proconsul to Swear, he denied it, and said, He was a Christian".[74] From more recent times they found supporters such as Wycliffe, John Hus and Jerome of Prague, as well as those to be found in the pages of Foxe's *Acts and Monuments*, who, "in Queen Mary's dayes suffered Martyrdome that refused to Swear".[75] Friends denied any form of sanction to add to Christ's words:

> For all Oaths, Vows, Promises, Types, Shadows, and Figures, which were among the Jews, Christ ends, and sets up Yea, yea, and Nay, nay, above them, which we shall stand by and to .... [76]

As they pointed out later in the pamphlet, anything more than this was superfluous, "for in our hearts God hath placed his fear, which brings us to obey Christ's Command, and we are sensible that he is a present Witness of all our Actions and Words".[77]

The "Declaration made in '66", upon which Lancashire Friends based their objection to any form of Affirmation containing phrases like "in the presence of God", provided powerful support for the dissatisfied Quakers. In a concise and cogent fashion it set the rigorist's position firmly in the mainstream of early Christian and Protestant thought; thus the rigorists were not, as Margaret Fell had claimed, inventing "a new doctrine", or "another gospel which … is accursed", but were rather maintaining one of the earliest publicly stated positions of Friends.[78] Not only was it the stated view of Friends in general, but also of George Whitehead in particular, a fact which must have caused both him and the Meeting for Sufferings considerable embarrassment. It was no doubt in order to exploit this embarrassment, and to support the case of the dissatisfied Friends, that *The Declaration from the People call'd Quakers* was republished anonymously as a broadside in 1700.[79] The text and signatories of the Declaration were in the main unaltered from that which appeared in *To the King and both Houses of Parliament in 1666*, with one significant addition at the end.[80] This, a short paragraph reproduced in bold Gothic type, put the content of the 1666 'Declaration' sharply in the context of the 1696 Affirmation:

This was Printed in the Year 1666, with a Representation of the Cause and Sufferings of the People call'd Quakers, and what they desired signified from those whose Names are above, etc.... By which it appears how ready and willing the said People have been to submit to the like Punishment for the breach of their Yea, yea or Nay, nay, as they that break their Oaths. And to put as great a Sanction on their Words by doubling their Yea and Nay, as the Lord Jesus Christ the Sanctifier of all true Christians hath directed, and whatsoever is more than Yea, yea, and Nay, nay, he hath declared cometh of evil. Now whether the making use in Temporal Affairs of the Sacred Name of God, in affirming or denying to bind the Speech, is more than Yea, yea, and Nay, nay and cometh of evil. And if that form of Words layd down by Christ is best as it is and declared to be, Whether than that form is not fittest to be kept, and all others (especially wherein the Sacred Name of God is made use of) avoided, by all that believe Christ's Precept to be binding.[81]

The Meeting for Sufferings' epistle of 1696 met with objections even before it was printed and circulated to the counties.[82] None was more eloquent that that from William Penn, who was himself cited in the epistle and had indeed on several occasions in the 1670s used words similar to "In the presence of God" in various proposed declarations.[83]

By the 1680s his views had changed, for in Pennsylvania witnesses were required to testify "by solemnly promising the speak the truth, the whole truth and nothing but the truth to the matter or thing in question".[84] In May 1696 Penn wrote to the Meeting for Sufferings, "hearing some Friends desire to print and disperse among Friends what some Friends and myself have said that may give any countenance to the form of words lately enacted in lieu of an oath".[85] First Penn argued a "forbearance [i.e. an inhibition] of such publication, ... because it will look as if Friends were divided, which should not be ... it tends to divide, by declaring or insinuating dissatisfaction, which should lie as hid or dormant as may be, in hopes of gaining more ground, or that Friends may feel more clearness". Secondly, Penn argued that in publishing what was apparently an incontrovertible justification for the Affirmation, Friends were creating a future danger:

> for if we go to show them by the authority of our own writers we can or may bring our consciences that length there can be no ground to hope for more from them, be it we shall shut the door upon ourselves

Finally, he urged that "the matter lie quietly as it is" and that Friends "should not grieve or offend those that cannot easily exceed those bounds least that look overdriving and impatient".[86]

The sentiments of William Penn, expressed in the face of the uncompromising attitude of the Meeting for Sufferings, were generally shared and repeated by the Yearly Meeting in as much as it sought to minimise conflict, its desire being "that all Friends be very careful how they expose this difference to the world, but by all means possible to endeavour to prevent it".[87] However, the issue of the Affirmation was to illustrate dramatically the tensions that could exist between those attending an annual delegate assembly and a standing subcommittee. The delegate assembly addressed itself to general issues, always seeking to reach a consensus "in that sweet and tender frame of mind and spirit which is upon this meeting".[88] The standing committee, in order to react quickly to changes in political climate and circumstance was prepared to ignore consensus and instead seek expedients.[89] The apparent inability of Friends from Lancashire and elsewhere in England, Ireland and Scotland to influence the behaviour of the Meeting for Sufferings through the Yearly Meeting was no doubt an additional factor in creating bad feeling within the Society. The absurd situation, whereby the Meeting for Sufferings, in theory on behalf of all Friends, solicited Parliament for a continuation of thie Affirmation, whilst the dissatisfied Friends solicited Parliament for an amended Affirmation, reflects not only the failure of dissatisfied Friends to influence the Yearly Meeting, but also the failure of the Yearly Meeting to control its executive.[90]

In 1696 the Yearly Meeting acknowledged that "it is evident that the words mentioned in the Act are not alike easy and satisfactory to all Friends".[91] It urged that all who "may be concerned therein on either hand will walk charitably and tenderly one towards another ...", urging that "Friends be very careful how they expose this difference to the world".[92] In the following year a select meeting of the Yearly Meeting was chosen to discuss complaints from Irish Friends led by William Edmundson concerning the behaviour of the Meeting for Sufferings during the campaign leading to the passing of the 1696 Act.[93] In its report the select committee could only suggest to

> the Friends of Ireland, whether they could be satisfied for peace and unity sake, to pass over and let fall their exceptions ... rather than hazard the widening of differences

In addition they warned "that nothing may be spread by word or writing, that may lend to beget or continue an uneasiness or dissatisfaction among friends".[94] In 1713 a complaint of a similar nature was made to Yearly Meeting by the Aberdeen Quakers.[95] In response they received not only a reply from the Yearly Meeting but also one from the Meeting for Sufferings itself. In its letter the Meeting insisted "that we are not of those that make the solemn Affirmation a bone of contention". They continued,

> We observe your hint about rending and dividing, and we are heartily sorry for it as well as you can be but do not esteem it to lie on the satisfied Friends, who adhere firmly to the expositions of Christ's words, according to the continued sense of faithful Friends from 1654 to 1696 and as you say, we are unwilling to any innovating there-from.[96]

One of the complaints of the Aberdeen Quakers concerned a letter which had been sent to the Quarterly Meetings in January 1712–13 by the Meeting for Sufferings.[97] Concerned that the Affirmation Act was about to expire the letter asked the Quarterly Meetings to:

> provide the Friends they send up with a full and brief answer in writing to this weighty point because as we conceive thereby unprofitable and tedious debates may in great measure be prevented, which several Friends cannot but remember did bring great exercise as well as take up much time in the last Yearly Meeting.

The Friends to be sent to the Yearly Meeting were

> to be duly qualified and fully instructed truly and impartially to give the sense of their several counties and to agree in this weighty point,

which was:

> That since the present solemn Affirmation has been and is of great service to the body of Friends, it be solicited to be renewed or accepted by us from the Government ....[98]

The import of the letter, that Friends in general used the Affirmation and that therefore its renewal should be sought without wasting valuable time on "tedious debates", was of course an extreme provocation to those dissatisfied Friends who were themselves seeking to lobby Parliament for a modified Affirmation in the approaching session.[99]

In response to this an anonymous letter was circulated to the Quarterly Meetings in February.[100] This letter complained first that the Meeting for Sufferings was exceeding its authority in attempting to influence a Yearly Meeting in this way. Secondly,

> In consideration whereof of the means whereby the said letter was obtained, we find ourselves concerned to let our brethren know that the Meeting in which the said letter had its rise and conclusion was very much made up of such Friends as do not usually attend the common service of the Meeting for Sufferings, and as well have reason to believe the matter was secretly concluded of beforehand because of their extraordinary attendance and resolution: for although the dissatisfied as well as some satisfied Friends, members of the said Meeting, objected against its being sent so hastily alleging it was a matter of great concernment and ought weightily to be considered yet they would by no means be prevailed upon to defer it seeing they had the majority.[101]

In addition, the letter argued that a renewal of the 1696 Affirmation Act would make an amendment at some point in the future difficult, if not impossible to obtain. The existing Affirmation was not consistent with previous practice, for "Friends then [in early times] could not then accept words of so high a nature as is the present for a common form of Affirmation".[102]

This circular letter was accompanied in the case of Lancashire and doubtless other dissatisfied counties, by a covering letter from John Whiting, possibly one of the letter's authors.[103] Whiting explained that the letter was being sent to prevent the Quarterly Meetings from being misled "'tho there may not be such immedaite need of it in your country as in some others ..." He reiterated the claim that the Meeting for Sufferings had been packed, and that its outcome was the work of an organised majority, something contrary to all accepted practice in Quaker business meetings.[104] This resort to decision-making by majority as opposed to consensus was being resorted to in a number of Meetings by those Friends who favoured the existing Affirmation:

> Things are at that posture among us, and such striving and contention already in Monthly Meetings about it, in some laid by, in others suspended, carried in few, in one by a poll though they mustered up all they could but by five in about sixty.[105]

In another letter written in the following year Whiting again emphasised the deceit of the Meeting for Sufferings in their attempts to renew the Affirmation. "They would", he wrote, "break over hedge and ditch to do it so that nothing will stop them unless the providence of God do ..." [106]

Although he was silent as to the authorship of the circular letter, there is strong reason to believe that Whiting was at least a co-author; he certainly acted within the Meeting for Sufferings with Henry Gouldney, the two of them stating "that they would appeal to the next Yearly Meeting against the proceedings of this meeting".[107] The Meeting for Sufferings had already determined, in response to the circular letter,

> to caution and entreat all Friends that they be very careful not to give any encouragement to such breach of civil society and disorderly spirits and practises by receiving and promoting them, but to stop and discourage them, that thereby the true Christian authority of meetings and peace of the Church may be preserved.[108]

Typically, to counter the threat of Whiting and Gouldney, the Meeting itself appealed to the Yearly Meeting that "strife and contention in the churches of Christ are sown and industriously spread, contrary to the wholesome advice of the Yearly Meeting".[109] They complained "of some who had in opposition to that Meeting [the Meeting for Sufferings] set up an independent power", and of those who were "setting up a separate authority differing from what is established among us".[110]

These matters were all discussed at the Yearly Meeting held in the summer of 1713 which appointed a special committee of six to consider the dispute.[111] The background to the committee's deliberations was a Meeting which heard "much discourse ... for more ease to Friends ... but nothing was *unanimously* resolved upon".[112] William Stout, who attended the Meeting, wrote in his diary that "it was by most Friends thought most proper to let it [the Affirmation] expire .... But Friends in London, and thereaway, were for the present solicitation, which was condescended to ..." [113] However, minutes of this meeting show less "condescension" than Stout suggests, for the dissatisfied Friends actually demanded a minute to be written "that it may not be thought they consented" to the minute approving a solicitation to Parliament for a renewal of the Affirmation.[114] In view of such a breakdown in the traditional procedures of Quaker Meetings, it is perhaps not surprising that the select committee looked to promote reconciliation, asking "that mutual forbearance be exercised ... that no occasion of offence be either given or taken". It concluded in an obvious reference to the 1712 protest letter:

> That no person or persons do presume to write circular letters to Monthly or Quarterly Meetings against regular constituted Meetings but any member of the Meeting for Sufferings may at any time write to their country correspondents,

asking once more "that every person offender or offended do freely forgive each other for what is past".[115]

For Lancashire Friends the Yearly Meetings at which the Affirmation was discussed were occasions of endeavour, dispute and frequently disappointment. However, the knowledge of this did not prevent a clamour from large numbers of Friends seeking to represent the Lancashire Quarterly Meeting in London.[116] The Quarterly Meeting could even find spiritual comfort and reassurance in the frustrations experienced there, as in 1702 when Robert Haydock and William Rawlinson gave

> account that according to the trust reposed in them they have faithfully discharged themselves and truly represented the sense of the county, and this meeting in the hearing of the report by them given of their exercise and labours in behalf of this county and Friends in general was deeply affected and sympathised with them in their faithful Friend's earnestness concerning the Affirmation it being continued, notwithstanding their and many faithful Friend's endeavours to the contrary, and the Lord's tendering presence attended this Meeting greatly to the bowing and confirming of Friends in their present sense touching the business.[117]

Generally, however, the Meeting was simply inclined to record that its delegates in London had met with "much labour and exercise", or "some exercise for some time" in debates. However, even at these Yearly Meetings there was some "warmness and unity" and "much tenderness" in the departure of the delegates.[118] Such phrases, however, should not be allowed to hide the deep concern felt by those Friends dissatisfied with the Affirmation, both at the apparent conduct of some of the Church's leadership and also at the malaise of which they felt this behaviour was symptomatic.

William Edmundson, with his Westmorland and Irish connections, was typical of those Friends, farthest from the metropolis, who were most unhappy with the 1696 Affirmation. On the face of it, Edmundson breathed ecstatic enthusiasm for the proceedings of the Yearly Meeting. In his *Journal*, published at the height of the Affirmation controversy in 1712, he described his attendance at the Yearly Meeting in 1697 thus:

> were at many Heavenly Meetings, both for the Worship of God and Mens Meetings for managing Truth's Affairs, relating to Church Government: I had great service on several Accounts in that City, and the Lord's Power went over all. When the Service was over I parted with Elders and Brethren in the tender Love of God ...

Here Edmundson omitted all mention of the debates surrounding the complaints from Ireland concerning the Meeting for Sufferings.[119] In the *Journal*, however, Edmundson was clearly writing an edifying account of a harmonious Yearly Meeting as it should have been. In his correspondence he was more forthright. In a letter written to Robert Haydock he complained that the Affirmation Act, which "that untimely birth at London brought forth" had hindered Irish Friends from gaining a more acceptable form of relief from the government there. "The greatest aggravation", he wrote, was that "we suffer under the act procured by our own brethren". Friends in Ireland generally refused both oaths and the Affirmation, and Edmundson noted that "where any amongst us ... darkens our general testimony in that particular it appears in that floating lofty high predominating spirit, that leads into inordinance after riches".[120]

Edmundson's observation, that the taking of the Affirmation was symptomatic of a "floating, lofty, high predominating spirit", was shared by many Friends. Isaac Alexander, described by Edmundson as "my Fellow-Labourer in the Gospel of Christ", wrote to Robert Haydock in March 1705 describing events in London:

> I hear many make a great noise about brotherly love and unity and the gospel fellowship and peace and concord and yet if they cannot have all to their own mind and to submit to their own ways and sense, both in spiritual and indeed in temporals, they are ready almost to bite the head off one another and the hot blood is quickly and highly raised. Many talk of the brotherhood and of the unity of it and hath known but very little if anything of the time and real work of regeneration.[121]

Henry Gouldney blamed "the mallancholly affliction of intestine trouble" on "a libbertine spirit ruleing in placed than were set up to prevent the occation of disorder". He added, with a touch of the cynicism present in many of his letters, that satisfied Friends were "inraged upon the apprehensions of looseing wt thy have or part with their darling, a libberty of voteing".[122]

This apparent desire on the part of some Friends to predominate over the dissatisfied, and introduce a uniformity of behaviour in the form of the Affirmation, was also perceived by Thomas Story. Following the Yearly Meeting of 1716, he complained of "rude and forward spirits" and those who "strenuously contended to force the Affirmation upon all, and charged all the ill Consequences of Division upon such as could not comply with it".[123] Two years later, he again wrote of some who had "more regard to Party than Unity, and to themselves, and what they had procured and set up, than the Peace of the Church".[124] Similar concerns were voiced by correspondents of Story. In 1707, when he was in Philadelphia, John Field had written to him that "we still have our exercises here, from some that do not abide in that love and sincerity as they ought considering their proffession".[125] Ten years later, when Story was in London, Thomas Chalkley wrote to him from America:

> I was glad to understand by thine that things were like to have a better turn about the Affirmation. I could wish it might be turned out of

doors and have been affected deeply with sorrow that ever it came within them ... it will be a means to hinder the convincement of the world.[126]

The danger then of the Affirmation, and the "predominating spirit" that supported it, was that ultimately it would hinder "the convincement of the world", the mission to which many of the dissatisfied Friends adhered, in a cluster of values that included integrity, consistency and propagation through suffering.

It is clear that apart from the intrinsic points, the oath-Affirmation controversy focused other issues in the Society, including the desire for confrontation and suffering, in partial detachment, perhaps, from the ostensible first cause of such collision, but as proof of persistent virtue, by whose means alone Friends could continue to recruit. This sense of mission and martyrdom was closely identified with the dissatisfied Friends. In 1712 Thomas Gwin, a Friend from Falmouth, drew a graphic portrait in his journal of the dispute at the Yearly Meeting over the sufferings on the Leather Act and the Affirmation.[127] The depth of disagreement clearly caused him profound distress, but even so the dissatisfied Friends' sense of falling standards was acute and poignant, leading Gwin to see failings even in the recognised spokesmen of the rigorists:

> The third day I was at Wheeler Street but I wanted time to clear myself and was not greatly pleased with what was spoke, the like 4th day at Grace Street. Patrick Henderson and Robert Haydock as sundry other of the dissatisfied seemed to be the most living ministers yet I still wanted what I found formerly in their meetings.[128]

Lydia Lancaster portrayed the dissatisfied Friends as of "the lambs nature", undergoing "a suffering time" at Yearly Meetings. She observed, however,

> that he who was called the lamb of God, was also termed the lyon of Juda, so there may be occasion sometime to roar out of sion and arise fearce in judgement against antichrist wherever he appears to exhalt his kingdom.[129]

To these dissatisfied Friends then at least the millenial images of early Quakerism and the consequent sense of mission had remained a vital, living reality.

These various issues relating to authority, suffering, eschatology and mission were all touched on in a letter written by John Haydock in 1702 to the Friends of Hardshaw Meeting.[130] At the time of writing Haydock was at Wigan, "under confinement upon a Commission of Rebellion (for denying the oath and solemn Affirmation)".[131] In his letter he stressed the importance of sufferings over material concerns, "Is it not the straight and narrow way that leads to the living well which springs up in us?". All the externals of life, although "precious to possess", were to be sacrificed for the commands of Christ, who "as the giver of all these, was before them all ...." This testimony was to be maintained "until the number and count be fulfilled",

> then shall our yea be yea, and nay nay instead of an oath in the usual form; instead of the solemn Affirmation (that oath though not in the usual form), and the multiplyings of zeal faith and hope abound in all our hearts ....

Interestingly, Haydock also portrayed the struggle amongst Friends over the Affirmation as one between the younger and the elder. Thus the Affirmation was the "uneasy yoke through the solicitation of our elder brothers that walks at large with a disteeme and slighting of us ...". When the time came, "Then shall the yoke be taken away, and the elder give place to the younger".[132]

Haydock seems to have been using the word 'elder' in two senses. First he was using it in a functional way that was to become common amongst Friends in the later eighteenth century, as a description of an office-holder or someone of authority amongst Friends.[133] Thus it was those elders, the members of the Meeting for Sufferings, who had solicited for the original Affirmation. Secondly, there appears to be a more figurative use of the word. Elder was being used to impart a sense of staleness or decay, whilst on the contrary younger represented strength and vigour. According to this view it was the elder Friends or brethren who were seeking a compromise with the world in order to pursue its material offerings. The younger remained the "children brought forth to God in the Gospel light and liberty".[134]

"The elder", Haydock complained,

> was on his way to possess himself of greatness by the solemn Affirmation and make his mount as high as Edam, yet fair flourishes, fine words and the cry of liberty cannot hide his dwelling place from that eye that God has opened in us, no, no neither can he in the choice of his payment of tithes and steeple-house lays which is in the body of the Affirmation, and wash his hands of our many sufferings we lye under upon that account in this north country ....

To frustrate the elders, Friends, he urged, should obey the commands of Christ, whose "time, not Man's time, is the time of perfecting ... not by might or polity, or Man's contrivance, but by his own spirit". Only in this way could Truth be protected against the encroachments of the world, and only by inheriting the mantle of the early Quakers could the younger brethren achieve it.[135]

The sentiments expressed in Haydock's letter can be taken as a fair representation of the views of the dissatisfied Friends, particularly those in

Lancashire, of the Affirmation and those who promoted it. In seeking to challenge the "predominating spirit" Friends placed strains on the organisation and decision-making processes developed during the 1670s. They also questioned the apparent assumption that there was an automatic right of leadership possessed by a small number of influential or weighty Friends, mainly resident in London, which was to be followed at national and local level. Implicit in this assumption was the idea of a single Truth, the interpretation of which also lay in the hands of these leaders.[136] They denied the pursuit of the expedient in favour of the more Quakerly leadings of the Inner Light, or of an interpretation of primitive Quakerism.

In doing so the dissidents threatened the basis of the fragile relationship with the national political establishment which had been built up by the London leadership. For although the two groups of Quakers shared common perceptions about the nature and obligations imposed by civil governments, they differed on the degree to which those governments could be accommodated according to Quaker precepts.[137]

To the dissatisfied Friends the dispute over the Affirmation had little to do with political allegiances, although not perhaps surprisingly some of them deprecated the lengths to which some of the London Friends were prepared to go in order to ingratiate themselves with Whig politicians or at the court.[138] The debate over a form of words which could "be taken and complied with by the least Child of God amongst us" had an import far beyond worldly politics, and in some senses little connected with the act of swearing or affirming.[139] To Friends in Lancashire, and also Ireland, Scotland and other English counties, the rejection of the 1696 Affirmation was part of a restatement of what they, led by the Inner Light, believed to be the fundamentalism of the early Quakers. This restatement was made against a background of growing wealth in the Society, particularly amongst its urban members, which was said to be leading many Friends to value material possessions above spiritual well-being.[140] The Affirmation was, at least in theory, a means by which Friends could secure their wealth and possessions, but to the dissatisfied Friends it was a security gained at the expense of the scriptural literalism propounded by their forbears, "yea yea and nay nay". As such, this relaxation compromised Quakers in the face of the world and devalued the evangelical mission of the Northern, Irish and other Friends. Far from being a "tedious tale", the controversy over the Affirmation is an essential element both in explaining the internal history of Quakerism, and also how internal problems determined relationships with both the political establishment and the wider world.[141]

REFERENCES

1. *Political Associations*, pp.32–42
2. 7 & 8 Will.III, c. 34
3. Those areas clearly identified with this critique were Cumberland, Cheshire,

Derbyshire, Dorset, Durham, Lancashire, Somerset, Westmorland, York-shire, North Wales, Scotland and Ireland; see, "The sense of the counties relating to the renewal or not of the present affirmation", LYMM, vol.5, pp.16–19, 1714. In addition, as will be seen below, the "sense" of those Quarterly Meetings which were in favour of the Affirmation should not necessarily be taken as reflecting the sentiments of the general body of Friends in those Meetings.

4. George Whitehead gave account of the proceedings as follows: "But then to make our Attestation, Affirmation, or Negation, as solemn as was expected from us by the Parliament, in Courts of Justice, etc. it was the Opinion of most of our Friends in Parliament, That there must be some solemn or sacred Expressions, religiously respecting God, as solemnly to declare the Truth in his Presence; which we durst not Gainsay, least we should be deemed Atheistical; the Bishops were caught upon these words to be added to the Word (God) viz. The witness of the Truth of what I say ... Those Lords that were most our Friends, were very earnest that we would admit of the Addition of the words which they proposed to be added, rather than to loose our Bill, or have it thrown out ..."; George Whitehead, *The Christian Progress of that Ancient Servant and Minister of Jesus Christ, George Whitehead* ... (London, 1725), pp.648, 654–55

5. MMS, vol.10, 12/12/1695

6. Thus it was stressed that Friends should "have a right and full sense of the great favour lately granted by the government ... and may be truly thankful to the Lord and to the government"; LYMM, vol.2, pp.140–41, 1696

7. MMS, vol.7, 19/9/1690

8. *ibid.*

9. *ibid.*

10. *Political Associations,* p 35

11. Henry Gouldney to Sir John Rhodes, London, 10/10/1690: in S. Locker-Lampson, *A Quaker Post-Bag* (London, 1910), pp.48–50

12. *DQB*; He had close connections with Lancashire through the marriage of his sister Margary to William Rawlinson, son of Thomas Rawlinson of Graythwaite. He may well have been influenced in his attitude to at least part of the Quaker establishment by the bitter dispute that had taken place between Thomas Rawlinson (a "first publisher of Truth") and the Fell family over the management of the Fell's iron interests at Force Forge. Through his marriage Gouldney became brother-in-law to the Quaker minister Lydia Lancaster, who was closely associated with Friends dissatisfied with the Affirmation. *DQB*; see Isabel Ross, *Margaret Fell, Mother of Quakerism* (London, 1949), pp.266–71, for an unsatisfactory account of the Force Forge incident. For Gouldney's description of his sister-in-law, "a woman of extreordinary qualifications ... she may well be accounted of the first ranck!", see Locker Lampson, *A Quaker Post-Bag*, p.98, where Gouldney is described by John Tomkins as having "such Power over his Frends (as I know none has the like) because of his loving disposition ...", *ibid.* p.117

13. The presence of businessmen like Gouldney in London, and William Stout and those other Quakers who formed such an extensive part of the Lancaster merchant community, among dissatisfied Friends, tends to throw doubt on one traditional interpretation of the Affirmation controversy. Isabel Grubb writes, "there was a long struggle within the Society itself to find an

affirmation which all Friends would be satisfied to make use of: broadly speaking, those who were becoming wealthy and engaging in extensive business transactions were in favour of being content with the form already granted, whilst those who wanted to tighten up the "discipline" desired a simpler form, which was not made legal until 1722". Although it was true, as we shall see, that dissatisfied Friends were also concerned with discipline, there is nothing to suggest that they were hostile either to "extensive business transactions" or the accumulation of wealth, provided that it did not lead to a neglect of the Truth, or "Truth's affairs" . The difference between the economic attitudes of the two groups probably lay in the fact that the dissatisfied, for example the Lancashire leather-tanners whose businesses were ruined in 1711 following their refusal either to swear or affirm, were prepared to sacrifice commercial gain before Truth's testimonies, which the satisfied were not. For Quakers in Lancaster's commercial life see *Stout*, pp.52–63. Isabel Grubb, *Quakerism and Industry before Eighteen Hundred* (London, 1930), pp.85–86. For discipline, see below and Chapter 7, *passim.*; for the Quaker leather tanners, see above, chapter 3

14.   Because "their Trades, and Industry (according to their capacities) advance the National Stock ..." it was not in "... the interest of the Government in general, that they should be any ways discouraged in their Honest Industry". *A Brief Representation of the Quakers Case for Not Swearing* (London, 1694), p.3; Friends had earlier argued that relief from oaths would put them "in a capacity to provide for themselves, and their present distressed Families, and may be enabled to pay such Taxes, for the maintaining the Peace and Government of the Kingdom, as they have been alwayes ready to do, when they were in a capacity ....": *To the King and both Houses of Parliament, Now Sitting at Westminster* (London, 1666), p.4. In stark contrast with this, non-Quaker opponents of the Affirmation argued later that "they are as great underminers of our Trades as they are of our Religion, and do brag that a Third of the Trade of the Nation is in their hands, and so will have a third of the Money, and by that do as much mischief as Guy Fawkes, with his Gunpowder, only not so speedily", *Some Reasons Humbly Offered ... why the Quakers Affirmation should Not Pass instead of an Oath, at Future Elections of Parliament* (London, 1708 ?), p.1

15.   See, for example, *Second Period*, p.181; for the Lancashire data see above chapter 3

16.   See, for example, *Besse, passim.*

17.   This idea of precision can also be seen in the Quaker attitude to the law, and their efforts to restrict Quaker sufferings to those laws which specifically applied to them. See above, chapter 2

18.   For an example of this unity see LYMM, vol.2, pp.107–125, 1696; at this Yearly Meeting immediately following the passing of the Affirmation Act there was a general acceptance and welcoming of the new legislation. No county spoke against the Act; Lancashire's representatives were "against oaths, and therefore the more glad to be eased from them", while the representative from Yorkshire observed: "As to what is obtained from the Government (so far as I know) Friends are glad of it". It was clearly only when the terms of the "ease" were conveyed to the counties that the problems began.

19.   Locker Lampson, *A Quaker Post-Bag*, p.50; LQMM, vol.1, 13/11/1693, 5/2/1694

20. LQMM, vol.1, 1/8/1696, 3/2/1701
21. LQMM, vol.1, 3/2/1701; in 1713 the Quarterly Meeting concluded "that if the present Affirmation Act cannot be made easy to Friends in general that the same may expire", LQMM, vol.1, 30/1/1713
22. Joseph Skidmore, *Essay upon the Vth of Matthew, From Verse 33d to 37th* (London, 1713); see also by the same author, *Primitive Simplicity Demonstrated* (London, 1714), *passim.*
23. See Braithwaite's summary of Skidmore's argument, in *Second Period*, pp.196–97
24. MMS, vol.21, 23/2/1714 "An Epistle from the Meeting for Sufferings, the 16th of the second month 1714. To the Friends and brethren at their several Quarterly and Monthly Meetings". A printed version of this is in LSF, Tract vol.G, no.2
25. LSF, Tract vol.G no.1, *Epistle from the Meeting for Sufferings* (London, 11/1/1715)
26. Thomas Story wrote that some Friends in London "charged all the ill consequences of Division upon such as could not comply ..." with the Affirmation, Thomas Story, *A Journal of the Life of Thomas Story* (Newcastle, 1747), p.529
27. This interpretation of the actions of the Meeting for Sufferings is in agreement with Thomas O'Malley's view that the Meeting was one of the tools used by George Fox and others to impose "notions of uniformity on the movement"; Thomas O'Malley, "'Defying the Powers and Tempering the Spirit", A Review of Quaker Control over their Publications 1672–1689', *Journal of Ecclesiastical History*, 33 (1982), pp.85–86
28. MMS, vol.21, 29/2/1715
29. *ibid* .
30. 8 Geo.III, c. 6. Following the passing of this Act the Lancashire Quarterly Meeting expresses its "gratitude, for the singular favour granted to us as a people in the provision made to us by law, that our solemn Affirmation and declaration in simple words of truth, such as with freedom and safety we can express, shall be taken in lieu of an oath". LYMM, vol.6, pp.79–80, 1722. The 1696 Affirmation Act had been renewed in 1702 and made perpetual in 1715 by I Geo. c. 26 see *Political Associations*, pp.49–54
31. Locker Lampson, *A Quaker Post-Bag*, p.49
32. LYMM, vol.4, pp.315–16, 1713; see also LFMH, 2Ai:27, Epistle from the Yearly Meeting, 30/4/1713
33. Locker Lampson, *A Quaker Post-Bag*, p.50. Clearly both the satisfied and dissatisfied Friends were concerned with the extent to which the Affirmation might affect the Quakers' public image. The satisfied saw it as a confirmation of Quaker respectability, a public recognition of Friends as peaceable conscientious citizens, proper beneficiaries of the Toleration of 1689. The dissatisfied, however, were less concerned with respectability than with reputation; the Affirmation, seen by some Anglicans as little different from an oath, was a threat to Truth's undefiled reputation, and, as we shall see, a hindrance to missionary activity; the theme of respectability versus reputation is dealt with more fully in chapter 7
34. Among those supporting this view in the debate were the Archbishops of Canterbury and York, the Bishops of Oxford, Titchfield, Coventry and Rochester, the Earls Strafford, Cowper, Scarborough and Sunderland, Lord

North and Grey, the Lords Trevor, Bathurst and Townshend, *Parliamentary History*, vol.7, p.943

35. *ibid.* vol.7, p.943

36. *ibid.* vol.7, p.943. "Petition of the London Clergy against the said Bill."

37. *ibid.* vol.7, p.946

38. *ibid.* vol.7, p.947

39. *Second Period*, pp.189, 206. Norman Hunt appears at least sympathetic to this view, writing of Quaker "Jacobite inclinations", *Political Associations*, p.72

40. *Second Period*, p.189

41. *Political Associations*, pp.1–112

42. *Second Period*, p.190. Penn's objections to the Affirmation were considerable, but his actual involvement in the dispute marginal. For his letter to the Meeting for Sufferings written in 1690 see below. William Penn's involvement with James II as an envoy to the monarch from Friends and as an envoy from the monarch to various political groupings, and his contacts with and continued affection for, the deposed sovereign after 1688 have earned him the appellation "Jacobite". There is, however, little or no evidence to suggest that Penn was ever actually involved in attempts to restore the Stuarts to the English, Scottish, and after 1707 British, throne, although some Quakers, mainly London merchants, did maintain treasonable contacts with the Court of St Germain. Penn's Jacobitism, in as much as there was any, consisted simply of a continued personal relationship. His political views, both before and after 1688, were aligned more closely with the traditional views attributed to Whigs, than probably were those of many leading Quaker Whigs themselves. However to some Friends, and notably to William Meade, Penn remained tarred with the brush of association. He was an embarrassment to their political aspirations on behalf of Friends as a whole, and was a continued rival to their particular ambitions for place and authority amongst the Quaker hierarchy. For some account of this see *Second Period*, pp.134–50; J.R. Western, *Monarchy and Revolution*, pp.167–68, 205, 231–33; Vincent Buranelli, *The King and the Quaker. A Study of William Penn and James II* (Philadelphia, 1966), *passim.* In Penn's own words "... since he had loved King James in his prosperity, he should not hate him in his adversity ... though he would not join with him in what concerned the state of the Kingdom", Gerard Croese, *The General History of the Quakers* (London, 1696), pp.112–13, quoted in *Second Period*, p.162. For Quaker support of the exiled court see, Pierre Burger, 'Spymaster to Louis XIV: A Study of the Papers of the Abbe Eusete Renaudot', in E. Cruickshanks (ed.), *Ideology and Conspiracy. Aspects of Jacobitism 1689–1759* (Edinburgh, 1982), pp.114–15. For a statement of Penn's Whig views see *One Project for the Good of England* (n.p.1679), *passim.* in Barbour & Roberts (eds.), *Early Quaker Writings*, pp 442–51, where he rehearses many of the later claims for toleration, particularly on economic grounds, made by John Locke. Hugh Barbour argues that Penn's support for James II when he was on the throne was simply a result of the pragmatism which came to form the basis of his search for toleration: see Hugh Barbour, 'William Penn, Model of Protestant Liberalism', *Church History* 48 (1979), pp.166–67

43. LSF, Miller MSS, no.89, Margaret Fox to Friends, 9/11/1697; *Second Period*, p.189

44. In effect Penn had fallen foul of the traditional Quaker establishment,

represented in this case by the Fell family, George Whitehead, etc., who were also among those Friends most strongly in support of the Affirmation: *Second Period*, p.174. The allegation is the substance of Margaret Fell's letter in LSF, Miller MSS 89, which criticises those Friends who refused the Affirmation. "This", she wrote, "is a new doctrine, and another gospel which the Apostle saith whosoever preacheth is accursed". Friends maintaining such views were "weak, and so childish in the Truth", evidence "that there is now many troublers as well as witnesses for the eternal Truth" (originally this had read "more troublers than there is witnesses") *ibid*.

45. MMS, vol.10, 10/12/1695, 12/12/1695. See, for example, John Tomkins' letter to Sir John Rhodes, London, 11/12/1697, where he writes that Margaret Fell, "by reason of her age, ... will be lead by her son Wm into something or other, which may not be of the best consequence to Truth, nor the quiet of the Church, nor her own honner": Locker Lampson, *A Quaker Post-Bag*, p.134; for Meade's involvement in the solicitations relating to the Affirmation, see, for example, HMC, Twelfth Report, Appendix pt.vi, *Manuscripts of the House of Lords 1688–89* (London, 1889), p.36; MMS, vol.10, 10/12/1695

46. For biographical data see Norman Penny (ed.) *Journal of George Fox* (Cambridge, 1911), vol.2, p.420, n.162 and the same editor, *The short Journal and Itinerary Journals of George Fox* (Cambridge, 1925), p.295, n.77; *Second Period*, p.207

47. Locker Lampson, *A Quaker Post-Bag*, p.134, John Tomkins to Sir John Rhodes, London 11/12/1697

48. Much of the authority claimed or assumed by authors for this and other letters of similar content written by Margaret Fell at this period of her life rest on the explicit assumption that they were circulated amongst, and that therefore their contents gained credence amongst, Friends in general. However, there is little or no evidence to support this contention. The letter in LSF, Miller MSS 89, is a transcript of an original manuscript that was destroyed by fire in 1940 and thus there is no way of checking the original for endorsements, directions etc. written on the verso. No other copy of the letter has been traced in LSF, although this does not preclude a copy's existence in loose or bound form amongst one of the Monthly or Quarterly Meeting collections held there. No copy has been found amongst the papers of the Lancashire Monthly or Lancashire Quarterly Meeting either bound or loose, held in LFMH. Clearly copies could exist elsewhere. However, the suggestion that the letter was not circulated, (possibly at the direction of Margaret Fell's daughter, Sarah Meade, to whom the letter was dictated and who can be seen from the transcript to have moderated some of the phrases originally used by her mother) must considerably reduce the authority of its contents. If it is possible that the letter's contents were not thought fit for general consumption by her daughter-in-law (who may have been trying to preserve her 83-year-old mother's considerable reputation and in John Tomkin's word "honner", by suppressing some of her more outspoken comments) then it is difficult to see how Margaret Fell's views at this stage of her life can be given any authority. For Tomkins see n.45 above

49. Bruce Lenman, *The Jacobite Rising in Britain 1689–1746* (London, 1980), pp.12–19

50. Lenman, *The Jacobite Risings in Britain*, pp.25–27

51. See above, chapter 2
52. A Jacobite view of the Quakers was provided by Sir John St. Aubyn, Member of Parliament for Cornwall, in 1736; the Quakers, he said, represented "the intemperate follies, the luxury, the venality and irreligion of the age, which have been long gathering like a dark thunder cloud in the sky ...." *Parliamentary History*, vol.9, p.1165, for St. Aubyn see Romney Sedgewick, *The House of Commons 1715–1754* (3 vols., London, 1970), vol.2, pp.401–02
53. For the Bradshaighs, see above, chapter 2
54. *Stout*, p.117
55. *Stout*, p.109
56. *Stout*, p.173
57. *Stout*, p.187
58. The nature and development of these principles are discussed in J.P. Kenyon, *Revolution Principles, The Politics of Party 1689–1720* (Cambridge, 1977), *passim*.
59. For a summary of Tory political attitudes during the period 1689–1740 see H.T. Dickenson, *Liberty and Property, Political Ideology in Eighteenth-Century Britain* (London, 1977), pp.13–56. The temper of the Tories during this period can be judged from the contents of the Occasional Conformity Act of 1711 and the Schism Act of 1714; see 10 Anne. c. 6 and 13 Anne. c. 7
60. "It is worthy of remark that the dissatisfied districts were those which, during the same period, were most zealously opposing the consequences of the growth of wealth and worldliness among Friends by pressing a searching discipline on the Church", *Second Period*, p.189
61. MMS, vol.10, 17/2/1696
62. MMS, vol.10, 17/2/1696, 1/3/1696, 8/3/1696
63. *An Epistle from the Meeting for Sufferings, by their order, the 17th of the Second Month, and 1st of the Third Month 1696* (London, 1696), *passim*.
64. *ibid.* p.4
65. *ibid.* p.14
66. *ibid.* p.15
67. SMMM, vol.3, 3/8/1693
68. LMMM, vol.1, 6/9/1693, 4/10/1693
69. *To the King and Both Houses of Parliament Now sitting at Westminster* (London, 1666), pp.7–9. Joseph Smith's *Descriptive Catalogue of Friends' Books* (2 vols., London 1867), p.65, suggests that the 'Declaration' was also printed separately in 1666. There is little doubt that this is the item referred to by Friends; the phrase contained in the 'Declaration', that yea, yea and nay nay "we will stand by and to" is repeated twice almost exactly in the Quarterly Meeting Minutes considering the Monthly Meetings' response to the circulation of the 'Declaration'. See *To the King and Both Houses of Parliament*, p.7, and LQMM, vol.1, 3/11/1693
70. The contents were: 'A Representation of the Cause and Sufferings of the People, called Quakers, and what they desire signified' (pp.3–6); 'A Declaration from the People, called Quakers, what they can say in stead of an Oath: Together with an Account of the Names of some of the Prisoners, called Quakers, in the several Gaols in England and Wales, who have had the sentence of Premunire etc', (pp.7–13); 'To the Committee for Grievances, some of the Grievances of the People called Quakers' (pp.13–15); 'Some Wholsome Advice and seasonable Considerations, lending to

Peace and Concord: which being tendred and delivered to some of the
Members of each House, only in Manuscript (with a desire they might so be
read among them) therefore that they may the better take notice of them;
they are tendred in Print, that they may peruse them, and consider the Cause
and Grievous Sufferings of the Innocent, herein hinted and partly related'
(pp.16–22)

71. The following names appear at the end of the 'Representation': Amor
    Stodard, George Whitehead, Gerard Roberts, Gilbert Latye, Thomas Loe,
    Samuel Newton, Ellis Hooks, Thomas Coveny, William Crouch Morgan
    Watkins, John Nelson, Josiah Cole, Walter Mires, Abraham Shapton,
    Thomas Yokeley: *To the King and both Houses of Parliament*, p.6
72. For the Quakers' view of history see Hugh Barbour, *The Quakers in Puritan
    England* (London, 1964), pp.188–92
73. *To the King and both Houses of Parliament*, p.9
74. *ibid.* p.7
75. *ibid.* p.8
76. *ibid.* p.9
77. *ibid.* p.17
78. LSF, Miller MSS, 89, Margaret Fell to Friends, 19/11/1697–98; the *Epistle
    from the Meeting for Sufferings* (1696), was at pains to stress that "as Friends
    have sometimes in Publick express'd themselves in the Words Yea and Nay,
    so have they many times express'd themselves in other Words, and offered
    divers Solemn Reverential Expressions, as in the Presence of God, in his
    Sight, in his Fear, and God is Witness, etc. .... Yet they did never therein
    believe they exceeded Christ's Command, or Yea and Nay or their own
    Testimony": *ibid.* pp.11–12
79. *A Declaration From the People call'd Quakers, to the King, and Both Houses of
    Parliament Then Sitting at Westminster, what they can say instead of an Oath*
    (n.p., 1700?)
80. The names of Gerard Roberts, Samuel Newton, Morgan Watkins, Abraham
    Shapton and Thomas Yokeley were omitted from the signatories: *The
    Declaration from the People call'd Quakers*, p.2
81. *ibid.*
82. MMS, vol.10, 1/3/1696
83. William Penn, *One Project for the Good of England*, in Hugh Barbour & Arthur
    Roberts (eds), *Early Quaker Writings* (Grand Rapids, Michigan, 1973), p.450;
    Epistle from the Meeting for Sufferings, (1696), p.11
84. *Second Period*, p.190
85. LSF, Port 41.35, William Penn to the Meeting for Sufferings, 4/3/1696
86. *ibid.*
87. See for example LYMM, vol.2, pp.140–41, 1696
88. *ibid.*
89. See the opening of this chapter
90. For this see *Political Associations*, pp.51–52
91. LYMM, vol.2, pp.140–41, 1696
92. *ibid.*
93. LYMM, vol.2, pp.179–81, 1697: Edmundson, a native of Westmorland, had
    moved to Ireland in 1652. He was closely identified with the imposition of a
    rigorous discipline amongst Friends, and was closely associated with Friends
    in the north of England. William Edmundson, *A Journal of the Life, Travels,*

Sufferings and Labour of Love in the Work of the Ministry of that Worthy Elder, and Faithful servant of Jesus Christ, William Edmundson (London, 1715), pp.1–7 for his early life and conversion; for his connection with the discipline and Northern Friends, see *ibid. passim.*

94. LYMM, vol.2, p.179, 1697
95. MMS, vol.21, 9/8/1713
96. *ibid.* The outcome of this disagreement was a severing of official links between the Aberdeen Quarterly Meeting and the Meeting for Sufferings which appears to have lasted for nearly twelve months. SRO CH10/3/55 (unnumbered bundle), Gilbert Mollison and others to Aberdeen Quarterly Meeting, London, 2/5/1714; *Second Period*, p.204
97. MMS, vol.21, 9/8/1713 "In as much as your said epistle takes notice of some epistles from this Meeting, dated the 16th and 30th of the 11th month and 20th 12th Month 1712 ..."
98. MMS, vol.21, 16/11/1712: LFMH, 2Ai:23, Epistle from the Meeting for Sufferings, 16/11/1712
99. *Political Associations*, pp.51–52
100. LFMH, 2Ai:24, Epistle from the dissatisfied Friends concerning an epistle from the Meeting for Sufferings, not dated; MMS, vol.21, 20/1/1713
101. LFMH, 2Ai:24, Epistle from the dissatisfied Friends.
102. *ibid.*
103. LFMH, 2Ai:24, John Whiting to William Stout, London, 14/12/1712. John Whiting's covering letter may have been sent to a number of counties, as the Meeting for Sufferings was to complain "that several letters were sent ... copies of some of which letters" it had obtained. None however, unlike Whiting's to Stout, were signed: MMS, vol.21, 20/1/1713
104. *ibid.* For an introduction to decision-making in Quaker business meetings, see Chapter 2 of L. Hugh Doncaster, *Quaker Organisation and Business Meetings* (Friends Home Service Study Papers No. 2, London, 1958). He concludes that "Because Friends believe that there is a will of God in part discernable by Man, and that unity in the discovery of this is possible, they refuse to divide a meeting by voting", (p.65). The experience of some eighteenth century Friends was clearly sometimes to the contrary and not only during the debates over the Affirmation. In 1735 Lancashire Quarterly Meeting directed its four representatives to that year's Yearly Meeting "to show the dislike this Meeting has of deciding controversial points by majority votes in [the] most pressing terms they are capable of", LQMM, vol.2, 14/2/1735. In the epistle circulated at the close of the 1735 Yearly Meeting Friends were cautioned "that nothing be done through strife and contention, nor from any private views, or the influence of numbers ..." in business meetings; rather "through meekness, humility, long-suffering, and forbearance one of another" would Friends "keep the unity of the spirit in the bond of peace". *Epistles from the Yearly Meeting of Friends, held in London, to the Quarterly and Monthly Meetings in Great Britain, Ireland, and Elsewhere, from 1681 to 1817* (London, 1818), p.224
105. LFMH, 2Ai:24, John Whiting to William Stout, 14/12/1712
106. LSF, Port 41.18 John Whiting to George Bowles, London, 13/3/1713
107. MMS, vol.21, 17/2/1713. The Meeting had noted earlier that "no person in this Meeting acknowledging himself to be the author, this meeting thereupon declares such clandestine practises and proceedings are unbecoming

the Truth": MMS, vol.21, 13/1/1713
108. MMS, vol.21, 20/1/1713
109. MMS, vol.21, 1/3/1713
110. LYMM, vol.4, p.318, 1713
111. The committee consisted of Thomas Aldam, Robert Haydock, James Pike, John Gurney, Edward Lloyd and Benjamin Coole. LYMM vol.4 , p.333, 1713
112. LQMM, vol.2, 2/5/1713 (my emphasis)
113. *Stout*, p.169
114. LYMM, vol.4, pp.332–33, 1713
115. LYMM, vol.4, pp.334–35, 1713
116. See, for example, LQMM, vol.1, 2/2/1702, here there were eighteen volunteers to attend the next Yearly Meeting. By 1736 this enthusiasm had waned and there were no volunteers to make the trip to London, LQMM, vol.2, 11/2/1736
117. LQMM, vol.1, 2/2/1702
118. LQMM, vol.2, 3/5/1712, 1/5/1714
119. William Edmundson, *A Journal of the Life*, p.169
120. LSF, Port 20.97, William Edmundson to Robert Haydock, (Dublin?), 18/12/1697
121. William Edmundson, *A Journal of the Life*, p.230: LSF, Port 20.105, Isaac Alexander to Robert Haydock, London, 17/1/1705. Alexander, a native of Westmorland, was a young convinced Quaker minister; he died in 1706 aged 25, *DQB*
122. Locker Lampson, *A Quaker Post-Bag*, pp.97–99, Henry Gouldney to Sir John Rhodes, London, 6/2/1714
123. Thomas Story, *A Journal*, p.529
124. *ibid.* p.617
125. LSF, Gibson TS. 432, John Field to Thomas Story, London, 22/7/1707
126. LSF, Gibson TS. 584, Thomas Chalkley to Thomas Story, Philadelphia, 5/7/1717
127. LSF, MS vol.77, Thomas Gwin's Journal, 10th & 11th June, 1712. A partial transcript of the relevant entry is in *Second Period*, pp.192–93
128. LSF, MS vol.77, 10th & 11th June 1712
129. LSF, Gibson TS. 472, Lydia Lancaster to Thomas Story, Kendal, 2/4/1715
130. LSF, Port 20.101, John Haydock to Friends of Hardshaw Meeting, Wigan, 10/1/1702. A copy of this letter also survived among manuscripts preserved at Liverpool Friends' Meeting House, see James A. Murphy, 'The Old Quaker Meeting House in Hackins Hey, Liverpool', *THSLC*, 106 (1954), p.81 n.17. For a complete transcript of the LSF copy see Appendix 2. Haydock, who died at Lancaster Castle in 1719 whilst imprisoned there for non-payment of tithes, was a member of one of the most prominent Quaker families in late seventeenth and early eighteenth century Lancashire. He travelled widely as a minister, both in England, Wales, Scotland and Ireland, and in America. He was closely associated not only with the campaign for a modified Affirmation, but also with the efforts to increase discipline and mission amongst Friends in the 1690s and early 1700s. See *Piety Promoted* (London, 1812), vol.2, pp.162–63; *A Collection of the Christian Writings ... of ... Roger Haydock* (London, 1700), pp.201–23; T.C. Porteus, 'Roger Haydock of Coppull', *TLCAS*, 52 (1937), pp.1–66; and below, chapter 7

131. This suffering does not appear amongst those entered in the Great Book Of Sufferings for Lancashire Friends, and consequently is not included in the figures presented in chapter 3, Table 2, above.
132. LSF, Port 20.101
133. The specific appointment of elders was not acknowledged by the Yearly Meeting until 1727; however their existence, both in name and function, had been recognised since before the Restoration: L. Hugh Doncaster, *Quaker Organisation and Business Meetings*, pp.21–23
134. LSF, Port 20.101
135. *ibid.*
136. In this the Friends were questioning the organisational and spiritual unity imposed on the movement by George Fox, George Whitehead etc. in the 1660s and 1670s, which is discussed by Thomas O'Malley in '"Defying the Powers and Tempering the Spirit". A Review of Quaker Control over their Publications 1672–1689', *Journal of Ecclesiastical History*, 33 (1982), pp.72–88
137. For these see above, Chapter 1, *passim*.
138. Locker Lampson, *A Quaker Post-Bag*, pp.101–02, Henry Gouldney to Sir John Rhodes, London, 31/3/1706
139. MMS, vol.21, 8/2/1715, letter from Somerset Quarterly Meeting, dated 24/1/1715, "That you will not either offer or accept of any form of Affirmation, but such as may be taken and complied with by the least child of God amongst us".
140. This is discussed in more detail below, chapter 7
141. *Second Period*, p.204, "The tedious tale of the Affirmation is now told".

5

Tithes

... and let no Man henceforth think it strange, that any should
refuse to pay Tithes; but rather wonder that any will do it.
          (Anthony Pearson, *The Great Case of Tithes*, p.66)

The Quaker refusal to pay tithes either to clerics or lay impropriators was
the main cause of friction between Friends and the established authorities
in the late seventeenth and eighteenth centuries.[1] In addition it could be a
major source of conflict in the communities in which Friends lived. Rather
than resort to the law, many tithe-owners would seize their tenth from a
Quaker's property, frequently using violence in the process and sometimes
earning the disapprobation of Anglican neighbours.[2] Family and social ties
could also be strained by the actions of non Friends (sometimes
maliciously motivated) who paid tithes on behalf of their Quaker friends
or relatives consequently bringing them under the discipline of their local
Meeting.[3] Maintaining their tithe testimony was not easy for Quakers, and
it was certainly not a simple way of evading an irksome expense.[4] For the
majority of Friends refusal involved either legal expenditure in excess of
the tenth demanded or loss through excessive seizures and damaged
property. Violence and psychological intimidation also frequently surrounded tithe proceedings, which at worst could end in death for the
Quaker involved.[5] Although the cases of Friends who lost their livelihoods
through refusing tithe payments were comparatively few, for the majority
of Quakers the annual collection of the tenth involved distress, loss and
not infrequently injury. The refusal to pay tithes was in every sense of the
word a suffering.[6]

    This, and the following chapter, will be devoted to a discussion of a
number of issues concerning the Quaker tithe testimony, particularly in
relation to Friends in Lancashire and the other North-West counties.
First, it is necessary to consider the arguments used by the Quakers to
justify their opposition to tithe payments. It will be shown that it was in
these arguments, as much as in any others concerning the nature of
government or the magistracy, that the Quakers revealed many of their

underlying attitudes, concerning the nature and basis of society and authority in seventeenth and eighteenth century England.

It has recently been suggested by Dr. Barry Reay that the Quakers' principal arguments against tithes were not scriptural, but rather that they rested on a "wide range of economic and social objections to tithes", which revealed both "rabid anti-clericalism" amongst Friends and also, most importantly, "a deep hostility towards the social order".[7] I will argue here that this view is misleading, and that it reveals a misunderstanding of the basis of Quaker beliefs. Moreover, I will show that, inasmuch as Quakers did present important economic and social objections to tithes, these arguments for the most part reflected fundamental support for the social order rather than opposition to it.[8] In many respects the Quaker's secular arguments echoed those put forward by political philosophers to justify the legitimacy and lawfulness of a society based on capitalist means of production. In this discussion I shall, like Dr. Reay, use the writings of Quaker propagandists published both before and after the Restoration.[9] In addition I will use material from the unique collection of tithe testimonies contained in the archive at Lancaster Friends' Meeting House which offer a rare opportunity to consult the views not of the Quaker propagandist, but of the mostly anonymous "Quaker in the street".[10] These will also allow some conclusions to be drawn as to the extent to which ordinary Friends drew on the official propagandists in order to formulate and justify their opposition to tithes.

Of course the main thrust of articulation of the Quaker case against tithes was scriptural and theological. Indeed, to suggest that secular arguments took precedence over scriptural arguments is to deny the fact that Friends were brought together initially by a shared religious experience which in turn led to shared theological beliefs. It was this shared experience and these beliefs which determined the Quaker view of the outside world.[11] Social assumptions held in common by Friends in particular parts of the country may well have been articulated by this experience and these beliefs. The resulting attitudes almost certainly attracted converts to Friends who already held similar social assumptions.[12] However, in the process of conversion these assumptions took on secondary status to the primacy of shared experience and belief.

Quakers believed that tithes should not be paid because, according to the Old Testament, they had been established by the Mosaic Law as a payment to the Levitical priesthood which had been abolished by the coming of Christ.[13] Far from being little used, this and a number of other theological arguments were always present in any Quaker criticism of the tithing system whether in general works or in those devoted solely to attacks on the tenth.[14] In *A Touch-Stone, or a Tryal by the Scriptures, of the Priests, Bishops and Ministers*, published in 1667, Margaret Fell explained, on the question of maintenance,

that we have a Testimony of our Lord Jesus Christ, our Everlasting

High Priest, that he is come, we cannot deny his Testimony, in paying Priests Tythes, which was paid under the Levitical Priesthood before he came ....[15]

Thomas Ellwood, who wrote extensively against tithes, shared this opinion:

For Tythes being a part of the Ceremonial Law, and peculiarly belonging to the Jewish Polity, which Christ came to end and take away; the continuing or restoring of Tythes is equally a denyal that Christ is come in the Flesh ....[16]

The refusal to pay tithes, then,was an acknowledgement of the coming of Christ and as such was a fundamental of Quaker religious belief. In contrast the acceptance of tithes was, according to Richard Hubberthorn, a denial that Christ had come "in the flesh".[17] Even Anthony Pearson, whose *Great Case of Tithes* is probably the most secular and legalistic Quaker work on the subject, stressed the role of

Christ Jesus ... who put an End to the first Priesthood, with all its Shadows, Figures and carnal Ordinances.[18]

There was no attempt, argued the Quakers, to replace the old form of maintenance. Thomas Ellwood succinctly expressed the Quakers' scriptural argument for a free ministry,

Freely ye have received, freely give, was our Lords Command to his Disciples when he sent them forth to preach, Mat. 10.8 and freely receive what is freely given by those that receive you and your Message, was the Provision he allowed them, Luke 10.7, 8. And a sufficient provision too it proved, even though they went as Lambs amongst wolves, vers. 3 for when they returned he asked them, Lacked ye anything? and their Answer was Nothing, Luke 22.35.[19]

Tithes were not introduced during what the Quakers called the time of "the Gospel", for members of the early church freely supported those in the ministry, sustaining themselves by living together, sharing "all things in common".[20] Thomas Ellwood spent the first 150 pages of his *Foundation of Tythes Shaken* proving that there was

no firm Foundations for a Divine Right to Tythes under the Gospel. No institution of them; No New Determination of them; No Establishment of them; No Mention of them in all the New Testament, as a Maintenance for Gospel-Ministers.[21]

Rather than being instituted "under the Gospel" the tithe system had been reintroduced "when the Apostacy came in".[22]

Tithes should not be paid, argued the Quakers, because they were a popish imposition with no place or authority in the reformed Church.[23] This was a view shared by many, for, as Christopher Hill has pointed out, the explanation of the "reluctance of Englishmen to pay tithes ..." could "conveniently be expressed in terms of anti-popery".[24] By accepting tithes, ministers in the Church of England further revealed their corrupt and popish tendencies. Does it become, asked Ellwood,

> a Protestant Ministry, who are so denominated from protesting against Popery, to receive and exact that Maintenance which was given by a Popish Prince to Popish Priests to uphold Popery?[25]

Ellwood carefully and tortuously side-stepped any controversy in civil matters by making a clear distinction between the civil and religious actions of papists and popish princes.[26]

Rather than question the validity of legislation such as Magna Carta, he conceded that "though in their Religious capacity they were wrong, yet in their civil capacity they were right ... they were truly Members of the political Body, though they were not truly Members of the Body of Christ".[27] Thus

> making void ... Tythes, which had direct Relation to their Religion, and was designed to support their Church and Worship ..., doth not at all shake, much less overthrow those civil Acts, Laws ... which in a civil capacity ... were made or enacted by them.[28]

These three strands linked together the Quakers' theological and historical arguments against tithes. In the first place tithes had been established under the Mosaical Law for the payment of the Levitical priesthood. This law had been abolished by the coming of Christ, who had established a free ministry, nowhere mentioning tithes as a source of income. Therefore, to uphold tithes was to deny the coming of Christ. The tithe system by which the Quakers suffered was a popish imposition, "a weight of oppression upon poor People", made under the auspices of Rome by Saxon Kings such as Ethelwolf.[29] But English history apart, tithes were a relic of the unreformed church, and as such had been denied by the Lollards such as William Thorpe "whom the Tithe Takers now own for a Martyr ..."[30] Thus for the Quakers the taking of tithes by the clergy was a mark of the degeneracy of the Established Church.[31] Friends added a further argument concerning the historical origin of tithes. Under the Mosaic Law, and even during the reign of the papacy, "the Poor were maintained out of Tythes", for the support of the needy was one of the purposes of the system.[32] Now, however, "the Priests have jostled out the poor ... and now Ingross all the Tythes to themselves, leaving the poor upon the Parish's charge".[33] Margaret Fell observed that:

these Tythe-mongers of the Gospel Times, have neither fed Widows
nor Fatherless; but what they could get of them, they have taken from
them.[34]

For Hubberthorn, this misappropriation of tithe was "one great yoke
of bondage which is upon the subjects and seed of God in this nation".[35]

Although these scriptural and historical points were to Dr. Reay, "the
Friends' least convincing arguments", to Quakers themselves, to possible
converts and to the layman at large these were no doubt forceful reasons
for not paying tithe.[36] Dr. Evans has pointed out that "however much the
defenders of the Church Establishment might wish to find them, it could
not be denied that the New Testament refused to provide any evidence of
payment of tithe by the early Christians".[37] This, as the Quakers realised,
was a powerful argument against those supporters of the tithing system.
However, although Quakers could be perfectly convinced of the wrong-
ness of tithe by the account of Christ's coming, and by the fact that the first
Christians did not pay tithe, laymen, they appreciated, might also hold
purely secular objections to the system. Many of these objections, although
worldly, were shared by Friends, and only served to confirm their religious
objections outlined above. Not surprisingly, therefore, Friends were
prepared to use these secular arguments in the propaganda they issued to
the world against tithe. It should be remembered, however, that no matter
how convincing these arguments were, the Quakers' objections were based
primarily on theological reasoning, whether or not the reasons for their
objections were religious or material.

The Quakers complained bitterly that in being forced to pay tithes
they were being asked to pay for something they did not get. They did not
attend the parish church, and neither did they receive the ministry offered
there; why then should the law demand that they pay towards the upkeep
of churches and maintain ministers?[38] Typically Hubberthorn argued
against this on the basis of the workings of a free market economy:

Is there ever a Tradesman in the Nation so unrighteous that sells his
wares on the week day as the Priests do on the first day, to take money
of them, and compel them to pay money they sell nothing to? Is there
ever a poor hireling or hedger or labourer in the Nation that will force
people that have not hired them, nor set them at labour, to pay them
money?[39]

To the Quakers, with their highly developed commercial sensibilities
and insistence on value for money, the bargain, or lack of it, implied in
tithe demands was outrageous. This can be compared with Margaret Fell's
frustrations at seeing honest tax-paying Quakers being disturbed by
soldiers in their Meetings; on this occasion a bargain paid for was not
being kept as Friends were paying soldiers to keep the peace, not to break
up their Meetings.[40] This question of payment of taxes was often closely

associated with Quaker arguments against tithes. Abolish tithes, said Hubberthorn, and revenue from taxation would be increased.[41]

Friends were at pains to stress that their refusal to pay tithes did not extend to tax payments, neither would the abolition of tithes lead to an abolition of taxation.[42] For Ellwood

> These were Taxes purely civil; which Tythes are not. And they were levyed for Civil Use, however afterwards disposed of; which Tythes are not.[43]

Anthony Pearson expanded this distinction between the civil and the religious:

> For civil Ends and Uses the People may give Power to their Representatives to raise Moneys, or any other civil Thing … But in Matters of Religion and Spiritual Things, no Man can give himself, or his Neighbour.[44]

Thus taxes could, and would, be paid after the abolition of tithes. In the absence of tithes the people "will be better able, and more willing, to enlarge the publick Treasury, if it be found wanting".[45] Thus, not only would the system be maintained, but any loss of income to the government through the loss of augmentations would be made good. To the rhymester John Raven the effect of abolition would be immediate,

> soon would the Country then look Brisk and Gay,
> And cheerfully their Debts and Taxes pay.[46]

Equally, Friends were not threatening rents when they refused to pay tithe: "Quakers are as willing to pay their rents, (or any other just dues) and are as good Tenants to their Landlords, as any others are …."[47] This, argued Ellwood, was because rents were paid "from a Principle of equity and justice". On the other hand, tithes were refused "which are against Equity and Justice".[48]

Tithes were unjust because, as explained above, the Quakers and others were being asked to pay for a service they did not receive. They were unequal because they penalised the countryside as against the city, and the poor as against the rich. Christopher Hill has shown how a growth in commercial and industrial activity in cities and ports led to a decrease in the collection of personal tithes in these urban centres during the sixteenth century.[49] In the absence of these, the tithes due from urban-dwellers were negligible.[50] Those who lived in the country, however, bore the full brunt of the tithing system. Pearson who had originally addressed his work to "the country-men, Farmers, and Husbandmen of England", and who carefully fashioned many of his arguments to appeal to this group, complained that

out of the Tithe of such Country Parishes of Tillage, generally great
sums are paid for Augmentations, to Cities and Market Towns, when
the Inhabitants, that have far greater Gain by Trading, go free.[51]

Tithes were also unequal in that they penalised the poor rather than
the rich:

the burden lies chiefly on the poor Farmers and Husbandmen, and
men of greatest Estates pay least: So that he that has many thousands a
year scarce pays so much Tythes, as he that Rents a Farm of fifty
Pounds a year.[52]

Pearson agreed with Ellwood that "The Rich generally pays little, and
the poor Husbandman bears the Burden".[53]

Arguments such as these should not be taken to represent an attack or
denunciation of the inequality present in seventeenth century society.
Although Friends had always attacked excessive materialism and
extravagance – the worldly riches which John Haydock denounced in his
letter to Hardshaw Meeting of 1702 – the unequal distribution of wealth
was never seriously questioned.[54] Friends were attempting to cultivate the
support and sympathy of small-scale farmers and property-owners by
presenting them with appealing secular arguments against tithe. An
Anglican neighbour might find little sympathy for a Quaker who refused
tithes on the basis of the abolition of the Mosaic Law: he would have far
more sympathy for someone who argued that he was a victim of common,
and naturally unfair, economic and social forces. After all, books such as
Pearson's were not intended to convert Anglicans to Quakerism but rather
to mobilise all opinion against the tithe system.[55] Similarly in their
statements concerning taxes and rents, Friends desired to reassure laymen
and authorities that their attack on tithes did not have any wider, more
sinister, implications. Ultimately their need to do this was probably
greater than their need to win the support of the rural bourgeoisie, for
their main secular argument against tithe rested on an easily
misunderstood interpretation of property rights.

Anthony Pearson, in *The Great Case of Tythes*, presents the most persua-
sive version of this argument. Although Pearson, himself a substantial
landowner, renounced Quakerism in around 1662, his definitive work was
republished by Friends nine times between 1657 and 1801.[56] That it still
held currency in the height of Quakerism's quietest period of conservative
respectability is indicative of the degree to which it faithfully reproduced
Friends' views of property.

Pearson's argument began with the coming of Christ and the abolition
of the Mosaic Law; however, throughout the rest of the book he
consistently returned to the question of property.[57] "Every man", said
Pearson "is the sole owner of his own labour and possession".[58] In
consequence of this every man was also sole owner of the "Increase or

Renewing" produced by virtue of his labour or property.[59] Tithe, representing as it did a claim to the tenth part of the annual increase of a man's stock or labour, was thus a claim against his property. Tithes could be upheld as a valid demand only if it could be shown that they too were held by a right of property. If this were the case, then "all scruples of conscience were answered, for if a true and legal property be in another person to the tenth of my increase, I ought in conscience to yield and set it forth, because it is not mine ...." [60] There was, however, no legal right to property in tithe. The laws which supported the tithing system were based on the (mistaken) assumption that "Tithes are due to God and Holy Church".[61] This assumption was disproved by Friends' crucial and fundamental argument that any spiritual claim to tithe had been lost with the abolition of the Old Law: subsequently the "popish" imposition of tithes rested on neither spiritual nor scriptural sanction. Thus,

> the Foundation of the Law being taken away, that they are not due to God and Holy Church, the Law falls to the Ground; for the Law not making them due, but supposing them due by former Right, if they were not so due, the Law cannot be binding.

The law could not be binding because of its function in a civil society. "The Law doth not give any Man a Property, either in Land or Tithes ... but only doth conserve to every Man his Property, which he hath in his Land and Possessions".[63]

Pearson's views were echoed by other Quaker propagandists. John Crook, like Pearson a former justice of the peace, followed Pearson's arguments in his *Tythes No Property*, published in 1659.[64] Property, he wrote, "is that which a man hath a just right to and interest in, without injury to another and is derived ... either by descent, purchase or gift and not by custom only ...." [65] Crook, like Pearson and many other of the Quaker writers quoted or invoked the Lollard William Thorpe extensively to support this view.[66] Ellwood argued that the owner or occupier of a piece of land purchased the whole of the profits or increase on that land that accrued by virtue of the expenditure of his labour (or property):

> he lays his Dung on all alike, he sows his Seed on all alike, he Plows all alike, he bestows Pain and Charge, and exercises his Skill and Care equally on all. Thus it appears that Tythes are really purchased by them, by whom the nine parts are purchased, and do really belong to them to whom the nine parts do belong.[67]

The consequence of this undermined any historical claim that might be made for tithes.

> A perpetual grant of Tythes implies a grant not only of other men's stock, in which the Granters had no property, but of other men's labours, care, skill, diligence and industry ...[68]

in which similarly no right could be claimed by custom; if such a right were allowed then all men had lost their freedom and "must be born slaves".[69]

Far from attacking property rights, the Quakers could claim to be arguing against tithe on the basis of a sustained defence of the right to property.[70] They were of course defending their own property rights, and those of other farmers and yeomen, at the expense of the parson. For him tithe was the property which provided his income.[71] The extent to which Friends were willing to take this is revealed in their attitude to lay impropriators. Pearson, who had himself purchased ecclesiastical estates and was thus probably as sensitive as any to the matter, denied that impropriators had any right to claim tithe.[72] However,

> seeing that it was the State that sold them, and that the whole Nation had the Benefit of their Moneys, it is equal and just, when they cannot have what is sold, that their Moneys be repaid.[73]

This repayment to impropriators would be funded by means of a general tax "wherein everyone must bear his Proportion, the very Impropriator himself" because all had benefited from the moneys which had originally gone to the state.[74] The collection of the tax would raise few problems, for as Hubberthorn explained, in the absence of tithes the population are "freely willing to part with Moneys for redeeming Impropriations".[75] Thus those who claimed a (mistaken) right to property in tithe through purchase would be offered compensation for any loss sustained by the abolition of tithes.

In their arguments against tithe which were based on property the Quakers reflected the basic assumptions of what C.B. Macpherson calls "possessive individualism".[76] These assumptions were "that man is free and human by virtue of his sole proprietorship of his own person, and that human society is essentially a series of market relations".[77]

Although writers as diverse as Hobbes and the Levellers shared these assumptions in varying degrees, it was in the writings of John Locke that they found their most articulate form.[78] In the stress that they laid on a man's labour as being a form of property, the Quakers shared Locke's view of property "in the bourgeois sense", as "not only a right to enjoy or use" but as "a right to dispose of, to exchange, to alienate".[79] According to Macpherson, "the free alienation of property, including the property in one's labour, by sale and purchase is an essential element of capitalist production".[80] Thus the very arguments that the Quakers were using to preserve property and abolish tithes in the pre- and post-Restoration periods were used by Locke in his *Two Treatises of Government*, published in 1690, to justify not only the Glorious Revolution, itself a revolution by the propertied classes for the propertied classes, but also the capitalist economy on which post-Revolution society would be based.[81] When Locke argued in 1688 that

> Man, by being Master of himself and proprietor of his own person and
> the actions or labour of it, had still in himself the great foundations of
> property,

he was echoing the earlier writings of Pearson which were still in
circulation amongst Friends, writings which themselves echoed the
Levellers and the Putney Debates.[83] Similarly, when Locke justified civil
society on the basis that it was formed by men coming together in order to
establish an authority to protect their property, he was sharing Pearson's
view that the law "only doth conserve to every man his Property".[84] In view
of this, the assertion that the Quakers in their action on tithes wished to
overthrow the social order must be treated with considerable reservation.

Yet for historians who have studied the tithe question and the Quaker
attitude to it, the overturning implication of Friends' philosophy seems
inevitable. Margaret James has argued that a "direct menace to society
arose through the close connection between tithes and other property".[85]
Barry Reay shows that a result of Quaker agitation was "to reinforce the
conviction of the propertied that opposition to tithes was the harbinger of
levelling, and to confirm suspicions that the Quakers were dangerous
social radicals".[86] For Christopher Hill the attack on tithes threatened the
concept of a state church, deprived the gentry of a variety of property
rights and undermined the financing of the universities.[87] The refusal to
pay tithes was synonymous with a refusal to pay rents.[88] Michael Mullett,
on a more general level, writes that "The primary expression of Quaker
disaffection was permanent hostility to the Church, though as the laws
made it plain that this Church was inseparable from state and society, so
state and society were necessarily involved in the Quaker repudiation of
the Establishment".[89] Nowhere, of course, was this permanent hostility
better expressed than in the refusal to pay tithes. But as we have seen,
when they used secular arguments the Quakers argued against tithes not as
part of an attack on property or the social order, but rather from a defence
of a certain definition of property rights, rights which they considered to
be the basis of civil society.

As we have seen, the logical conclusion of the Quakers' argument, as it
appeared both to most of their contemporaries and to current historians,
was that the attack on tithes ultimately led to an attack on all property
rights and consequently the social order. However, this was not a view
shared by the Friends themselves, whose logical reasoning led them to
another conclusion. This was that tithes, the maintained ministry and by
implication the Established Church (neither of whom, as the Quakers had
shown, had a right to the property they claimed in tithe) could be abolished without disturbing the social equilibrium.[90] Those lay impropriators
who had purchased a right to tithes would be duly compensated for any
loss they sustained.

Only in this way could property, particularly the property of the
"middling sort", and consequently the social order, be maintained. With

property thus preserved from the unjust, unequal, and illegal claims made upon it by the Church, the social order was safe and the free market economy would flourish. In addition, the disestablishment of the Church would allow Friends and others to enjoy fully another property, that of their conscience. Although Hugh Barbour was shocked by William Penn's articulation of this view – the identification of property with conscience – seeing it as a product of the material sufferings imposed upon Friends by the Second Conventicle Act, Penn was doing no more than extending the secular arguments which Quaker propagandists had presented against tithe.[91] "I am sure", wrote Penn, "'twas to enjoy Property with conscience that (Protestantism) was promoted, nor is there any better Definition of Protestancy, than protesting against spoiling Property for Conscience".[92] It was never the intention of the Quakers to overturn property rights, let alone what they perceived as the social order. For Friends, property was the basis of the established legal authority to which they looked for preservation of both their civil and spiritual rights. As they were later to prove, the Quakers were the bastion of the propertied classes.

It remains to be seen how far the arguments presented by Quaker polemicists both to Friends and the world were reflected in the views of Friends themselves. A source which enables us to consider the objections to the tithing system presented by many Quakers in Lancashire, is the collection of tithe testimonies contained in the archive of Lancashire Quarterly Meeting. It should be stressed from the outset that this collection is incomplete, and the problem of missing data makes it unsuitable for any form of rigorous statistical analysis.[93] The system of collecting the testimonies grew out of the discipline enforced by Meetings in respect of tithe payments. In 1669, for example, two Friends from Swarthmore Monthly Meeting were ordered to "inquire of the faithful- ness of Friends in their testimonies against tithes … and to give an account thereof at the next Monthly Meeting".[94] Similarly, the Quarterly Meeting for the county ordered that each Particular Meeting should appoint a number of Friends "to go to all Friends of their Meeting and know their clearness in their testimony for God in denying to pay tithes". The Friends so instructed were "to bring up their particular answers to the next Quarterly Meeting".[95] By 1674 the system of collecting individual testimonies, rather than simply inquiring as to the maintenance of the discipline, seems to have been established. In September the Quarterly Meeting ordered

> that every Monthly Meeting within this county do take care to bring in their testimonies concerning their clearness against tithes against the next Quarterly Meeting, and further that every Monthly Meeting do take care that every Particular Meeting appoint a Meeting of Friends upon some day in the week for the end that Friends that are concerned in tithes or anything tending to that priesthood may give in their testimonies of their clearness[96]

Five years later the procedure was fixed: Particular Meetings first collected the testimonies, they were then taken to the Monthly Meeting where they were checked and "perfected" and thence to the Quarterly Meeting, to "be recorded in a book there to be kept".[97]

A parallel system of collecting testimonies from women Friends was developed by the Women's Quarterly Meeting. The first recorded minute in the Women's Quarterly Meeting Minute Book, dated 4th month, 1675, ordered

> that there be some women from every Particular Meeting in the county, at every General Women's Meeting, [i.e. Quarterly Meeting] to give an account, how things are in every Meeting, and that they bring in testimonies touching the payment of tithes … so all may be kept in good order.[98]

By 1675 at the latest, the testimonies were being recorded together in "the General Women's Meeting Book". As the testimonies accumulated, so it was decided that "there will not be a necessity to bring them in writing every year", rather that

> where any are convinced, they are to give in their testimonies in writing against tithes etc to be recorded with the rest, that so all may be kept in good order, and that we may stand one by another and join in our testimony for Christ Jesus, our redeemer and saviour.[99]

Thus the testimonies came to be regarded as the equivalent of a solemn statement of membership.[100] Were they complete, the testimonies of both the Men's and Women's Quarterly Meetings would provide the equivalent of a list of members for the county, some fifty years before the concept of membership is generally acknowledged to have been defined and accepted amongst Friends.[101] It was in 1737, the same year that membership was defined, that London Yearly Meeting recommended that the practice of collecting testimonies, used in "several parts of the nation", be generally adopted throughout the country.[102]

The original book of the Men's Quarterly Meeting in which tithe testimonies were recorded has not survived in the Meeting's archive. Instead, various pages from this book can be found bound in with volume 1 of the Quarterly Meeting Minute Book and in the first Lancaster Monthly Meeting Minute Book.[103] In addition, various loose papers containing rough (and possibly the original) copies of testimonies are contained in bundles of documents dealing with tithe matters.[104] The women's tithe testimonies are included in the first Women's Quarterly Meeting Minute Book.[105] For the whole of the county there are 630 male testimonies recorded between 1679 and 1703: for women Friends there are 778 testimonies which were recorded between 1675 and 1710.[106] These totals, particularly those for the women's testimonies, contain a number of statements from the same individual brought in and recorded at different dates. Thus the actual totals for the number of individuals bringing in testimonies would be less than those given above. In addition there are omissions in the testimonies brought in from various parts of the county. This appears to have been caused either through non-survival, as in the case of the Cartmel Meeting, or faulty and casual recording procedures, as in the case of Manchester Meeting.[107] In addition, although the last recorded male testimony is dated 1703, the various minute books make it clear that testimonies were brought to the Meetings and recorded after this date.[108] The same is the case for the Women's Meetings.[109] Nonetheless, those testimonies which have survived provide a graphic portrayal of the reasons held by Quakers in Lancashire for not paying tithe.

The elaborate denunciation of the tithing system, given by Margaret Fell's son-in-law Thomas Lower of Marsh Grange near Ulverston, is typical for its content rather than its length and style:

> From the beginning of my convincement and conversion to the Truth, by and in which my understanding was and is illuminated, I have seen that the legal right and claim the priests and levites had to tithes is of the old law and covenant, was abolished, ended and determined by Christ offering up himself once as a sacrifice and a ransom for all mankind, who being the substance of the new covenant ended all types and shadows of the old. And in my measure being a witness that Jesus Christ the substance is come in the flesh and manifested in me by his light and spirit, grace and truth, which is come by him, therefore I cannot uphold nor maintain the old priests, nor the old law, which gave them their tithes, nor any novice upstart priest that derived a right, or claim to tithes from the Jew's old law, lest I be found denying Christ that bought me, with the dearest price of his own precious blood, but have and still do, and I trust ever shall while I have a being here, deny the payment of tithe, or any other paying for me, and all steeple-house or church-rates, the market houses of the priest, which as the truth and knowledge of the Lord increases, will decay and tumble down, as the idol's temples of old did when the shepherd and bishop of souls did appear. Which is the full belief and testimony for the Lord, of him who knows himself to be under the new covenant and the law of words.
>
> Thomas Lower.[110]

Christopher Simson of Swarthmore offered a crisp denial of the same import, "I pay no tithes nor steeplehouse lays, nor none for me with my consent, but bear my testimony against it knowing the priesthood is changed, and Christ Jesus is come, of which I am a witness".[111]

The importance of the coming of Christ and the consequent abolition of tithes was predominant in the testimonies recorded in Lancashire. For Friends it was vital to "witness in measure the one offering ever, Christ Jesus come" which "puts an end to all offerings, tithes as well as others".[112]

It was precisely because Christ "hath enlightened my understanding and brought me to see that false priesthood which does receive tithes and other offerings" that John Moone of Wyreside, as with many other Friends, was led to refuse their payment.[113] When Henry Lampe of Swarthmore gave in his testimony in 1698 it was because to do otherwise seemed "an implicit denial or at least an undervaluing of" Christ, who had "put an end to all Mosaical rites, shadows and lies".[114]

Of almost equal concern to Friends was the historical origin of the specific tithing system they suffered under. James Smith, from Fylde, was "willing to bear my testimony against all those things set up by the Pope in the dark night of apostacy ...."[115] Christopher Thornton's analysis of the Romish origins of the tithing system given in by Wray Meeting in 1702, breathed the millenial expectations of the earliest Friends:

> I testify against tithes as an antichristian custom introduced by the Pope in the dark night of apostacy and continued by those who notwithstanding their specious pretences of reformation are found in the same spirit with them who set up these idolatrous practices by the spirit and power of antichrist, and seeing it hath pleased the Lord to let me see that tithes was so brought in, I hope he will so preserve me in a clear testimony against these antichristian impositions upheld by the power of darkness.[116]

Mary Taylor of Cartmel similarly testified against "all idolatrous worships in the world ... for in the light, life and power the Lord God is about to establish his truth, and to reign over all tithe payers and tithe receivers".[117] For the most part, those Lancashire Quakers whose tithe testimonies have survived were concerned to witness the coming of Christ through non-payment of tithes, and to testify against the unreformed nature of the Anglican Church which depended upon "popish" imposition for its financial support. Clearly, though, the tithe issue, and more acutely than any other, focused Quaker attention on an eschatological scheme. If the Inner Light did not always lead to this position, then it could be arrived at through a literal interpretation of the scriptures. According to the brothers Thomas and Richard Hynd of Wray Meeting, "as we do not read neither do we believe that the apostles either took tithes or payed tithes but as they had freely received they freely ministered therefore we cannot pay tithes ...."[118]

In a number of cases Friends revealed an objection, possibly secular, to tithes that pre-dated their conversion to Quakerism. Margaret Holmes of Knowsley Meeting paid "no tithes, nor steeplehouse lays", and "did believe it was not right to pay them before I came to meetings".[119] Bridget Soraw of Cartmel Meeting, in a testimony given in 1712 "had a testimony in my heart against tithes before I came among Friends".[120] Elizabeth Lucas of Blackrod Meeting simply explained that "I never paid tithes in all my life".[121] These, however, were exceptional instances, and in the majority of testimonies Friends stressed the importance of conversion in shaping their attitudes to the tithing system. Jane Cannby of Knowsley had not paid tithe "ever since convinced of the blessed Truth".[122] Henry Clare of Sankey had not paid tithe "since the Lord God by his heavenly gift has so far opened my understanding".[123] Similarly, John Chorley of the same Meeting had refused "since I was convinced of God's Truth".[124]

A few Friends revealed clearly expressed social, along with scriptural, objections to the payment of tithe. "Tithes in the first covenant", wrote James Harmson of Coppull, "Was the portion of the tribe of Levi ... and the widow, fatherless and poor strangers was relieved out of them so that there was no beggars". The current system was thus wrong in its "rise and end".[125] Thomas Fletcher of Lancaster complained that the clergy "make a prey of widows' goods for what they call their dues as tithes". "They have not", he added, "received their ministry without money and therefore cannot give it without the same".[126] George Benson of Hawkshead had "suffered imprisonment for not paying tithes ... because I could not satisfy those who claim a right to the tenth part of my labours ...."[127] Mary Flemming of Cartmel refused to give her "labour for that which satisfied not", a return to the idea discussed earlier, of payment for services rendered.[128] Basic social objections to the whole system were expressed by Isobel Dillworth who believed that "tithes are unequal" and her sister, Elizabeth, who believed that "tithes are very unequal".[129] Other Friends, such as Mary Ratcliffe, simply wished to express their objection to tithes and testify to the material sufferings to which this could lead. "I do not pay tithes", she wrote, "hoping never to be of that mind, for the denying of which the bailiff, this year, has taken my petticoats".[130]

In their emphasis on the theological and historical basis of the Quaker objection to the tithing system the surviving tithe testimonies of the Lancashire Friends entirely contradict Dr. Reay's argument concerning the predominance of secular arguments in Quaker thought on this matter.[131] Neither did the Lancashire Friends reveal a hostility towards the social order, although, as mentioned above, their hostility towards the established Church, clearly articulated in the testimonies, could ultimately lead to a repudiation of the Establishment.[132] Rather the use of secular arguments against tithe was generally confined to the published writings of Quaker propagandists, and in particular in the writing of those who addressed themselves less to Friends and more to the world at large. Typical of these was the often quoted Anthony Pearson, whose concern with functional arguments against tithe was unrepresentative of Friends' views. Even then, Pearson's arguments, far from being hostile to the social order, were in fact a sober defence of all property rights against illegal incursions, particularly by the Church. Perhaps more representative of the arguments of Quakers, at least in Lancashire, against the tithing system are those contained in the testimony of John Fell of Swarthmore:

These are to certify where it may come that I do pay no tithes, neither any for me, nor any steeple-house rates, for in the strength of him, that has manifested them, never intend to pay anything of that nature, that priesthood being ended which was for a time and did serve, till the good Christ Jesus came, which is come many years since, and now in these later days had he who is priest for ever raised up Apostles to bear a testimony against them, who put an end to all outward offerings whatsoever by offering up himself, once for all praise be unto this high priest for ever; and this is it which lives in me and in my desire that I and every one that profess the name of him and his truth may bear a living testimony for him against tithes and other things which is in measure to many made manifest.[133]

There was clearly, at least at one level, an interaction between Quaker propagandists and Friends in the counties. The Lancashire tithe testimonies suggest that many Friends there borrowed heavily from the likes of Pearson and Ellwood in order to elaborate their objections to the tithing system. A few examples here must suffice, but similarities are clear in those already quoted above. Henry Clare from Sankey may well have read Foxe's *Book of Martyrs*, but his reference to William Thorpe (a favourite subject for Quaker writers) in his tithe testimonies suggests a debt owed to Pearson's *Great Case of Tithes*.[134] Clare wrote that his testimony was "the same with the several of the martyrs in Queen Mary's days as to William Thorpe for one who was burned for the testimony of a good conscience".[135] Pearson had written of "our famous Reformers, John Wickliffe, William Brute, William Thorpe, and others", who "did in their Days bear their Testimony against Tithes, for which some of them suffered in the Flames".[136] Pearson had also explained in his book that Jesus, neither "of the Tribe of Levi nor consecrated after the order of Aaron", had abolished tithes; Mary Bispham from Bickerstaffe wrote in her testimony that Christ has ended tithes, being "not after the order of Aaron".[137] This repetition of material may in part be a consequence of the fact that both authors and the givers of tithe testimonies were drawing on a limited pool of suitable scriptural and historical materials. In addition, Friends in Lancashire may have been able to draw from memory on a restricted number of themes and phrases which were apparently repeated in the public-speaking of ministering Friends.[138] Whatever the reason, the Lancashire tithe testimonies show a strong correlation with the works of Quaker polemicists in the use of scriptural and historical references.

The testimonies retained, however, a strong degree of personal commitment against the tithing system. As we have seen, this was frequently accompanied by an urgent eschatological note, even in the eighteenth century. Although the declarations may have been elaborated by scriptural and historical references (possibly cribbed from popular Quaker authors) they remained in essence statements, testimonies, of individual belief. Nor should we expect anything different from a group who believed "that Christians are always led inwardly and immediately by the spirit of God dwelling in them; and that the same is a standing and perpetual ordinance".[139] Christopher Thornton could have picked up the phrase, that tithes were "an antichristian custom introduced by the pope in the dark night of apostacy", from any number of Quaker sources. But the import of his testimony lay not in this but rather in that "it hath pleased the Lord to let *me* see that tithes was so brought in".[140] Mary Rosthorn from Rossendale argued that "the Lord *I have found* to be a better priest than that which received tithes".[141] Richard Armistead of Twisden, drawing on his own previous experience, refused to pay clerics who never "did *me* any good as to *my* soul's health".[142] Henry Lampe was concerned that the payment of tithes "seemeth to *me* an implicit denial" of Christ's coming.[143] Margaret Dawson from Hawkshead, "seeing how it is with me in this matter, [found] rest and peace because the Lord has required *me* to give *my* testimony against tithes".[144] Christopher Duckworth, from Chipping, had been "persuaded in *my* heart ever since I knew the Truth" that tithes ought not to be paid.[145]

The Quakers constructed a complex, although not always convincing, set of arguments against the tithing system to present to the world. They attacked the legality of tithes primarily on the grounds of scriptural and historical precedent, adding a number of purely secular arguments, the most important of which related to their individualistic concept of property rights. Although this view of property threatened the Church's right to maintain itself through tithes, it presented no threat to society. Friends were preaching the sanctity of private property within the context of the modern secular state which so many of their ideas and attitudes demanded.[146] In a state which still relied in part on spiritual sanction for its legitimacy the Quaker view of property was seen as a threat which had to be countered, regardless of any considerations of toleration. In Lancashire the denial of tithes was used by Friends as a badge of membership, and they consequently devised a typically elaborate scheme for recording testimonies against tithe. Although they shared and reproduced many of the arguments presented by the propagandists, the Lancashire Friends revealed in their testimonies an underlying individual opposition to tithes.

We shall see in the following chapter how this theoretical opposition was put into practice.

REFERENCES

1. For a background to the tithing system in Europe see Joseph Goy's essay on 'Methodology' in Emmanuel Le Roy Ladurie and Joseph Goy, *Tithe and Agrarian History from the Fourteenth to the Nineteenth Centuries* (Cambridge, 1982), pp.14–24. Christopher Hill deals with the English background in *Economic Problems of the Church* (Oxford, 1956), chapters 5–6, *passim*. This is also dealt with by Rosemary O'Day, *The English Clergy, the Emergence and Consolidation of a Profession* (Leicester, 1979), pp.190–98. Margaret James, in 'The Political Importance of the Tithe Controversy in the English Revolution 1640–1660', *History*, 26 (1941), pp.1–18, discusses the general

opposition to tithes during the Revolution period. In *The Contentious Tithe* (London, 1976), Eric Evans deals with the tithe problem from 1750 to 1850. Dr. Evans' Ph.D. thesis, 'A History of the Tithe System in England, 1690–1750, with Specific Reference to Staffordshire' (University of Warwick, 1970), deals also with the earlier eighteenth century, chapter 5 being devoted to a study of Quakers and tithe payments in Staffordshire. This is expanded upon in Eric Evans, '"Our Faithful Testimony" The Society of Friends and Tithe Payments, 1690–1730', *JFHS*, 52 (1962), pp.106–21. The most recent work on Quakers and the tithe question is Barry Reay, "Quaker Opposition to Tithes, 1652–1660", *Past and Present*, 86 (1980), pp.98–120

2. For the many accounts of violence used in tithe seizures, see LQMS, vols.1 and 2, *passim.*; Evans, ' "Our Faithful Testimony" ', pp.109–10

3. See, for example, the case of John Proctor of Wyreside, whose Anglican brother-in-law, Richard Hathornwaite had paid tithes to the vicar of Lancaster for several years prior to 1679 "under a fear, lest this wicked priest … should endeavour to ruin me". Proctor condemned and testified against Hathornwaite's actions, as did William Baines and Thomas Hathornwaite, two other Friends whom he had attempted to assist: LQMM, vol.1, T/T: Wyreside, 13/5/1679

4. As Thomas Ellwood argued, "Do not the Quakers know beforehand that if they refuse to pay tithe, they incur the penalty of treble damages which by that time it is levied seldom comes to less than five or six times the single value of the tithes demanded, besides imprisonment. Is this the way to save charges?", *The Foundation of Tythes Shaken* (n.p., 1678), p.265

5. Dr. Evans has argued to the contrary that "There can be no doubt that many Quakers were able to avoid payment of any tithe without damage either to their conscience or their pocket": '"Our Faithful Testimony"', p.113. John Haydock, who died in 1719, was the last Lancashire Friend to do so whilst imprisoned for non-payment of tithes: see, LYMM, vol.5, p.406, 1720

6. Amongst the definitions given for the word "suffering" in the *Shorter Oxford English Dictionary* one refers explicitly to the prosecution or persecution of Quakers for non-payment of tithe

7. Reay, 'Quaker Opposition to Tithes', p.105. Dr. Reay's statement was made in response to a contrary statement made by M.G.F. Bitterman in 'The Early Quaker Literature of Defence', *Church History*, 42 (1973), p.211, that the Quakers' main arguments were scriptural. Ms. Bitterman's conclusions were based on a quantitative analysis of early Quaker writings

8. See below pp.339–40

9. Although Dr. Reay's title confines him to the period 1652–1660 he cites authors such as Francis Howgill, *The Great Case of Tythes … Once More Revived* (London, 1665), Thomas Ellwood, *The Foundation of Tythes Shaken* (London, 1678), and Thomas Rudyard and William Gibson, *Tythes, Ended by Christ* (London, 1673): 'Quaker Opposition to Tithes', p.105, n.39; p.106, n.40; p.107, n.48

10. Other smaller collections of testimonies have been located by researchers; see Hugh Barbour, *The Quakers in Puritan England* (London, 1964), p.175; Helen Forde, 'Derbyshire Quakers 1650–1761' (University of Leicester, Ph.D. thesis, 1977), p.154

11. Barbour, *The Quakers in Puritan England*, pp.83–84; *Second Period*, pp.376–77

12. This subject is dealt with at length by B.G. Blackwood, 'Agrarian Unrest and

the Early Lancashire Quakers', *JFHS*, 51 (1965), pp.72–76; see also Barbour, *The Quakers in Puritan England*, pp.83–84 and Reay, 'Quaker Opposition to Tithes', pp.100–104

13. This was a view Quakers shared with many critics of the tithing system, notably Selden; Ellwood, *Foundation of Tythes Shaken*, p.88

14. This view is formed by a wide reading of seventeenth and eighteenth century Quaker pamphlets and books. It is supported by Ms. Bitterman's quantitative analysis, see above, n.9

15. Margaret Fell, *A Brief Collection*, pp.444–45

16. Ellwood, *Foundation of Tythes Shaken*, p.515

17. Richard Hubberthorn, *A Reply to a Book set forth by the Priest of Berwick ....* (1654), in *A Collection*, pp.10–11

18. Anthony Pearson, *The Great Case of Tithes* (London, 6th ed., 1732), p.4. So, as we have seen, Friends argued that the liberation of Christ's coming, renewed in the Reformation, freed them from obedience to coercive laws whose basis lay either in the Old Testament, or in papal innovation

19. Ellwood, *Foundation of Tythes Shaken*, p.66

20. Pearson, *Great Case of Tithes*, p.5

21. Ellwood, *Foundation of Tythes Shaken*, p.147

22. Margaret Fell, *A Touch-Stone: or, A Tryal by the Scriptures of the Priests, Bishops, and Ministers etc* (1667), in *A Brief Collection*, p.437

23. "By means of such historical analysis radical religionists were able to condemn the magisterial churches of the Protestant Reformation as being fundamentally unreformed": Michael Mullett, *Radical Religious Movements* (London, 1980), p.136

24. Hill, *Economic Problems of the Church*, p.162

25. Ellwood, *Foundation of Tythes Shaken*, pp.306–07

26. Dr. Reay suggests that Quakers did not "distinguish between the spiritual and the temporal in their refusal to pay", 'Quaker Opposition to Tithes', p.107

27. Ellwood, *Foundation of Tythes Shaken*, p.222

28. *ibid.*

29. *ibid.* p.513

30. Henry Mollineux, *Antichrist Unvailed by the Finger of God's Power* (London, 1695), p.157

31. Ellwood, *Foundation of Tythes Shaken*, pp.306–07

32. *ibid.* p.451: Pearson, *Great Case of Tithes*, p.6, 7. The omission of poor relief was a common complaint against the tithing system; see, for example, Felicity Heal, 'Economic Problems of the Clergy', in Felicity Heal and Rosemary O'Day, *Church and Society in England, Henry VIII to James I* (London, 1977), p.100. For the threefold division of tithes see Evans, *The Contentious Tithe*, p.17 and p.37, n.6

33. Ellwood, *Foundation of Tythes Shaken*, p.451

34. Margaret Fell, *A Touch Stone*, in *A Brief Collection*, p.439

35. Richard Hubberthorn, *The Real Cause of the Nation's Bondage and Slavery* (1659), in *A Collection*, pp.218–19

36. Reay, 'Quaker Opposition to Tithes', p.105

37. Evans, 'A History of the Tithe System in England', pp.1–2

38. Ellwood argued that "Priests do not labour spiritually for the Quakers" but rather "do often labour against them", *Foundation of Tythes Shaken*, p.433

39. Richard Hubberthorn, *Truth and Innocency, clearing itself and its Children* (1657), in *A Collection*, p.47

40. Margaret Fell, 'Abstract of a Letter given by M F to the King at Hampton Court, 1662', in *A Brief Collection*, p.37

41. Hubberthorn, *The Real Cause of the Nations Bondage*, in *A Brief Collection*, p.220

42. For Quaker views on the legitimacy of taxation see above, chapter 1

43. Ellwood, *Foundation of Tythes Shaken*, p.465

44. Pearson, *Great Case of Tithes*, p.40

45. *ibid.* p.59. Pearson added, however, "its hoped, our State rather looks at the Freedom of the People, than the increase of the Revenue ....", *ibid.* p.60

46. John Raven, *The Substance of a Discourse ... Concerning Tithes* (London, 1701), p.1

47. Ellwood, *Foundation of Tythes Shaken*, pp.317–18, 399

48. *ibid.* p.318

49. Hill, *Economic Problems of the Church*, pp.81–90

50. Evans, *Our Faithful Testimony*, p.113. Richard Vann has argued that "it is easy to observe the withdrawal of Friends from the countryside" during the late seventeenth and early eighteenth centuries, a trend partly caused by the difficulties that tithe demands presented to rural and isolated Friends. Although his argument is partly vitiated by the manner in which he described the predominantly agriculturally based village of Adderbury in Oxfordshire as a town, whose development as a Quaker centre typified this "urbanising" trend, there is nonetheless much in what he says. However in Lancashire, where Friends remained concentrated in rural settlements such as Yealand or Coppull, the mixed nature of the economy guaranteed that most Quakers faced tithe demands. Even urban Friends such as William Stout were liable to the payment of small tithes. Richard T. Vann, *The Social Development of English Quakerism 1655–1755* (Cambridge, Mass., 1969), pp.163–65. For the mixed North-West economy see for example W. King, 'The Economic and Demographic Development of Rossendale' (University of Leicester, Ph.D. thesis, 1979), p.60: "most local farmers had some income from textiles by-employment, whilst the majority of textile workers had some agricultural by-employment"; J.V. Beckett, 'Landownership in Cumbria c.1680–1750' (University of Lancaster, Ph.D. thesis, 1975), p.154: "the yeomanry's increasing wealth must have originated from non-agricultural sources of income"; For William Stout see *Stout*, pp.292–93

51. Pearson, *Great Case of Tithes*, pp.vii, 64

52. Ellwood, *Foundation of Tythes Shaken*, p.514

53. Pearson, *Great Case of Tithes*, p.64

54. This letter is transcribed in full in Appendix 2. See also, for example, Barclay, *Apology*, p.517 and p.533, where he offers the following rationalisation of economic inequality: "we shall not say, that all Persons are to be cloathed alike, because it will perhaps neither suit their Bodies, nor their Estates. And if a Man be cloathed soberly, and without superfluity, tho' they may be finer than that which his Servant is cloathed with, we shall not blame him for it. The abstaining from superfluities, which his Condition and Education have accustomed him to, may be in him a greater Act of Modification, than the abstaining from finer cloathes in the Servant, who never was accustomed to them". See also Barbour, *The Quakers in Puritan England*, pp.249–50

55. Hence the book's dedication, p.vii
56. *DNB*; Joseph Smith, *Catalogue of Friends Books* (2 vols., London, 1867), vol.2, pp.275–76
57. Pearson, *Great Case of Tithes*, p.4
58. *ibid*. p.33
59. *ibid*. p.46
60. *ibid*. p.28
61. *ibid*. p.38; Ellwood, *Foundations of Tythes Shaken*, pp.513–14
62. Pearson, *Great Case of Tithes*, p.38
63. *ibid*. p.37
64. *Second Period*, pp.358–59
65. John Crook, *Tythes No Property* (London, 1659), p.1
66. *ibid*. pp.5–8; Pearson, *Great Case of Tithes*, p.24
67. Ellwood, *Foundation of Tythes Shaken*, p.420
68. *ibid*. p.355
69. *ibid*.
70. For this view see Alan Cole, 'The Quakers and the English Revolution', in T.H. Aston (ed.), *Crisis in Europe, 1560–1660* (London, 1965), p.347
71. It was argued in the House of Lords in 1736 that the "incumbent has generally, by law, a right to the tythes within his parish, he has as much a property in them as any man in the parish has to the estate he enjoys": *Parliamentary History*, vol.9, p.1185
72. He had purchased Manors at Aspatria, Cumberland and Marrowlee, Northumberland, "with other delinquent estates" in 1650, *DNB*
73. Pearson, *Great Case of Tithes*, p.56
74. *ibid*. p.62
75. Richard Hubberthorn, *The Good Old Cause Briefly Demonstrated* (London, 1659), p.12
76. See C.B. Macpherson, *The Political Theory of Possessive Individualism* (Oxford, 1962), *passim*.
77. *ibid*. p.270
78. *ibid*. p.321
79. *ibid*. pp.214–15
80. *ibid*. p.219
81. For this view see Angus McInnes, 'The Revolution and the People', in Geoffrey Holmes (ed.), *Britain After the Glorious Revolution* (London, 1969), pp.80–95
82. John Locke, *The Second Treatise of Government* (ed. J.W. Gough, Oxford, 1956), p.24
83. See, for example, the speech by Captain Clarke during the Putney Debates, who argued that "the Law of Nature does give a principle for every man to have a property of what he has, or may have, which is not another man's": A.S.P. Woodhouse (ed.), *Puritanism and Liberty* (London, 2nd. ed., 1974), p.75. C.B. Macpherson noted that the "proprietorial quality of the Leveller's individualism ... was ... at first sight, even more extreme than Locke's", *The Political Theory of Possessive Individualism*, p.142
84. C.B. Macpherson, 'The Social Bearing of Locke's Political Theory', *The Western Political Quarterly*, 7 (1954), p.11; Pearson, *Great Case of Tithes*, p.37
85. James, 'Political Importance of the Tithe Controversy', p.6
86. Reay, 'Quaker Opposition to Tithes', p.117

87. Christopher Hill, *The World Turned Upside Down* (Pelican ed., London, 1975), p.99
88. Hill, *Economic Problems of the Church*, p.164
89. Mullett, *Radical Religious Movements*, p.84
90. This is reflected in the Quaker distinction between the civil and the spiritual
91. Barbour, *The Quakers in Puritan England*, pp.245–45
92. Quoted from Ralph Perry, *Puritanism and Democracy* (New York, 1964), p.297, in Barbour, *The Quakers in Puritan England*, p.246
93. A table of those testimonies surviving in given in Appendix 3
94. SMMM, vol. 1, 9/9/1669; the first recorded minute of Lancaster Monthly Meeting "ordered that Henry Coward and William Gunson should see and be careful to bring in Friends' testimonies against tithes or steeple-house dues ... and to bring their answers up in writing to the next Monthly Meeting" LMMM, vol.1, 20/8/1675
95. LQMM, vol.1, 24/7/1673
96. *ibid*. 30/7/1674
97. *ibid*. 2/5/1679
98. LWQMM, vol.1, 25/4/1675
99. SWMMM, vol.1, 5/8/1675; LWQMM, vol.1, 2/5/1679
100. All Friends were required to give in their testimonies, regardless of whether or not tithes were demanded of them, see for example, the testimony of Richard Coward, LQMM, vol.1, Fylde, 4th mo. 1679
101. Richard T. Vann, *The Social Development of English Quakerism 1655–1755* (Cambridge Mass., 1969), pp.155–56. The importance of the tithe testimonies to Friends is reflected in the exact arrangements made for their collection; this tends to support the view that the testimonies represented statements of membership (of a suffering community) and thus the arrangements are described here in some detail.
102. LFMH, 2Ai:40, Yearly Meeting Epistle, 1737
103. LQMM, vol.1, 1669–1711; LMMM, vol.1, 1675–1718
104. These are LFMH, 2Bxv:l; 2Bxv:2, 2Bxv:3, 2Bxv:5; 2Bxv:6; 2Bxv:7; 2Bxv:25; 2Bxv:48; 2Bxv:50
105. LWQMM, vol.1, 1675–1777
106. See Appendix 3
107. Only 2 testimonies for men from Cartmel Meeting survive in LFMH: in 1674 the Quarterly Meeting complained of Manchester Friends' "neglect in coming to the Quarterly Meeting with the rest of Friends in the county to give in your testimony concerning your faithfulness in denying to pay tithes ....". LQMM, vol.1, 30/10/1674
108. See, for example, LQMM, vol.2, 1/11/1712
109. See, for example, LWQMM, vol.1, 20/2/1738
110. LQMM, vol. 1, T/T: Swarthmore, 4th mo. 1679
111. *ibid*.
112. *ibid*.: Yealand, 4th mo. 1679, testimony of Richard Lancaster
113. *ibid*.: Wyreside, 4th mo. 1679
114. *ibid*.: Swarthmore, 3/10/1698
115. *ibid*.: Fylde, 4th mo. 1679
116. LM, vol.1, T/T: Wray, 2/10/1702
117. LWQMM, vol.1, T/T: Cartmel, 23/7/1675
118. LMMM, vol.1, T/T: Wray, 1690

119. LWQMM, vol.1, T/T: Knowsley, 1678
120. *ibid.*: Cartmel, 1712
121. *ibid.*: Blackrod, 1675
122. *ibid.*: Knowsley, 1678
123. LFMH, 2Bxv: 3, T/T: Sanky, 8/7/1679
124. LQMM, vol.1, T/T: Sankey, 30/4/1679
125. *ibid.*: Coppull, 4th mo. 1679
126. *ibid.*: Lancaster, n.d. (1679?)
127. *ibid.*: Hawkshead, 4th mo 1679
128. LWQMM, vol.1, T/T: Cartmel, 1678
129. *ibid.*: Chipping, 17/7/1675
130. *ibid.*: Rossendale, 1675
131. Reay, 'Quaker Opposition to Tithes', p.105
132. Mullett, Radical Religious Movements, p.84
133. LQMM, vol.1, T/T: Swarthmore, 4th mo. 1679
134. For a few of many references to Thorpe see Pearson, *Great Case of Tithes*, p.24: *Reasons given for refusing to pay Tithe to Priests or Impropriators*, (n.p., 1700?), p.1; Henry Mollineux *Antichrist Unvailed*, pp.156–57; Ellwood, *Foundation of Tythes Shaken*, pp.322–25; John Crook, *Tythes No Property*, pp.5–8
135. LFMH, 2Bxv:3, T/T: Sankey, 8/7/1679
136. Pearson, *Great Case of Tithes*, p.24
137. *ibid.* p.4; LWQMM, vol.1, T/T: Bickerstaffe, 1678
138. Richard Bauman, *Let Your Words Be Few, Symbolism and speaking and silence among seventeenth-century Quakers* (Cambridge, 1983), pp.74–78
139. *Apology*, p.47
140. LMMM, vol.1, T/T: Wrea, 2/10/1702 (my emphasis)
141. LWQMM, vol.1, T/T: Rossendale, 1675 (my emphasis)
142. LQMM, vol.1, T/T: Twisden, 18/4/1679 (my emphasis)
143. *ibid.*: Swarthmore, 3/10/1698 (my emphasis)
144. LWQMM, vol.1, T/T: Cartmel, 23/7/1675 (my emphasis)
145. LQMM, vol.1, T/T: Chipping 10/6/1679 (my emphasis)
146. This point is discussed earlier in this chapter

6

Distraint and Discipline: Lancashire Tithe Sufferings 1660–1740

The general pattern of Quaker tithe sufferings in Lancashire between 1650 and 1690 has been established by the work of the late Alan B. Anderson.[1] Anderson's analysis of all sufferings during this period was made from three volumes of transcripts of material contained in the first volume of the Lancashire Quarterly Meeting Book of Sufferings (LQMS). These transcripts had been made by Giles Howson, then curator of the archive at the Lancaster Friends Meeting House.[2] While some of Anderson's conclusions (particularly those concerning Quaker attitudes to unsolicited assistance from the community aimed at reducing the severity of prosecutions or distraints for tithe) are vitiated by his lack of access to the various Quarterly and Monthly Meeting minute-books contained in the archive, his analysis of the sufferings remains a pioneering piece of work.[3] In all, Anderson identified 1,203 sufferings of which 525, or 43%, involved tithe.[4] Anderson observed that throughout his period the emphasis of the sufferings shifted quickly away from imprisonment for offences towards fines and distraints. Financial penalties, he noted, could be just as crippling as incarceration.[5] Part of the explanation for the trend he observed was the gradual increase in tithe cases over the forty years he studied, from some 10% of all cases in the years 1650–1659 to 91% in the years 1685–1690. Of the 525 tithe cases that he identified, only 35, or some six per cent, involved imprisonment. Anderson's findings led him to conclude that "the worst persecution of members in Lancashire took place not under the Conventicle Act or for dissent from public worship but for non-payment of tithes".[6] This in turn led him to argue that for the Lancashire Quakers "the Act of Toleration proved to be of little benefit" because "those areas of persecution covered by the Act were declining well before 1690, while the bulk of the sufferings undergone by, and after, that date were for tithe avoidance ...."[7]

Anderson's observation of a steady increase in sufferings for tithe over the period 1650–1690 is confirmed by my own analysis of the first recorded sufferings for each Lancashire Quaker involved in tithe seizures or litigation between 1650 and 1700. The source for this study was LQMS volume one, with Joseph Besse's *Collection of the Sufferings of the People Called Quakers* (1753) being used as a check for the early part of the period when Quaker record-keeping appears to have been erratic.[8] The following details were recorded for each Quaker's first suffering for tithe: the date (year) of the incident; the name of the Friend involved; the Meeting to which that Friend belonged; the amount taken in pounds; whether or not the amount taken was in excess of the original cost; the method by which the Quaker suffered; and the description of the tithe-owner. When calculating whether or not an excess was taken, any costs awarded following legal proceedings were taken to form part of the original amount demanded. In determining the method by which Quakers suffered, three simple categories were employed. First, that of tithe taken in kind, which seems to have been used as a residual category by the Quaker record-keepers.[9] The second category was tithe taken by legal action, either in ecclesiastical courts, local inferior courts or in the Courts of Exchequer or Chancery under the Edwardian statute of treble damages.[10] The third category employed consisted of cases where tithe was taken by distraint under justice's warrants granted in accordance with the two statutes of 1696.[11] Tithe owners were divided into three groups, impropriators, farmers, and members of the clergy or clerical institutions. The term tithe farmer was used widely and not always precisely by Friends in their accounts of sufferings; it is clear that on many occasions tithe farmers were in fact tithe gatherers, whilst on others they were more accurately described as impropriators. The term tithe farmer has been used here only where it has not proved possible to identify either the impropriator or cleric to whom the tithe was ultimately being paid.

Several problems accompany the use of data obtained in this way from Quaker records.[12] The first relates to the duplication of names in the many small and self-contained communities of Quakers throughout Lancashire. Sons were sometimes distinguished from their fathers by the use of "senior" and "junior" as in the case of William Skirrow and William Skirrow junior of Wrea Meeting. It was possible to distinguish between the two Leonard Fells of Swarthmore Meeting on the basis of both address and occupation. Such indications of uniqueness are not, however, always available. Friends might have moved between sufferings, and thus appear at different times at different addresses as apparently first-time sufferers.[13] In contrast, a Friend could remain at the same address and yet have his suffering recorded under the heading of a variety of Meetings; such was the case with William Walker of Priest Hutton, a village nine miles to the north-east of Lancaster, who had sufferings entered under the headings of Lancaster, Yealand and Chipping Meetings. Similar confusions can arise between Friends who were entered as sufferers under one Meeting, who subsequently attended another Meeting. This was the case with Sankey Meeting, whose existence was overtaken in the mid 1680s by Penketh Meeting.[14] A further consideration is that although it was the intention to record details only of those Friends involved in cases of non-payment of tithe it is possible that some sufferings, particularly during the earlier period, were recorded as being for tithe when they were in fact for church-rates. These difficulties should all be borne in mind when considering the following results.

In all, a total of 509 Friends were identified as having been involved in tithe proceedings of some sort on at least one occasion between 1650 and 1700. A comparison with Besse's *Collection* revealed the names of a further thirty-six Friends who suffered for refusing to pay tithe between 1650 and 1689: thirty-two of these were involved in cases prior to 1685, the date at which Lancashire records become "fairly complete".[15] The distribution of these initial sufferings identified in LQMS, volume one, is outlined below in Table 3.

Table 3   Distribution of initial tithe-sufferings 1650–1700

	1650 –54	1655 –59	1660 –64	1665 –69	1670 –74	1675 –79	1680 –84	1685 –89	1690 –94	1695 –1700	Total
No.	1	12	10	17	17	56	42	88	86	180	509
%	0.2	2.3	2.0	3.3	3.3	11.0	8.2	17.3	16.9	35.4	100

(source: LQMS, vol.1, 1645–1700)

The gradual increase in the number of Friends being involved in tithe cases for the first time correlates closely with Anderson's findings of an increase in the overall number of tithe cases during this period. The only significant difference to arise from Table 3 is the suggestion of a larger number of tithe cases (13 as opposed to 5) in the period 1650–59 than was identified by Anderson.[16] The most striking similarity is to be found in the large increase in tithe sufferers in the period leading up to the Toleration Act of 1689. There is a clear upsurge in the number of Friends becoming involved in tithe cases after 1689 (a period not covered by Anderson). This is even more dramatic in the period following the passing of legislation introducing summary proceedings in tithe cases in 1696.

The first of these two Acts was the Act for the more easie Recoverie of Small Tythes.[17] This Act introduced an optional summary procedure that could be used in cases involving small tithes claimed up to the value of 40 shillings which were outstanding for two years or less. Cases brought under this legislation were to be heard by two justices of the peace who were empowered to award the plaintiff costs of up to 10 shillings. If an award was followed by a further refusal to pay, the justices were enabled to issue a warrant ordering distraint of the defendant's goods sufficient to realise both the amount originally claimed and also unspecified "reason-able charges" to cover the costs of the action. An extension of this Act, applicable only to Quakers, was made in two clauses contained in the Affirmation Act of the same year.[18] The Affirmation Act extended the summary procedure to cover cases involving both great and small tithes and church rates claimed up to the value of £10. There was no limit on the number of years' tithes or rates which could be claimed. Goods could be distrained from Friends refusing to pay a claim confirmed by the justices, with the "necessary charges of distraining" also being met from the proceeds of the sale of these goods. Any "overplus" remaining was to be returned to the owner.

Eric Evans has suggested that these two items of legislation, passed as a Whig reaction against "the pretensions of the church courts", were of "limited usefulness since the sums involved were so small".[19] In Lancashire, however, the £10 limit seems to have been sufficiently large to enable many clerics and impropriators to take advantage of the legislation in order to press claims that had lain dormant for some years. Clearly the expense of the legal alternatives available to tithe owners prior to 1696 discouraged tithe owners from using the courts to pursue amounts under £10 when there was no guarantee of success.[20] In addition tithe in kind could be taken easily only from those Friends involved in arable-farming; whilst the whole process was strictly illegal, there was clearly far more risk involved for the owner or farmer who broke into a house or farm-property to remove goods or livestock than to the one who removed crops from the field at the time of harvest.[21] Thus the 1696 legislation was a great boon to those tithe owners who had to deal with the Quaker's refusal to comply with their demands. A few other observations should be made at this point. Firstly, few of the seizures under the 1696 legislation in Lancashire even approached £10 in value. The mean value of distraints made from those 112 Friends (in the 1650 1700 group) whose initial tithe-suffering was under the new legislation was £1.6s. Secondly, £10 was by no means a small sum; the suffering records for Lancashire show that cows and oxen were valued at between 3 or 4 pounds, lambs at between 2 and 3 shillings each, horses at up to 7 pounds in 1696. The economic implications of losing a horse, three cows or six dozen lambs would surely have been considerable for any small-scale farmer. Even to William Stout, a prosperous merchant, the loss of 12.5 cwt. of English iron (Stout had 56lb taken from him in 1698 valued at 1 shilling per 7lbs) would have robbed him of one tenth of his annual profits.[22] Ten pounds, then, was not a small sum in the late seventeenth and early eighteenth century. However, it is apparent that the success of the summary procedure in recovering tithe under the value of £10 was sufficient to encourage some justices to extend its competence to amounts in excess of £10. In 1698 Daniel Abraham of Swarthmore had a warrant granted against him for £16 15s 6d for small and great tithes by Charles Rigby and Thomas Shearson, both justices of the peace from Lancaster.[23]

The extent of the sufferings under the two Acts of 1696 only added to the indignation that was clearly felt by many Friends who were dissatisfied with the form of words to be used in place of an oath contained in the Affirmation Act.[24] The Lancashire Quarterly Meeting reorganised its method of recording sufferings in order to emphasise the degree to which the new legislation was being used against them.[25] Friends in the county were also to complain of excessive costs being awarded against them.[26] In Westmorland the situation was possibly worse. Thomas Camm wrote to the Meeting for Sufferings that

> the old informers are now witnesses for the priests against Friends upon the late Acts for the Recovery of Small Tithes, and the justices Daniel Fleming and son and Edward Wilson, being on their sides, do prosecute Friends for small matters as 3d, 7d, 9d etc. claimed for tithes, and do award £10 costs for each suit being the utmost extent of the Act, and the priests' multiplying complaints against one and the same person and take excessive distress to double the value awarded.[27]

Similarly, Friends in Cumberland complained of "the great and heavy sufferings sustained by the late Act". Friends there alleged that "Priests and tithe-mongers ... appoint set days and times to feast and drink, and set Friend's costs so high to pay for the same".[28] Nor were such things confined to the North; in Somerset the Quarterly Meeting noted "the great havock" caused by the new law.[29] The Meeting for Sufferings received similar complaints from Norfolk, Essex, Gloucestershire, Wiltshire, Hampshire and Lincolnshire.[30]

Nor was the effect of the 1696 legislation shortlived, as has been suggested by Norman Hunt.[31] Rather it initiated a sustained increase in the level of distraints for tithe which did not reach its peak for some twenty years after the passing of the two Acts. This is clearly shown by an analysis of the yearly value of distraints and seizures for tithe in Lancashire for the years 1700–1740. The data for this analysis are drawn from the minutes of the London Yearly Meeting, and more particularly from that section headed "Sufferings Brought In".[32] Under this heading are listed the annual returns from each Quarterly or Yearly Meeting in England, Wales and Scotland dealing with the previous year's sufferings within the compass of that Meeting. Originally these returns concentrated on a general description of the types of sufferings undergone by Friends, listing as well the names of any imprisoned. From 1698 onwards each Meeting also gave the value of any fines or seizures for non-payment of tithes, the change of emphasis in itself being a belated acknowledgement of the changed nature of Quaker sufferings. In order to prevent any spurious conclusions being drawn by concentrating overmuch on one county, it was decided to present comparative data alongside that relating to Lancashire. The counties included in this comparison are Lincolnshire in the east of England, Somerset in the southwest of England and Staffordshire in the Midlands.[33] In addition the aggregate totals for England and Wales are also given.

The results of this analysis are presented in Tables 4 and 5. Table 4 shows the size of the four counties' sufferings relative to the total for England and Wales. Three – Lancashire, Lincolnshire and Somerset –

Table 4   Tithe sufferings 1700–1740
(Total value of seizures and distraints in £)

	Total	Mean	% England Total
Lancashire	10,847.4	264.5	6.3
Lincolnshire	13,637.9	332.6	7.9
Somersetshire	9,234.1	225.2	5.3
Staffordshire	1,164.0	28.4	0.7
England & Wales	173,046.0	4,220.6	100.0

(Source: London Yearly Meeting Minutes, vols.2–8)

Table 5   Tithe sufferings 1700–1739
(Ten yearly mean value of seizures and distraints in £)

	Lancs	Lincs	Soms	Staffs	England & Wales
1700–09	264.8	320.4	217.7	20.8	4,314.9
1710–19	305.2	431.6	262.5	24.3	4,885.3
1720–29	279.0	391.8	210.1	32.1	4,338.9
1730–39	212.8	219.0	220.7	36.2	3,384.2

(Source: London Yearly Meeting Minutes, vols.2–8)

each recorded large sufferings, between them accounting for some 20% of the total for England and Wales, leaving some 39 Meetings to account for the remaining 80%. At the other end of the scale was Staffordshire, itself accounting for only 0.7 of the *national* total over the period 1700 to 1740. During this period Staffordshire recorded a mean annual total of some £28.4, in comparison with Lancashire's £265.4. Clearly, even after accounting for a probably substantial difference in the number of Friends in each of these counties, and for the apparently large amount of tithe free land occupied by Friends in Staffordshire, the sufferings for tithe experienced by Friends in this county can in no way be regarded as typical of the country as a whole.[34] Table 5 presents the tithe sufferings for the four counties in terms of the ten-yearly mean value of seizures and distraints. The figures contained in this table confirm that the increase in the value of sufferings instigated by the two Acts of 1696 continued well into the second decade of the eighteenth century. It was only in the period 1730–39 that the average value of sufferings in Lancashire fell below the figure for the start of the century. This decline coincides with a gradual fall in the overall number of Friends in Lancashire during the early eighteenth century, a fall which accelerated dramatically after 1730.[35] Lincolnshire and Somerset also reached their peak of sufferings in the decade 1710–19 and this reflected the experience of the figures for England and Wales. A yearly breakdown of the figures for each of these counties and England

and Wales reveals that Lancashire and Somerset each returned their largest amount of sufferings for the year 1716, whilst Lincolnshire recorded its largest annual figure 3 years later in 1719.[36] The aggregate figure for England and Wales reached its peak of 5,370 in 1711; in 1716 the figure stood at 5,290.

Clearly some explanation needs to be sought for this peak at both the local and national level, and the subsequent fall. Recently, historians have been all too ready to attribute the decline in sufferings for non-payment of tithes (which is generally and incorrectly assumed to have followed the passing of the 1696 legislation) to an increased laxity amongst Friends with respect to their testimony against tithes.[37] It is possible, however, to see the influence of both internal and external forces in producing both the increase, and subsequent decline, in tithe sufferings that Friends experienced in the late seventeenth and early eighteenth century. The following discussion will concentrate on some of these different influences. First, and at greatest length, the role of tithe owners will be considered, and particularly that of lay impropriators. Secondly, I will examine the role of the agencies of enforcement in tithe cases. Thirdly, I will consider the degree to which the Quakers' successful recourse to legal defences in tithe cases led to a decline in sufferings. Fourthly, and finally, I will assess the degree to which laxity contributed towards the down-turn in sufferings in the mid-eighteenth century.

If the role of personality played a major part in shaping the course of tithe disputes then no less important was the role of economic necessity. The degree to which tithes contributed towards the income of the tithe owner could clearly determine the extent to which he or she might press a Quaker to yield his tenth. For the clergy the need both to collect their tithe and at the same time protect the interests of future incumbents could be tempered by a desire to retain the goodwill of their parishioners.[38] This sentiment, of course, might not have extended to Friends. It was certainly not a sentiment that was likely to influence a lay impropriator or farmer. Evidence abounds, for example, as to the extent to which landlords in the North-Western counties were prepared to alienate their tenants by increasing entry fines and customary payments in order to maximise incomes from their estates.[39] Many of these alienated tenants, it has been suggested, became some of the earliest converts to Quakerism in the late 1640s and early 1650s.[40] The Quaker attitude to property, outlined above, was certainly not sympathetic to arbitrary impositions of this nature.[41] Some of these oppressive landlords were also impropriators or farmers of tithe.[42] For Eric Evans "the most rapacious tithe collectors were lay impropriators", a view shared by Felicity Heal who argued that "it was frequently they, rather than the clergy, who were involved in litigation with parishioners to extract the full economic value of the tithe".[43] Nor should this be in any way surprising. As Christopher Hill has pointed out "in the days before the establishment of a funded national debt ... the leasing of tithes (or the purchase of an impropriation) offered a convenient, safe and not unprofitable form of investment".[44] No-one would expect an investor to waive his dividend, or a broker to decline his commission, on the basis of a scruple which they did not share. Neither should we expect impropriators or farmers to do anything other than realise the greatest possible return on their investments or leases. Good housekeeping demanded that impropriators and farmers (whether leasing from laymen, clerics, or clerical institutions) collected their tithe as efficiently and cheaply as possible.

It was estimated that by the mid-seventeenth century some 3,845 livings out of a total of 9,284 were held by impropriators.[45] This figure of 41% was exceeded in the diocese of Chester, the unit of ecclesiastical administration which governed Lancashire. There it was said that 133 rectories out of a total of 248 were impropriate, "and those the best".[46] In some areas of the county the situation could be even worse; in Furness, for example, seven out of eight parishes were held by impropriators.[47] Such a high degree of lay involvement in clerical livings, inevitably determined the character of the Anglican ministry in the county.[48] For Quakers it was also likely to influence the nature of the tithe disputes in which they were involved. The degree to which impropriators were involved in Quaker tithe disputes is revealed by an analysis of tithe owners in the 509 first-recorded tithe sufferings identified in Lancashire between 1650 and 1700 (for which see Appendix 4). In the 448 cases where it was possible to identify the tithe owner, 152 or 34%, involved impropriators. A further 168 cases, or 37.5%, involved tithe farmers. This category could vary from individuals leasing tithes for substantial periods (perhaps more correctly described as impropriators) to those who farmed the tithe on an annual basis, receiving a proportion of the tithe determined by the total recovered. Whatever their exact nature, these farmers were subject to the same economic pressures as impropriators, and we can speak of a lay involvement in some 71% of these initial tithe sufferings. Nor should the total be left at that, for in many of the 128 cases where clerics or clerical institutions were involved, farmers were employed to recover the tithe at source. This, for example, is true of the Dean and Chapter of Worcester who owned the tithe of the rectory and parsonage of Warton, six miles to the north of Lancaster. They collected tithe through a number of agencies, variously described as "agents", "farmers", "attorneys" and "impropriators".[49] For the purpose of this analysis the owner was identified as a clerical institution, but for the Quakers the collectors were men with motives little different from the impropriators of tithe farmers mentioned above.

The involvement of impropriators and tithe farmers in Quaker tithe sufferings is also revealed in a detailed breakdown of all sufferings recorded for the year 1716, the point at which the value of seizures and distraints from Quakers in Lancashire reached their peak. Table 6 contains these data, and in addition contains a similar breakdown for the year 1738, when Lancashire recorded its lowest value of seizures and distraints for tithe between 1700 and 1740. In 1716, 62% of all cases involving tithes or

Table 6   Lancashire tithe sufferings 1716 and 1738

	1716				1738			
	Cases	%	£	%	Cases	%	£	%
Tithes in kind								
Impropriators	42	14.7	60.65	16.5	51	33.6	68.65	37.4
Farmers	24	8.4	47.35	12.9	–	–		
Clergy etc.	27	9.5	32.35	8.8	13	8.5	35.3	19.2
(sub-total)	93	32.6	140.35	38.2	64	42.1	103.95	56.6
Tithes by warrant								
Impropriators	112	39.3	155.6	42.3	24	15.8	34.5	18.8
Clergy etc.	51	17.9	55.8	15.1	50	32.9	38.85	21.2
(sub-total)	163	57.2	211.4	57.4	74	48.7	73.35	40
Church-rates by warrant								
Clergy	29	10.2	16.4	4.4	14	9.2	6.1	3.3
Totals	285	100	368.15	100	152	100	183.4	99.9

(source: GBS, vol.14, pt.1; LQMS, vol.2)

church-rates were brought by impropriators and tithe farmers, accounting for 72% of the value of goods and produce taken from Friends. If cases involving church-rates are excluded then the percentages are 70 and 75 respectively. These figures confirm the results of the analysis of the first-recorded sufferings of Friends involved in tithe proceedings between 1650 and 1700. Between 60 and 70% of those Quakers liable to pay tithes in Lancashire owed their tenth to a lay impropriator or tithe farmer. The evidence for 1716 seems to suggest that these impropriators were anxious to recoup their due. It is therefore interesting to note that in 1738 the main difference in the breakdown of sufferings from that of 1716 is the reduction by 88 of the number of cases brought against Friends by impropriators using the summary proceedings. Although the clergy were slightly more active in this year, it is at first sight in the failure of lay owners to recover their tithe that we should seek the explanation of the decline in the overall value of goods and produce taken from Quakers in Lancashire at the end of the period 1700–1740.

The motivations of impropriators, beyond the simple desire to reap the maximum yield from a piece of property, are not always easy to discern. They, like the clergy, would have been influenced to some degree by fluctuations in the economic climate, but it is not easy to see this reflected in the seizures taken from Friends. 1716, for example, the peak year of seizures, was neither a year of bad harvests (when scarcity might have induced owners to press for their tenth) or good harvests (when over-abundance might account for the large amount taken).[50] Rosemary O'Day has suggested that bad harvests, leading to increased need for the tenth on the part of the owner and an increased reluctance to part with it by the farmer, could lead to a larger number of tithe cases being brought into the courts than was usual.[51] It is not clear how far this was reflected in Friends' experiences, although it is perhaps worthy of note that the peak of seizures at the national level was reached in 1711 following two years of bad harvests.[52] This approach offers little explanation for the slump in seizures that was experienced in Lancashire in 1738, which again was neither a period of paucity nor plenty.[53] The most that can be said is that these influences were among a larger number which could determine an impropriator's actions. A revealing case study of the Prestons of Holker Hall shows how important individual circumstance was in these cases.

Thomas Preston of Holker leased the tithes of the parish of Cartmel, said in 1650 to be worth some £350 per annum, from the Bishop of Chester.[54] This was common enough amongst the gentry in the North-West, many of whom leased the tithes of their own demesne or of land near to their estates.[55] One estimate suggests that leased tithes could yield vast profits, while the more conservative B.G. Blackwood wrote that some families made "fair profits from impropriations".[56] For Thomas Preston tithes formed an essential part of his income; clearly little of the proceeds were diverted towards the spiritual needs of the parishioners. In 1644 the people of Cartmel were described as "exceeding ignorant and blind as to religion"; some sixty years later, by which time the tithes had descended through marriage to the Lowthers of Marske, the ministry in the parish was still being described as inadequate.[57]

Preston's need to retain all his tithe, and to collect as much of it as was possible, was dictated by continual financial pressure. In 1649, for example, he was forced to pay a composition fine of £1,592, which he attempted to recoup by increasing tithe payments in the parish.[58] The response to this was a refusal to pay by over 100 of his parishioners, led by Thomas Atkinson, later a prominent Quaker in Cartmel.[59] Preston's dire financial straits did not end with the Restoration; in 1667 when he arranged the marriage of his son, George, to the daughter of John Lowther he also negotiated a loan with the bride's grandfather.[60] In addition to paying a portion of £2,000 Sir John Lowther lent Thomas Preston "the old Man", £3,150 to redeem a mortgage over the Holker estate.[61] The loan was to be repaid at £400 per annum for fourteen years, but Preston soon had difficulty meeting his payments and the terms of the loan had to be re-negotiated.[62]

It was during this period that Preston began what was to be a long battle between himself and his family, and the Quakers of Cartmel. Clearly, he needed to ensure not only that the Quakers paid their tithe, but also that their bad influence did not spread to Anglican neighbours, some of whom must have been amongst the refusers of 1649. Thus the Quakers were to be made an example of, and he "presented them in the King's Courts at Westminster and county court, whereby many suffered tedious imprisonments, spoil of their goods, and much waste by his prosecutions".[63] He also sued Friends in the Wapentake court for the hundred of

Lonsdale, and "after that, by the advice of some moderate person sued them in Cartmel court where the spoil was little less".[64] Preston's contact with the Quakers ceased in 1674, four years before he died, when the lease for the tithes was renewed by his son Thomas Preston the younger.[65] Preston the younger,

> since he came in, sued the said people in a court baron held within the said parish of Cartmel. And for some good reasons in or about the 5th month 77, some of them did demurr to their proceedings in the said court as not having jurisdiction in the case of tithe. Upon which demurrer the said Thomas Preston, farmer, brake furth into great wrath and rage as he has expressed himself at several times and places.

Preston was not, however, to be confined to wrath and rage. His response to having his cheap, speedy and illegal method of ordering distraint for non-payment of tithe challenged by Friends was to proceed against them under the terms of the Conventicle Act of 1670, "to get his Tythes out of the Goods which might be taken upon that Act".[67] Having sent his tithe gatherer and a neighbour to Friends' Meeting at Height to act as informers, Preston himself accosted the Quakers as they were leaving the Meeting, abusing them and calling particularly for "Thomas Atkinson, that old rogue of all rogues".[68] Preston then offered the Quakers a bargain, which revealed both his need for the Friends' tithe, and his comparative indifference to their form of worship:

> he said this was his business with us to show us this civility, and to take our answer that if we would submit to the court at Cartmel and let him recover his tithe there, well, if not he would prosecute us so that he would root us out root and branch, foundation and generation, and that he would pull the Meeting house down over our heads and trail us in carts.[69]

The Quakers "knowing it not to be according to the king's laws to try cases of tithe in Cartmel court nor in any other inferior court" refused his offer, with the consequence that in October, thirty-five of them were convicted for attending a conventicle at Height on a warrant granted by Myles Doddin, Preston's brother-in-law.[70]

Preston had expressed his determination to "root the Quakers out of Cartmel" and later in the same month he again sent informers to attend the Height Meeting.[71] John Armstrong, Anglican minister of the parish explained that this was because "the Quakers had purely or merely provoked Mr Preston because they would not pay him tithe nor suffer him to recover them in Cartmel court". If Preston "set the informers against the Quakers he might get his tithe out of the informers".[72] Rather than proceed on the Conventicle Act, however, Preston again summonsed the Friends into the court baron to answer a suit of non-payment of tithes.

The Friends again challenged the competence of the court to hear matters concerning tithe,

> whereupon Thomas Preston grew rageous, saying 'In the court house is the jury called? If not call the jury, for I hear they will demur again, which if they do I will prosecute them as long as they have a groat', saying further 'I vow and protest I will spend my whole estate but I will root you out of your whole estates, and bring in others that will pay me tithes'.[73]

The Conventicle Act was to be his weapon, for

> he would prosecute us by the Act – having it in his hands – 'till he had not left us a groat, if it was not repealed, unless we would submit to the court, and let him have his tithes ....[74]

Nonetheless, the steward of the court, Curwen Rawlinson, accepted the Friend's demurrer and they were dismissed.[75] Thomas Atkinson complained that Thomas Preston was abusing the Conventicle Act, using it to "maintain the usurpation of inferior courts, to brow-beat the Law, to inforce the payment of his illegal Demands, a shoeinghorn for his Interest".[76]

Preston's failure to convince either the Quakers or the court steward to proceed with tithe cases in the court baron led him to seek alternative means of pressing his claims. In May 1678 he summoned the Quakers at short notice to appear at the Wapentake court for the hundred of Lonsdale. There six Friends were sued for debt, arising out of their failure to pay a composition for tithes allegedly made between Thomas Preston senior and the inhabitants of the parish.[77] The Friends, who anyway denied the legality of the composition,

> desired as their Right to appear by their Attorney, one Edmund Gibson, who, as formerly, offered a Demurer to the Jurisdiction of that Court, which the Steward refused to accept (although by Law he ought not to deny it) – but the steward pressing for another Answer, they desired a copy of the Plaintiff's Declaration in writing, and Time to plead till next Court, both which Requests although by the Law the Steward could not deny (as he was often told) yet he arbitrarily against Law, Right and Custom, over-ruled them ....[78]

In Thomas Lampugh, steward of the court, Preston had found a willing ally. Judgement was passed against the Friends for a total demand of £6 10s 9d, "without giving any Copy of the Plaintiff's Declaration, or Time to plead", and on the following day the Friends were distrained of goods worth in total £19 11s 8d.[79]

Between 1679 and 1683 Thomas Preston spent much of his time in London, pursuing another course to improve his financial position.[80] In

1674 his cousin, Sir Thomas Preston of Furness, granted the iron-mines he had developed in the manor of Furness as a charitable bequest to the Society of Jesus, of which he had become a member in 1672 following the death of his second wife.[81] Thomas Preston of Holker challenged the bequest in the Court of Exchequer, claiming that the estate of Furness was forfeit as it has been granted by his cousin for superstitious uses.[82] It was in pursuit of this claim that Preston travelled to London. The outcome was a success, and in 1683 he was granted a crown lease of Furness Abbey at £500 per annum.[83] The estate was said to be worth £177 per annum, and the iron mines, although apparently little worked since 1666, were worth some £1,300 per annum.[84] This stroke of good fortune was matched by a general improvement in the economic condition of the Holker estate, where rents rose steadily through the 1680s and early 1690s.[85] Preston, however, was still determined to make an example of the Quakers, and shortly after his return from London he commenced a suit against nine Friends for tithes of corn, wool and lamb. He chose to bring his case in the Court of Exchequer, possibly as a result of the experience he had obtained of its workings over the previous four years. The Cartmel Friends were anxious with regard to the outcome of the proceedings, and George Barrow of Newton wrote to London Friends desiring

> if they think it convenient and stand with the truth that they would do so much for our Friends in the North that some Friend that hath any acquaintance with the Chief Baron of the Exchequer that gives judgements of actions that are tried in the Court, and if any Friends speak to him and reason the matter concerning our suit that is against us ....[86]

Ultimately Barrow's fears were justified, for five Friends were prosecuted "and by a false Return of *Non est Inventus* (though they were so far from absconding, that they offered themselves to the Bayliffs) a Sequestration was obtained against them, by which their Cattle and Goods were carried away to the value of £82 1s 8d".[87]

Following this case, Preston apparently had little difficulty in persuading Cartmel Friends to defer to the jurisdiction of the hundred court. It was following

> one of their private sessions at Cartmel town where his ill-gotten money was brought in for the sale of poor Friends' goods of Cartmel for non-payment of tithes being illegally prosecuted in his Wapentake court there, and very outrageous distress taken upon his ill-gotten verdicts and judgements

that Preston, "seeming overcome with drink", was thrown from his horse, breaking his leg and endangering his life, "so as he hath small cause to rejoice in his tithe money etc., though he made a feast, when it was brought in, but it was accompanied with a bitter sauce".[88] In 1691 Preston again resorted to the Exchequer Court, suing Edward Britton, James Britton and John Gurnall for non-payment of tithes.[89] He followed the same course as previously, his attorney making returns of *non est inventus* against the three Friends "although the persons were always to be found", until he got sequestrations out against their estates (having formerly done the like against several Friends) and put in Commissioners for Execution of the sequestration "certain persons of evil fame, being bailiffs and very unreasonable men".[90]

Preston clearly scored a major victory in bringing the action of 1691. In January 1692/93 Swarthmore Monthly Meeting, to which Cartmel Particular Meeting belonged, ordered two Cartmel Friends, George Barrow and John Gurnall "to speak to the Friends of Cartmel Meeting that have not given in their clear testimony but have suffered others to agree for them for tithes".[91] The following month the Meeting noted that some of the transgressors "as are here have declared how they have been troubled in their spirit" concerning the agreement; they were "tenderly admonished to clear the Truth".[92] Barrow and Gurnall, along with fellow tithe sufferers Miles Birkett and James Birtton were ordered "to speak to the rest and admonish them and make what enquiry they can to know how the matter began to be put forward ...."[93] The following month the four Friends reported that they had spoken with a number of Friends, "but they seem unwilling to receive their reproof, and to sleight Friends' care".[94] By May no satisfactory explanation had been received and the Monthly Meeting urged the estranged Friends "to clear Truth's testimony from their agreement for tithes" and bring or send to the next meeting "their testimonies against or condemnations".[95] This more severe attitude apparently succeeded where tender admonition had failed, for in July there "appeared before this Meeting some of the Friends of Cartmel Meeting whose tithes were agreed for and seem willing to do anything that Friends think convenient for clearing the Truth".[96] The Meeting was also closer to identifying the instigators of agreement; in August, Friends were instructed to "assist James Harrison in drawing up a paper for clearing the truth concerning his son's agreeing for his tithes".[97] When, after the harvest and annual tithing, Harrison produced a satisfactory paper he was desired "to deliver a copy to the said Thomas Preston and others as there may be service in it".[98] As Preston was absent from Holker it was noted that "James Harrison is willing when Preston returns to deliver him that, his paper, formerly signed ...."[99]

The threat of legal action, to recover tithe in a superior court had been enough to win Preston some respite from the tribulations which the Quakers caused him. It was only after a difficult struggle that the Cartmel Quakers re-imposed discipline to maintain the testimony against tithe. In the long run, however, Preston appears to have been the winner of the drawn-out disputes. When he died in January 1696/97 his estate, far from being over-burdened with mortgages, brought his daughter and her husband Sir William Lowther a fortune of some £30,000.[100] While some of Thomas Preston's good fortune may have been the result of generally improving economic conditions and the leasing of the Furness estate, part of it must have been due to efficient housekeeping and good management. In his workmanlike attitude towards Quakers who refused to meet tithe demands he exhibited both these characteristics to the full. Nor is there any reason to suppose that he was exceptional. At Holker his son-in-law, William Lowther, took full advantage of the 1696 legislation to press home his newly inherited claims against Friends.[101] By 1716 his wife, Elizabeth, was equally active in collecting tithe in her role as guardian to his son, Thomas Lowther.[102]

Nor should the Prestons be considered exceptional. In the east of the county, for example, two families, the Ashtons of Whalley and the Ashtons of Middleton were equally aggressive in pursuit of their tithe. The Ashtons of Whalley leased the tithes of this extensive parish from the Archbishop of Canterbury; in 1650 they were estimated to be worth in excess of £550, in addition to which the Ashtons also received various prescription payments, tithe-rents and fees.[103] Sir Ralph Ashton, who died in 1679, was described by B.G. Blackwood as a "kindly and considerate" landlord; "landlords such as these", he wrote, "seem to have been rare".[104] Whatever his behaviour to his tenants during the Civil War years, his attitude to Quakers, and their refusal to pay tithes, was no less harsh, and no less understandable, than was that of the Prestons. Amongst the earliest recorded Lancashire tithe sufferings are those of a group of Friends from Marsden Meeting sued for treble damages by Sir Ralph.[105] His name appears frequently in the suffering records, and rarely did he proceed against Quakers except it was in a superior court. His successor, his brother Edmund, was no less intransigent.[106] In 1684 he imprisoned 12 Friends at Lancaster upon a writ *de excommunicado capiendo* following their failure to answer his suit for corn-tithes upon oath in the ecclesiastical court.[107] These Friends were released under the terms of James II's General Pardon of 1686.[108] Ashton however renewed his suit against them and by 1687 the number imprisoned had increased to 19, at which point the Quarterly Meeting appealed to London "to know of Friends here what may be done for the getting their enlargement".[109] The following year the number stood at 23 imprisoned, and Friends were seeking out the judges assigned to the Northern circuit to "be spoken to to be favourable to Friends".[110] In 1688 the 23 Quakers were released, but in 1691 Ashton again sued members of the Marsden Meeting for tithes, imprisoning 33 Friends on an Attachment following their failure to enter an answer upon oath in the Exchequer Court.[111] In 1691 four of those imprisoned died, leaving, as Friends were anxious to note, three widows and nineteen children.[112] In 1692 one Friend, Ann Whalley, who had been amongst those first imprisoned in 1694, died leaving four small children.[113] Nineteen of the Friends were still in prison in 1694, and it was not until 1695 that they were released following the death of Sir Edmund in a duel.[114]

Sir Ralph Ashton of Middleton held the impropriate great tithes of the parish of Middleton, which were estimated to be worth £188 in 1650, and some £250 in the early eighteenth century.[115] In 1697 he inherited the Whalley estate by virtue of his maternal links with the Ashtons of Whalley. Although he was apparently little troubled by Quakers at Middleton, his inheritance carried with it a large number of still intransigent Friends. Edmund Ashton's suits, apparently aimed at winning the eventual submission of Friends rather than any immediate financial gain, had had little effect.[117]

Rather than follow the course of his kinsman Sir Ralph, Ashton instead chose to take full advantage of the new laws passed in 1696, maintaining his annual income by making regular distraints from Friends by justice's warrants. His pursuit of this aim made him one of the most persistent prosecutors of Lancashire Friends, and his substantial territorial interests ensured that he came into conflict with more Friends than any other single impropriator.[118] Forty-seven of the tithe cases brought before justices in Lancashire by impropriators in 1716, or some 41% of the total involving laymen, originated with Ashton or his estate.[119]

The role of the clergy should not be ignored in this discussion of the motivations behind tithe prosecutions. Although they were not protecting an investment in the way that impropriators were, clerics were defending what many of their propagandists claimed was a property right.[120] In claiming tithe, whether from a Quaker or anyone else, they were also protecting the property rights of their successors, whose income could decline dramatically as a consequence of neglectful incumbents.[121]

Moreover, clerics, perhaps particularly in Lancashire, were subject to their own particular set of economic problems which in many ways mirrored those of laymen such as Thomas Preston.[122] These too could be equally as imperative as any vindictive desire to persecute Friends. Richard Clegg, for example, the vicar of Kirkham from 1666 to 1720, was well known for his hostility to all forms of Dissent.[123] In 1682 he had complained to Roger Kenyon about the Friend's burial ground at Brewers-Yard; the Quakers "the most incorrigible sinners that I know" were holding burials there which were not registered in accordance with the Act for Burying in Woollen. In addition they were holding conventicles there.[124] He was responsible for the imprisonment of the Quaker Margaret Coulburn of Freckleton in 1692, following her trial at Preston on a charge of blasphemy.[125] In 1709 he petitioned the Quarter Sessions not to license a Quaker Meeting house at Clifton or Greenhalgh in the Fylde, subsequently complaining that "yet at Clifton they doe meet and draw people about them after a very unchristian like manner".[126] He was also one of a number of clergymen in the North who had instigated prosecutions against Friends under the 1670 Conventicle Act after the passing of the Toleration Act in 1689.[127] It would thus be tempting, and convenient, to explain any actions taken by Clegg against Quakers to recover tithe in terms of his unreasonable and intolerant hatred of Friends.

Quakers, however, were of peripheral interest to Clegg during his incumbency at Kirkham. His main concern, in addition to ministering to the needs of his parish, was his battle to maintain his income which had been eroded by his predecessor's agreements to composition payments, and by significant changes in the agriculture of the area.[128] He was also concerned to combat the indifference of the lay impropriator, Sir Thomas Clifton, who ignored appeals to meet his responsibilities either to maintain the minister's living or the fabric of the parish church.[129] This course of action involved Clegg not only in litigation with Quakers but also with the majority of his parishioners.[130] Moreover, the Quakers with whom Clegg had to deal were not always as fast in their refusal to comply with his demands as Friends might have desired. He was involved in proceedings involving the summary procedure in 1696, 1698 and 1710. He again sought judgement against them in 1712, 1718 and a number of subsequent years.[131] However, although twelve male Friends from Freckleton entered tithe testimonies before 1700, only seven of these (and Alice Sharples, a woman Friend) are recorded as suffering for tithe (owed either to Clegg or Clifton) during this period.[132] At least one Friend, Lawrence Coulburn, was disciplined by Lancaster Monthly Meeting for dishonouring his testimony. In 1692, the same year that he had suffered distraint following his wife Margaret's prosecution, the Meeting received information "that Lawrence Coulburn was contracted with the priest for his tithes and steeplehouse lays".[133] Clegg's attention had clearly proved too much for Lawrence, for two months later the Meeting ordered two Friends "to speak to Lawrence and to exhort him concerning his weakness in paying tithes and leaving Friends' Meetings ...."[134] The next month Lawrence replied to the Meeting that "he could not stand against the law" and he was ordered to be admonished, apparently with some degree of success.[135] However, as Cunliffe-Shaw has suggested, Clegg apparently did not always have to resort to law in order to persuade the Quakers amongst his parishioners to maintain his meagre income.[136]

Although possessed of a larger income than his impecunious colleague in Kirkham, James Fenton, the vicar of Lancaster between 1684 and 1714, and his son and successor, also James Fenton (who was vicar from 1714 until 1767) were no less anxious to press their claims against the Quakers.[137] Whilst the great tithes of the parish were impropriate, the vicar received tithes on corn and grain, plus various small tithes, arising out of his glebe lands in Lancaster. These were estimated at £280 per annum in 1650. He also received small tithes and fees from various chapels within the parish.[138] If Clegg's actions can be explained by both necessity and a fear and dislike of Quakerism, then the Fentons' seem to have been motivated more by hostility towards Dissent in general. To be sure, James Fenton senior found himself in a position where he needed to reassert his rights to protect his income. Although Edmund Garforth, "this wicked priest of Lancaster", had been "seveir for his pretended dues", his successor, Seth Bushell, had "discuraged persecution for religion or prosecution of any in his parish for what was customary due".[139] Bushell only served for two years, but Fenton senior may well have felt he had ground to make up.[140] Although not all attributable to Fenton, 87% of those Friends who suffered for tithe in Lancaster between 1650 and 1700 were first recorded as suffering between 1687 and 1700. He also recovered tithe from Friends in Wyresdale. Fenton was, wrote William Stout, "a haughty man, and very seveire in exacting his pretended dues, to imprisonment of sevral".[141]

Fenton certainly approached his task with a severity that must have both surprised and shocked Friends, as the following account shows:

> James Fenton, priest of Lancaster, came with three men, his wife and a boy, and forced his way into the ground of Henry Coward of Lancaster, where he and his servants were loading his corn. And Henry came to him and would have persuaded him to have taken his men and horses away, but he forcibly broke in and sent his servants Robert Parkinson and Thomas Thompson to load his corn, and the said Henry offering to stop them, the priest in a great fury stripped off his outward garment and run upon him and took him by the throat, and with great violence used all endeavour to strangle him, and keep him fast 'till his carts were gone away with the corn. The Priest's wife all the whole laughing at his actions ....[142]

He had clearly, and correctly, identified Coward, who acted as clerk both to the Monthly and Quarterly Meetings, as an influential man to be made an example of.[143] Four months after the above incident, in December 1693, Coward wrote to the Meeting for Sufferings from Lancaster Castle. He had been sued for tithe with another Friend in one of the Palatine courts and was being kept a close prisoner. Fenton, he wrote, "threatens he will hew out such a way that no priest of the parish that succeeds him shall have any more trouble with Quakers".[144] Fenton had certainly done enough to persuade some of Coward's many Anglican acquaintances that he should cause the vicar, and himself, no further trouble. In May of the following year the Monthly Meeting noted that "some of the relations or others of the world have undertaken to pay or agree for some tithes on the behalf of Robert Lawson and Henry Coward, contrary to their minds".[145] Both Friends were ordered "speedily" to prepare a denial of these actions to present "to the neighbourhood and the world and also of their denial to make any recompense for the same".[146] Such was the sensitivity of Friends regarding the compromising of Coward's reputation that the matter was also dealt with by the Quarterly Meeting.[147]

Fenton died in 1713, Stout's obituary for him being that he was "a great exacter of his demands from his own poor hearers and Dissenters, by prosecution and law, and afected rather to be feared than loved".[148] His son, he noted, "shared much of his disposition".[149] However, rather than use the violence that his father had been forced to employ in his early years at Lancaster, Fenton instead made full use of the summary procedure of 1696. He made annual complaints to the justices of the peace, claiming both small tithes and church-rates.[150] He was assisted in his actions, as Stout complained, by the justices of the peace:

> James Fenton now prosecuted his neighbours the Quakers for tyths befor Charles Rigby and Thomas Shearson, Justices, for smal tyths for two years, of about 4d a year, in two actions who grant him costs each 9s 6d, the law not allowing above 10s [costs] under ten pounds proved; and for about 20s demanded, granted ten pounds costs ....[151]

Whether resulting from collusion between the plaintiff and the bench, or simply from the hostility of the bench towards the defendant, the attitude of the justices responsible for enforcing the summary procedures of 1696 could manifestly alter the proceedings of the law. This, the extent to which the agencies of enforcement might have determined the overall level of tithe prosecutions, is the second point to be considered in this discussion.

There is a possibility that the general downturn in the value of seizures and distraints made from Friends for nonpayment of tithe after 1716 may have been influenced by the changing political complexion of the bench in Lancashire. J.H. Plumb has suggested that Toryism amongst the gentry was at its strongest between 1689 and 1715 in the South-West, the Marches, and the North-West.[152] Many, if not all, lay impropriators, were country gentlemen.[153] Moreover, Lionel Glassey has shown that between 1702 and 1715 Tories dominated the commission of the peace in Lancashire, particularly so at the start and end of this period.[154] In 1715 the bench was purged, although not completely, of Tories, so that "the bench at quarter sessions in January 1716 was as Whig as that in July 1714 had been Tory".[155] Clearly the presence of a hostile bench could be expected to lead to increased distraints against Friends, if only on the basis of awards of heavy costs against them. As we have seen, the Lancashire Quakers frequently complained of just this.[156] Moreover, although Stout's complaints against Rigby and Shearson concerned their activities in 1716, they had both been active on the bench before this date. They were, for example, the justices who had granted a warrant against Daniel Abraham in 1698 for an amount in excess of the maximum specified by the Act.[157] In 1716 they heard cases both in Lancaster and Yealand. The motives of these two Justices were probably varied; Stout questioned their political honesty "who pretend to be loyal yet oppress some of the best friends of the King" and they may indeed have shared Fenton's crypto-Jacobite sentiments.[158] They were both men of the law, Rigby being "an encourager of litigious suits, and espetially in forwarding prosecutions against the Quakers for their conscientious refusall of paying tyths and the clergy's demands", whilst Shearson, a former mayor of Lancaster was impropriator of tithes in Lancaster parish.[159]

The presence of a tithe owner on the bench was by no means unusual. The dangers which this might present to the fair passage of justice had been recognised by the legislators, who had included a clause in both Acts preventing Justices who had an interest in the tithes claimed in any particular case from acting at its hearing.[160] There was, however, a strong thread of interest in tithes which connected many members of the bench in Lancashire. Both Thomas Prestons, for example, served as justices for lengthy periods, and the younger Preston also served as deputy lieutenant for the county.[161] Sir Edmund Ashton had also been on the bench, while his eventual successor, Sir Ralph Ashton, served between 1675 and 1716 with a break of only two years at the end of James II's reign.[162] The respect and deference due to such a senior member of the bench by his junior colleagues must surely have manifested itself in partiality when the matter of awarding costs arose. At some points the relationships could become incestuous, as when we find Thomas Shearson, impropriator of great tithes in Lancaster, hearing cases concerning small tithes in the parish.[163] A similar situation arose within Swarthmore meeting where John Braddyl heard cases for small tithe and church-rates brought by Thomas Inman, curate of Aldingham. Braddyl, lay impropriator of tithes in the area, awarded costs in these cases which were virtually equal to the amount demanded.[164] It was in the mutual interest of both Braddyl and Inman, and Shearson and Fenton, that heavy costs might be awarded, so as to act as a disincentive to future intransigence on the part of the Quakers. Such a network of interest would ensure that the value of tithe taken from Friends, particularly under the summary procedures of 1696, would remain high, especially when the political complexion of the law-enforcement agencies was hostile to Quakers or Dissenters in general.

If due process of the law could be abused by a network of self-interest to act against Friends, then equally the Quakers could manipulate the law on their own behalf. One way this could be done was to challenge proceedings when they appeared to contravene either the spirit or letter of the law. Early Friends had complained against the complexities of the legal system, of

> The people's ignorance of the Laws under which they live, because of the multiplicity thereof, and contradictions therein. Of some Statutes part repealed, and others part continued; some before repealed, again revived, or part revived; some limited to time, some otherwise .... Courts so divers and different in their manner of proceeding and tryals ....[165]

In particular Friends attacked "the wretched Lawyer",[166] "which would devour the Creation to spend upon their own lusts".[167] However, such publicly expressed views had never prevented even the earliest Friends from taking advantage of the law where it seemed appropriate and "consistent with Truth". As we have seen, Friends at Cartmel (with the assistance of their attorney) were well able to challenge the jurisdiction of the variety of courts employed by Thomas Preston by demurring to their competence to hear cases for tithe.[168] The other technicality that Friends frequently employed was to challenge writs and judgements on the basis of errors sometimes as slight as spelling mistakes, in order to halt proceedings.[169] The success which Friends might experience could clearly be a body-blow to the tithe-owner, particularly if the suit had involved considerable expense. When Jeffery Alcock, a Cheshire Friend, was released from prison following the intervention of lay judges in a case brought originally in the ecclesiastical court, his prosecutor, the vicar of Wilmslow, complained that

> if things go thus, Quakers being prosecuted in the Bishop's courts and flung in prison and forthwith released by the judges, all the small tithe will be lost etc. And upon hearing of his [Alcock's] discharge talked of shutting up the church-door, and spoke as if he would preach no more.[170]

A successful intervention in proceedings by Friends could act as a strong discouragement of future action against them.

It will be recalled that not all Friends could in conscience use legal contrivances to lessen their sufferings. Many were prepared to "wait upon the Lord" and let proceedings take their full course rather than be seen to have compromised their testimonies.[171] Others, however, were prepared to use the law not only to challenge the proceedings against them on technicalities, but also to challenge the right which was claimed by the owner to his tithe. A success in a case of this nature automatically reduced the liability of a particular Friend or group of Friends to pay tithe. At least one such case was fought by Friends in Lancashire in the early eighteenth century involving Friends from Yealand. Josiah Lambert, who farmed the tithes of the parish of Warton for the Dean and Chapter of Worcester, made complaint to the Court of Exchequer in January 1721 against twenty–two of the inhabitants of the parish who had refused to pay various tithes for five years or more.[172] It has not been possible to identify all of the individuals concerned, but at least half of them appear to have been Friends.[173] Lambert complained that the parishioners had failed to pay tithes of grain worth at least £10 per annum each; they had also neglected to pay tithes on livestock worth at least £5 per annum each. Similarly, he complained of neglect to pay tithes on wool, hemp, flax and a variety of root crops; fruit; pigs horses and poultry, and also church rates. This, he claimed, was as a result of the parishioners "having entered into combination and confederacy amongst themselves ... together with several other persons unknown". They had refused to pay the tithes, and endeavoured "to conceal the same and the particular values thereof" and similarly refused to "discover which lands, tenements, and heritages in particular they severally or jointly or otherwise hold occupied".[174]

The alleged conspiracy extended to a variety of deeds, for

> to give colour to such their citings and refusals sometimes the said confederates pretent that they have severally duly paid and answered unto your orator [Lambert] his agents or servants the tithes of all and singular the said tithable matter and things ....

This, argued the tithe farmer, was not the case, for

> though it may be true that they severally set out yielded and delivered unto your orator his agents or some of them in every of the said years some small and inconsiderable parts of the tithes of their corn and hay ... yet they and each of them in every of the said years concealed and withheld many of the said tithable matters and subtracted and withheld a great part of the tithes justly due from them respectively ....

Lambert appealed to the Court to enquire into the exact amounts of tithe which were owed to him and to order recovery of the same. His aim was not "to take advantage of the treble" but rather to assert his right to the tithes which the "confederates" had refused to pay.[175]

Of the Friends named in the original complaint only two, Edward and Hannah Cumming, were proceeded against in the Exchequer.[176] Lambert had claimed that the two had grown corn and hay on their estate within the rectory of Warton called Hilderstone, "which they pretend to have been some antient glebeland therefore exempt from payment of tithes in kind". They had also pastured sheep on the same land, refusing tithes of lambs and wool "on the same pretence". He also alleged that they pastured ewes on common ground in Yealand, moving them to the alleged exempt ground to yean, in order to deprive him further of tithe.[177] In all, by the time the case was heard against the Cummings in November 1723 Lambert was claiming seven years' great tithe from their estate at £20 per annum, tithes of sheep and cattle, Easter offerings at 12 shillings per annum, and tithes for two years on "four or five acres of land" for which distraint had previously been made by justice's warrant.[178] The Cummings defence was that their estate "was part and parcel of the Abbey of Cockersands in the said county of Lancaster, which was one of the greater abbeys", and thus not liable to tithe. The right to pasture on the common ground was "an appurtenance to said estate", and "the said estate with all its appurtunances was exempt from payment of tithes".[179] In support of their claim the Friends produced from the Augmentation Office a copy of the surrender of the abbey to the crown, and a valuation of its rents in order to prove it was a "greater abbey".[180] A copy of the grant of the Cumming's estate by the Crown to the Braddyl family, from whom they held it, was also exhibited.[181] In addition, depositions were made by residents of Yealand (non-Friends), showing that the estate had not paid tithes for some forty years, and that it had always enjoyed rights to pasture on the common ground.[182]

Rather than wait on the Lord, the Cummings, with the support of the Meeting for Sufferings, had chosen instead to wait upon the law. Moreover, in this case the law proved more effective than the spirit, at least in material terms. The Barons of the Exchequer

> decreed that the estate called Hilderstone, with its appurtenances, are free and exempt from all manner of tithes, the right of common on Yealand Common was an appurtence to said estate, that the plaintiff's bill be dismissed with cost of this suit.

Lambert, in response, "dropped his further proceedings".[183] Although the success of Friends in this case probably had negligible impact on the overall sufferings for the county (the tithes having apparently never been previously claimed nor paid) it did act as a dissuasive to Lambert to pursue similar claims, contenting himself instead with the occasional seizure of tithes in kind and more commonly distraint by justices' Warrant.[184] The law and its officials could, and did, work in favour of Friends. The outcome might also have acted as a restraint on other tithe-owners seeking either to confirm or extend their income. If Lambert had had the benefit of William Stout's thoughts he might have regretted having employed as his attorney Robert Gibson, described by Stout as "a lawyer of the most reputt of any in this county", "a discurager of vexatious suites and the extortions of the atturneys", and who, whilst a justice of the peace, had "acted very impartialy, and particularly in prosecution of the Quakers for tythes etc...."[185]

It has been suggested by at least three writers that the history of the Quaker tithe testimony in the late seventeenth and eighteenth centuries was marked by a sharp downturn in the number of sufferings for tithes, which was caused by a growing laxity amongst Friends with regard to this particular aspect of their faith and practice. Barry Reay, for example, has suggested that "in general, then, the early Quakers seem to have borne a firmer testimony than their descendants". This, he continues, was because these "were first-generation members of the sect, more committed to Quaker principles" than later, "cooler", generations of Quakers.[186] Eric Evans, having examined in detail the sufferings of Staffordshire Quakers between 1690 and 1730, has concluded that connivance with tithe owners, community sanction operating on their behalf, and occasionally continuous tithe payments by Friends, typified the response to the demand for the tenth at the turn of the seventeenth century.[187] For Evans, like Norman Hunt, one of the most striking illustrations of this was the sharp decline in the number of Friends imprisoned for non-payment of tithes following the introduction of the summary procedure in 1696.[188] Hunt reached the same conclusions that "many Friends were willingly finding, or conniving at, ways of meeting these dues".[189] So widespread was this neglect of the testimony, argued Hunt, that the Meeting for Sufferings launched a campaign in Parliament in order to obtain legislation abolishing the right of ecclesiastical, Exchequer and Chancery courts, to hear tithe cases.[190] The only way to ensure adherence to Friends early principles was to ensure that they posed no real danger to the pockets or persons of the sufferers.

Although superficially attractive, there are a number of weaknesses in such an approach. Underlying the view of Evans and Hunt, for example, is the assumption that whilst imprisonment for not paying tithes was a persecution, the seizure of produce or distraint of goods from Friends either to the value or in excess of the tenth, was not.[191] Now, although persecution is an emotive word which is perhaps best dropped from this discussion, to the Quaker who scrupled the payment of tithes,

> believing Christ's coming in the flesh effected freedom both for his ministers to preach freely without money and without tithes, and for his disciples to hear and learn freely without being imposed upon to pay money, or tithes, or steeple-house rates[192]

there was little or no difference between physical incarceration and material loss. Imprisonment, as we have seen, was sometimes less a product of the titheowner's actions than a result of a particular Friend's or group of Friends' reluctance to involve themselves with the law.[193] Either way, the penalty was unjust because Friends were being penalised for refusing to pay for something which their conscientiously held beliefs prevented them from condoning or financially supporting. One penny or one hundred pounds, one day, one year or even one life: for Friends, acting in the sight of God, each was an equal suffering; each sufferer an equal victim of "persecution".

The second weakness of this view relates to the summary procedures introduced in 1696, and the consequent impact they had on Friends' sufferings. The general observation that imprisonments decreased after the mid-1690s is reflected in the data for Lancashire.[194] However, as we have seen, the main reason for the sudden drop in imprisonments in Lancashire was not the new legislation, but rather the fact that Sir Edmund Ashton, fatally, came second best in a duel.[195] Ashton alone had been responsible for the majority of imprisonments of Lancashire Friends in the 1680s and 1690s, and his absence accounted for the dramatic reduction in 1696.[196] Moreover, as we have also seen, far from alleviating the sufferings of Friends for tithe the new legislation sharply increased the number of Lancashire Friends who became involved in tithe cases. Far from instigating a period of laxity amongst Friends, the 1696 legislation appears to have created an atmosphere of stringency, or severity, amongst tithe owners.[197] Indeed, Alan B. Anderson's observation, that the Act of Toleration was "of little benefit" to Quakers might be enlarged to suggest that rather than 1689 being a turning point for Friends in Lancashire, 1696 instead marked a fundamental change in their situation.[198] This change was two-fold. First, as we have seen in an earlier chapter, the passing of the Affirmation Act provoked nearly thirty years of sometimes bitter conflict between Friends in Lancashire (and elsewhere) and the Quaker establishment in London. Secondly, the two clauses added to this Act concerning the recovery of tithe by summary procedures provoked an upsurge of tithe prosecutions in the county which continued well into the eighteenth century.[199] The angry reaction to this on the part of Lancashire Friends no doubt contributed to their hostility towards both the Affirmation, and the proceedings of the Meeting for Sufferings. It is thus not surprising that in 1706, when the Meeting for Sufferings solicited the Quarterly Meetings for support in obtaining "an Act to restrain the priests or impropriators of tithes ... from suing for the same except upon the late Act", Friends in Lancashire replied that such solicitation will not consist with our Christian testimony against tithes.[200]

Table 7   Lancashire Friends imprisoned for non-payment of tithes, 1692–1700

1692	28	1695	21	1698	1
1693	22	1696	6	1699	2
1694	28	1697	6	1700	1

(source: London Yearly Meeting Minutes, vols. 1 & 2)

A third weakness in the argument of Evans, Hunt and Reay is that whilst it emphasises evidence of apparent neglect in the Quaker's tithe testimony, scant regard is given to other causes which might either increase or decrease the general level of tithe prosecutions and the value of seizures and distraints. Some of these have already been alluded to: for example, the degree to which general or personal economic circumstances could influence the decision to claim tithe. Changing economic conditions could likewise tend to reduce the liability of Friends to pay tithes. In the east of Lancashire the years 1715 to 1780 saw "a period of massive long-term expansion" in the textile industries, particularly in the production of worsteds. Many Friends who had previously been involved in both agricultural production and the textile industries may have been tempted to forgo the former (titheable) income in favour of the latter. The increasing involvement of Friends in the Lancaster and Liverpool districts in trading may also have drawn them away from agriculture.[202] The law could be abused to Friends' disadvantage or manipulated by them to their benefit. The gradual decline in the number of Friends in the county might also affect the total of distraints.[203] The political climate, at both national and local levels, and the extent to which it influenced the officers of law enforcement, also influenced the level of seizures and distraints. Finally the sentiment of a particular community or neighbourhood might deter an owner, particularly a cleric, from pressing home claims against Quakers which might have earned him the disapprobation of his Anglican parishioners.[204]

A fourth weakness of this traditional view of the easing of hardship, and perhaps the most fundamental, is that it neglects to consider the development and practice of the tithe testimony amongst Friends. Reay's conclusion implies the assumption that the refusal to pay tithes was a general practice amongst Friends prior to the Restoration, which in turn suggests that they had also constructed a system of discipline by this time to deal with transgressors.[205] On the other hand it is implicit in both Hunt's and Evans' argument that the laxity in discipline which they both identify after the passing of the Toleration Act was not present before 1689. Moreover, no consideration is given to the extent to which laxity, when it appeared, was successfully combated by Friends in their various business Meetings.[206] The remainder of this chapter will be devoted to a study of the development and enforcement of the discipline respecting the tithe testimony amongst Friends in Lancashire. I will show that there was by no means unanimous agreement amongst early Friends relating to the practice of the tithe testimony, and that this was not established until the late 1670s, by which time Friends had also established a discipline to deal with transgressors. The very presence of a code of discipline suggests that it was required to meet a need, as indeed it was. Friends paid tithe, or it was paid (innocently or otherwise) on their behalf throughout the seventeenth and eighteenth century; this was as much the case in Lancashire which was a county with a high level of sufferings and a well maintained discipline as it was in, for example, Staffordshire, a county which was not.[207] This was recognised by the Yearly Meeting, which noted in 1723, the height of the "lax" period, that "we have no reason to believe otherwise than that Friends *are as faithfull in their testimony as in former years*".[208] The presence of transgressors did not, however, mean the end of the testimony. In Lancashire, maintained by a searching discipline, the testimony against payment of tithes was still held forth by Friends in the eighteenth century as a banner in their crusade to overcome the world.

Hugh Barbour has pointed out that, in the case of tithes, "a general principle felt from the beginning was only later formulated in terms of patterns and conduct".[209] Early Friends had found a shared social concern in their objection to the tithing system, but there is little evidence to suggest that before the Restoration Friends' testimony automatically extended as far as refusing to pay tithes. To be sure, a large number of Friends were prosecuted for such refusal, but an equally large number were not.[210] Nor does what survives of the code of discipline practised amongst early Friends suggest that refusing to pay tithes was a major concern. At the famous meeting held at Balby in Yorkshire in November 1656, one of the earliest codes of discipline was formulated by a group of Northern Friends. Of the twenty clauses, many of which reappeared in later formulations of faith and discipline, there is no mention of tithes, or enquiring into Friends' faithfulness in not paying them.[211] "Disorderly walking" is to be disciplined, but this was not a phrase normally used by Friends with respect to tithe.[212] There is evidence to suggest that in 1657 a number of Friends, among them ministers from the North, were advocating the payment of tithes, at least to lay impropriators.[213] Thomas Budd, a Friend from Somerset said in the same year "if any are free to give their tithes, I have nothing against it".[214] It was probably not until two years later, at the earliest, that Friends began to formulate a coherent and consistent position on tithes. In May 1659 Friends in Lancashire, Cumberland and Westmorland were asked to "take subscription of all those persons that will give in their testimony against the oppression of tithes ..." in order to prepare a petition which was to be presented to Parliament.[215] This petition was probably the immediate forebear of the process of collecting individual testimonies stating "clearness" in the payment of tithes. The collection, reading, and recording of testimonies, detailed in the previous chapter, was one of the most important parts of the discipline concerning tithe.[216]

It is not until the Monthly Meetings began to be held regularly that we see Friends stating the need for a clear testimony against tithe payments. Appended to the first Lancaster Monthly Meeting Minute Book is a paper written by George Fox, probably in 1669, setting out the scope of the Meeting's authority.[217] It was amongst other things, he said, to make enquiries "concerning all such as do pay tithes which makes void the testimony and suffering of all our brethren who have suffered, many of them to death ... all such is to be enquired into, and to be exhorted".[218] In 1675 the Yearly Meeting advised

> that our ancient testimony against tithes, which we have borne from the beginning, and for which many have deeply suffered, some not only the spoiling of their goods, but imprisonment even unto death, be carefully and punctually upheld and countenanced, in the power of God; and that all those who oppose, slight, or neglect that testimony, be looked upon as unfaithful to the ancient testimony of Truth, and dealt with according to gospel order established among us.[219]

Friends in Lancashire enquired into each other's faithfulness at the Meetings which received tithe testimonies; if a testimony was scrutinised or heard and found to be wanting, then a Friend might receive further attention from his or her Particular or Monthly Meeting. Not all Quakers, however, were easy with this form of interrogation. As early as June 1676 the Women's Quarterly Meeting noted that women Friends from Fylde, Rossendale, Marsden and Oldham had neglected to bring in testimonies, and their Monthly Meetings were ordered to "admonish such as have been backward".[220] In the following year it was again noted that there were some women from Marsden Meeting "who scruples to give in their testimonies against tithes ... what their grounds and reasons are for it, we know not".[221] At the following Meeting Friends from Marsden reported that they "have endeavoured to give them satisfaction and to move that which stood in opposition", and "that they are come to see the mistake they were in, and have sent in their testimonies in writing".[222]

These objections to the system of taking in testimonies were similar to those raised by the parties involved in the major separation which took place amongst Quakers in Westmorland in 1675.[223] They appeared again in 1678 when it was noted that

> we understand that there are some women in several particular meetings who seem to join with us in worship that refused to give in their testimonies as others do against the payment of tithes, some pretending they cannot freely do it, and some that they are not clear in the payment of them.[224]

Some of the testimonies which were recorded were not as forthright as previously: Mary Pickupp from Rossendale declared that "I have not been concerned in tithes. If I were, I could not tell how it might be with me".[225] Friends were urged

> to endeavour to satisfy them, of the weakness and danger they are in, in that unstable, hypocritical mind, for if they be given up to serve the Lord, it must be with their whole heart, and not think to serve him with one part and the world with another. [226]

This approach proved partly successful, for it was reported in 1679 that some Friends saw "their weakness and error", one, Jane Canby of Knowsley bringing her testimony "for the Lord and his Truth in this matter".[227] However, at the same Meeting a widow from Rossendale who "being under the power of the enemy to mankind" refused to end an agreement made by her late husband for the payment of his tithe.[228] The response of Friends was to disown her, that they were "clear of her in the sight of God, having discharged our consciences of her in this matter".[229] Indeed it was not until 1681 that the Meeting, could, for the first time, record that all Meetings stood "faithful and upright" in their testimony against tithes,

> for which we bless the Lord and give him the prayers for the preservation of his children; and we can say of a truth his presence attends us and he is in the midst of us and overshadows our assembly; glory over all ascends unto him from the arisings of his heavenly life in our souls.[230]

The Men's Meetings in the county appear to have had less difficulty than the Women's in establishing the regular scrutiny of written and verbal tithe testimonies. As we have seen, Friends' earliest Men's Meetings in the county were concerned to put this procedure into practice.[231] The importance of this was two-fold: not only did it allow Friends' faithfulness to be monitored, but also it enabled them to maintain a register of membership on the basis of the record of acceptable testimonies. There were, however, early problems with Friends who had paid, or allowed their tithe to be paid for them, some of whom were unwilling to accept the discipline of their Monthly Meetings particularly at Swarthmore and Cartmel. In November 1668 Swarthmore Monthly Meeting was informed that three Friends from Swarthmore, Thomas Goad, Thomas Borwick and Richard Ashburner, had paid tithes or had tithes paid for them

> which is a grief and trouble to others that are faithful sufferers in that particular, and it opens the mouths of the priests and others who are ready to say we are not all of one mind and so gives them occasions to speak evil of the ways of the Truth and those that walk in it.[232]

The three Friends sent written explanations of their behaviour to the next Meeting, but "Friends being not satisfied with the answer" they gave, they were ordered to be dealt with further.[233] The Meeting was still dissatisfied with the response of the three Friends in February when it was reported that Thomas Goad had taken "an oath lately at the Commissary Court and how he was clear himself to Friends concerning the said report, and of his buying the priest's tithes at Sunbrick".[234] The following Meeting, "having not received any satisfaction or answer" from the three, declared that in the absence of a written answer the next Monthly Meeting would "have just cause to declare against them and deny them to be any of us or our judgement".[235]

Early in 1670 Friends at Swarthmore were again troubled by a number who "have paid tithes, or consented to the payment of them".[236] Of particular concern was Richard Myers, who gave in a testimony to the Meeting "concerning the payment of his tithes, that he has more peace in letting it go quietly than in striving against him [the tithe] collector".[237] Friends attempted to reason with Myers without success, and he was asked to explain "why he reviled Truth's messengers who was in love sent to him, or else it will appear rebellion".[238] Almost twelve months passed before a testimony from Myers was presented to the Quarterly Meeting to be recorded; it was, however, refused.[239] Friends from Swarthmore again spoke with Myers but concluded

> after several admonitions he says he has peace with God and unity, both either concerning tithes or any other transgressions that may be laid against him, which answer and spirit we cannot but deny, and him also while he says he had peace with God and lives in transgression and disobedience. [240]

By allowing the inner light to lead him into paying tithes, Myers had taken the individuality inherent in Quaker belief to a point which by 1670 was no longer acceptable. The collective self-discipline which had in part been forced upon Friends by a hostile world could not tolerate such a breach, for it was in their opposition to tithes that Friends presented their most united face to the political and religious establishments.[241]

It was not easy for a Friend who paid tithes to escape the notice of his or her Particular or Monthly Meetings. If fault was not found with a testimony, then a Meeting might receive "a report" or "information" concerning the alleged transgressions of its members.[242] In 1700 Daniel Abraham gave to Swarthmore Monthly Meetings the names of "some Friends whom he observed to be crossed out of the justices warrants about steeplehouse lay".[243] Similarly, Friends enquired whether any were seeking to avoid the liability of making tithe payments. Following advice from the Yearly Meeting, Friends in Lancashire were warned against leaving tithable land uncultivated or leasing it to non-Friends "to avoid sufferings and so weaken their testimony".[244] The Quarterly Meeting ordered that

if any Friend or Friends be apprehended to be under any such weakness it is desired that Friends be very careful to advise them to the contrary unless they can give a satisfactory reason to Friends for their so forbearing to plough or sow or letting their lands to lease.[245]

Behaviour was also monitored in relation to the illegal seizure of tithe in kind which before 1696 was probably the most common form of suffering in the county.[246]. There is no suggestion that this was, as Eric Evans has written, "the most satisfactory arrangement on both sides", or that Friends entered into "explicit agreements" with tithe owners to adopt this course.[247] Any such arrangement would have led to the offender's coming under the discipline of his or her Monthly Meeting, with the subsequent requirement for a testimony to be brought in.

In 1687 the Quarterly Meeting advised that Friends

do take care as much as in them lies to keep up their testimonies against tithes etc., and to keep their conscience clear by taking a due care over their corn that they see what quantity of corn they have and see how it is gone that they as far as they have freedom in the truth resist them that would take it and bear up their testimonies against them.[248]

Six years later Friends were reminded to "keep their gates locked" at tithing; they were to "bear a testimony by word against them in meekness and not to strive or struggle with them or be in any way harsh therein except they found it required of them ...."[249] Such a stance, however, was frequently accompanied with violence; for example, when Mary Fletcher of Knowsley refused to allow tithe-farmers to enter her property they "broke the gate open upon her and flung her down, and had like to have gone over her with the cart".[250] John Haydock of Coppull told the farmers "they should not come further but by force" at which "Richard Wilkinson violently broke the chain with an axe and John Lowe struck his servant and cut him with an axe and violently they forced open his gate".[251] John Tomlinson was another victim of James Fenton and his servants; "they came to me where I and my wife were working at the hay and smote me very sore and abused my wife", later they "forcibly took away my beans holding their pitchforks against me when I came to hinder them".[252]

The refusal of Friends to countenance the seizure of tithe in kind could have far-reaching consequences, as John Moore's case illustrates.

> Thomas Butler of Kirkland in the parish of Garstang and County of Lancaster (called justice of the peace) did come to John Moone's house of Cabus ... and the said Thomas Butler did demand tithe ... and John said he would not give him any, Thomas answered he would have it, but John Moone did forwarn him not to meddle of it, but forcibly the said Thomas Butler entered into the said John's ground and marked with other two men with him and a carriage his corn. Then John locked up his gate and did endeavour to keep his conscience clear in the sight of God, and so went away to plough. The said Thomas Butler and his men came to the gate and found it locked, and he called to my wife to unlock the gate and let them go. And she said she could not; then the said Thomas Butler said for the preservation of thee and thy children, open the gate. John's wife said the safest way for the preservation of me and my children is to be faithful to what the Lord has made known to me. So when the said Thomas Butler could not prevail with her he went to my husband where he was ploughing. And he pressed on him to let the carriage go with the corn; John said he would not, except they would lay down the corn, so when he had tired himself he was willing to leave my corn, and then John did let them go, but the said Thomas Butler was very angry.[253]

This success was tempered by Butler's long-lasting anger. Later in the same year Butler sued and imprisoned Moone for non-payment of tithes, eventually making distraints worth £20 for a demand of £6 4d.[254] Fifteen months later Butler sued Moone in the Exchequer at Westminster, but following his refusal to give a bond to appear he was committed to prison at Lancaster, where he spent the winter "sick and weakly".[255] In 1683 Butler sued Moone for treble damages, "the goods they took at this time (having often spoiled him of his goods before) amounted in value to £35 leaving him naked, not a bed to lie upon".[256]

The greatest difficulty for Friends, however, was not to ensure that seizure of tithe in kind became a covert method of tithe payment, but rather to deal with the difficulty posed by Friends whose tenth was paid for them by relatives or friends and neighbours. The involvement of the latter brings us to a consideration of the community sanction, which Eric Evans identifies as having "operated in favour of Friends, who seem to have been generally popular, at least when combating the demands of tithe owners".[257] For Friends, however, such sanction, or intervention, in breach of their testimony against tithes was unwelcome. Few Friends sought such assistance without coming under the discipline of their Meeting; even when the Meeting was convinced of a Friend's innocence in the matter they were required to produce "a paper to the world and neighbours of their clearness against such things, and of their denial of making any repayment for the same".[258] The consequence of failing in this was that "their said testimonies will not be taken as worthy to be recorded amongst those that are faithful, but denyed".[259] If tithes were paid for Friends because they were popular, then they were forced to deny the same in a way that left little room for easy friendship. In 1697 it was ordered that Friends should "give out a paper against them" that paid their tithes. In the following year the Particular Meetings were advised to "take care that Friends do show their dislike to those who pay tithes, steeplehouse-lays etc. for them by not being so familiar as before, before they show their remorse for their so doing".[261] Later in the same year the Quarterly Meeting expanded upon this:

> where any Friends are concerned on that account they may be careful not to give any encouragement to such either by words or conversation or trading but rather to withdraw till they do perceive them to show some remorse for what they have done and promise of not doing so for the future.[262]

Eventually those that had tithe paid for them were obliged to bring in not only their own testimony but also one from those who had paid, repudiating their actions in writing.[263] The enforcement of this discipline saw Friends acting in an anti-social manner, denying the courtesies and kindnesses of common-life in a brusque and ungrateful fashion.[264] There was often a reluctance on the part of Friends to act in this manner, particularly, no doubt, when important social or commercial links were at stake. In July 1698 Lancaster Monthly Meeting noted that "some Friends … was found not readily to answer advice in giving forth a testimony against those that may in anywise have paid or compounded for them in the behalf of tithes etc"; five months later the testimonies were delivered.[265] In 1708 three prominent Lancaster Friends, William Stout, Edward Wallbank and Robert Lawson jointly put forward a paper against Edmund Cole for paying a church-rate for them.[266] Cole was high-sheriff for the county in 1707 and mayor of Lancaster in 1716, 1725 and 1736.[267] It may well have been Cole's intention to embarrass Friends by his actions, but, as in the case of another Meeting clerk, Henry Coward, Stout was not deflected from restating his testimony.[268] Friends often spoke harshly of those who had offered them misguided kindness. George Holm of Ulverston gave in a testimony against one Thomas Mann who had paid his small tithe, in which he indicated his "dislike of such sort of civility, taking it as a diskindness and shall rather withdraw my former familiarity with him".[269] Alexander Rylands denied the action of the constable of Winstanley, who had paid his church-rate, adding that "neither shall I take him to be my friend till he promises to do no more".[270] Thomas Askew of Cartmel received a paper not from Richard Brittain, whose tithe he had paid, but from the Monthly Meeting, which warned

> If Richard Brittain bids thee pay his tithes in that thing we do deny him
> to be in God's eternal truth, for Christ Jesus the end of tithes is our
> minister and teacher, and if thou pay them without his consent it is just
> and right thou loses them because thou endeavours to murder and
> betray the just in him.[271]

In such an atmosphere community sanction was not likely to be offered
to a Friend twice.

The involvement of a close relation in a disciplinary measure over tithe
payments could place an even greater strain on both the Friend and the
tithe payer. Quakerism had traditionally cut across family ties, sometimes
abruptly, in attracting its converts and it continued to do this in Lancashire
when enforcing the tithe testimony.[272] Elizabeth Lucas from Blackrod
wrote in 1675

> I never paid tithes in all my life, nor did never give my consent to the
> payments of any, and before I was married to this man, I spoke to him
> much about tithes, whether he could suffer his goods to be taken for
> tithes, and he said, he would do as other Friends did, but now he lets
> them take his corn away, but as for me, I believe I shall never consent
> to the payment of any.[273]

William Kippax from Marsden admitted that "my wife, not being
conformable unto the Truth, does pay [tithes] although I have requested
her to the contrary".[274] When Henry Clare's stepson gave the tithe farmers
a bond to pay his stepfather's tithe for his lifetime Henry wrote "I do not
count him my friend but an enemy to the living testimony that is in my
heart".[275] In 1704 Thomas Robinson testified against his mother, who was
also required to attend the Meeting at Yealand to "confess I did wrong".[276]
Friends were required to rupture the most delicate bonds in order to be
seen to be maintaining their opposition to the tithing system. Both
community and family sanctions operated in Lancashire but Friends did
not perceive them as operating in their favour. Rather they were to be
curtly, not to say rudely, denied and condemned both in private, and often
to the humiliation of those who offered help, in public.

The disciplinary procedure operated by Friends in respect of tithes was
nonetheless a caring process, aimed at persuading the transgressor to
acknowledge both his fault and his or her determination to live according
to Truth's precepts for the future. Rather than rush to a quick denial or
disownment, Friends instead were prepared to labour long to bring about
a proper understanding of the tithe testimony. This was reflected in the
length to which the Quarterly Meeting might go in order to record only
"acceptable" testimonies. To the extent, then, that a Friend like Richard
Myers might be under the care of a Meeting for a year or longer, Friends
tolerated tithe-payers amongst their midst.[277] However, as with Myers,
those who refused to conform to the testimony would ultimately be

disowned. Richard Eccles, for example, first came to the attention of Swarthmore Monthly Meeting in June 1701 as a person "that is not so clear as they could desire concerning the payment of tithes".[278] Joseph Goad and Matthew Fell were delegated to speak with Eccles, but two months later they could report only that he refused to attend the Meeting to explain himself.[279] By December Friends had concluded that "a paper should be drawn signifying Friends disunion with him in his payment of tithes"; the paper was to be read to Eccles as a last opportunity for him to show remorse.[280] His response, however,was that he did "not seem to own nor acknowledge the justice of the said paper", with the consequence that in March 1702, some nine months after the case first arose, Richard Eccles was publicly disowned.[281]

In 1706 it was noted by Swarthmore Monthly Meeting that "Swarthmore Meeting gives account that they have something under their care".[282] This matter was minuted for six months until June 1707, when the Particular Meeting reported that

> they have spoken pretty fully to the persons within the compass of that Meeting who is short in bearing their testimonies against tithe and also they give account that they returned the collection of one of them, viz. Abraham Clayton, who seemed to be hard and not to accept Friends' advice and the other being John Goad Jnr. seemed to be more tender ....[283]

Friends were advised to visit the two, to "read to them the paragraph relating to that matter out of the manuscript of the last yearly epistle".[284] Clayton and Goad, however, did not "incline to Friends' advice any further" and were ordered to be spoken to again.[285] In addition, William Satterthwaite was

> desired to search the book wherein condemnations is recorded and to take out a copy of a paper formerly given forth by Abraham Clayton.[286]

This having been done, in August 1707, the Meeting decided to rest the matter "till after harvest time, that it may be seen whether the late visits and advices which have been bestowed upon them have any effect ...."[287] Clayton and Goad were still found "deficient in their testimonies against tithe", but the Friends dealing with them "desired Friends' forbearing 'till they may be further tried in that matter", although the Meeting did send papers of advice to both of them.[288] A year later Goad had apparently reconciled himself to the Meeting, but Clayton had not, "so the issue of the matter is left 'till they have made some proof of their testimonies in the matter ..."[289] The proof was not forthcoming; Friends had

> spoken to Abraham Clayton and advised him further with respect to his testimony and to use more diligence in coming up to Meetings but

he did not seem inclinable to accept Friends advice at that time but made some very weak and impertinent excuses which gives this meeting small hopes of his coming up in more faithfulness.[290]

Consequently, in June 1710, some three and a half years after the matter first arose, Clayton was disowned by the Monthly Meeting.[291]

In enforcing the discipline in this way Friends ensured that they faced the world with a united opposition to the tithing system. Friend's opposition to tithes was still a banner around which they rallied, a banner which was by the early 1700s more firmly held than it had been in the 1660s. Moreover, such was the firmness of Friends in Lancashire on this matter that at the turn of the century, in the face of opposition from both London Friends and from Margaret Fell, they sought to redefine their testimony in order to include a refusal of payments which had previously been tolerated. The incident which sparked off this matter was the refusal of Margaret Fell's son-in-law, Daniel Abraham, to pay fee-farm rents due from his estates at Swarthmore.[292] Isobel Ross, in her recently re-published biography of Margaret Fell, touches briefly on this matter.[293] "Daniel's overconscientiousness was quite unnecessary" she writes, adding that he, and "some other Swarthmoor Friends who had taken the same line" were persuaded to see the error of their ways.[294]

Another biographer of Margaret Fell has written that Daniel's "more clear-sighted and practical brothers-in-law … showed him his mistake". Daniel was "not very practical and perhaps over-conscientious".[295] Whether through a misunderstanding of the materials they consulted, or possibly through a desire to impose a unity where none existed, both these writers have been guilty of a clear misrepresentation of the facts. As the following short narrative shows, Daniel Abraham's "over-conscientiousness" was the over-conscientiousness of Lancashire Quarterly Meeting, his refusal to pay fee-farm, or "rectory rents" being shared by Friends throughout the county.

In August 1699 Daniel Abraham wrote to the Meeting for Sufferings having been served with a writ of rebellion at the suit of John Woods, impropriator of tithes at Swarthmore.[296] Abraham was advised by the Meeting to appear at the Exchequer to answer the suit; his brother-in-law, Thomas Lower, a prominent member of the Meeting for Sufferings, asked him to search out the facts of the case, obtaining where possible witnesses to act on his behalf.[297] However, his failure to answer the writ led to his arrest on a commission of rebellion in October, when he was transported to London and imprisoned in the Fleet.[298] Although there were apparently errors in the proceedings Abraham appeared before the Barons of the Exchequer in December, when an action was begun for his seques-tration.[299] Later in the month, however, Lower reported to the Meeting for Sufferings

that his brother-in-law Daniel Abraham upon his new search in the Dutchy office (in his case) finds it is a fee-farm rent belonging to the

King out of his estate at Swarthmore, within the rectory of Ulverston upon which he has suffered, and upon his understanding it is not tithe has paid the cost of suit and its now at end.[300]

The conclusion of the case was described by Thomas Lower and another brother-in-law, William Ingram, in family correspondence.

Ingram had written to Daniel Abraham's wife, Rachel, early in December, that "we have dealt very plainly with my brother in this affair and hope it will have a good effect, being done in love".[301] On the 16th he wrote to his mother-in-law, Margaret Fell, explaining how the matter had been resolved following a meeting with Sir Thomas Rawlinson, the owner of the disputed rents.[302] Rawlinson had been "exclaiming against brother Abraham for putting him to so great trouble and calling his title in question ... he would by no means be persuaded but it was a dishonest design in him to defeat him of his right". Ingram and Lower had "laboured much to bring my brother to an understanding" in the matter, "being satisfied it could not be tithes because there is tithes paid besides this incumbrance out of the estate". Ingram confirmed that Lower had paid the costs in the case, complaining:

It has happened very strangely that this damage and loss should be sustained without a due enquiry into the nature of the claim ... we hope for the future that it may be avoided.

He also indicated that to prevent any further difficulties Lower was attempting to buy the right to collect the rent.[303] Lower had also written to his mother-in-law, explaining that he had given the Meeting for Sufferings a satisfactory account of the matter, "excepting some few that would be jangling according to their wonted manner".[304] The opinion that the rent was not a tithe had not been accepted without "agitation in the Meeting". However as the business was now "allayed and quiet at present" Lower had determined not to present the Meeting with a letter which his mother-in-law had passed to him on the subject. The letter, he said, might "by some of our carping folk may be made a matter of dispute and controversy"; there were, he added, other reasons for not presenting the letter, "too large to mention".[305]

The debate in London over the exact nature of the rent was no doubt fired by the difficulty in determining the origins of the particular fee-farm rent in question. "The true meaning of fee-farm is a perpetual farm or rent", and it was a term used to cover a variety of payments including in Lancashire "corn mill rents", "priest's land rents' and "Wapentake tithes".[306] There were probably other fee-farms which had had their origins in tithes which had been alienated to the crown; clearly Friends' scruples would not extend as far as the payment of these. In Lancashire the Quarterly Meeting invited those Friends who were concerned in the payment of the disputed rent to offer their deeds for inspection, so its origin could be discovered.[307]

Rachel Abraham wrote that "several of the Quarterly Meeting were well satisfied that our rent is nothing of tithes although there was some appeared disquieted in the matter".[308] The inspection of the deeds on 3rd May 1700 restored unity to the Meeting, for

> several deeds and instruments having been read and considered, by all that appeared for the information of Friends in this Meeting, this Meeting's sense is that the rent demanded and chargeable upon the lands of Swarthmore Friends is of the nature of tithes and therefore cannot be paid without invalidating the testimony of Truth.[309]

Robert Haydock, who had organised the inspection of the deeds, wrote to the Meeting for Sufferings giving the opinion of the Meeting at Lancaster, asking that the suffering undergone by Daniel Abraham in the previous year (which had been "suspended" following the delivery of Lower's opinion) should be entered in the Great Book of Sufferings.[310] An additional note from "the Friends of Swarthmore Meeting that are concerned in that matter" stated that "they were more easy and clear in their minds to suffer for it, than to pay it".[311]

The Meeting for Sufferings had concluded "thus the matter is settled".[312] This was not, however, the opinion of a number of Friends at Swarthmore, most notably Margaret Fell. On 2nd December 1700 the Particular Meeting there appointed seven Friends, including Daniel Abraham, "to inspect into the debates which of late have appeared in our Meeting".[313] These Friends reported that they found "Friends to differ about the rectory-rent" and the matter was referred to the Monthly Meeting.[314] There the Meeting was informed that

> some Friends are under some apprehension that the said (Quarterly) Meeting was not altogether fully informed so this Meeting agrees that if any Friends can produce anything that may better inform Friends therein that they make the same appear at our next Monthly Meeting and in the interim stand clear of paying or consenting to the payment thereof. And this Meeting appoints Daniel Abraham, Joseph Goad and Henry Lampe to speak to such persons as are under that apprehension to make ready what they have ....[315]

At the next Meeting nothing was forthcoming from the objectors, but it was reported "they believe there is an expectation of something coming from London in order thereto" and the matter was left for the following month.[316] It was not until 31st March 1701 that John Fell "brought a paper to this Meeting signed by Margaret Fox and directed to Friends of the Monthly and Quarterly Meetings". The paper was read "but the matter therein contained not clearing the matter", it was referred to the Quarterly Meeting for a decision.[317] The Quarterly Meeting, however, was equally "not satisfied thereby that the said rent is not of the nature of tithes".[318]

The paper which Margaret Fell presented to the Meeting at Swarthmore is not extant, but its content was probably influenced by a letter sent
to her earlier in the month by George Whitehead.[319] He had, at her
request, investigated the nature of fee-farm rents by consulting various
statutes, concluding that "if they had been originally part of the tithes or
church-rents, their property is altered by converting them into a rent to
the crown". The rent had thus become a civil payment, "and I see not how
a reason of conscience can be placed upon refusing payment any more
than to refuse the payment of taxes or poor rates". Friends, he warned,
"had need to have good reason for conscience and see the same be
consistent with our Christian profession in every case where they profess a
conscientiousness, and not to strain that to dubious cases". Margaret Fell
had clearly given him a hostile account of proceedings in Lancashire, for
he was

> truly sorry to understand that there are some among you that are
> zealous but not according to true knowledge and divine wisdom; which
> is poor and peaceable, low, and seeks peace and concord, and admits
> not of strife or self exaltation, nor seeks to pick occasion against faithful
> brethren or sisters in Christ. And I am sorry that any should take upon
> them so hardly to censure or judge any of you.

There were, he continued, dangers in such matters, "where either civil
or Christian reputation is concerned".[320] Whitehead was clearly anxious
lest the refusal of Lancashire Friends to pay rectory-rents breached the
delicate line which had been drawn (partly by him) between those civil
payments which ought to be paid by Friends, and those spiritual payments
which ought not.[321] It was partly on the basis of this consensus that Friends
had made themselves acceptable to those politicians who were prepared to
further their aims in Parliament. By questioning civil payments Friends
thus endangered their political respectability.[322]

Although Margaret Fell's paper to the Monthly Meeting (like that
which Thomas Lower suppressed) has not survived, one letter by her on
this subject has. It was written in November 1701, sometime after the
Monthly and Quarterly Meeting had decided to support the refusal to pay
fee-farm rents. No manuscript copy of this document survives, but a
transcript was printed in Maria Webb's *The Fells of Swarthmoor Hall*,
published in 1865.[323] As with other letters written by her at this time, there
is no guarantee it was ever distributed among Friends. Maria Webb
interprets the letter as showing that "there had arisen among the Friends
some narrow, fault-finding, dividing spirits, which were giving trouble to
the right-minded portion of the Society".[324] As we have seen, however, the
"narrow, fault-finding, dividing spirits" belonged exclusively to Margaret
Fell and her few isolated supporters in Lancashire. She wrote of a "false
lying spirit gotten up amongst us to oppose and withstand our gracious,
blessed Truth". Thwarted once more by the majority of Friends in the

county, she complained bitterly of "an imagining, false, and untrue spirit" who she clearly felt was challenging Friends' precious political accept-ability. God commanded, she wrote,

> that we should render to Caesar the things that are Caesar's, and to God the things that are God's: which I shall by His holy assistance and power endeavour to fulfil both to God and Man.[325]

Neither the sentiments of George Whitehead, nor those of Margaret Fell and most of her family were sufficient to persuade the Quarterly Meeting other than that the rectory rents were tithes. As such, they were not to be paid, and any who transgressed in this was liable to the discipline of the Monthly Meeting. The atmosphere that this decision was taken in was one of unprecedented sufferings for non-payment of tithes following the introduction of summary procedure for their recovery in 1696. In this testing time Friends responded not with a growing laxity towards their tithe testimony but rather with a greater stringency. In many respects Friends entered into a battle with the Establishment in the same way that they had done during the fierce persecution following the Restoration. This battle with the Establishment over tithes was paralleled with a battle with the Quaker establishment in London over the Affirmation. On both these counts Margaret Fell was alienated from the Friends of Lancashire Quarterly Meeting. She responded to this with considerable personal bitterness, censure and judgement.[326] What she wrote has been taken at face value by historians who have failed seriously to consider the events that were taking place in Lancashire, and possibly throughout the North, at this time.[327] This is particularly so in the case of the strict discipline which was imposed at this time by Friends in Lancashire, a discipline which, along with their testimonies against oaths and tithes, was to be their vehicle to convert the world.

REFERENCES

1. Alan B. Anderson, 'Lancashire Quakers and Persecution', (University of Lancaster, MA thesis, 1971), *passim*.; Alan B. Anderson, 'A Study in the Sociology of Religious Persecution: The First Quakers', *Journal of Religious History*, 9 (1977), pp.247–62
2. Anderson, 'A Study in the Sociology of Religious Persecution', p.250, n.11
3. For a discussion of "community sanction" see below, this chapter
4. Anderson's main findings are reproduced in tabular form above, Table 1.
5. Anderson, 'A Study in the Sociology of Religious Persecution', p.253
6. *ibid*. p.259
7. *ibid*. p.261
8. Lancashire Quarterly Meeting Book of Sufferings, vol.1; for problems with early record keeping in Lancashire see above, chapter 4
9. Eric Evans, "'Our Faithful Testimony'" *JFHS*, 52 (1969), writes of "the

frequency with which incumbents and impropriators took tithe in kind ..."
during the period 1690–1730, p.110

10. 2 & 3 Edw. VI, c. 13
11. 7 & 8 Will. III, c.6, c. 34
12. For this see also Anderson, 'A Study in the Sociology of Religious Persecution', pp.248–50
13. It has been suggested that in the Lakelands there was a "relative absence of great geographical mobility" – this may well have applied to parts, if not all, of Lancashire. J.D. Marshall, 'Agrarian Wealth and Social Structure in Pre-Industrial Cumbria', *Economic History Review*, 2nd series, 33 (1980), p.505
14. The latest suffering recorded for Sankey is 1684, whilst the earliest for Penketh is 1687. A breakdown of tithe sufferings, 1650–1700, by Meeting is presented in Appendix 4
15. *Stout*, Appendix B, 'Distraints suffered by William Stout, 1698–1747', p.292
16. See above, Table 1
17. 7 & 8 Will. III, c. 6
18. 7 & 8 Will. III, c. 34
19. Eric Evans, *The Contentious Tithe* (London, 1976), pp.43–44
20. For the expense of tithe proceedings, see *ibid*. pp.44, 50–53
21. For the illegality of this procedure, see Alfred W. Braithwaite, 'Early Tithe Prosecutions, Friends as Outlaws', *JFHS*, 49 (1960), p.149. Braithwaite suggests, in contrast to the findings presented here and by Eric Evans, that this was a little used procedure; see above, n.9
22. *Stout*, p.292
23. LQMS vol.1, Swarthmore 10th month 1698
24. See above, chapter 4 *passim*.
25. LQMM, vol.1, 7/11/1696
26. LQMM, vol.1, 3/5/1706
27. MMS, vol.11, 25/7/1696; see also MMS, vol.12, 24/7/1697
28. MMS, vol.11, 25/10/1696
29. Stephen C. Morland (ed.), *The Somersetshire Quarterly Meeting of the Society of Friends 1668–1699* (Somerset Record Society, vol.75, 1978), p.245
30. MMS, vol.11, 1/11/1696
31. *Political Associations*, p.63, n.6
32. LYMM, vols.2–8
33. A breakdown of the sufferings of Friends in Staffordshire for tithes only can be found in Eric Evans, 'A History of the Tithe System in England 1690–1850' (University of Warwick Ph.D. thesis, 1971), Appendices IV–V, pp.427–33
34. This therefore modulates most of the conclusions arrived at by Eric Evans in "'Our Faithful Testimony", *passim*. Figures given by Michael Watts suggest a total of 1,460 Friends in Lancashire in the early eighteenth century, as opposed to 170 in Staffordshire: *The Dissenters* (Oxford, 1978), p.509
35. For this see the figures in John Stephenson Rowntree, *Quakerism, Past and Present* (London, 1859), p.81; for some of the weaknesses in these data see *Second Period*, p.458; see also above, Introduction
36. See Appendix 5
37. Especially Barry Reay, 'Quaker Opposition to Tithes 1652–1660', *Past and Present*, 86 (1980), pp.118–20; Eric Evans, "'Our Faithful Testimony"', *passim.*; *Political Associations*, pp.64–72

38. Rosemary O'Day, *The English Clergy. The Emergence and Consolidation of a Profession 1558–1642* (Leicester, 1979), p.198; for the particular problems of tithing in kind see Evans, *The Contentious Tithe*, pp.22–26

39. B.G. Blackwood, 'Agrarian Unrest and the Early Lancashire Quakers', *JFHS*, 51 (1965), pp.72–76; B.G. Blackwood, 'Economic State of the Lancashire Gentry on the Eve of the Civil War', *Northern History* 12 (1976), pp.60–64; J.V. Beckett, 'Landownership in Cumbria 1680–1750' (University of Lancaster, Ph.D. thesis, 1975), pp.150–51; C.B. Phillips 'The Gentry in Cumberland and Westmorland 1600–65' (University of Lancaster, Ph.D. thesis, 1974), p.137

40. Blackwood, 'Agrarian Unrest', p.75; Barry Reay provides evidence of the same in Cumberland, Essex, Kent, Somerset and Suffolk, 'Quaker Opposition to Tithes', pp.100–104

41. See above, chapter 5

42. For example, Thomas Preston of Holker. See below, this chapter

43. Eric Evans, 'Some Reasons for the Growth of English Rural Anti-Clericalism c.1750–c.1830' *Past and Present*, 66 (1975) p.86; Felicity Heal, 'Economic Problems of the Clergy', in Felicity Heal and Rosemary O'Day, *Church and Society in England, Henry VIII to James I* (London, 1977), p.110

44. Christopher Hill, *Economic Problems of the Church* (Oxford, 1956), p.117

45. *ibid.* p.144

46. R.C. Richardson, *Puritanism in north-west England* (Manchester, 1972), p.2

47. *ibid.*

48. "The unsatisfactory state of a great many of the clergy of the diocese was, in part at least, the result of this situation", *ibid.* p.3. For some comments on the state of the Church in Lancashire, and efforts to remedy it, see Christopher Hill, *Change and Continuity in Seventeenth Century England* (London, 1974), pp.3–47

49. For the Dean and Chapter of Worcester and the case of Robert Hubberstey see above, chapter 2; for the case of Edward and Hannah Cumming see below, this chapter

50. The price of both corn and bread was falling in 1716, whilst wages had risen since 1715; B.R. Mitchell and Phyllis Deane, *Abstract of British Historical Statistics* (Cambridge, 1962) pp.346, 486, 497

51. Rosemary O'Day, *The English Clergy*, pp.192–94

52. Prices for corn and bread had peaked in 1709, but were still high in 1711; Mitchell and Deane, *op.cit.* pp.486, 497

53. Although the period was one of falling prices and agricultural depression; G.E. Mingay 'The Agricultural Depression, 1730–50', *Economic History Review*, 2nd Series, 8 (1955–56), pp.323–38

54. Henry Fishwick (ed.), *Lancashire and Cheshire Church Surveys 1649–55* (Record Society of Lancashire and Cheshire, 1, 1879), p.141

55. C.B. Phillips, 'The Gentry in Cumberland and Westmorland', p.172

56. *ibid.* pp.172–74; B.G. Blackwood, 'Economic State', p.63

57. 'The Life of Master John Shaw', in *Yorkshire Diaries* (Surtees Society, 65, 1875), p.137, quoted in Richardson, *op.cit.* p.4; *Diary and Letter Book of Thomas Brockbank 1671–1709* (Chetham Society, n.s. 89, 1930), pp.310–11. Although Thomas Preston's father had effected a "general restoration" of Cartmel Priory in 1618; *VCH Lancs*, vol.8. p.259

58. B.G. Blackwood, *The Lancashire Gentry and the Great Rebellion 1640–60*

(Chetham Society, 3rd Series, 25, 1978), p.145

59. *ibid.*; B.G. Blackwood, 'Agrarian Unrest', p.73

60. C.B.Phillips, *Lowther Family Estate Books* (Surtees Society, 191, 1976–7), p.251

61. *ibid.*

62. *ibid.* pp.186–87

63. GBS, vol.3, pt.2, Cartmel, 1676, p.790. An almost identical version of this account, taken from a manuscript then at Cavendish House, is reproduced in *TC&WA&AS*, n.s.20 (1920), pp.246–51. The conflict between the Cartmel Quakers and Thomas Preston is also detailed in Thomas Atkinson, *The Christian Testimony Against Tythes* (no place, 1678), *passim*. For details of pre-Restoration tithe prosecutions at Cartmel see GBS, vol.3, pt.2, p.696

64. *ibid.* vol.3, pt.2, p.790. The Wapentake court was the equivalent of a hundred court, having "jurisdiction in debt, covenant and trespass not exceeding 40 shillings". The court at Cartmel was the manor court, known also as court leet or court baron. The lord of the manor or his steward acted as judge; it "tried all personal actions where the cause of action did not exceed 40 shillings". David M. Walker, *The Oxford Companion to Law* (Oxford, 1980), pp.595, 803. For the court leet, see S.A. Peyton, *Minutes of Proceedings in Quarter Sessions held for the Parts of Kesteven in the County of Lincoln 1674–1695* (Lincoln Record Society, 25, 1928), pp.lviii–lix

65. J.V. Beckett, 'Landownership in Cumbria', p.275. The lease was for three lives.

66. GBS, vol.3, pt.2, p.790; a demurrer was "a defence pleading seeking discharge on grounds of want of jurisdiction by the court or technical insufficiency". W.J. Jones, *The Elizabethan Court of Chancery* (Oxford, 1967), p.500. For counsels' opinion sent to Lancashire Friends by Thomas Corbett in London in July 1676, that court leet, court baron or other inferior courts have no jurisdiction in matters of tithe, and advice to Friends on how they should proceed in such cases see LFMH, Yearly Meeting Minutes and Epistles, vol.1, pp.31–32

67. Thomas Atkinson, *The Christian Testimony*, p.6

68. GBS, vol.3, pt.2, p.791

69. *ibid.*

70. *ibid.*

71. Atkinson, *The Christian Testimony*, p.9

72. GBS, vol.3, pt.2, p.791

73. *ibid.* p.792

74. *ibid.*

75. Atkinson, *The Christian Testimony*, p.10

76. *ibid.*

77. *ibid.* p.12

78. *ibid.* p.11

79. *ibid.*; *Besse*, vol.1, p.323

80. Basil Duke Henning, *The House of Commons 1660–90* (3 vols, London, 1983), vol.3, p.283

81. Michael J. Galgano, 'Iron-Mining in Restoration Furness. The Case of Sir Thomas Preston', *Recusant History*, 13 (1975–76) p.215

82. *ibid.*

83. *ibid.* p.216

84. Henning, *op.cit.* vol.3, p.283; Galgano, *op.cit.* p.217
85. J.V. Beckett, 'Landownership in Cumbria', p.278
86. LSF, Port 16.35, George Barrow to the Yearly Meeting, Newton (near Cartmel), 1/3/1684; *Besse*, vol.1, p.329
87. Besse, vol.1, p.329. *Non est inventus* was a "formal return by the sheriff, to a writ ordering him to arrest a person, that the person specified could not be found": Jones, *The Elizabethan Court of Chancery*, p.502. This formal return could lead to Friends being declared outlaws, for which, see, Alfred W. Braithwaite, 'Early Tithe Prosecutions', pp.152–53
88. MMS, vol.5, 31/10/1686
89. LQMS, vol.1, Cartmel Meeting 1693, p.228
90. *ibid.*
91. SMMM, vol.3, 3/11/1692
92. SMMM, vol.3, 6/12/1692; it was noted at the same Meeting that at "Cartmel Meeting they give account that the upper-end is pretty well and some in the other part seem to sleight Friends care and admonition ...."
93. *ibid.*
94. SMMM, vol.3, 7/1/1692–93
95. SMMM, vol.3, 2/3/1693, "against or condemnations" was later scored out of the minute
96. SMMM, vol.3, 5/5/1693
97. SMMM, vol.3, 1/6/1693
98. SMMM, vol.3, 3/8/1693
99. SMMM, vol.3, 5/10/1693
100. Henning, *op.cit.* vol.3, p.283; but for the later financial problems of the Holker Estate see J.V. Beckett, 'The Lowthers at Holker. Marriage, Inheritance and Debt in the Fortunes of an Eighteenth Century Landowning Family', *THSLC*, 127 (1977), pp.47–64
101. For example, LQMS, vol.1, Cartmel Meeting, 25/8/1698
102. GBS, vol.14, pt.1, Cartmel Meeting, 1716
103. Fishwick, *Lancashire and Cheshire Church Surveys*, pp.161–63; *VCH Lancs*, vol.6, pp.356 n.52, 382
104. Blackwood, *The Lancashire Gentry and the Great Rebellion*, pp.14–15
105. LQMS, vol.1, Rossendale Meeting, 1658
106. He succeeded to the estate in 1680, W. Pink & A. Beavan, *The Parliamentary Representation of Lancashire* (London, 1889), p.256
107. *Besse*, vol.1, p.329. Failure to answer in an ecclesiastical court led to excommunication; the writ was "directed to the sheriff requiring him to arrest a person who had stood excommunicated for forty days", Jones, *op.cit.* p.500
108. MMS, vol.5, 7/3/1686; *Second Period*, p.125
109. MMS, vol.6, 11/9/1687
110. MMS, vol.6, 8/4/1688, 13/5/1688
111. GBS, vol.7, pt.1, 1693, p.313
112. *ibid.*
113. *ibid.*
114. GBS, vol.7, pt.1, 1694, p.332: Henning, *op. cit.* vol.1, p.561
115. Fishwick, *Lancashire and Cheshire Church Surveys*, p.23; *VCH Lancs*, vol.5, p.157
116. Henning, *op.cit.* vol.1, p.562

117. Alfred W. Braithwaite concluded his discussion of *de excommunicado capiendo*, "all this did not produce any payment, and the justices had no power to issue any warrant for distress. The defaulters remained in prison; the tithe-owner remained unpaid; and the impasse was often only relieved by the death of one or other of the parties": 'Early Tithe Prosecutions', p.151

118. Whalley parish, for example, extended "almost incredibly" to 106,000 acres: Richardson, *op.cit.* p.15

119. Ashton died in May 1716, cases during this year being brought by both him and his executors, GBS, vol.14, pt.1, Marsden and Rossendale Meetings, 1716.

120. This was one of the arguments which Thomas Ellwood wrote against in the *Foundation of Tythes Shaken* (no place, 1678), *passim*

121. Hill, *Economic Problems*, pp.98–99

122. "Because of impropriations, clerical incomes in the diocese of Chester tended in many cases to be very low", Richardson, *op.cit.* p.3

123. B. Nightingale, *Early Stages of the Quaker Movement in Lancashire* (London, 1921), p.193, n.1

124. *HMC Kenyon MSS*, pp.146–47; for Brewers Yard see Nightingale, *op.cit.* p.195; 'Brewers Yard Burial Ground', *JFHS*, 4 (1907), p.37

125. See above, chapter 2

126. R. Cunliffe-Shaw, *Kirkham in Amounderness, the Story of a Lancashire Community* (Preston, 1949), p.651

127. LQMS, vol.1, Freckleton, 1692, p.226; GBS, vol.7, pt.1, Freckleton, 1692, p.295

128. Cunliffe-Shaw, *op.cit.* pp.154–66

129. *ibid.*; Henry Fishwick, *History of the Parish of Kirkham* (Chetham Society, 92, 1874), pp.108–09

130. Fishwick, *History of the Parish of Kirkham*, pp.82 83 131. LQMS, vol.1, Freckleton, 30/7/1696, 2/1/1698, vol.2, Freckleton, 31/5/1710; Cunliffe-Shaw, *op.cit.* p.154

132. LQMS, vol.1

133. LMMM, vol.1, 1/6/1692

134. LMMM, vol.1, 3/8/1692

135. LMMM, vol.1, 7/9/1692; he gave in a tithe testimony to Lancaster Monthly Meeting in 1699, LMMM, vol.1, T/T: Freckleton, 29/2/1699

136. The Quakers "appeared to have made a small annual payment to the church", Cunliffe-Shaw, *op.cit.* p.154

137. Clegg's income was estimated at £60 per annum in the early eighteenth century, whilst Fenton's appears to have been well in excess of £250 per annum; *VCH Lancs*, vol.7, p.146; W.O. Roper *Materials for the History of the Church of Lancaster*, vol.3, (Chetham Society, n.s. 58, 1906), p.599 vol.4 (Chetham Society, n.s. 59, 1906), p.776

138. W.O. Roper, *Materials for the History of the Church of Lancaster*, vol.3, pp.598–600

139. LQMM, vol.1, T/T: Wyreside 13/5/1679, testimony of John Proctor; *Stout*, p.78

140. *Stout*, p.250 n.52

141. *Stout*, pp.78–79

142. GBS, vol.7, pt. 1, Lancaster, 13/6/1693; see also the case of John Tomlinson below

143. Coward held this position until 1696, when he was succeeded by his former apprentice William Stout, *Stout*, p.117

144. MMS, vol.9, 29/10/1693, 2/12/1693

145. LMMM, vol.1, 2/2/1694

146. *ibid.*

147. *ibid.*; Coward's reputation suffered eventually, his replacement by Stout being due to his unacceptable "circumstances, as also his conversation", *Stout*, p.117

148. *Stout*, p.170

149. *ibid.*

150. See, for example, the annual distraints of William Stout's goods, *Stout*, pp.292–93

151. *Stout*, p.177

152. J.H. Plumb, *The Growth of Political Stability in England 1675–1725* (London, 1967), p.22

153. For the status of tithe owners in Staffordshire, for example, see Evans, 'A History of the Tithe System in England' p.26

154. Lionel Glassey, *Politics and the Appointment of Justices of the Peace 1675–1720* (Oxford, 1979), pp.285–94

155. *ibid.* p.294

156. SMMM, vol.3, 5/1/1705–06; LQMM, vol.1, 3/5/1706; SMMM, vol.4, 5/11/1730

157. LQMS, vol.1, Swarthmore, 10th month 1698

158. *Stout*, p.177; Fenton was asked to preach to the Jacobite rebels in 1715, "it seems that he was not so averse to it any more than some of his brethren, but he wanted to see how the scales would turn ....", Roper, *Materials for the History of the Church of Lancaster*, vol.4, p.778

159. *Stout*, p.183; *VCH Lancs*, vol.8, p.41, n.124; LQMS, vol.1, Lancaster, 7th month 1691. Shearson and Fenton were among a small number of Lancastrians who presented a loyal address to James II in 1687. In answer to the three questions concerning the penal laws and tests he had answered that he favoured removing the former, but not the latter. Michael Mullett, 'Conflict Politics and Elections in Lancaster 1660–1688', *Northern History*, 29 (1983), p.79

160. 7 & 8 Will.III, c. 6, c. 34

161. Pink & Beavan, *op.cit.* pp.78, 121

162. Henning, op.cit. pp.561, 562–63; "Only one justice in the commission, Sir Ralph Assheton, had been a Lancashire magistrate continuously since the Revolution", Glassey, *op.cit.* p.293

163. See for example, *Stout*, p.177

164. GBS, vol.14, pt.1, Swarthmore, 1716

165. Richard Hubberthorn, *The Good Old Cause Briefly Demonstrated* (London, 1659), p.11

166. Edward Billing, *A Word of Reproof and Advice to my Late Fellow-Souldiers and Officers of the English, Irish and Scottish Army* (London, 1659), p.76

167. Richard Hubberthorn, *The real cause of the Nations Bondage* (London, 1659), in *A Collection*, p.222

168. See above. Alfred W. Braithwaite suggests that Friends rarely employed lawyers prior to the Restoration, although he neglects to consider the advantage they took of legal minds such as Judge Fell, Gervase Benson, John

Crook and Anthony Pearson; 'Thomas Rudyard Early Friends' "Oracle of Law'"; *JFHS*, supp.27 (1956), pp.2–3. For contradictions in the early Quaker attitude to the law, see above, chapter 2

169. A writ of error was used "to reverse judgement on grounds of error in pleadings, process, or the record of the judgement": Jones, *op.cit.* p.501. See for example, "a letter from Henry Coward to John Hall with the case of one Bickerstaff inclosed, showing that the said Bickerstaff was arrested by the name Beckhusstaff ....", MMS, vol.6, 4/3/1688

170. MMS, vol.7, 8/3/1691

171. See above, chapter 2; as late as 1724, John Cartmel, a Friend imprisoned at Lancaster Castle upon a writ *de excommunicato capiendo* in a tithe case refused legal advice from the Meeting for Sufferings, "he is willing rather to continue as he is, a prisoner, than stir in it", MMS, vol.23, 29/11/1724

172. LPL, MS 5447, Papers concerning the tithe dispute between Josiah Lambert and Edward Cumming; Petition of Josiah Lambert

173. These were Edward and Hannah Cumming, John Burrow, Richard Hadwen, Ann Hadwen, John Hutton, Robert Jackson, William Jackson, Jennet Robinson, Robert Waithman, William Waithman

174. LPL, MS 5447; Petition of Josiah Lambert.

175. *ibid.*

176. LSF, Book of Cases, vol.2, p.265

177. LPL, MS 5447: Petition of Josiah Lambert

178. LSF, Book of Cases, vol.2, p.265

179. *ibid.*

180. *ibid.*; for categories of lands exempt from tithe see Evans, 'A History of the Tithe System in England', pp.7–8

181. LSF, Book of Cases, vol.2, p.265

182. LPL, MS 5447: depositions concerning tithing of land occupied by Edward Cumming, January 1722. For the importance of customary usage in tithe disputes see Evans, 'A History of the Tithe System in England', p.18

183. LSF, Book of Cases, vol.2, p.265

184. For example LQMS, vol.2, Yealand, 1738

185. *Stout*, p.208

186. Reay 'Quaker Opposition to Tithes', p.120

187. Evans, '"Our Faithful Testimony"', p.121

188. *ibid.* pp.114–15, *Political Associations*, pp.65–66

189. *Political Associations*, p.68

190. *ibid.* p.70

191. For example, Evans, *The Contentious Tithe*, p.59: "There is no evidence of persecution of Friends ....'

192. LMMM, vol.1, T/T: Coppull, 10/1/1703, testimony of John Haydock Junior

193. See above, n.171

194. For the national figures for imprisonments, 1691–1710, see Evans, '"Our Faithful Testimony"', p.114

195. See above, this chapter

196. Twenty-one prisoners released between 1695 and 1696 were being held at the suit of Ashton, some 16% of the national total, LYMM, vol.2, p.112, 1696

197. See Table 3

198. Anderson, 'A Study in the Sociology of Religious Persecution', p.261
199. See Table 5 and Appendix 5
200. LQMM, vol.1, 4/5/1706
201. W. King, 'The Economic and Demographic Development of Rossendale' (University of Leicester, Ph.D. thesis, 1979), p.299
202. For the development of the Quaker merchant community in Lancaster see *Stout*, pp.52–63; Nicholas J. Morgan, 'The Social and Political Relations of the Lancaster Quaker Community', in Michael Mullett (ed.) *Early Lancaster Friends* (Lancaster, 1978), pp.22–33. For the move towards trade in Liverpool see for example, Thomas C. Porteus, 'Roger Haydock of Coppull, A Brief Biography', *TLCAS*, 52 (1937), pp.31, 37
203. See above, Introduction
204. See above, this chapter
205. He identifies "a firmer attitude among early Friends"; Reay, "Quaker Opposition to Tithes", p.119
206. Eric Evans addresses himself specifically to the period after 1690; Hunt writes that "by the 1730s the Quaker objection to tithes was not being accompanied by anything like a completely unanimous refusal to pay", *Political Associations*, p.66
207. I base this statement on a reading of Evans, "'Our Faithful Testimony" *passim*.
208. *Epistles From the Yearly Meeting of Friends Held in London* (London, 1818), p.178 (my emphasis)
209. Hugh Barbour, *The Quakers in Puritan England* (London, 1964), p.162. He also applies this observation to the Quaker peace testimony.
210. For the low level of recorded tithe prosecutions in Lancashire before the Restoration see Tables 1 and 3 above
211. *Beginnings*, pp.311–13
212. *ibid*. 'Disorderly walking' was more likely to have been applied to Ranterism than non-payment of tithes. For Quaker views of Ranters at this time see Christopher Hill, *The World Turned Upside Down* (Penguin edition, London, 1975) chapter 10, *passim* .
213. *Beginnings*, pp.345–46
214. *ibid*. p.387
215. *ibid*. p.458
216. See above, chapter 5
217. This is probably the paper written in January 1669 mentioned by Braithwaite, *Second Period*, p.256
218. LMMM, vol.1, p.6
219. *Extracts from the Minutes and Advices of the Yearly Meeting of Friends* (London, 1802), p.184
220. LWQMM, vol.1, 22/4/1676
221. LWQMM, vol.1., 27/7/1677
222. LWQMM, vol.1, 18/4/1677
223. *Second Period*, p.297; for a survey of the Wilkinson-Story Separation see Chapter 11, *passim*. It could be argued, perhaps, that the refusal to pay tithes was one of the marks of uniformity which Fox stamped on the movement in the 1670s, see Thomas O'Malley, "'Defying the Powers and Tempering the Spirit". A Review of Quaker Control over their Publications 1672–1689' *Journal of Ecclesiastical History*, 33 (1982), pp.72–88

224. LWQMM, vol.1, 18/7/1678
225. LQMM, vol.1, T/T: *Rossendale*, 1678
226. LWQMM, vol.1, 18/7/1678
227. LWQMM, vol.1, 2/5/1679
228. LWQMM, vol.1, 18/7/1678, 2/5/1679
229. LWQMM, vol.1, 2/5/1679
230. LWQMM, vol.1, 6/8/1681
231. See above, chapter 5
232. SMMM, vol.1, 10/9/1668
233. SMMM, vol.1, 8/10/1668
234. SMMM, vol.1, 9/12/1668
235. SMMM, vol.1, 11/3/1669; as the minutes for the next two Meetings are missing the outcome of this case is not clear. However both Borwick and Ashburner do appear as tithe sufferers after this date, whilst Goad does not.
236. SMMM, vol.1, 8/1/1669–70, 10/3/1670
237. SMMM, vol.1, 8/12/1669
238. SMMM, vol.1, 12/2/1670
239. SMMM, vol.1, 9/11/1671
240. SMMM, vol.1, 12/1/1671–72
241. According to the most recent view, Friends had to adopt "the same sort of discipline, as all other nonconformist sects (except the Muggletonians) had to adopt in order to survive in the hostile post-restoration world", Christopher Hill, *The Experience of Defeat* (London, 1984), p.165
242. See for example SMMM, vol.1, 10/9/1688 (my emphasis), 'We being *informed* ..."; in 1707 it "*appearing* that Richard Lawson has been active in executing some warrants against Friend upon the account of tithes ...", LMMM, vol.1, 29/10/1707 (my emphasis).
243. SPMM, vol.1, 4/9/1700
244. LQMM, vol.1, 2/2/1696
245. *ibid.*
246. See above, this chapter
247. Evans, "'Our Faithful Testimony'", p.111
248. LQMM, vol.1, 6/2/1687
249. SMMM, vol.3, 6/12/1693
250. LQMS, vol.1, Knowsley, 1676, p.45
251. LQMS, vol.1, Coppull, 1677, p.60
252. LQMS, vol.1, Lancaster, 6/6/1686
253. LQMS, vol.1, 1675, p.46
254. *ibid.*
255. LQMS, vol.1, 1677/78, p.60
256. LQMS, vol.1, 1683, p.92
257. Evans, "'Our Faithful Testimony'", p.121; for this see also Anderson, 'A Study in the Sociology of Persecution', p.258
258. LQMM, vol.1, 5/2/1677
259. *ibid.*
260. LMMM, vol.1, 5/5/1697
261. LMMM, vol.1, 6/2/1698
262. LQMM, vol.1, 6/8/1698
263. For example, LQMM, vol.1, 9/2/1713
264. "Blunt and spikey, in an age of stylised social behaviour they upheld an

aggressive incivility that was neither quaint nor acceptable", Michael
Mullett, *Radical Religious Movements*, (London, 1980), p.90. For Quaker
rudeness see also Richard Bauman, *Let Your Words Be Few* (Cambridge,
1983), pp.55–56

265. LMMM, vol.1, 4/5/1698, 3/8/1698, 5/10/1698
266. LMMM, vol.1, T/T: Lancaster, 6/7/1708
267. *Stout*, pp.265–66. If Edmund Cole shared the views of his father, Thomas,
      election agent to Lord Brandon in the 1680s, then his actions were probably
      prompted more by a general sympathy towards Dissent than by
      mischievousness. See Michael Mullett, 'Conflict Politics and Elections in
      Lancaster', p.77; *VCH Lancs*, vol.8, p.135, n.41
268. For Coward see above; in 1698 James Wayles presented a testimony
      "Whereas I do understand that Thomas Walker now Mayor of Lancaster
      hath payed the steeplehouse 'sessment for me contrary to my mind and I
      never will give him any satisfaction for so doing", LMMM, vol.1, T/T:
      Lancaster, 1698
269. LMMM, vol.1, T/T: Swarthmore, 31/6/1704
270. LMMM, vol.1, T/T: Coppull, 15/5/1708, Rylands promised "I will do no
      more".
271. SMMM, vol.1, 13/2/1669
272. *Beginnings*, pp.488–89
273. LWQMM, vol.1, T/T: Blackrod, 1675
274. LQMM, vol.1, T/T: Marsden, 1679
275. LFMH, 2Bxv:3, T/T: Sankey, 8/7/1679
276. LMMM, vol.1, T/T: Yealand, 22/8/1704
277. See above and Richard T. Vann, *The Social Development of English Quakerism
      1655–1755* (Cambridge, Mass., 1969), pp.128–31
278. SMMM, vol.3, 3/4/1701
279. SMMM, vol.3, 5/6/1701
280. SMMM, vol.3, 4/9/1701, 31/10/1701
281. SMMM, vol.3, 30/1/1702
282. SMMM, vol.3, 3/10/1706
283. SMMM, vol.3, 3/4/1707
284. *ibid.*
285. SMMM, vol.3, 1/5/1707
286. *ibid.*
287. SMMM, vol.3, 5/6/1707
288. SMMM, vol.3, 2/1/1708, 1/4/1708
289. SMMM, vol.3, 7/4/1709
290. SMMM, vol.3, 2/3/1710
291. SMMM, vol.3, 6/4/1710
292. Daniel Abraham had purchased the Swarthmore Hall estate in 1691, Isabel
      Ross, *Margaret Fell Mother of Quakerism* (London, 1949), p.22 (the second
      edition was published at York, 1984)
293. *ibid.* pp.338–39
294. *ibid.*
295. Helen G. Crossfield, *Margaret Fox of Swarthmoor Hall* (London, 1913),
      pp.222–23
296. MMS, vol.13, 18/6/1699. A writ, or commission of rebellion, was issued if a
      person refused to give securities to appear in a superior court. The writ

normally authorised the person's arrest: W.J. Jones, *op.cit.* p.500

297. MMS, vol.13, 18/6/1699, 25/6/1699
298. MMS, vol.14, 27/8/1699
299. MMS, vol.14, 1/10/1699
300. MMS, vol.14, 29/10/1699
301. LSF, Abraham MSS, 40, William Ingram to Rachel Abraham, London, c.10th month 1699
302. LSF, Abraham MSS, 39, William Ingram to Margaret Fell, London, 16/10/1699
303. *ibid.*
304. LSF, Gibson MSS vol.1, 231, Thomas Lower to Margaret Fox, London, 9/11/1699
305. *ibid.* Lower's actions in attempting to restrain his mother-in-law from publishing her views to Friends may be compared with those of her daughter Sarah a year or so earlier, see above, chapter 4, n.48
306. Sidney J. Madge, *The Domesday of Crown Lands* (London, 1938), pp.234–35
307. SMMM, vol.3, 26/1/1700
308. LSF, Miller MSS Transcript no. 9, Rachel Abraham to William Ingram, Swarthmore n.d., c. 1699–1700
309. LQMM, vol.1, 3/2/1700
310. *ibid.*; MMS, vol.14, 3/3/1700
311. *ibid.*
312. *ibid.*
313. SPMM, vol.1, 2/10/1700
314. SPMM, vol.1, 27/10/1700
315. SMMM, vol.3, 31/10/1700
316. SMMM, vol.3, 4/12/1700
317. SMMM, vol.3, 31/1/1701
318. SMMM, vol.3, 6/3/1701
319. LSF, Port 42.35, George Whitehead to Margaret Fell, London, 15/1/1700–01
320. *ibid.*
321. See above, chapter 1
322. See above, chapter 1 (for the case of Elizabeth Redford)
323. Maria Webb, *The Fells of Swarthmoor Hall and their Friends* .... (London, 1865), pp.404– 05. The letter was "copied and furnished by Hannah Thorp of Halifax". The letter was dated 24/9/1701
324. *ibid.* p.404
325. *ibid.*
326. For example, LSF, Port 25.66, Margaret Fox to Friends, no place 2nd. month 1700 (see Appendix 6)
327. Hugh Barbour and Arthur Roberts (eds.), *Early Quaker Writings* (Grand Rapids, Michigan, 1973), consider that Margaret Fell "in her old age still personified the free spirit of early Friends", p.565. See also below, chapter 7

7

Discipline, Decline and Mission

The Quakers' relationship with the political establishment was determined by the subjects dealt with in the preceding chapters. Their view of the state and the role of the magistrate, their contacts with governing institutions and individuals, their testimony against taking and making oaths and their refusal to pay tithes all helped to shape this relationship. Ultimately, however, this relationship was regulated by the discipline exercised among Friends in both their local and national Meetings. We have seen how the discipline was operated in Lancashire in relationship to oaths and tithes.[1] Its influence extended further than these two fundamental testimonies. The Quakers' discipline governed all aspects of their behaviour and thus shaped the face which Friends presented to the Establishment, and to the world in general. It is the purpose of this chapter to describe some aspects of this discipline and its operation in Lancashire, to complement the data already presented on oaths and tithes. I will also examine the use to which the discipline was put in Lancashire, and will show that its maintenance in the county, at least up until the late 1730s, was crucial to the continuation of a sense of outward mission among Friends. First, however, it will be necessary to discuss the place of discipline in Quaker historiography and explain why many historians, rather than seeing discipline as a vehicle of outward aggression and missionary intent, have viewed it instead as a means of retreat from the world, and a sign of resignation from the early Quaker wish to convert the world .

In 1858 an anonymous benefactor, concerned that the "witness" of the Society of Friends "has been gradually becoming more and more feeble" offered a prize of one hundred guineas to the author of the best essay on the subject of the "Causes of the Decline in the Society of Friends".[2] Two essays were selected from a large number of entries as joint prize winners, John Stephenson Rowntree's *Quakerism Past and Present*, and Thomas Hancock's *The Peculium*.[3] The former, written by a Friend, contained a plea for the reinvigoration of Quakerism by "resuming the aggressive spirit of olden times": the latter, written by an Anglican clergyman called for an end to "the Quaker Schism" and its reunion "in the unchanging Catholic

Church".[4] Both authors, however, despite their radically different positions, shared broadly similar views on the causes of the Society's decline.

Clearly charted in Rowntree's carefully prepared membership statistics, the fall in the number of Friends and the apparently corresponding decrease of zeal amongst them was ascribed by both authors to be the failure of second generation Quakers to capture the enthusiasm (Hancock chose to label it "fanaticism") of their earliest forbears.[5] This lack of aggression was mirrored by the cessation of persecution which, "except such as was occasioned by the refusal to pay ecclesiastical demands, virtually ceased in the reign of James II, the newly obtained liberty being confirmed by the Toleration Act of William and Mary". So, continued Rowntree, "the Society, when no longer kept watchful by persecution, sank into a state of lukewarmness".[6] Hancock argued that when "the missionary aggression of Quakerism upon every other body ceased, the persecution of the Quakers by every other body ceased. They neither attacked as they used, nor were they attacked as they had been".[7] In this era of ease came commercial success, wealth and a growing indifference to religious matters.[8] The organisation which Friends had developed was incapable of combating this trend, for according to Rowntree it was not centralised and expansive, but rather localised and seclusive. This seclusive system was "a powerful cause of the society's first stationary, then retrograde condition", and out of this organisation came "the seclusive influence of the discipline".[9] For Hancock the "establishment of a Discipline was, in itself … an unconscious prophecy of decay".[10] Aggressive growth could be maintained only whilst "Quakerism proclaimed itself the restored church of God; but its Discipline regards it as a private religious family".[11] Discipline traditionalised and preserved the Society, however "preservation by Discipline alone", was "but a temporary arrest of decay".[12]

Rowntree identified two contradictory strands in the operation of the discipline which contributed to the decline in zeal and in membership of the Society. Firstly there was the maladministration of the discipline, which saw the testimony against tithes compromised and the plain dress and language of the early Friends disregarded. Hand in hand with this "extended conformity to the practices of the world, inconsistent with the Christian character" there was a decline in the numbers and efficacy of those in the ministry.[13] In stark contrast to this numbers declined, particularly after the so-called revival of the discipline in 1760, due to the severity and lack of charity with which it was enforced.[14] "We shall", wrote Rowntree, "frequently have to draw attention to the loss of numbers and of influence which it [i.e. the Society] has continually suffered through attempting to enforce compliance with modes of action not immediately connected with moral duties …"[15] This was a "contraction of the basis on which Christian fellowship rests".[16] Serious injury was inflicted "by compelling persons, irrespective of individual conviction" to refuse payment of tithes; the strict rules against marriage outwith the society was "the most influential proximate cause of the numerical decline of the Society".[17]

Both these writers conceded, fleetingly, that their generalisations were subject to regional variation. So Hancock allowed that "the strong walls of the Discipline also kept many, as it were, in the Seventeenth Century after the Eighteenth had begun"; whilst Rowntree conceded that "some lights still shone amongst the prevailing dimness".[18] However such remarks were not allowed to prejudice the seemingly overwhelming cases they had presented. These two essays were landmarks in the authorship of Quaker history, and in their interpretation of the course of two hundred years of Quakerism Rowntree and Hancock did much to establish the framework which subsequent historians were to follow and elaborate upon. Moreover, in the stress they laid upon the discipline which developed during the 1690s, as being the cog around which Quakerism made its downward turn, the two were responsible for creating one of the great unchallenged myths of Quaker history.

Much could be written to question the account of early Quaker history given by these two authors, and many of the assumptions upon which they rest. The view, for example, that Friends were "no longer kept watchful by persecution" as early as 1685 has been shown in the chapters above to be entirely inappropriate to their experience in Lancashire, and probably many other counties. Friends were "kept watchful" over the use of both the oath and the Affirmation in Lancashire until 1722, as were Quakers in other dissatisfied counties or Quarterly Meetings.[19] As we have seen, the level of distraints for non-payment of tithes rose steadily in Lancashire until 1716, and remained at a high level throughout the 1720s. This was an experience shared with other counties, notably Lincolnshire and Somerset.[20] As the level of distraints remained high, so "watchfulness" was maintained.[21] If missionary zeal, as Hancock suggested, could be measured in relation to the degree of persecution endured by Friends, then we should expect to see it at a high level for at least the first quarter of the eighteenth century. Any lukewarmness in Lancashire must be traced to the 1730s and 1740s, and not fifty years earlier.[22] The alleged failure of second generation Quakers to recapture the zeal of the first Friends is a matter that requires the support of extensive research into Quaker demography before it can be shown to be true.[23] It is not always easy to identify between the first and second generation of Friends (outside of a number of very notable founders of Quakerism), and it has yet to be established how many of the first generation dropped out during the persecution of the early 1660s, and how many second generation Friends joined during this period. There is much to suggest that in Lancashire Quakerism was sustained by the enthusiasm and labours of second generation converts such as the Haydocks and William Stout.[24] The Haydocks in particular were associated both with the enforcement of the discipline in the county in the 1680s and 1690s, and also with the continued missionary efforts of the Meeting.[25] John Lawson, the first Lancaster Quaker, was not the only heroic Friend of the first generation to renege on his beliefs when the going got tough after the Restoration.[26]

However, it is in the central position which they give to the development of the discipline in the 1690s as a cause of introspection and decline that Hancock and Rowntree are most mistaken. In this, moreover, they are guilty of allowing their historical perspective to become confused. It was clear to them, as it has been to subsequent historians, that the events of 1760, when the Yearly Meeting began a process of restating the Quaker codes of practice, "marks an epoch and is the beginning of a new stage in the importance of the discipline".[27] Prompted by the poor and declining condition which a number of concerned Friends perceived the Society to be in, the Yearly Meeting looked to the reinvigorated discipline for "the purpose of improving the condition of the Society".[28] It was in the enforcement of this discipline, and particularly in the gradually increasing number of transgressors who were disowned, that Rowntree's answer to the cause of decline lay.[29] However, both he and Hancock attributed characteristics of the post-1760 discipline to that which was practised among Friends in the late seventeenth and early eighteenth century. It is here that both he and Hancock were mistaken. For as it has already been suggested, and as we shall see below, the discipline used by Friends in Lancashire at this period was intended to enhance Friends' missionary drive. Its whole emphasis was outward looking; it was a tool to improve the condition of the world, and not of the Society of Friends.

If Hancock and Rowntree established the framework for future Quaker historians to follow, then it was a framework which was perhaps to find its fullest expression in the historical writings produced by the spiritual awakening which took place among Friends in England and America during the later nineteenth century.[30] History was at the core of this awakening, whose leaders "drew their inspiration from the historic days of early Quakerism".[31] One man in particular, John Wilhelm Rowntree, can be identified as being responsible for this historical revival, out of which came the works of W.C. Braithwaite, "still indispensable volumes for students of the early history of Quakerism" and Rufus Jones, published in the Rowntree series of Quaker History.[32] Both these authors, and particularly Braithwaite, followed the course of history determined by Rowntree and Hancock, although it was presented with a different emphasis. In order to understand this emphasis and to appreciate the influence it had on the interpretation of discipline in Quaker history, it is necessary first to consider what John Wilhelm Rowntree wanted his history to achieve.

Crippled by deafness from birth, and afflicted by a creeping blindness and ill health which was to lead to his death at the age of only 36 years; trained in all aspects of cocoa manufacture in his father's firm and noted as an innovator in the commercial side of that business; possessed of a deep, almost unique, spiritual insight and a keen wit and sense of humour; John Wilhelm Rowntree blended these assets and liabilities to make himself one of the most remarkable figures in late Victorian and Edwardian Quakerism.[33] At one time he had been a sceptic on the verge of renouncing his membership of the Society of Friends; however, he came to see that what the Society needed was a revitalisation of its message, particularly if the ministry was to reach the younger generations of Quakers in a meaningful way.[34] History, a knowledge and appreciation of the Quaker spiritual heritage, was the rich soil that would allow a strong ministry to grow.[35]

What he sought for Quakerism "was not to be a revival, but a new revelation of the power of the Spirit".[36] The recorded experiences of early Friends were to be a guide to this revelation, although its effects were to be directed to the present and the future.[37] "Shall we", wrote Rowntree,

> win back the fervours of the seventeenth century, make good our spiritual connection with the primitive giants who, wrestling mightily for the Lord, bore unflinching a cruel persecution, and in the twentieth century give such an interpretation to the Christian Gospel as may move the England of King Edward VII as Fox moved the England of Cromwell and the Stuarts?[38]

If the answer to this rhetorical question was in the affirmative, then what was needed was the means to disseminate the inspirational and guiding history. Much of Rowntree's later life was dedicated to this dissemination; in personal speeches and publications, in the setting up of Quaker summer-schools, (later formalised in the foundation of Woodbrooke College in Birmingham), and in planning a comprehensive history of Quakerism, from its pre-history to the present.[39]

For Rowntree, Quaker history had two parts; the inspirational rise and the dismal decline. For his special purpose the one was no less important than the other, both were to be stressed. The first called Friends to "climb Pendle Hill with Fox and see once more his vision"; they were to "enter in the spirit the dungeons of the past and learn why they were palaces, and the bolts precious jewels ...."[40] However, it was equally important that they should know that "we stopped thinking in the seventeenth century", that "the thought-stuff of Fox, Penington and Barclay was never properly worked out".[41] The historical landmarks were clear; "we may say that from the time of James Nayler's fall, the Whitfield in Fox is gradually subordinated to the Wesley".[42] The end of the early inspirational period was sudden, "when in 1689 the Toleration Act was passed, the Quakers, like a rowing crew after a fierce race, rested on their oars".[43] From this followed the "paralysing discipline, typified by the obsession with the minutiae of conduct", particularly in respect of dress.[44] So the eighteenth century was marked by a "narrow rather than a broad interpretation of the meaning of inspiration, coupled with a mistaken and restrictive idea of the purpose of discipline ...."[45] But Friends needed to know: "we can afford to study the history of the great decline and to take its lessons to heart, because we have hope in the future and faith in the great renewal".[46] Moreover, the stress laid on the decline served another purpose; the darkness only served to emphasise the light which it had overtaken. Furthermore, if the coming of the darkness could be brought forward, to 1700, 1691, 1689 or even earlier, then the light became more concentrated, more clearly defined, more inspirational.

W.C. Braithwaite was an exact fit for the mould of a historian prepared by John Wilhelm Rowntree. Possessed of immense scholarly prowess he also shared completely Rowntree's view of the course of Quaker history, and the function of the Quaker historian.[47] For Braithwaite, Rowntree himself was a figure belonging more properly to the inspirational period than the twentieth century. Following his death Braithwaite wrote that he had "ridden forth into the fuller day, as it seemed to us before his time, like Burrough and Audland, Caton and Barclay ...."[48] However, it was not only these inspirational figures which concerned Braithwaite, for one of the objects of his history was "to examine the changes ... which slowly turned the aggressive Quaker movement of 1654 into the hermit-like Society of Friends of the eighteenth century".[49]

These were changes of organisation and practice, mostly confined to the Restoration period, whose study would offer great rewards to Braithwaite's readers. It would "afford much help, both in guidance and in warning, for the task which awaits the Christianity of the twentieth century – the task of transferring institutional religion into a church of prophetic and apostolic type ...."[50] If, said Braithwaite

> our hearts were open to the pulsating life which filled the First Publishers of Truth with ardour and dedication, we who share the priceless heritage and know something of the inward experience of Quakerism could go forth with joy to the new era of service and sacrifice that awaits the disciples of Christ.[51]

"The time is come" he wrote, "for the feet of a new band of Publishers of Truth to be shod with the preparation of this gospel of peace ..."[52]

Braithwaite unfolded the history of Quakerism in two volumes, the first, some 560 pages dealing with the first ten years of the movement, and the second, 650 pages dealing with the years 1660 to circa 1700.[53] It was in this second volume that the sorry tale was told, of how Quakerism, "driven in on itself by storms of persecution and by the growth of a narrowing discipline, was no longer aflame with a mission to the world".[54] Such developments in the seventeenth century condemned Friends to "years of outward respectability and inward spiritual decline" in the eighteenth.[55] A better historian than either Hancock or the two Rowntrees, Braithwaite searched for contemporary support for sustaining the view that the "narrow discipline" was at the root of the late seventeenth century decline. He found it in the writings of one of the few survivors of the inspirational period, Margaret Fell, who in her last years fiercely criticised her co-religionists in Lancashire over matters of discipline such as dress. In particular, Braithwaite seized upon a letter written by her in 1700 to

Friends in Lancashire, "one of those rare documents in which a whole life's rich experience flames out in passionate wisdom".[56] As we have seen, however, the context in which this letter was written (a context which eluded Braithwaite's researches) suggests an alternative interpretation; that of an elderly lady, possibly in her dotage, thwarted in the exercise of an authority which she believed to be hers of right, venting her anger and frustration by bitterly criticising those who thought differently from her.[57] However, with the Mother of Quakerism to support him, Braithwaite's view of the narrow discipline of the 1690s slipped into Quaker historical orthodoxy, as did the importance which he attributed to Margaret Fell's later writings.[58]

Braithwaite's history was followed by the writings of Rufus Jones, a more thoughtful writer but possibly less of a scholarly historian, who in two volumes of *The Later Periods of Quakerism* charted the history of the Society of Friends from 1725 to "the present", 1921.[59] Although more cautious in his dating of the decline of Quakerism, and although he is generally less critical of eighteenth century Friends than either Braithwaite, Hancock or the two Rowntrees, Jones was nonetheless at one with J.W. Rowntree's view of the spiritual dimensions of historical research.[60] He wrote that

> History itself is a revelation of God. Its processes are sometimes stern and tragic. Its judgements are often severe. But it is always cathartic and clarifying. It arouses attention. It awakes consciousness. It drives home great realities. It demonstrates moral laws. It unveils the truth and it makes the fact of God's imminent presence as sure and certain as it can be made in a world like ours.[61]

This historical knowledge was to help guide Quakerism in the future:

> We want now a Quakerism which fulfils the early promise, which gathers up the vital features of the different epochs and movements, and which will be a genuine spiritual religion for the times that are now ....

However, history could only guide if it was joined with first-hand religious experience; "no reinterpretation of message will do for us unless at the same time it springs out of great experience ..."[62]

Between them W.C. Braithwaite and Rufus Jones fully articulated John Wilhelm Rowntree's conception of a history of Quakerism which was both scholarly and inspirational. Braithwaite in particular poured lavish praise on the spiritual endeavours of the earliest Friends, and then clearly signposted the paths which took Friends from their heroic missionary age to an era of inward-looking sterility.[63] Like J.S. Rowntree and Thomas Hancock before him, he identified the discipline introduced in the late seventeenth century as the main cause of this decline, citing to support him the writings of Margaret Fell, identified in the early twentieth century as the heroine of the early Quaker adventure.[64] It is to Braithwaite that all subsequent Quaker historians have turned for their framework and it should not be surprising that his views remain largely unchallenged. Indeed the author of the most recent comprehensive study of early Quakerism to be published, Hugh Barbour, is fully in accord with Braithwaite's analysis.[65]

Although at pains to "caution against seeing early Friends in terms of modern religious experience", Barbour wrote that "if the faith and experience of early Friends can be allowed to speak in their own terms, they may bring real guidance to modern Quakerism as well as to the historian".[66] Allowing Friends to speak in their own terms leads Barbour to write not of decline but of change. However, it was change that occurred at the same time as Braithwaite's decline. "As the hope of conquering the world faded, the meaning of Quaker customs and testimonies quietly changed".[67] These customs and testimonies, the outward manifestation of the discipline "lost their sharp power for piercing the conscience of the unconverted" when persecution ended with the Toleration Act.[68] They "became the badge of peculiarity for a sect ...", marking a turn inwards by Friends.[69] In Early Quaker Writings, jointly edited with Arthur Roberts, Barbour is even more explicit as to the effect of this change.[70] Its consequence was to compromise the "freedom of the spirit" by imposing outward uniformity. This was the uniformity of the discipline of the 1690s which partly originated in Lancashire.[71] To illustrate their point Barbour and Roberts "give the last word to a woman, who in her old age still personified the free spirit of early Friends" by quoting from the letter written by Margaret Fell to Friends in 1698.[72] Their change is Braithwaite's decline; both rest on the writings of a contemporary critic of the discipline whose motives and prejudices neither has fully appreciated.

A final word must be saved for the contribution of Christopher Hill and other modern historians to this framework of Quaker history. For ironically, Hill's perceptive and provocative work has only served to perpetuate the traditional view of Quaker history propounded by J.W. Rowntree.[73] To be sure, Hill is not writing about Friends during the English Revolution in order to provide us with the inspiration to lead more Quakerly lives. Rather, in The World Turned Upside Down, for example, his professed aim is to obtain an insight into English society by examining the ideas of the free-thinking purveyors of radicalism who fill his pages.[74] Friends, in as much as they come into this category, are naturally among his subjects of study. However, in his attempt to stress the social radicalism of early Friends, Hill places their history firmly in the context of all the other radical groups of the 1640s and 1650s. This context demands that 1660 and the Restoration should be viewed as a defeat for radicalism, Quakers included, with an implicit decline in the life of any of those groups which survived into the later seventeenth century.[75] Such decline is typically marked by a growth in organisation and discipline, a discipline which, in the case of Friends, Hill traces back to 1656 and the trial of James Nayler, "a tragedy for the Quaker movement". So, "Nayler's case strengthened the arguments for more discipline, more law and order in the Quaker movement".[76]

Nayler's trial was the Quakers first defeat, the Restoration of the monarchy their second. Post-1660 Friends "came down on the side of discipline, organisation, common sense" whilst "the eccentricities of Quakerism were quietly dropped" in favour of the standards of a commercial world.[77] This "was simply the consequence of the organised survival of a group which had failed to turn the world upside down".[78]

For historians such as Christopher Hill the apparent radicalism of Friends during the Commonwealth era, particularly with regards to matters of social justice, is only emphasised by their apparent retreat into quietism after 1660. In harmony with the view of John Wilhelm Rowntree, the early period is concentrated and bright, the later period drawn out and dismal.[79] "First-generation members of the sect", writes Barry Reay, who shares many of Hill's perspectives, were "more committed to Quaker principles, not yet subjected to the cooling-off process, institutionalization and birth into the sect that characterizes the later generation of Quakers ...."[80] This haunting echo of the work of Quaker historians of preceding generations is not repeated by the most recent writer to deal in any way with this subject, Tom O'Malley. In an important article published in the *Journal of Ecclesiastical History* O'Malley sets the development of post-1689 Quakerism in the context of George Fox's attempts to impose a uniformity on the movement in the 1670s, primarily through control of the Quaker press.[81] He argues that

> One of the major reasons for the famous decline of Quakerism into the respectable quietism of the eighteenth century was the successful attempt to delimit political and religious speculation within the movement, implemented through the system of press controls in operation after 1672.[82]

Decline, therefore, was not in this view an accident of a discipline which allegedly forced Friends to turn in on themselves; rather it was a result of a deliberate attempt to limit Friends' sphere of thought and action. Fox and his colleagues had, according to O'Malley, stamped the spirit of the earlier Friends out in favour of a uniformity that was agreeable to the Establishment.[83] However, even in his interpretation O'Malley is pointing the finger of guilt at the discipline, if only in respect of its operation relative to printing and publication. Moreover, his remarks suggest that the uniformity that led to decline in the post-1689 era was without challenge; that the decline was universal.

It can thus be seen that there is a corpus of material relating to Quaker history, dating from the mid-nineteenth century to the present, which has created certain orthodoxies in relation to the course of that history during the seventeenth and eighteenth centuries. Briefly stated these are that the first twenty years of Quakerism witnessed the growth of a movement brought together by a ferment of radical religious and social ideals which, in its inward worship and outward actions, encapsulated a living example of the Quaker ideal. These first twenty years formed what we might call the inspirational period of Quakerism. One of the effects of the persecution which Friends underwent during the second twenty-year period of their history was the development of what was essentially a defensive, and not offensive, organisation. This organisation led to an increasing uniformity and respectability among Friends, enhanced by a discipline which gradually began to govern all aspects of Friends' lives. In the years immediately before and after the Toleration Act of 1689 persecution ceased and Friends sank into a torpor of spiritual indifference and missionary inactivity. This condition was sustained by a discipline which led Friends to become obsessive about their own outward appearance and behaviour whilst ignoring the spiritual condition of either themselves or the world which their forbears had sought to overcome. In consequence the eighteenth century witnessed Friends retreating into quietism, when "the life that was in the open is in secret".[84] Attempts to halt this decline in the 1760s by means of reinvigorating the discipline only served to aggravate the problem, and led ultimately to widescale disownments from the Society for breaches of its various rules and regulations.

It has already been suggested at various points throughout this book that many of the assumptions upon which such a view of Quaker history is based are in need of revision or correction. These suggestions are based on evidence relating to Quakerism in Lancashire, and to a lesser extent other North-Western counties of England. It may well be the case that the generality of Friends in, say, London or Bristol did follow a course similar to that outlined above. In Lancashire they did not. Nor is there any reason to think that Lancashire was atypical of counties with dense Quaker settlements outwith the immediate orbit of the growing metropolitan centres in the south of England. More in-depth regional studies could test such a hypothesis to the full. Moreover, the extent to which decline and discipline went hand in hand in the late seventeenth and early eighteenth century is not simply a matter of interest to the student of the internal history of Quakerism, for, as stated at the start of this chapter, discipline regulated the Quaker relationship with the world and the Establishment. Decline in turn marked an adjustment by Friends to the state. It was, in the words of Rufus Jones, "a passing over from a movement charged with potential energy to a stage of arrested development and cooling enthusiasm".[85]

Those Friends who typified the period of decline, such as George Whitehead, "the embodiment of worthy and drab respectability" (and yet ironically "the leading survivor of the First Publishers of Truth") sought areas of common ground with the authorities.[86] Early Friends had found only conflict. "They had no thought of compromising at any point, of yielding any ground or bending around any obstacles, or of ceasing the fight they would had said ceasing to 'bear their testimony' ...."[87]

In 1698 the Lancashire Quarterly Meeting offered to the Yearly Meeting in London a complete restatement of the discipline then practised in the county, and of the various testimonies that it encompassed. Written against the background of the first stirrings of the Affirmation controversy, and the increase in tithe prosecutions following the legislation of 1696, the Quarterly Meeting's epistle stated the belief that

> the faithfulness of God fails not the people who in heart trust the Lord God who have nor neither dare make flesh their own arm, who have not neither dare not trust in the princes or nobles of the earth, nor yet in the mountains of Israel, but with a single eye have looked and still look to the invisible God over and above his workmanship for deliverance and salvation.[89]

This was a stinging rebuke of the tendency (most clearly expressed in the activities of the Meeting for Sufferings) to look to the expedients of the world for temporary relief from sufferings, in particular by securing the passage in Parliament of legislation favourable to Quakers. As we have seen, such legislation as had been obtained offered little favour to Friends in Lancashire.[90] The rebuke was followed by a call for the maintenance of Friends' testimonies:

> we have renewed reason to commemorate the eternal life made manifest by its mighty works in us and to us from the beginning, and to be zealously affected for the testimony thereof in its several branches both in life and practice lest the simplicity of the gospel and offence of the cross should be trampled upon and cease, and that spirit take place which advised master save thyself.[91]

Like those early Quakers described by Rufus Jones, who "had no thought ... of ceasing the fight – they would have said ceasing 'to bear their testimony'", the Lancashire Friends rejected compromise, with the inevitable result that they courted conflict.[92]

Having conducted "a strict enquiry ... how Friends uprightly bear their testimonies for Truth", the Quarterly Meeting could write that Friends refused to pay tithes or any other form of spiritual payment.[93] Neither did they swear, nor involve themselves in war or fighting. They testified "against giving or taking of hat honour, bowings or feinting titles to or from the children of men, or using corrupt language of the world".[94] Friends had no involvement in plots, either against the government "or against the welfare of our neighbours".[95]

They refused to observe public holidays, fasts and days of prayer. They avoided

> all excess and superfluities of meat, drink, apparel, together with vain and foolish customs, fashions and observances at births, marriages and burials, and fellowships of the world.[96]

Friends were married only with and by Friends, after due enquiry had been made with the parents of both parties. Friends were "examples of plainness both in deportment, habit and speech to their children, teaching them to speak thou and thee to a single person".[97] Schools and masters were maintained for their education, and when put out to apprenticeships they were always placed with a Friend. Provision was made for poor children. Parents made wills which deprived any of their children who "goes out to the world, or admits the world to come in", of "their patrimony and deprives themselves of any portion from their parents". Parents who allowed their children to fraternise with the world "are dealt with as offenders".[98] Care was taken to supervise the business conduct of Friends, particularly in relation to contracting debt or committing fraud. Good order was maintained in all Meetings, "strife and contention is watched against, and such are judged that go thereinto", whilst disputes between Friends were settled (if possible) by Friends rather than the law.[99] Meetings, both Men's and Women's, were "encouraged and duly kept up".[100]

The Quarterly Meeting concluded their account of the discipline and "of the state of Friends in our county of their love and zeal for Truth and testimony of it" with a suggestion. This was that the Yearly Meeting should instigate a nationwide investigation into the maintenance of testimonies and administration of the discipline in all Friends' Meetings,

> a due inspection to be made how Truth's testimony is born and Friends' advice taken and practised in all respects in all counties and countries that the zeal of God's house may more and more be kindled, that Friends' love may more and more spring up and shine, that self-love and exaltation be mortified, and self cast out of the very suburbs belonging to the holy city, that the lamb may ascend to sit upon the throne in majesty and glory in the midst of his saints.[101]

The suggestion was not, to any great extent, taken to heart, the Yearly Meeting simply being "comforted in the salvation of your tender love and your tender zealous care in church discipline or order to keep the testimony of Truth according to the simplicity thereof ...."[102] It was this church discipline which Margaret Fell attacked in a letter written to Friends some two months after the Quarterly Meeting epistle had been sent to the Yearly Meeting.[103] She asked that Friends should "keep to the Rule and Leading of the Eternal Spirit, that God hath given us to be our Teacher" rather than depending on "Legal ceremonies".[104] "Let us beware", she wrote, "of being guilty, or having a hand in ordering or contriving that which is contrary to Gospel Freedom". "I would be loth", she concluded, "to have a hand in these things".[105] Two years later she again broached the subject in the letter written to "Friends and Brethren and Sisters" which Braithwaite quotes to support his interpretation of the relationship between discipline and decline.[106] Written in the midst of her dispute with Swarthmore Monthly Meeting over the decision by Friends to refuse the payment of fee-farm rents, and also against the background of her continuing disagreement with the Quarterly Meeting in the county on the matter of the Affirmation, the letter is one of the less charitable pieces to come from the pen of the Mother of Quakerism.

She complains that "there is a spirit got up amongst Friends in some places, that would make and medle in their imaginations, in leading of Friends into things outward". These were, she said, "whimsical narrow imaginations". Monthly Meetings, originally set up to look into "sufferings or disorderly walking, and such to be admonished and instructed in the truth", were now dominated by "private persons", who took "upon them to make orders, and say this must be done, and the other must not be done" Under this discipline Friends

> must look at no colours, nor make anything that is changeable colours as the hills are, nor sell them, nor wear them. But we must be all in one dress, and one colour. This is a silly poor gospel, it is more fit for us to be covered with God's eternal spirit, and cloathed with his eternal light, which leads us, and guides us into righteousness ....

If Friends subjected themselves to this spirit, she continued, then they would rekindle their sense of mission; it would make their "light shine forth before men, that they may glorify our heavenly fathers ...." She wrote because she saw "that our blessed precious holy Truth, that has visited us from the beginning, is kept under, and those silly outside imaginary practices is coming up, and practised with great zeal, which has often grieved my heart".[107]

In point of fact, Friends in Lancashire had done little more than formulate into a code what had been the practice among them from the earliest times. Where new circumstances or difficulties arose, and this is probably particularly the case with business and commercial matters, then Friends adapted their practice to meet them. There were few, if any, "imaginary practices". The emphasis on plainness, and the rejection of the world's fashions, had been one of the most forceful messages of the earliest Quakers. In 1653 in Yorkshire, after first hearing the Quaker message "the men of Malton burnt their ribbons and silks and other fine commodities, because they might not be abused by pride".[108] Such outbreaks of popular sanction against extravagant finery, representing as it no doubt did for many the worldly pursuits of the upper classes, were apparently a common result of early Quaker Meetings.[109] James Nayler, in *The Lambs War Against the Man of Sin*, published in 1658, wrote that in Christ's war, "all things of this old world, the ways and fashions of it will he overturn, and all things will he make new, which the god of this world has polluted".[110] So Friends were to war against

> whatever the flesh takes delight in, and whatever stands in respect of persons (as says the scripture) the lust of the eye, the lust of the flesh, and the pride of life, these are not of God.[111]

"Inventions in meats and drinks, inventions in apparel, inventions in worship, in sports and pleasures ..."; by such means the "whole creation" was "captivated under the spirit of whoredom".[112]

Robert Barclay, in his *Apology*, put the discipline in the centre of the Quaker stage

> seeing the chief end of all Religion, is, to redeem Man from the spirit and vain Conversation of this world, and to lead into inward Communion with God ..., therefore, all the vain Customs and Habits thereof, both in word and deed, are to be rejected and forsaken by those who come to this Fear.[113]

He wrote that "the use of Ribbands and Lace, and much more of that kind of stuff" were "the fruits of the fallen, lustful and corrupt Nature, and not of the new creation ..."[114]

Gilbert Latye and a group of Quaker tailors in London warned that "Lace, Ribbons, and needless Buttons and such like things ... the Light does not Justifie".[115] Friends in the clothing trades, by "way of Answering the World in making their clothes ...", were urged to "beget them into Moderation". They themselves ought "not desire, nor weare anything unconvenient ..."[116] This stress on plainness and simplicity was, then, a hallmark of early Quakerism; "Let none despise these lines for their plainness", wrote John Crook in a pamphlet written in 1686 which criticised growing worldliness among Friends, "for we were a plain people at the beginning".[117] It was partly this growing worldliness which, as we saw from John Haydock's letter of 1701, was associated in the minds of Lancashire Quakers with the acceptance of compromising offers of relief from the authorities, that Friends were trying to combat in their restatement of the discipline in 1698.[118] Rather than adopting the political conformity and urbane habits in use by their co-religionists in London, Friends in Lancashire set themselves against an increasingly fashionable public display of conspicuous consumption, against moving with the times in sartorial as well as political fashion, and against the kind of easy converse with polite society into which London Friends were drifting.

This was apparent to John Kelsall, a Lancaster Quaker who was resident in Wales. He confided to his journal that "the government and better sort of people are very kind and civil to Friends, and they have respect and interest in them ... now I greatly fear that too many Friends being unwilling to give them offence (as they call it) are too easy towards them in respect of religious matters ..."[119] According to the Quaker minister George Knipe, from Hawkshead, in London "this world is like to prevaile"; the world, he wrote, "gets into the hearts of many and becomes their master ... this earnest pursuit of the world eats out true love ...."[120] The world that was being sought after is illustrated in the warning of the Yearly Meeting of 1691. Friends were "to keep to plainness in language and habits, and avoid pride and immodesty in apparel and extravagant wigs"; they were also to avoid those peculiarly metropolitan vices, coffee houses.[121] Plainness, as the Lancashire Quaker Robert Haydock observed in 1698, was but too frequently overtaken in London by an "opposite spirit" which "did too much appear there which caused disorder ...." This opposite spirit was identified as being kindred to the political ambitions of the Meeting for Sufferings.[122] Eventually the Meeting itself was the target for criticism: its members no longer had the "gravity, humility and plainness which adorned our worthy elders in the beginning ..." [123]

A paper was read at the Lancashire Quarterly Meeting in 1688 concerning the use of tobacco; "Friends generally was against the excess in taking of it, or the smoking of it frequently in alehouses or in the streets or on the highways".[124] In 1689 a query was introduced in the Quarterly Meeting "about Friends care in exhorting Friends in their Particular Meetings ... to keep out of the fashions and customs of the world".[125] In the following year it was decided at the Quarterly Meeting, in response to the question "whether Friends at the burying of their dead or at marriages, may give or receive ribbons, gloves or rings?", that "they ought neither to give nor receive any such things neither from Friends nor their neighbours that are people of another persuasion".[126] In 1691 the practice of erecting headstones over Friends' graves was abandoned, as was the covering and colouring of coffins.[127] Two years later in 1693, a paper from Hardshaw Meeting

> desired that such as might be concerned about frequenting the burials of others ... do consider how far the freedom of attending such burials may consist with the honour of Truth ... since too familiar an use thereof has already emboldened some and may be in danger to draw more to go with them into their worship houses and conform to their ceremonies ....[128]

In the same year the Meeting judged against "Friends making, selling, or wearing striped cloths, skirts, or striped silks, or any sort of thing of different colours".[129] This was but a logical progression from the decision of Swarthmore Women's Monthly Meeting, ever the domain of Margaret Fell, in 1674 to reprove Bridget Cowell and Sarah Benson "for their selling of lace, which is needless, and Friends cannot own them in it, nor that covetous spirit that sells it for advantage".[130] Indeed Margaret Fell's signature was to be found on a minute of the same Meeting, dated 1694, "that all who profess Truth keep out of fashions and costumes of the world in their habits and language".[131] In the following year hers was the first signature on a minute of the women's Quarterly Meeting

> to all young people in our sect to walk so as becomes the Truth in their conversations and behaviours; not fashioning themselves according to the customs and ways of the world, but be redeemed out of the pollutions thereof, not spotted thereby with their vain corruptable ways or words, that so we may appear before the Lord holy and unrebuteable.[132]

In 1697 she similarly signed a minute "that all superfluities in enter-
tainment at marriage, births and burials" be laid aside.[133]

As the apparent dangers of fraternisation with the world or the
adoption of its fashions increased, so Friends in the Quarterly and various
Monthly Meetings continued to redefine and restate the discipline. The
method of quarterly household visitations "to see how their children is
educated and that no superfluous things be used in their houses ..." was
perfected.[134] Friends were cautioned against "the use of guns, greyhounds
or hounds, to be used or followed by Friends".[135] A paper from Hardshaw
Meeting was circulated in 1704 "as being of service to prevent any
professing Truth from breaking in debt to the reproach of Friends and
Truth ..."[136] In 1711 the Women's Quarterly Meeting advised that
"Friends dress themselves modestly and fashion not themselves like unto
the world".[137] The Quarterly Meeting warned men, apparently with
reason, against wearing "unnecessary and superfluous wigs".[138] Three
years later women Friends were desired to "have no unnecessary
conversation with the world's people and to keep out of all things that may
spot or defile".[139] In 1718 the Quarterly Meeting noted a complaint from
Hardshaw Monthly Meeting "relating to some amongst us who go to the
burials of their neighbours and take liberty to sit under their ceremonies
and sermons of the priests in their steeplehouses which liberty this
Meeting advised against".[140]

There is little evidence to sustain the view that the discipline practised
in Lancashire was based on "imaginary practices", or that it was a discipline
forced upon Friends by "private persons". Its basis lay firmly in the practice
of the earliest Quakers. The clearer formulation of these practices into a
code was partly in response to the growing threat of incursion by the world
into Quaker lifestyle, mainly at the end of the seventeenth century. The
structure of Meetings within the county allowed the discipline to filter
upwards from Particular and Monthly Meetings to the county as a
whole.[141] Rather than the view of "private persons", the discipline
represented the cumulative sense of all business Meetings throughout
Lancashire. As we have seen, Margaret Fell, although claiming to be "loth
to have a hand in these things", was closely involved in both the operation
and formulation of this discipline until at least 1697.[142]

Few could claim that her desire that Friends should be allowed to
attend the funeral services of Anglican neighbours was consistent with the
practice of the earliest Quakers. [143] On the contrary, most of the things she
pleaded for in her famous letters were symptomatic of the corrupt
Quakerism which was such a cause of concern in Lancashire at the time.
However, they were also things which she personally, as a person of some
social rank in Furness, had probably managed to mix comfortably with her
Quakerism ever since the 1650s.[144]

By the late 1690s her declining influence in all but Swarthmore
Women's Monthly Meeting, combined with the growing self-assertiveness
of Friends in the county, had possibly led to criticism of her worldly

lifestyle.[145] All the issues which contributed to the vitality of Quakerism in Lancashire in the late seventeenth and early eighteenth centuries had witnessed the thwarting of Margaret Fell's influence among Friends in the county. In many ways she was the unfortunate representative of the "London" Quakerism which Lancashire Friends were rejecting. She reacted to this rejection with the bitterness of a mother scorned.

Inasmuch as the discipline was a reaction against the growing incursion of worldly ways into the Quaker lifestyle it could be viewed as a defensive device. The desire that "all the Lord's people may be cleansed, not defiled by the customs of the world, but a people separated from them in all things" may simply have been the expression of a wish to isolate Quakerism, to make it inward-looking and, in the words of its nineteenth century critics, sterile.[146] Defence was a matter of concern. Michael Mullett has shown for example that Quaker economic regulations were designed both to protect Friends from business failure and also from the excessive accumulation of wealth.[147] To defend them from the world lest "their great enjoinments proves a snare that holds them so fast they neither serve God or the church".[148] When the Quaker Oliver Atherton was in dispute with Hardshaw Monthly Meeting, William Edmundson, the Irish Friend noted for his association with the discipline of the 1690s, was asked to arbitrate.[149] Edmundson, who had close links with many leading Lancashire Friends, warned Atherton of the danger he was in:

> that spirit that draws people so inordinately after and into the things of this world is the chief obstruction betwixt Friends and Christ's kingdom which is not of that world neither does consist in the things of that world, and therefore I advise thee give not way to that worldly spirit neither contend with Friends to thy own ruin but study to be quiet in thyself and subject to Friends in the council of God.[150]

In other words, Atherton's only defence from the allurements of the world lay in being "subject to Friends" and their discipline.

Nor were the dangers of such allurements imaginary. William Stout's *Autobiography* provides a catalogue of downfalls and disasters caused by Friends (and non-Friends) subjecting themselves to the ways of the world. Henry Coward's case is worth quoting at length: Coward, at one time clerk of the Quarterly and Monthly Meeting, was an ironmonger in Lancaster whose entrepreneurial skills seem to have taken him into rudimentary banking:

> he affected popularety, and to be drawn into some gentleman's company and to pretend skill in horses, which drew him from his nessesary business: which whilst I was with him was very good. And his creddit so good that if any had money to dispose of, if the[y] got it into his disposal they concluded it was safe. But this large credit, and his freedom in conversation in company and in some houses of no good

caracter, hurt his esteem of his best friends. He also delt in merchandize with loose partners and became concerned much with persons of declining circumstances, where neither profit nor credit could be got; and he gave uneasiness to his wife, by his frequenting some houses of no good caracter. And she was a very indolant woman, and drew money privetly from him, and his circumstances became so burdensome to him that he daily expected to be made a prisoner. Which, with the shame of forfeting his former reputation, it drew him into despair and broke his hart, so that he kept to his house for some time and dyed for greif or shame.[151]

Robert Lawson of Sunderland Point was one of the leading Quaker merchants in Lancaster, but he "imployed the proffit in superfluety of buying land at great prices, and building chargeable and unessary houses, barns, gardins, and other fancies, and costly furnature ...."[152] These and other worldly extravagancies, said Stout, led to his business failure in 1728.[153]

Stout was also aware of the dangers of a relaxed social intercourse with the world. He observed the way in which young and married people "entertain each other in a bantering way in such tearms as could only tend to beget evil thought and excite to lewdness".[154] This lewdness, he concluded, was "mostly the effect or consequence of exessive eating and drinking of both men and woman, and want of lawfull exercise".[155] Thus Stout, in accordance with the directions of his Monthly Meeting, regulated his life so as to avoid these dangers. His main recreation was walking, only occasionally in the company of a "sober" friend.[156] In the spring he

> got up as it was day, and in summer at sunrising, and took a walk a mile out of town by my selfe each day in the week, if fair, sundry ways, and returned in time to open the shop. And in the evenings, after nine, took a walk upon the Green Aire, alone, if fair. Otherways, when out of busnes, passed my time in reading religious books, or history, geography, surveying or other mathamatical sciences.[157]

Stout's walking was seclusive, unlike the promiscuous strolling and social fraternisation which was becoming increasingly common in early modern towns.[158] As he became older much of his walking was confined to "an hower or more in my gardin" or in the winter evenings to walking "upon the floor" in his house "rather than sit by the fire".[159] His diet also reflected the discipline of the Meeting; he was "content with simple and plaine meat and drinke, such as was the product of our own country, without any sauces, even potatos without butter".[160] He ate "flesh, fish, butter, cheese, milke, etc., all without sugar or seasoning except salt".[161]

Stout's business conduct and lifestyle exemplified the attempts by the Quarterly and Monthly Meetings in Lancashire to regulate Quaker behaviour, in both public and private, in order to prevent Friends from succumbing to the temptations of the world. However, the concern of the Meetings went further than protecting the spiritual virtue of individual Friends, for at stake was the reputation of Truth. When Emy Hodgson gave in a paper to Swarthmore Meeting condemning her action of swearing in front of a justice on the Act for Burying in Woollen, it was "to clear the Truth and people of God of this transgression".[162] When William Harrison, a weaver from Ulverston, was disowned for immoral behaviour he "brought shame and dishonour both upon himself and the profession of the holy and spotless Truth". Friends were "obliged in conscience to clear ourselves and that holy principle which we make profession of of all such unbecoming and ungodly practices".[163] Elin Hadwen bore an illegitimate child, "to the great dishonour of Truth which with us she made profession of".[164] When Friends failed to maintain the testimony against tithes they were disciplined in order "to clear the Truth from the reproach they have brought thereon".[165]

Richard Vann has argued that "the effects of religious persecution and the nature of eventual religious toleration conspired to rivet the idea of group respectability into the structure of Quaker discipline".[166] According to this view, persecution "was so often based on the identification of Friends with such disreputable groups as the Fifth Monarchy men, whilst toleration "was a privilege which might be revoked".[167] Both consider-ations pushed Friends to maintain a discipline which had respectability, presumably in a guise that was acceptable to the world, as its end.[168] We have seen that in Lancashire the worst sufferings experienced by Friends were as a result of refusal to pay tithes; distraints for non-payment of tithes, and the number of Friends concerned in tithe cases, increased steadily after the granting of toleration, with a spectacular rise in the late 1690s.[169] The concern with reputation, which is reflected in the discipline of the Lancashire Meetings was very different from the concern for respectability which Vann claims to have identified in the Meetings he studied. Both concerned the face which Friends presented to the world. However whilst respectability meant meeting the world on its terms, reputation meant meeting the world on the Quakers' terms. The consequence of respectability was that "the moral precepts of Christianity ... dwindled into the peculiar roles of the Society".[170] The consequence of reputation was that Friends were

> like a city set on a hill, or a candle lighted, burning and shining about
> for the good and benefit of others ... [171]

It was in maintaining reputation that discipline ceased to be a defensive device employed by Friends, and became instead the primary tool in their missionary kit.

By strictly enforcing a discipline which they collectively imposed on themselves, the Lancashire Quakers were consciously attempting to maintain the lines of conflict which formed the the boundary between Friends and the world. This is clear from the Quarterly Meeting's epistle to the Yearly Meeting in 1698.[172] Rather than being viewed as a symptom of decline, the discipline of the 1690s and early eighteenth century including the simple regulations against dress; against fraternisation with members of other denominations; against debt and the excessive accumulation of wealth; for a simple diet; against the adoption of worldly affectations; and most crucially, the testimonies against the oath, Affirmation and all forms of tithe payment, should rather be seen as a clear restatement of the original and fundamental outward manifestations of the movings of the Inner Light. The discipline did not mark an inward turning in the attitudes of Friends, but rather an outward turning, a bold missionary statement to the world.

"We who profess the blessed Truth", wrote John Kelsall,

> ought all of us to be preachers of the gospel, or evangelists, which preaching consists not in words only when met together or asunder but much more, in our lives and conversations, behaviour and communications everywhere and in all companies, where we ought still to bear in mind and look upon ourselves as preachers of the gospel and consequently see that we be careful truly to perform such a great office and answer such a high and heavenly calling.[173]

In their outward garb Friends were ambassadors for the inner light, their function "to inform, reprove, direct or advise everyone we are concerned with and so leave some mark, impression or taste with them of the virtue of that holy Truth".[174] So Roger Haydock, one of the leading Friends in late seventeenth century Lancashire, who also travelled a staggering 32,727 miles in the ministry visiting 2,609 Meetings before his death in 1696, was remembered by Friends of Hardshaw Meeting because "all superfluities of Meats, Drinks, Apparel and Furniture, as well as Feastings at Births, Marriages and Burials, and other needless worldly customs, he lived to see put a stop to, and which he in the Lord's hand was made an instrument to effect".[175] In the words of his brother John, he was "instrumental in turning many to Christ, zealous for improvement of Church Discipline, that all superfluities might be at an end; and so the Church and Family of God appearing in brightness, might occasion many eyes to look after that God that lives forever and ever".[176] Paradoxically Roger Haydock's concern in the exercise of discipline was to strive for that which Margaret Fell had claimed could only be achieved through laxity, to "make our light shine forth before men, that they may glorify our heavenly father ..."[177]

John Haydock, himself an active minister until his death in Lancaster gaol in 1719, was noted for "his great humility, pious and godly walking", which "adorned the doctrine of the gospel of Christ, so that by his example he recommended that which he was called to preach in the power and demonstration of the spirit, and did shew forth the good effects of true religion ...." [178] We have seen that Haydock, by his ministry and personal example upheld the Quaker testimony against swearing (and affirming): this was a testimony "born of that seed which envys not, though its sufferings be many, yet it bears all things and suffers through things until its brightness and beauty shine over the earth and over waters". [179]

William Edmundson, a frequent visitor to Lancashire, was a "faithful and valiant Labourer, and an instrument in the Lord's Hand, to the convincing and gathering many to the Lord, both by Doctrine and Discipline ...." [180] Robert Haydock, Roger Haydock's son, wrote to Edmundson in 1697 that his "last visit in England hath been of great service to Truth and Friends ... several of our Friends are become engaged in a war against the world and spirit of it in order to the rooting of it out from having such a place amongst Friends". [181] Edmundson replied that "that spirit of the world that is so earnest after earthly things is the chief obstruction in Friends progress and works in a ministry". [182] Robert Haydock himself was a minister of repute whose ministry was sought after in London. [183] When he spoke in London during the Yearly Meeting of 1712 it was he and others who were there as representatives of counties dissatisfied with the Affirmation, who "were the most living ministers". [184] For many Friends the Affirmation typified the lax and worldly Quakerism which was obstructing continued mission; "it will", wrote Thomas Chalkley, "be a means to hinder the convincement of the world ...." [185]

The sense of mission was given urgency by the strong current of eschatological thought which was present in Lancashire Quakerism in the late seventeenth and early eighteenth centuries. "And now is at hand", wrote Henry Molineux,

the great and notable Day of the Lord, wherein he will try and weigh all People in the just Ballance of his sanctuary; and it will come as a Thief in the Night, in an unexpected and terrible time and manner, upon all the Children of Disobedience. [186]

For Molineux, a Friend active both in the ministry and the administration of the Society, who belonged to Hardshaw Monthly Meeting, the belief in an impending day of judgement was yet another reason for the world to follow the Quaker discipline. [187] For those who did not, "in that great Day of the Lord (which hasteth apace) such will be found in Antichristian Estate, and Partakers of the sins of Babylon, and consequently must receive of her Plagues". [188] Mollineux turned to the world with a sense of mission, "being Concerned in Love and Pity towards Multitudes; who under a large profession of Christianity, are yet going on in the broad way, which leadeth to Destruction ...." [189] He called them to "return to him in his straight way that teacheth to Life, and so escape falling headlong into remidiless Destruction ...." [190] Nor were Friends entirely free of such dangers, particularly those who succumbed to the pressures of the world. "All who in any manner disobey the Light of Christ in their Hearts, for fear of the Cruelty of Men, they worship this Image of the Beast, and must drink of the Wine of the wrath of God".[191]

It has been suggested that eighteenth century Quaker eschatology, expressed "in an authentically seventeenth-century language" was closely related to the continued sufferings Friends experienced for non-payment of tithes.[192] It was, in this view, an expression of frustration at the refusal of the political establishment to relieve Friends from the burden of making payments to the Established Church. This was a frustration borne out of the inability of the early-modern state to incorporate groups like the Quakers within its polity. We have seen from the tithe testimonies given in by Friends in Lancashire that these eschatological beliefs were widespread amongst the generality of Friends in the county.[193] However, they were beliefs which sprang not only from grievances over the tithe. John Haydock seems to have linked them both to Friends' sufferings for not swearing, and also to the worldliness among Friends, typified by the Affirmation:

> In our servitude, in our suffering state, until our return be through a full resignation to God, thy will O God be done in all things until the number and count be fulfilled. Then shall the yoke be taken away and the elder give place to the younger, then shall our yea be yea, and nay nay, instead of an oath in the usual form, instead of the solemn Affirmation that oath though not in the usual form, and the multiplyings of zeal faith and hope abound in all our hearts through the sweet attendance and enjoyment of God's presence ....[194]

In their denunciations of the tithing system Friends found an opportunity to express ideas which were fundamental to their Quaker beliefs and traditions; John Haydock could do the same in his denial of oaths and the Affirmation. William Edmundson showed that Quaker eschatological beliefs were linked closely with the discipline and its missionary purpose in the battle against the world: "The Lord", he wrote,

> according to his promise is lifting up his spirit as a standard that will stand his holy and heavenly testimony ... the Lord will overturn it with the breath of his mouth and clean the beauty and glory of it with the brightness of his coming in the day of his bright, glorious appearance in which he is and will discover everything according to its own nature and manifest clearly those that serves God in true and single self-denial.[195]

Whatever its context, the expected day of reckoning only served to enhance the missionary zeal of Lancashire Friends. Such zeal could lead Friends to repeat the extravagances and enthusiasms of the earliest Quakers, resulting in a reaction from the authorities no less hostile than that encountered by the earliest missionaries.[196] In 1686 Thomas Sanderson, "a very sober man", was publicly whipped at Dalton "for speaking in the steeple-house to the priest and people".[197] In 1694 William Wylde and three other Friends were arrested after Wylde had spoken to people gathered at the funeral of his Anglican house servant at Lancaster.[198] In the same year two young Friends, John Danson and Isaac Pennington (both of Lancaster Monthly Meeting),

> went into the steeple house at Burton where the priest, by name Jackson, gave them leave to speak. Notwithstanding they were afterwards prosecuted for it, and fined at the sessions at Appleby £20 each and committed 'till payment.[199]

There is evidence of official and popular hostility even to the most moderate manifestations of missionary zeal. When in 1692 John Haydock spoke to a group at the open-air funeral of a Friend's child he was convicted of preaching to a conventicle, and fined twenty pounds under the legislation of 1670.[200] Those Friends amongst his audience were similarly fined for attending a conventicle.[201] Friends in Liverpool and Manchester who refused to observe public holidays and celebrations were subject to harassment and the threat of prosecution.[202] In 1707, at Ecclefechan in Dumfries, Friends from Carlisle who were holding a "Fresh Meeting", "met with rough treatment from the priest of that place and the rabble, who tore their clothes off their backs and knocked one Friend down dead for some time".[203] When, in 1720, Friends at Brerton in Cheshire held a well-attended public meeting they received the hostility of the local landowner, Lord Brerton, who "fell into a great passion and said his tenants were all turning heathens, and that therefore there should be no Quaker stay in that town".[204] Few, however, could compare their experiences with the Quaker minister Thomas Rudd.

In 1699 Rudd, a miller from near Settle in Yorkshire, a Quaker "of a sober life and Christian Conversation",

> had a Concern upon his mind, in a Serious and Religious Manner, to go through the Streets of Liverpool in Lancashire, to warn the People to Fear and Dread the great God.[205]

The authorities responded to this manifestation of radical religious enthusiasm by arresting Rudd for a breach of the peace and he was imprisoned in the house of correction at Preston.[206] His release a month later saw him return to Liverpool as "he could not be clear till he went again to the said town to warn them".[207] His attempts to interrupt an Anglican service led to a second arrest and imprisonment at Lancaster.[208] The justices in Liverpool eventually decided that he should be returned to Settle as a vagrant, but not before he was "whipped … through some of the streets" of the town at the order of the mayor Thomas Sweeting.[209] Unbowed by his experiences at Liverpool, Rudd having a Concern upon his Spirit, that Vice and Wickedness, Pride, Drunkenness, Immorality, and all Profaness might be abandoned by all his Countrey-Men of this Nation,

next visited Chester in May 1700.[210] He "Exhorted the People, to fear God, and depart from Evil" with the consequence that he was put first in the public stocks and then into the town prison, where he remained for two months.[211] On his release he "went into the cathedral at Chester and spoke to them how could they sing in pride, it was more fit to go to the house of mourning".[212] He was again arrested, and eventually ordered to be whipped as a vagrant and returned to Settle. At Chester "in a most Cruel, Barbarous, Tyrannical Manner without Mercy, did they whip him on his Naked Body, with a Whip of strong Cord, and many knots in it ... until his Flesh was bruised like a Jelly".[213]

Rudd's next journey saw him crossing the Channel to Dunkirk, where he "had a service through the streets and to their great steeplehouse, where they was not so rude as at Liverpool [or] Chester ...."[214] Nonetheless Rudd was imprisoned for refusing to return home and was eventually transported to London where he "had a service through most of the chief streets ...."[215] From London he went into Kent, to Rochester and then Canterbury where, after "going through the streets and warning the people to fear and dread the Lord", he was imprisoned.[216] Rudd had been supported in his testimony in Lancashire by the Quarterly Meeting for the county. In Kent, however, his missionary zeal was so alien to the temper of Quakerism practised there "that a Friend represented Thomas Rudd to a justice of the peace at Canterbury, as if he was not in unity with Friends".[217] The Meeting for Sufferings assured the Kentish Friends that so far as they knew Rudd was "in unity", although their letter was considered with one advising "caution" to "such Friends that are forward to go into public places of worship".[218] Rudd's imprisonment at Canterbury exceeded two years.[219]

Rudd's concern for his fellow Englishmen was that

being made sensible of thy State and Condition, and Oh of that which is more, the Day that is coming upon many of thy Inhabitants, and will overtake, overtake them, as a Thief in the Night; Oh what will the unfitted and unprepared do in that Day.[220]

The nation, he wrote, should speedily "turn to the Lord, by true and unfeigned Repentance, and Amendment of Life ... For the Day that is approaching calls for it".[221] He criticised the failure of both civil and religious authorities to effect a reformation of manners, who would rather see a man "Imprisoned and Whipped, for Exhorting People to fear God", than prosecute offenders "for Swearing, Cursing, or any other Vile or Lewd Disorderly Practises...."[222] Rudd's complaint, made in 1700, differed little from Richard Hubberthorn's, made in 1656, that justices of the peace maintained a "peace which is kept with drunkards, swearers strikers and fighters, and is disturbed by the Word of the Lord".[223] If Rudd's message was the authentic message of early Friends then so was his mode of delivery. In 1651 Fox had gone through the streets of Lichfield crying "woe unto the bloody city of Lichfield", and the giving of such prophetic warnings was a hallmark of early Quaker behaviour.[224] In 1700 Rudd's message, (and it should be borne in mind that he was an intimate of Friends such as Robert Haydock), was welcomed in Lancashire. In Kent his testimony led Friends to think "he was not in unity with Friends".[225]

Rather than being marked by a growing insularity or any manifestation of decline, Quakerism in Lancashire in the late seventeenth and early eighteenth century was characterised by a lively sense of mission. This mission was sustained by the discipline practised by Friends, which, whilst it separated them from the world, did so only to ensure that "the Church and Family of God appearing in brightness, might occasion many eyes to look after that God that lives for ever and ever"[226]. The annual 'Accounts of Truth's Prosperity', sent by Lancashire Quarterly Meeting to the Yearly Meeting in London, suggest that the sustained missionary drive was not without a degree of success.[227] In 1696 the Meeting stated that "Truth prospers", its prosperity being manifest both "in doctrine and discipline": in 1701 that there was "great comings in and some increase since last year".[228] Three years later the report was that "Truth prospers and gains reputation and people ready to come to meetings, especially in fresh places; some convinced".[229] In the following year it was that "Truth prospers, some increase and meetings in several new places".[230] In 1709 there were "divers convinced in some parts of the county and an openness more than formerly in some places to hear the testimony of Truth declared"; in 1710 there was "considerable resort by people of most persuasions to Friends' Meetings".[231]

These optimistic accounts of the results of Friends' continued sense of mission continued throughout the second decade of the eighteenth century. In 1715 "there had been some convincement in places since last year, also that the testimony of Friends in fresh places or at marriages and burials are quietly heard and seem delightful to many people".[232] Three years later it was reported that there was "some convincement since last year, that many people flock to Friends' Meetings where Meetings are appointed in fresh places, especially on the south side of our county, and are attentive to hear the testimony of Truth declared".[233] These accounts, which suggest a peak in the responsiveness of the Lancashire population to the Quaker message coincident with the peak in distraints made against Friends for non-payment of tithe, bear testimony to the extent to which Friends were still aggressively outward looking. In particular, the zeal for doctrine and discipline displayed by Friends from Hardshaw Monthly Meeting in the south of the county where the Haydocks were so influential, appears to be reflected in the reports.[234] By 1722 Friends could still report that "Truth is in good reputation, and many people opened free to hear the testimony of it and some convinced".[235] It was not until 1727 that the first note of pessimism was struck, when Friends reported that "a considerable openness appears in divers places, many being ready to come to bear the testimony of Truth" declared, "though not many convinced so as to join publicly in society with us".[236] In 1733 there "was not much convincement since last year, yet there is an openning in diverse places to hear Truth's testimony".[237]

However, there was still optimism, and clearly a desire to reach the world still existed among some Friends. By 1740, the end of our period, it could still be reported that there were "several convinced since last year", although the account "that Friends are generally preserved in unity, and 'tis hoped do prosper in the Truth" was far less emphatic and confident than that given, say, ten years earlier.[238] There were difficulties in some parts of the county at this time, particularly amongst women Quakers in the north of the county where minute books reveal the survival of only a "remnant" of active Friends.[239] Numbers were falling, with a particularly sharp drop in the decade 1740–1749.[240] In 1740 distraints for tithe had fallen by about one third since 1720.[241] So it is possible to discern a decline in the vigour of Quakerism in Lancashire in the eighteenth century. It is a decline that can probably be dated to the fourth decade of that century. It is difficult to see from the evidence presented here, however, that it was a decline prompted by an over-seclusive discipline. The many historians who have reached this conclusion have probably been guilty, for a variety of reasons, of attributing the characteristics of the revived discipline of the 1760s to that of the 1690s or 1720s. And yet the two were very different creatures. As we have seen, the discipline of the 1690s or 1720s was a weapon to keep worldly decline at bay, and a tool to stimulate spiritual growth, particularly by going out to the world with a sense of mission.[242] Moreover, it was this same discipline, and the sense of mission which it engendered, which in keeping the lines of conflict between Friends and the world clearly drawn, served to perpetuate the difficulties which Lancashire Quakers experienced in their relationships both with the Quaker and civil establishment in the late seventeenth and early eighteenth centuries.

REFERENCES

1. See above, Chapters 3, 6
2. J.S. Rowntree, *Quakerism, Past and Present* (London, 1859), pp.v–vii
3. Thomas Hancock, *The Peculium* (London, 1859)
4. J.S. Rowntree, *op.cit.* p.188; Hancock, *The Peculium*, pp.211–12
5. J.S. Rowntree, *op.cit.* pp.77–88, 92–93, 121; "Fanaticism always decays. When the primitive generation of Quakers had passed away, their doctrinal and scholastic successors were ashamed of the conduct which had been so helpful in the upbuilding of their own schism", Hancock, *op.cit.* pp.166–67
6. J.S. Rowntree, *op.cit.* p.94, 178
7. Hancock, *op.cit.* p.192

8. J.S. Rowntree, *op.cit.* p.94
9. *ibid.* pp.63–65, 122
10. Hancock, *op.cit.* p.100
11. *ibid.* p.101
12. *ibid .* pp.96–97
13. J.S. Rowntree, *op.cit.* p.106
14. *ibid.* pp.42–43, 168
15. *ibid.* p.26
16. *ibid.* p.168
17. *ibid.* pp.153, 168
18. Hancock, *op.cit.* p.197; J.S. Rowntree, *op.cit.* p.111
19. See above, Chapter 4
20. For these figures, see Appendix 5
21. See above, chapter 6
22. Hancock, *op.cit.* p.149; see below also
23. The only published work as yet to deal with this subject is Richard T. Vann, *The Social Development of English Quakerism 1655–1755* (Cambridge Mass., 1969); for problems of methodology see his Appendix, pp.212–14
24. John and Roger Haydock became Quakers in 1667, Stout in 1685: T.C. Porteus, 'Roger Haydock of Coppull' *TLCAS*, 52 (1937), p.2; *Stout* p.83
25. See below, this chapter
26. LMMM, vol.1, George Fox to John Lawson, 5/9/1669 (bound as last page of this volume). Notable desertions in the North were Gervase Benson and Anthony Pearson, for whom see above chapter 1. However, there was a major desertion from Swarthmore Meeting in c.1669, caused in part by a wish to evade persecution, and also as a result of a dispute between Margaret Fell and her non-Quaker son George. Many of the Friends involved were early first generation converts. See "The confession of such as went from Swarthmore Meeting in the time of persecution, and fled the sufferings", in LMMM, vol.1, p.11; Isabel Ross, *Margaret Fell, Mother of Quakerism* (London, 1949), pp.224–26
27. Rufus Jones, *The Later Periods of Quakerism* (2 vols., London, 1921), vol.1, p.138
28. *ibid.*; for a general survey of the revival of 1760 see also *ibid.* pp.131–45
29. For an examination of some of J.S. Rowntree's data on disownments during this period, see David J. Hall, 'Membership Statistics of the Society of Friends, 1800–1850', *JFHS* 52 (1969), pp.97–100
30. This is summarised in Jones, *The Later Periods of Quakerism*, vol.2, pp.961–79
31. Elfrida Vipont, *George Fox and the Valiant Sixty* (London, 1975), p.xv
32. *ibid.*
33. Anne Vernon, *A Quaker Businessman. The Life of Joseph Rowntree 1836–1925* (London, 1958), pp.88–90, 105–06, 120–24, 151
34. Jones, *The Later Periods of Quakerism*, vol.2, pp.970–71
35. Joshua Rowntree (ed.), *John Wilhelm Rowntree, Essays and Addresses* (2nd ed., London, 1906), p.124
36. Sylvanus P. Thompson, 'John Wilhelm Rowntree', *Friends Quarterly Examiner*, 4th month 1905, p.264
37. Jones, *The Later Periods of Quakerism*, vol.2, p.951
38. Joshua Rowntree (ed.), *Essays and Addresses*, p.238
39. For some of his publications, and details of his various plans see *ibid. passim.*

40. *ibid*. p.76. "'The Lord let me see a-top of the hill in what places he had a great people to be gathered'", *Journal*, p.104
41. Joshua Rowntree (ed.), *Essays and Addresses*, pp.242–43
42. *ibid*. p.8
43. *ibid*. pp.64–65
44. *ibid*. p.60
45. *ibid*. p.69
46. *ibid*. p.61
47. See below, this chapter
48. *Second Period*, p.646
49. *Beginnings*, p.309
50. *ibid*. p.528
51. *Second Period*, p.644
52. *ibid*. p.641
53. In *Second Period* Braithwaite does not explicitly refer to the dates covered by the volume, but his final section (Book III) carries the title 'Position and Outlook at Close of the Century'. Nonetheless, he includes some material, for example relating to the Affirmation controversy, which belongs firmly in the eighteenth century. *Second Period*, p.xviii, 183–94
54. *Second Period*, p.179
55. *ibid*.
56. *ibid*. p.517; the letter is LSF, Port 25.66, Margaret Fox to Friends, and Brethren and Sisters, 2nd. mo., 1700. A transcript of this can be found in Appendix 6
57. See above, chapter 4 and this chapter
58. So Margaret Fell's most recent biographer has used this and similar letters unquestioningly; see Ross, *Margaret Fell*, pp.337–38, and especially "she saw … a spirit which was sowing the seeds of deterioration. These seeds grew in the next century into a quietism, a separation from the world …", p.378
59. Like Braithwaite in *Second Period*, Rufus Jones does not explicitly refer to the dates covered in his two volume *The Later Periods of Quakerism*. However, he suggests at various points in the text that his starting point is 1725; see, for example, vol.1, p.32. In his preface to *Second Period* Braithwaite states that Jones will be "covering the period from 1725 to the present day", p.vi. Given Braithwaite's own less-than-systematic treatment of the period 1700–25 (see above n.53) it could be suggested that the history of Quakerism in this crucial period has yet to be written.
60. Jones at one point dates the decline to the middle of the eighteenth century: "the Quakerism of 1752 was quite unlike the dynamic Quakerism of 1652", whilst among Friends there was "no striking decrease in zeal. There was rather a change of aim and purpose towards which the zeal was directed". *The Later Periods of Quakerism*, vol.1, pp.2, 3
61. Rufus Jones, introduction to *Second Period*, p.xlvii
62. Jones, *The Later Periods of Quakerism*, vol.2, p.989
63. The early years of Quakerism were "aglow with a wonderful vitality, which marks them off from the days of tradition and institutional rigidity which quickly followed", *Beginnings*, p.513
64. For an example of the popular literature published by the Society of Friends which cast her in that mould, see J.H. Midgley, *Margaret Fell (afterwards Margaret Fox), Mother of the Early Quaker Church* (Friends Ancient and

Modern No. 11, London, 1916) *passim.*

65. Hugh Barbour, *The Quakers in Puritan England* (London, 1964); Geoffrey Nuttall has written of Friends that, "before they had succeeded in shaking men's suspicion of sincerity, let alone in overcoming the world, the restoration shivered their bright hopes to dull endurance of an all-engulfing suffering". 'Overcoming the world: the early Quaker programme', in Derek Baker (ed.), *Studies in Church History*, vol. 10, (Oxford, 1973), p.16

66. Barbour, *The Quakers in Puritan England*, p.x

67. *ibid.* p.241

68. *ibid.*; so Friends' testimonies, which were originally "aggressive, not defensive ... and were seen as instruments of conversion" ceased to be so under the "tolerant rulers" of the 1690s; the Affirmation of 1696 was an indication that Friends had "given up hope of winning the world"; "The original Quaker Testimonies were no longer expected to offend or convert anyone", pp.162, 173, 242

69. *ibid.* p.241

70. Hugh Barbour and Arthur Roberts (eds.), *Early Quaker Writings* (Grand Rapids, Michigan, 1973)

71. *ibid.* p.565

72. *ibid.* pp.565–66; this letter is printed in *A Brief Collection*, as 'An Epistle to Friends', dated Swarthmore,4th month 1698, pp.534–35

73. See for example Christopher Hill, *The World Turned Upside Down* (London, Penguin ed., 1975), especially pp.231–58, and his *The Experience of Defeat* (London, 1984), especially pp.129–69

74. Hill, *The World Turned Upside Down*, p.18

75. Defeat, and "how some individuals coped with the experience of living through a revolution which they initially welcomed, and with the defeat of that revolution", an experience summarised as "the desolation of defeat", is the subject matter of Hill's *The Experience of Defeat*; see pp.17, 28

76 Hill *The World Turned Upside Down*, pp.250–51

77. Hill, *The Experience of Defeat*, p.129; *The World Turned Upside Down*, p.256

78. Hill, *The World Turned Upside Down*, p.256; "Organisation came too late or too early: it was a part of their defeat", *The Experience of Defeat*, p.292

79. The explanations, of course, are very different. Hill suggests at a number of points that the Quaker decline through organised respectability was a result of the influence of wealthy, commercially orientated Friends of gentry status: so George Fox, he adds darkly, "was at home with gentry sympathizers". *The World Turned Upside Down*, p.254, 374; *The Experience of Defeat*, pp.153–54, 166

80. Barry Reay, 'Quaker Opposition to Tithes 1652–1660', *Past and Present*, 86 (1980), p.120

81. Thomas O'Malley '"Defying the Powers and Tempering the Spirit". A Review of Quaker Control over their Publications 1672–1689', *Journal of Ecclesiastical History*, 33 (1982), pp.72–88

82. *ibid.* p.87

83. *ibid.* pp.87–88

84. Joshua Rowntree (ed.), *Essays & Addresses*, p.63

85. Rufus Jones, introduction to *Second Period*, p.xlvi

86. *Second Period*, p.178

87. *ibid.* p.xlvi

88. LSF, LYM Epistles Received, vol.1, pp.269-73. Epistle from the Quarterly Meeting in Lancashire, 7/2/1698, to Friends and brethren at the Yearly Meeting in London. This is reproduced in full in Appendix 7
89. LSF, LYM Epistles Received, vol.1, pp.269-70
90. See above, chapter 6
91. LSF, LYM Epistles Received, vol.1, p.270
92. *Second Period*, p.xlvi
93. LSF, LYM Epistles Received, vol.1, pp.270-71
94. *ibid.* p.271
95. *ibid.*
96. *ibid.*
97. *ibid.* p.272
98. *ibid.*
99. *ibid.* pp.272-73
100. *ibid.* p.273
101. *ibid.*
102. LSF, LYM Epistles Sent, vol.1, 1698, pp.301-03, To Friends and Brethren at the Quarterly Meeting in Lancaster. 103. *A Brief Collection*, pp.534-35
104. *ibid.* p.534
105. *ibid.* p.535
106. LSF, Port 25.66, Margaret Fox to Friends, and Brethren, and Sisters, 2nd. mo. 1700; this is transcribed in full in Appendix 6
107. *ibid.*
108. Joshua Rowntree (ed.), *Essays & Addresses*, p.17
109. *Beginnings*, pp.72-73, 75-77, 166, 169-70, 181
110. Barbour and Roberts (eds.), *op.cit.* p.114
111. *ibid.* p.106
112. *ibid.* p.115
113. *Apology*, p.14
114. *ibid.* p.533
115. Gilbert Latye et al., *A Salutation or Testimony of True and Brotherly Love* (London, 1672), p.1
116. *ibid.*
117. John Crook, *Epistle to Young People* (London, 1686), in Barbour and Roberts (eds.), *op.cit.* p.549
118. See Appendix 7
119. LSF, Kelsall MSS, vol.1, Journal, pp.238-39, 1725
120. LSF, Port 23.136, George Knipe to Daniel Taylor, London, 15/9/1708
121. LYMM, vol.1, 1691, p.266
122. LSF, Port 20.99, Robert Haydock to William Edmundson, Liverpool, 25/1/1698
123. 'Meeting for Sufferings: An Eighteenth Century Criticism', *JFHS*, 33 (1936), p.65
124. LMMM, vol.1, 3/10/1688
125. LQMM, vol.1, 2/11/1689
126. LMMM, vol.1, 5/11/1690. For some comments on Lancashire funeral customs see *Stout*, p.107; and more generally Claire Gittings, *Death, Burial and the Individual in Early Modern England* (London, 1984), *passim.*
127. LQMM, vol.1, 18/8/1691
128. SMMM, vol.4, 4/9/1718

129. LQMM, vol.1, 7/2/1692
130. SWMM, vol.1, 5/3/1674, 2/4/1674
131. SWMM, vol.1, 2/8/1694
132. LWQMM, vol.1, 3/5/1695
133. LWQMM, vol.1, 1/2/1697
134. SMMM, vol.3, 3/3/1698
135. SMMM, vol.3, 29/1/1703; "except where the good of the public may urgently require it", *ibid.* 1/3/1703
136. LQMM, vol.1, 4/8/1704
137. SWMM, vol.2, 1/6/1711
138. SMMM, vol.3, 30/5/1711; for an earlier statement of the "Superfluity of Naughtiness" involved in wig-wearing see Ambrose Rigge, *A Faithful Testimony against Extravagant and Unnecessary Wiggs* (London, 1699), *passim.* For a description of one late seventeenth century Lancashire wig see, John Fell, 'Some Illustrations of Home Life in Lonsdale North of the Sands in the 17th and 18th Centuries' *TC&WA&AS*, 11 (1891) pp.385–86: "Its powder was scented with ambergris musk and violet orris root rose bergamot orange flowers and jessamine and it was of different colours". The wig belonged to Curwen Rawlinson of Cark Hall.
139. SWMM, vol.2, 3/6/1714
140. LQMM, vol.2, 2/8/1718
141. This can be seen in the way initiatives from Hardshaw Meeting went up to the Quarterly Meeting for general approval and were then circulated to the various Monthly Meetings for implementation, see LQMM, vol.2, 2/8/1718, SMMM, vol.4, 4/9/1718
142. *A Brief Collection*, p.535, and above, this chapter
143. Few that is, except her biographers; see Ross, *Margaret Fell*, p.379. Incidentally, Margaret Fell's claim that Friends prevented the world coming to Quaker funerals is incorrect (LSF, Port 25.66, see Appendix 6). On the contrary the opportunities presented by such events were used to the full by Friends as opportunities to convert, or at least impress, the world. See *Stout*, p.191 for an account of his sister's funeral, where Lydia Lancaster and James Wilson gave a "public exhortation" to "some hundreds of Friends, neighbours and relations". It is clear that the design of Friends' discipline was to encourage the avoidance of excessive eating and drinking, and attendance at Anglican services. See SMMM, vol.4, 4/9/1718
144. For the use by the Fell family of lace, ribbons, etc, and their concern in following London fashions, see for example, Ross, *Margaret Fell*, pp.260–61, 348–49. For the arrangements made by the family for the funeral of Margaret Fell's Anglican brother-in-law, Matthew Richardson, including the purchase of beer, biscuits, wine and cheese, see Norman Penney (ed.), *The Household Account Book of Sarah Fell of Swarthmoor Hall* (Cambridge, 1920), pp.415–16
145. In April 1699 the Lancashire Women's Quarterly Meeting noted that "at our last Quarterly Meeting we found some not so condescending to our Truth-like practice and advice as we could have desired; yet have that faith and belief that the Lord in due time will further open upon their minds, and let the evil of those practices be clearly seen by them, which in our last paper we did admonish to abstain from. And again this day have in the love of God with regard to his honour, laboured to satisfy those who are yet in the practice and holds up those things, which are not to the honour of God

neither the practice of his faithful people … of this county. But do refer the further advice touching it to our next Meeting,and it is the further desire and breathings of the faithful in this Meeting that all the Lord's people may be cleansed not defiled by the customs of the world, but a people separated from them in all things". The minute was signed by Elizabeth Green, Rachel Abraham (Margaret Fell's daughter), Eleanor Haydock and Martha Haydock (Roger Haydock's wife and sister), LQMM, vol.1, 5/2/1699. This minute was written shortly before the dispute between Margaret Fell and the Men's Monthly and Quarterly Meeting over the refusal by the majority of Swarthmore Friends to countenance the payment of certain fee-farm rents, for which, see above chapter 6. In the midst of this dispute, but after Margaret Fell had written her famous letter criticising the discipline, Swarthmore Women's Monthly Meeting recorded that "It is the desire of the honest and upright hearted that the ancient unity in the love of God may continue among us and the regard and honour which is due and doth belong to the elders and those that hath been as mothers in Israel and have bore the burdens and exercises in the morning of the day and have washed their garments in the blood of the lamb, passing through many tribulations. That the younger generation may not hurt themselves nor grieve the Lord by their disregard and ungratefulness towards his worthies who are clear and precious in his sight and who are known unto him." The minute was signed by Margaret Fell and a number of other Friends, although a notable absentee from the signatories was her daughter Rachel Abraham (whose husband Daniel was so prominent in the dispute over fee-farm rents, see above, chapter 6). Three months later the same Meeting desired "that Friends may be preserved in love and concord out of jarring and bitterness"; Margaret Fell was the first signatory but again her daughter Rachel was absent; SWMM, vol.1, 5/9/1700; vol.2, 4/12/1700

146. LWQMM, vol.1, 6/2/1699
147. Michael Mullett, *Radical Religious Movements in Early Modern Europe* (London, 1980), pp.42–43, although the assertion that those Friends "who ran their businesses on the lines of credit and debt were, however solvent they were, disowned by the Society ..." cannot be sustained. For the importance of credit to William Stout see *Stout*, pp.89, 96, 120. Some general indication of the extent to which Friends were involved in credit transactions can be gained from a survey of the inventories contained in J. Somervell, *Some Westmorland Wills 1686–1738* (Kendal, 1928), *passim.* and W.G. Collingwood, 'A Book of Old Quaker Wills', *TC&WA&AS*, n.s. 29 (1929), pp.1–38. J.V. Beckett has stressed the importance of credit to the yeoman class in Cumbria: it "enabled them to accommodate each other in times of financial hardship" which were often unforseen; 'Landownership in Cumbria 1680–1750', (University of Lancaster, Ph.D. thesis,1975), p.156
148. LSF, LYM Epistles Received, vol.1, pp.272–73
149. LSF, Port 20.98, Robert Haydock to William Edmundson, Liverpool 5/9/1697; *Second Period*, pp.503–05
150. LSF, Crossfield MSS, 15, William Edmundson to Godfrey Atherton, 13/9/1697. Atherton's offence apparently involved his refusal to pay Friends a sum due to them from a legacy in his possession.
151. *Stout*, pp.120–21
152. *ibid*. pp.201–02

153. "If he had not been soe extravigent ... he might have been worth 3 or 4 thousand pounds", *ibid*. p.202

154. *ibid*. p.104

155. *ibid*. p.105

156. For his occasional companions see, for example, *ibid*. p.99, 168

157. *ibid*. p.96. The Green Aire was a piece of flat ground in Lancaster leading down to the River Lune.

158. Peter Borsay, 'The Rise of the Promenade: the Social and Cultural use of space in the English Provincial Town c.1660–1800', unpublished paper presented to the Urban History Group Colloquium, 'Urban Space and Building Form', held at the Institute of Historical Research, 21/9/1984

159. *Stout*, pp.231–32

160. *ibid*. p.227

161. *ibid*. p.237

162. LSF, Dix *MSS*, F2, Emy Hodgson's Testimony, 7/2/1679; see above, chapter 3

163. LSF, Dix *MSS*, G18L, Disownment of William Harrison by Swarthmore Monthly Meeting, 4/6/1702

164. LSF, Dix *MSS*, G22L, Disownment of Elin Hadwen by Swarthmore Monthly Meeting, 2/3/1727

165. SMMM, vol.3, 6/4/1693

166. Vann, *op.cit*. p.140

167. *ibid*. p.141

168. *ibid*.

169. See above, chapter 6, and Appendix 5

170. Vann, *op.cit*. p.142

171. LSF, Kelsall MSS, vol.1, *Journal*, p.187, 1719

172. See Appendix 7

173. LSF, Kelsall MSS, vol.1, *Journal*, p.187, 1719

174. *ibid*.

175. *A Collection of the Christian Writings ... of ... Roger Haydock*, (London, 1700), sig. C1, pp.216–17

176. *ibid*.

177. LSF, Port 25.66, Margaret Fox to Friends, and Bretheren, and Sisters, 2nd, mo. 1700, See Appendix 6

178. *Piety Promoted*, (London, 1812), vol.2, p.161. For an account of John Haydock's ministry see LSF, Kelsall MSS, vol. beginning "An account of Friends that have visited Dolobran", pp.1–10, 1702

179. LSF, Port 20.101, John Haydock to Friends of Hardshaw Meeting, Wigan, 10/1/1702, See Appendix 2

180. William Edmundson, *A Journal of the Life ... of ... William Edmundson* (London, 1715), p.xvii

181. LSF, Port 20.98, Robert Haydock to William Edmundson, Liverpool, 5/9/1697

182. LSF, Port 20.97, William Edmundson to Robert Haydock, 18/12/1695

183. LSF, Port 20.107, John Tomkins to Robert Haydock, London, 6/6/1700, that Friends and brethren in London "want help and shall be glad of thy assistance, both in public and private ...

184. LSF, MS vol.77, Thomas Gwin's Journal, 10–11/4/1712

185. LSF, Gibson Ts, 584, Thomas Chalkley to Thomas Story, Philadelphia, 5/7/1717

186. Henry Mollineux, *Antichrist Unvailed by the Finger of God's Power* ... (London, 1695), p.272
187. For an account of Mollineux's life, see LSF, Port 13.43, 'A short account concerning our dear Friend Henry Mollineux deceased', 15/1/1719–20; *DNB*
188. Mollineux, *Antichrist Unvailed*, pp.268–69
189. Henry Mollineux, *An invitation from the Spirit of Christ* ... (London, 1696), p.vii
190. *ibid*. p.viii
191. Mollineux, *Antichrist Unvailed*, p.204; his was not the only warning, see also, Eleanor Haydock Junior, *A Visitation of Love*. (London, 1712), *passim*.
192. Mullett, *Radical Religious Movements*, pp.93–94
193. See above, chapter 5; the widespread survival of these beliefs contradicts the assertion that Quakerism lost or was robbed of all its "enthusiasms" soon after 1660, see Hill, *The Experience of Defeat*, pp.167–69; *The World Turned Upside Down*, p.256
194. LSF, Port 20.101, John Haydock to Friends of Hardshaw Meeting, Wigan, 10/1/1702; see Appendix 2
195. LSF, Crossfield MSS, 15, William Edmundson to Godfrey Atherton, 13/9/1697. For the continuation of this eschatological tradition among some Friends in the late eighteenth and early nineteenth centuries, see J.F.C. Harrison, *The Second Coming. Popular Millenarianism 1780–1850* (London, 1979), pp.28–29, 252 n.57
196. This again tends to contradict views such as those expressed by Christopher Hill, see above, n.193; see also Barbour, *The Quakers in Puritan England*, pp.234–35
197. MMS, vol.5, 28/11/1686, 4/1/1687
198. MMS, vol.9, 27/5/1694
199. MMS, vol.9, 26/8/1694, 21/10/1694; LQMM, vol.1, 3/5/1695
200. GBS, vol.7, pt.1, pp.294–95, 31/12/1692: MMS, vol.8, 17/12/1692
201. GBS, vol.7, pt.1, p.282; LQMS, vol.1, p.226
202. GBS, vol.7, pt.1, p.266; MMS, vol.17, 30/4/1704, 7/5/1704
203. MMS, vol.18, 20/4/1707, 4/5/1707. Compare this with examples of early violence to Friends in *Besse*, vol.1, p.304
204. MMS, vol.23, 22/7/1721
205. Thomas Rudd, *An Account from the City of Chester of a Barbarous Persecution* .... (London, 1700), p.4; *The Cry of the Oppressed for Justice, or the Case of Thomas Rudd* .... (London, 1700), p.3; Rudd had earlier paid a similar visit to Bristol, Barbour, *The Quakers in Puritan England*, p.235
206. LFMH, 2Bxxv, "The Suffering Case of Thomas Rudd", 1699
207. *ibid*.
208. *ibid*.
209. Rudd, *The Cry of the Oppressed for Justice*, p.4
210. Rudd, *An Account from the City of Chester*, p.4
211. *ibid*.
212. MMS, vol.14, 14/14/1700; he also complained "How doth pride abound, people; how doth pride abound for all their teachers teaching, how doth pride abound a fore runner of destruction, how does it abound?", *ibid*. 19/5/1700
213. Rudd, *An Account from the City of Chester*, p.5

214. LSF, Crossfield MSS, 8, Thomas Rudd to Robert Haydock, Canterbury, 12/8/1700
215. *ibid* .
216. MMS, vol.14, 27/10/1700
217. See LFMH, 2Bxxv, "The Suffering Case of Thomas Rudd"; MMS, vol.14, 27/10/1700
218. MMS, vol.14, 3/11/1700
219. Thomas Rudd, *A Lamentation Over, and a Further Warning to England's Inhabitants* (no place, 1701), p.4
220. *ibid.* p.1
221. *ibid.* p.2
222. Rudd, *The Cry of the Oppresed for Justice*, p.5: he repeats the complaints in *An Account from the City of Chester,* p.6
223. Richard Hubberthorn, *The Distance between Flesh and Spirit etc.* (London, 1656), in *A Collection*, p.69
224. *Journal*, p.71; Kenneth L. Carroll, 'Quaker Attitudes towards Signs and Wonders', *JFHS*, 54 (1977), pp.70–84
225. MMS, vol.14, 27/10/1700
226. *A Collection of the Christian Writings ... of ...Roger Haydock*, (London, 1700), p.219
227. These accounts are contained in the LYMM series, entered annually along with returns of sufferings etc.
228. LYMM, vol.2, p.113, 696; p.329, 1701
229. LYMM, vol.3, p.140, 1704
230. LYMM, vol.3, p.166, 1705
231. LYMM, vol.4, p.26, 1709; p.115, 1710
232. LYMM, vol.5, p.104, 1715
233. LYMM,vol.5, p.319, 1718
234. See above for disciplinary initiatives from Hardshaw Monthly Meeting.
235. LYMM,vol.6, p.79, 1722
236. LYMM, vol.6, pp.425–26, 1727
237. LYMM, vol.7, p.392, 1733
238. LYMM vol.8, p.500, 1740
239. SWMM, vol.4, 5/7/1738; see also SWPMM, vol.1, 1/8/1732, 28/7/1735, 3/4/1739
240. J.S. Rowntree, *Quakerism Past and Present*, p.81
241. See Appendix 5
242. So Lancashire Friends were, like those early Quakers described by Geoffrey Nuttall, "world seeking" and "world overcoming": 'Overcoming the World', p.148

Conclusions

Quakers faced the Restoration with an equanimity which is surprising given their alleged radicalism during the Interregnum. The restored state was less magnanimous, and Friends throughout the country bore the brunt of a royalist backlash. In Lancashire this was enforced by established gentry families whose motives comprised personal dislike, social fears and economic envy. However, publicly expressed dislike of Dissent and hatred of Quakers frequently concealed acts of kindness which were offered to Friends by their gentry neighbours.

Friends met the sufferings imposed upon them by a persecuting state with a mixture of stoicism and outrage. Stoicism, because persecution merely confirmed the Quaker belief that Friends made up the "suffering seed" of the true Protestant church: persecution was but a prelude to liberation. Outrage, because Friends saw the state as a purely civil institution which they loyally supported by the payment of taxes and the disavowal of insurrection. By so doing, Friends were entering into what they saw as a purely secular contract with the state. This was a contract which the state, dependent as it was on spiritual sanction for its legitimacy, was unable to fulfil.

The sufferings imposed upon the Quakers by a hostile state stimulated the revival of an organisation that had existed among the earliest Quaker groups. Created by George Fox, the sophisticated structure of central and local Meetings served both to ensure the survival of the Movement and also to ensure the dominance of his own view of the Quaker Truth. The Meeting for Sufferings, the most important Quaker committee in London, became the mouthpiece through which the Friends spoke to the authorities. However, in seeking to find common ground with the authorities the Meeting for Sufferings gradually eroded the basis of Quaker testimonies, particularly against oaths, in favour of expedients offered by their political allies in Parliament and at court. The form of words contained in the Quakers' Affirmation of 1696 was generally unacceptable to all but those Friends in the metropolitan centres. The acceptance of the Affirmation marked a growing accommodation of the world's values by those Friends who dominated the central administration of the Society. It also marked the triumph of metropolitan attitudes over those of the less urbane Quakers who still (in the early eighteenth century) made up the bulk of the Society's membership.

In Lancashire, where Quakers appear to have maintained a high level of commercial intercourse with the world, Friends nonetheless refused the acceptance of standards which compromised the precepts of their earliest co-religionists. On the contrary, Friends in Lancashire and elsewhere in the North and in Ireland, sought to maintain the missionary dynamic which had marked the earliest Quakers off from the world. It was a dynamic sustained in part by sufferings, which although they were generally avoided for not-swearing, increased for tithes following the acceptance by the Meeting for Sufferings of a clause in the Affirmation Act which had been intended as a form of relief. In addition, the missionary impetus was sustained by the maintenance of a rigorous discipline among Friends which set them apart from their Anglican or Presbyterian business partners or contacts. Friends lived the Truth, and in their strictly regulated outward behaviour were the visible manifestation of God's workings through the Inner Light, the light within all men.

The consequence of this maintained sense of mission was conflict, both with the civil authorities and the Quaker establishment. Civil conflict is illustrated by the increasing level of tithe prosecutions during the first quarter of the eighteenth century, and sporadic outbursts of prosecutions following refusals to swear. It can be seen on a more general level by the hostile response of the local authorities to the attempts of Friends such as Thomas Rudd to carry the Quaker message to the population at large. Conflict among Friends was centred in Lancashire on the bitter disputes which raged between Margaret Fell, a loyal supporter of the London Quaker establishment, and the Quarterly and Monthly Meetings. She opposed their attempts to maintain the Quaker testimony against swearing, to maintain the Quaker testimony against the payment of tithes, and to maintain a discipline which marked Friends out as visible tokens of God's presence.

History, however, has dealt the majority of Lancashire Quakers a cruel hand. Overwhelmed by the charisma of the early Quaker leaders, and shamefaced at the Quietism of Friends in the second half of the eighteenth century, historians have chosen to ignore or misinterpret the missionary efforts of the Northern and other Friends who were attempting to sustain the Society through suffering and discipline. Instead they have chosen to see Margaret Fell as a lone survivor of the heroic age of Quakerism, fighting against a stifling discipline that could lead only to the dullness and decline of the 1760s. This was a reverse of the actual state of affairs.

In contrast to the accepted view of late seventeenth and early eighteenth century Quakerism, it has been shown here that, in Lancashire, Friends continued during this period to exhibit many of the characteristics more commonly associated with the earliest Quakers. This continuation of the early Quaker mission to overcome (but not to overturn) the world lasted well into the 1730s. As a consequence, the relationship which existed with the Establishment contrasted sharply between Friends in London and Friends in Lancashire. In London it was a relationship based on the Quakers' increasing acceptance of courtly manners, metropolitan values and the political judgement of Sir Robert Walpole. In Lancashire contacts were based on conflict: the annual round of tithe seizures, court appearances and occasional imprisonments. The special flavour of early Quakerism survived in the North, and the light of the star which had arisen in the 1650s was still shining in the 1700s.

Appendix 1

The Quakers' Address to George II on his accession to the throne

MMS, vol.24, 21/5/1727

Joseph Wyeth reports that according to the appointment of the Meeting the King was attended with the Address the 14th instant by the body of Friends of this Meeting; the encouragement given by its having been intimated that the King would receive the Address in the public room, where it was presented by Joseph Wyeth who, having spoke a few words to introduce the same to the King, then read it, and is as followeth:

"To George the second, King of Great Britain etc.: the humble Address of the people called Quakers:
Gracious sovereign; it having pleased almighty God in whose hand is the breath of the greatest monarch, to remove by death our late gracious King, thy royal father, an affliction in which we, thy dutiful subjects deeply share, as sensible that his reign was one continued blessing to all his people, and in which we enjoyed not only the indulgences granted us in the reigns of his royal predecessors, but also fresh marks of his own clemency and goodness.

We have therefore great and just cause to condole the loss of a prince, so gracious and beneficent: but when we consider that the merciful hand of divine providence hath placed peaceably on the throne a son, the successor of his royal virtues, (the earnest whereof we behold with pleasure, during the short experience of thy prudent administration when regent) it is cause sufficient to abate our grief, and asswage our sorrow. And the hopes we then conceived are fully confirmed by thy gracious declaration from the throne to make all thy subjects happy and secure, in the full enjoyment of their religious and civil rights.

Wherefore great prince, we, though a small part of thy dutiful subjects, humbly beg leave to approach thy royal presence with sincere and hearty congratulations on thy ascending the British throne in perfect tranquility, and to declare our entire affection and dutiful obedience to thy royal person and government, as our christian and peaceable principles enjoin. And we greatly hope thy hand will be the happy instrument to finish that good work, begun by thy royal father, of calming and composing the differences of Europe, and preventing the calamities of war which were so lately threatened.

We also humbly beg leave to express the joyful sense impressed upon our minds of the princely virtues of our gracious Queen thy royal consort, and of the pleasing prospect of your numerous and hopeful issue, who whilst they are shining and illustrious ornaments around the throne, are valuable pledges of the future peace and security of these kingdoms.

May the almighty and allwise God shower down on thy royal head and family his divine as well as temporal blessings. May he, by his wisdom, guide thee in thy counsels to the promoting religion and virtue, the support of the Protestant cause in general, and the good of all thy subjects. And may the weight and care usually annexed to a crown be lightened, and made easie by the dutiful and cheerful obedience of a great and free people".

Which said Address was very kindly received by the King, who gave the following gracious answer: "This dutiful and loyal address is very acceptable to me, and you may depend upon my protection". After which the Friends were introduced to the Queen to whom John Eccleston made the following speech, to which the Queen gave a gracious answer:

"May it please our gracious Queen,
As we have been favoured with the liberty of access to our gracious King, to condole the death of his royal father, to congratulate his accession to the British throne, and to tender the assurances of our affection and fidelity to his royal person and government.

We beg leave, with great deference, humbly to approach thy royal presence on the same solemn occasions, which we now do, with all the affection and regard due from dutiful and obedient subjects. Gracious Queen, may thy enjoyment of the royal dignity be long and happy, and may our present gracious King long possess the British throne in peace, 'till future time and maturity of years shall transfer it in safety to your royal and hopeful offspring, formed and nurtured for government by thy virtuous care to be fit examples to future princes, a blessing to late posterity, and the effectual security under divine providence of our present happy constitution".

Appendix 2

John Haydock to Friends of Hardshaw Meeting, Wigan 10/1/1702

(for John Haydock see above pp.310–14) LSF, Port 20.101

Brethren,
Born of that seed which envys not, though its sufferings be many: yet it bears all things and suffers through things untill its brightness and beauty shine over the earth and over the waters, that the children brought forth to God in the gospel light and liberty might rejoice and therein be glad. You are my companions and fellow helpers to bear and hold forth that testimony against all swearings which sprang up in our infancy – and has enlarged and spread itself in our riper years over the subilty, and still is bounded with the commands and precepts of Christ. Is it not the straight and narrow way that leads to the living well which springs up in us? Is it not that spring of life which enjoins us to observe and keep to the commands of Christ? Whose command is swear not at all, but let your yea be yea and your nay nay. See what is now come of us? – [edge of manuscript torn], and is from that ground master save thyself. Well then my brethren, let's wait for that spring of virtue and life in our hearts that will refresh us – augment our strength, increase our faith and hope in Christ Jesus unto obedience that the swelling waters drown not, the lofty winds upon the rocks split not, the wily foxes spoil not that greeness, tenderness and zeal amongst us for the commands of Christ. You know our unity hitherto has been precious: the general account from all our Particular and Monthly Meetings in this county that stands recorded in our Quarterly Meeting book bespeaks it, the giving up to suffer for the keeping of Christ's commands, confirms it. Yea, in this is our love manifest to Christ our Lord, that we sincerely keep his command, which is swear not at all. Is not the formal oath now used by many in this nation, that we have denied and suffered because thereof from the beginning, is not that oath, although not in the usual form, called the solemn Affirmation now usually taken by some Quakers that with many elder brethren, substantial Quakers and sincere friends to Christ denied and opposed before it was a law, denys and suffers because of their refusal to take it since it was a law. And is not this made use of now by envious and malicious men, as the formal oath has been, to get their ends of sincere Quakers and such as baulk not their testimony, by imprisoning and robbing such of them as come to the proving, who for Christ's sake and in good conscience to God can no more take the solemn Affirmation, than take the oath, in the usual form because not bounded within the precepts and commands of Christ. And although wife and children, family, friends, houses, lands, enjoyments, liberty and life be precious to possess and remain with, yet Christ the Lord the giver of all

these, was before them all, is the sweetness and life of the circumcision to God in the midst of them all, remains to be the rest and solace of the free-born (who are not subject to vanity) although removed from them all.

Surely Rebecca the wife of Isiah the son by promise felt the struggling of old and out of one womb Esau came forth first, and ranged the fields at large and became mighty; but Jacob came forth the latter, kept at home with the mother till by her counsel the blessing was gained; though he suffered for a season, yet the time of his return came and he became more mighty, for Edam's mount was fired, so that no shelter was therein for the wily foxes or beasts of prey. What was now is and will be. Read, you that can read, though the foxes have holes for shelter under the earth, yet the birth of God has not thereon to rest. And though its beauty be marred and besmarred by the puddles of envious minds and such as lurks in secret to spill blood, yet the time of washing comes in the stillness, when proud flesh is silent and Shilo in the lowly heart springs up and runs. Then shall the shelter of the running foxes vanish away, the foxes shall be taken, but the pure in heart shall see God. Then shall the keepers of Christ's precepts and commands shine forth, because of the smiles of Christ that have supported in the fiery trials: to the washing of their robes in the blood of the lamb and giving them dominion. Now brethren, although the Solemn Affirmation is likely to be continued as an uneasy yoke through the solicitation of our elder brothers that walks at large with a disesteem and slighting of us, yet let us remember still that the womb that brought us forth, that breast that nourished us that free spirit that has helped us hitherto and will help us still and counsel us to take such measures as daily to meet in our hearts with the smiles of life with the warming and melting of God's presence that blessing which has and will bear up in our afflictions.

In our servitude, in our suffering state, untill our return be through a full resignation to God. Thy will O God be done in all things until the number and count be fulfilled. Then shall the yoke be taken away and the elder give place to the younger, then shall our yea be yea, and nay nay; instead of an oath in the usual form, instead of the solemn Affirmation (that oath though not in the usual form), and the multiplyings of zeal faith and hope abound in all our hearts through the sweet attendance and enjoyment of God's presence, in standing for the precepts and commands of Christ, swear not at all, That the Lord God more and more may make manifest who are his. Verily God is the Lord, his time not man's time, is the time of perfecting what he will bring to pass; not be might or polity, or man's contrivance, but by his own spirit. I am your brother, now having offered my all a sacrifice to God in testimony against the oath in the usual form against the solemn Affirmation (that oath though not the in usual form), and waits to receive an inward supply through your prayers put up to God on my behalf who at Wigan am under confinement upon a Commission of Rebellion (for denying the oath and solemn Affirmation) by John Brown this 10th first month called March 1701–2

John Haydock

A Postscript

Brethren, consider your station and call to liberty in the gospel of Christ and beware least any of you contribute to your own thraldom through gratifying the flesh. For when the solicitation was to the King and Parliament to be freed from the burden of oaths, and that which was obtained was the solemn Affirmation, was not this accepted of contrary to the minds of many Friends? So as it was, And did not this cause a great uneaseiness in Friends so that further solicitation was to be made by agreement to the Government in order to obtain that which might be for the general ease of Friends' consciences in the case of oaths? And since opportunity has offered for a further solicitation to the government as aforsaid and yet the same way has been taken to circumvent us as was before, which makes our uneasiness the more and gives us ground of complaint for what unfair dealings we have had both at first and last relating to this weighty affair. Are we the younger, even so are we dealt with all by the elder [brethren – crossed out in manuscript] thats on his way to posses himself of greatness by the solemn Affirmation and make his mount as high as Edam. Yet fair flourishes, fine words and the cry of liberty cannot hide his dwelling place from that eye that God has opened in us, no, no neither can he in the choice of his payment of tithes and steeple-house lays (which is in the body of the Affirmation) and wash his hands of our many sufferings we lie under upon that account in this North country. No, no neither can he with endeavourings to over bear us [by laying his rough and cruel hands upon us – crossed out in manuscript] bring us to comply and fall down to his idol and break the precept and commands of Christ no, no. Therefore brethren, let us stand fast in the love of God; within your hearts spring up to confirm our faith in keeping the precept and command of Christ to the end, and let us not look out at man and men, what they do [though we be counted the younger brother yet the blessing we witnessing in us, this will prevail – crossed out in the manuscript] but let us look to Christ to follow Christ before whom all must appear. Yea the elder [brethren crossed out in manuscript], [crossed out] must to Christ give account, but who shall rise to make an account for him or who can stand when the fire of jealousy breaks forth in the midst of the younger [brethren – crossed out] that will fasten upon the elder in his high places. God is the Lord

John Haydock

To Friends at Hardshaw Monthly Meeting and such as they think meet

Appendix 3

Lancashire Friends' Tithe Testimonies 1675–1710

Meeting	Men	Women
Bickerstaffe	45	85 (21)[1]
Blackrod	–	19
Cartmel	2 (2)	49 (1)
Chipping	16 (2)	23 (1)
Coppull	52 (2)	18 (2)
Freckleton	21 (2)	–
Fylde	25 (4)	28 (1)
Hawkshead	23 (2)	58 (7)
Kellet	2 (2)	–
Knowsley	31 (2)	37 (1)
Lancaster	53 (3)	46 (3)
Manchester	21	20 (1)
Marsden	21 (1)	46 (12)
Oldham	15 (1)	11
Penketh	–	12 (1)
Rossendale	19	38 (11)
Sankey	46	89 (5)
Swarthmore	77 (3)	69 (7)
Trawden	–	5
Twiston	8	17 (5)
Waddicar	–	2 (2)
Wray	31	9
Wyrebridge[2]	–	23
Wyresdale[2]	15	–
Wyreside[2]	10 (1)	–
Yealand	97	74 (8)
Totals	630 (35)	778 (89)

(Compiled from LQMM, vol.1, 1669–1711; LMMM, vol.1, 1675–1718; LWQMM, vol.1, 1675–1777; LFMH, 2Bxv:l, 2Bxv:3; 2Bxv:5; 2Bxv:6; 2Bxv:7; 2Bxv:25; 2Bxv:48, 2Bxv:50)

1. The figures in parenthesis represent the number of Friends who indicated that they were not possessed of titheable property
2. These three names are probably variants for the same Meeting, Wyresdale, to the east of Lancaster

Appendix 4

Lancashire Tithe Sufferings 1650–1700
Individual tithe sufferers (one or more cases) 1650–1700

| Meeting | No | Cases involving | | | |
		Impropriators	Farmers	Clergy	Not Known
Bickerstaf	65	7	30	2	26
Blackrod	1	–	–	1	–
Cartmel	24	14	5	3	2
Chipping	8	3	4	–	1
Coppull	16	1	7	7	1
Freckleton	8	–	3	4	1
Fylde & Waddicar	33	8	8	6	11
Hawkshead	19	18	–	–	1
Knowsley	24	8	3	13	–
Lancaster	38	8	17	13	–
Manchester	10	–	–	9	1
Marsden	46	33	–	11	2
Oldham	9	–	7	1	1
Penketh	53	4	40	2	7
Rossendale	21	11	6	3	1
Sankey	21	–	13	3	5
Swarthmor	42	19	2	21	–
Twiston & Sawley	12	10	2	–	–
Wray	13	3	8	1	1
Wyresdale	5	–	–	5	–
Yealand	41	5	13	23	–
Totals	509	152	168	128	61

(source LQMS, vol. 1, 1654–1700)

Appendix 5

Annual Value of Tithe Sufferings 1700–1740

Year	Lanca- shire	Lincoln- shire	Somerset	Stafford- shire	England & Wales
1700	263.4	432.3	263.1	25.8	5,000
1701	309.5	266.8	206.6	16.9	4,500
1702	267.3	326.9	174.8	16	4,200
1703	261.1	292.7	170.3	15	4,260
1704	277	240.5	201.5	12	4,000
1705	219.6	n/a	138.1	20.4	3,884
1706	260.3	328.7	226	24.6	3,865
1707	265.8	300.8	256.5	18.2	4,000
1708	231	349.3	294	26.1	4,440
1709	293.5	345.8	247.1	33.6	5,000
1710	335.6	335.7	290.5	22.5	5,000
1711	345.7	382.7	266.2	31.1	*5,370*
1712	289.4	296.8	235.9	24.4	4,700
1713	223.7	431.6	281.9	22.2	4,460
1714	329.6	414.9	282.1	25	4,900
1715	237.3	461.1	268.9	20.1	4,630
1716	*372*	456.6	*326.1*	16.8	5,290
1717	279.9	500.9	275.2	18.8	5,193
1718	309.2	476.3	195.1	22.2	4,620
1719	330	*559.5*	203.1	40.8	4,690
1720	318.1	420.9	180.3	31.9	4,770
1721	332	508.9	257.6	37	4,666
1722	271	458.1	182.9	34	4,369
1723	266.2	434	212.1	15.9	4,204
1724	315.6	432.7	206.6	34.4	4,720
1725	234.7	450.3	257.4	29.1	4,519
1726	266.9	411.4	218.6	25.9	4,012
1727	245.1	295.5	231.4	34.8	3,914
1728	287.2	300.4	172.7	39.7	4,130
1729	253.9	205.8	182.1	38.6	4,085
1730	211.4	218.7	174.7	26.4	3,305
1731	243.6	218.7	144.2	*144.1*	3,419
1732	265.4	179.8	290.2	26.5	3,458
1733	211.7	226.1	178.2	23.6	3,188
1734	200.3	223.7	295.9	17	3,545
1735	208.6	246.3	241	22.5	3,332

Year	Lanca-shire	Lincoln-shire	Somerset	Stafford-shire	England & Wales
1736	204.6	293.6	192.9	28.2	3,565
1737	189.8	204.2	192.8	33.5	3,365
1738	183.2	239.5	301.4	17.5	3,365
1739	209.5	189.8	196.2	23.3	3,300
1740	227.7	329.6	121.9	27.6	3,813

(Source: LYMM,vols. 2–8, *Political Associations*, p.67 n.15; in calculating his annual totals Hunt has presented the figures entered in, for example, the Yearly Meeting Minutes of 1700, as representing the value of tithe taken in that year. However, the figures presented to the Meeting in 1700 represented the amount taken in the previous year (1699). His figures have consequently been adjusted here so that the figure presented for England and Wales in 1700 represents the amount taken in that actual year.)

Appendix 6

Margaret Fox to Friends, and Brethren, and Sisters. 2nd. month 1700.

LSF, Portfolio 25.66

Friends, and Brethren, and Sisters
We are the people of the living God, and God has visited us and brought us out in an acceptable day of salvation, a gospel day in which the eternal God is gathering his elect from the four winds of heaven and from the four corners of the earth. And he has shined from the throne of his glory in our hearts, in his spiritual light, and given us the true knowledge of himself in the form and image of Jesus Christ. He has made us partakers of his divine nature and he has given us his good and holy spirit to lead us and to guide us, into all Truth in all things.

Now dear Friends, brethren and sisters, let us all beware of limiting the holy one of Israel or tampering with anything contrary to this holy spirit, for the grace of God is sufficient to teach us to deny all ungodliness and unrighteousness and will teach us to live holily and righteously, unto God and his Truth in this present and evil world. And let us beware of meddling with the things of God otherwise than his spirit leads and guides. Now there is a spirit got up amongst Friends in some places that would make and meddle in their imaginations in leading of Friends into things outwardly, which our Lord Jesus Christ never commanded for he always testified against the Jews' manner of making and proscribing of things outwardly, for his testimony is in every heart to work inwardly, and make clean the inside. So let us beware of imitating and fashioning after the Jews' manner in outward things and ceremonies: for though it be said in scripture, that his people should dwell alone, that was in that time under the law, when he had chosen them out of all the families of the earth, yet he would punish them for their transgression.

But now our blessed Lord is come, and its but a small thing to him to gather together the tribe of Israel, and the dispersed of Juda: he is also given for a light to the gentiles and to be for salvation to the ends of the earth. He would have all to be saved, and to come to the knowledge of his blessed Truth; and he testified against the Pharisees, that said, I am more holy than thee. Let us beware of this of speaking or looking upon ourselves to be more holy than in deed and in truth we are, for what are we, but what we have received from God, and God is all sufficient to bring in thousands into the same spirit and light, to lead and to guide them, as he does us. And let us frame and fashion ourselves unto the apostle doctrine and practice, who was in a glorious shining light, read 1 Cor., chap.9, 19 ver., and so to the end.

Now see how contrary our practice is to the apostles, when we must not go to a burial of the people of the world, nor bid them to any of our burials, nor do that which is moderate and of a good report as to meats or drinks etc. Again read 1 Cor., ch. 10, ver. 27: if any of them that believe not bid you to a feast and you be disposed to go, whatsoever is set before you, eat, asking no question for conscience sake. This is more than a birth or a burial which is needful and necessary? Away with those whimsical narrow imaginations, and let the spirit of God which he has given us lead us and guide us: and let us stand fast in that liberty where with Christ has made us free, and not be entangled again into bondage, in observing proscriptions in outward things which will not profit nor cleanse the inward man. It is the work of Christ Jesus in this his day, and by this let everyone do as they are persuaded in their own minds, for the apostles said, he was not to rule over anyones faith.

For it is now gone 47 years since we owned the truth, and all has gone well and peacably till now of late, that this narrowness and strictness is entering in, that many cannot tell what to do, or not to do.

Our Monthly and Quarterly Meetings were set up for reproving and looking into superfluous [?] or disorderly walking, and such to be admonished and instructed in the Truth. And not private persons to take upon them to make orders, and say this must be done, and the other must not be done. And can Friends think that those who are taught and guided of God, can be subject and follow such low, mean orders? So its good for Friends in our county to leave these things to the Lord who is become our leader, teacher and guider, and not to go abroad to spread them, for they will never do good, but has done hurt already. We are now coming into Jewism, into that which Christ cried "woe" against, minding altogether outward things, neglecting the inward work of almighty God in our hearts. If we can but frame according to outward proscriptions and orders, and deny eating and drinking with our neighbours, in so much that poor Friends is mangled in their minds, that they know not what to do, for Friends says one way, and another, another, but Christ Jesus says, that we must take no thought what we shall eat, or what we shall drink, or what we shall put on: but bids us consider the lilies how they grow in more royalty than Solomon. But contrary to this we must look at no colours, nor make anything that is changeable colours as the hills are, nor sell them, nor wear them. But we must be all in one dress, and one colour. This is a silly poor gospel. It is more fit for us to be covered with God's eternal spirit, and clothed with his eternal light, which leads us and guides us into righteousness, and to live righteously and justly and holily in this present evil world. This is the clothing that God puts upon us, and likes and will bless. This will make our light shine forth before men, that they may glorify our heavenly father, which is in heaven; for we have God for our teacher and we have his promise and doctrine, and we have the apostles' practice in their day and generation. And we have God's holy spirit to lead us and guide us and we have the blessed Truth, that we are made partakers of, to be our practice. And why should we turn to men and women teaching, which is contrary to Christ Jesus' command and the apostles' practice, here is the [blank] where these things before mentioned stands upon: where have we had these whimsical and imaginations. Friends, we have one God and one mediator betwixt God and man, the man Christ Jesus. Let us keep to him or we are undone.

This is not delightful to me, that I have this occasion to write to you, for wherever I saw it appear, I have stood against it several years. And now I dare neglect no longer, for I see that our blessed precious holy Truth that has visited us from the beginning is kept under, and these silly outside imaginary practices is coming up and practised with great zeal, which hath often grieved my heart.

Now I have set before you life and death, and desires you to choose life and God and his Truth,

The 2 mo. 1700,   Margaret Fox

Appendix 7

Epistle from the Quarterly Meeting in Lancashire the 7th 2 mo. 1698 to Friends and brethren at the Yearly Meeting in London

LSF, LYM Epistles Received, vol.1, pp.269–73

Brethren,
In the ancient love which reaches many hearts, at the beginning broke down the partition wall and raised a pure mind that inclined to wait upon God to be encouraged and supported in the trials of that day, we tenderly salute you, having in our hearts thanksgiving and acknowledgement to God our father and Christ Jesus our redeemer and saviour for the continuation of this love which enables to bear all things, suffer through all things until the lamb of God arise, to raise over all things that remnant who have self in no repute, o its God's free love – precious in our hearts now as ever, soul affecting as ever – heart overcoming as ever, surely the faithfulness of God fails not the people who in heart trust the Lord God who have not neither dare make flesh their own arm, who have not neither dare not trust in the princes or nobles of the earth, nor yet in the mountains of Israel, but with a single eye have looked and still looks to the invisible God over and above his workmanship for deliverance and salvation, surely God is this peoples' only saviour, this ancient love shed – now abroad in our hearts to us doth declare it, so that we have renewed reason to commemorate the eternal life made manifest by its mighty works in us and to us from the beginning, and to be zealously affected for the testimony thereof in its several branches both in life and practice lest the simplicity of the gospel and offence of the cross should be trampled upon and cease, and that spirit take place which advised master save thyself, and said not have not I brought mighty things to pass, have not I built thee a flourishing city, whose merchandise make rich and nobles of the earth my own arm sustains me, for which the vials of God's wrath are prepared and ready to be poured upon without mixture.

Therefore having considered the many branches of our Christian testimony, the several admonitions, requests and friendly advices, which have from year to year come to the Yearly Meeting having unity therewith, concluded to recommend a strict enquiry to be made in all the Particular Meetings in our county, how Friends uprightly bear their testimonies for Truth and answered Friends' advices, which accordingly was done, and the account now returned to this Meeting is that where any Friends come short in his known duty, or in answering friendly advices, such hopes for future to redeem the time, and show forth the praises of the Truth both in life and practice, that generally our Friends are clear in their testimonies

295

against the hireling Priests, against their doctrine of imperfection against payment of tithes of all sorts, against their forced maintenance or any payment for reading or preaching; – against their marrying people, sprinkling or baptising children or others with visible water, reading before or praying over the dead, or prayers after a set form or in their own wills, and taking payment because thereof – against their communion in visible bread and wine, or any payment therefore, or payment for or towards the building or repairing their steeplehouses or chapels, fencing their yards, making or hanging their bells, organs, fonts, or what relates to their worships, against any payment either to clerk or sexton for what relates to their office, against oaths or swearing in any case whatsoever or taking the name of God in vain, against wars and fighting with any carnal weapons whatsoever in order to destroy men, women or children: against giving or taking of hat honour, bowings or feinting titles to or from the children of men, or using corrupt language of the world the double and deceitful tongue, against all plotting, contriving or abetting against the King, government or peace thereof, or against the welfare of our neighbours, against observation of days, both as to the fasts, feasts, and prayers of the world, against all excess and superfluities of meat, drink, apparel together with vain and foolish customs, fashions and observances at births, marriages and burials, and fellowships of the world, against going to the world or taking of the world in marriage – we likewise have account that meetings are constantly kept up both week days and first days, and the 10th hour to be observed through our county; That diligent schoolmasters and mistresses are provided to teach Friends' children, and that Friends comply with advice not to send their children for teaching nor bind them but apprentice to the world, that Friends are examples of plainness both in deportment, habit and speech to their children, teaching them to speak thou and thee to a single person, and call the days and months distinct from the world's, allowing the necessary and plain habit; that no friend make any offer or account of marriage without first acquainting parents or guardians, and obtaining their consent, and that none marry with near kindred or make too early procedure in marriage. That poor children are bound apprentices, and that poor Friends' children partake of that schooling and education which may fit them for apprentices, upon Friends charge, that many Friends by will or otherwise have settled their estates that where any professing Truth goes out to the world, or admits the world to come in and carry such away, such forfeits their patrimony and deprives themselves of any portion from their parents unless by unfeigned repentance such manifest themselves worthy – and if parents countenance any such running out for covetousness and earthly preferment, such are dealt with as offenders, that whispering, talebearing, backbiting and evil speaking, strife and contention is watched against, and such are judged that go thereinto; that care is taken, and in taking that Friends launch not into things of the world either to endanger their reputation by what may happen through going into debt, and also hinder many from their just rights in outward things, or by defrauding and over-reaching through coveting what is others to possess themselves thereof, or that their great enjoinments proves a snare that holds them so fast they neither serve God or the church – That Women's Meetings are both encouraged and duly kept up, that Meeting Houses are mostly recorded, that what makes for peace is generally pursued and Friends are still and quiet under the government. That if any misunderstanding or difference happen concerning anything between Friend and Friend way is considered upon which consents to put it to rights, that Friends go not to law by suing and arresting one another, until such have had gospel advice – That sufferings are kept account of and that now the greatest sufferings are upon the two late Acts which together with other sufferings we have sent you. That no Meeting Houses are built, no public Friend died since the last account. James Backhouse a prisoner died the 13th 4 mo. 1697. Four prisoners discharged, viz. Robert Hubberstey, William Braithwaite, James Braithwaite, and Robert Braithwaite, only William Dawson remains prisoner. That some are convinced since the last account, Truth is of good repute and Friends are at unity and peace one with another, blessed to God forever and ever.

Thus having given you dear brethren a brief account of the state of Friends in our county of their love and zeal for Truth and testimony of it, and their readiness to comply with friendly advices, together with our salutations in that ancient love that prevailed over us to love and to do good works, we leave you to that ancient love, and therein to your care and a due inspection to be made how Truth's testimony is born and Friends advice taken and practised in all respects in all counties and countries that the zeal of God's house may more and more be kindled that Friends love may more and more spring up and shine, that self love and exaltation be mortified, and self cast out of the very suburbs belonging to the holy city, that the lamb may ascend to sit upon the throne in majesty and glory in the midst of his saints.

Bibliography

MANUSCRIPT SOURCES

1.   Lancaster Friends Meeting House (LFMH)

a.   Bound volumes of minutes books etc:

Lancashire Quarterly Meeting Minutes: vol.1, 1669–1711; vol.2, 1711–1776

Lancashire Women's Quarterly Meeting Minutes: vol.1, 1675–1777

Lancashire Quarterly Meeting Book of Sufferings: vol.1, 1654–1700; vol.2, 1701–1717; vol.3, 1717–1743

Lancaster Monthly Meeting Minutes: vol.1, 1675–1718; vol.2, 1718–1767

Lancaster Women's Monthly Meeting Minutes: vol.1, 1676–1749

Lancaster Particular Meeting Minutes: vol.1, 1698–1740; vol.2, 1740–1795

Lancaster Women's Particular Meeting Minutes: vol.1, 1737–1799

Yearly Meeting Minutes and Epistles (including legal advices): vol.1, 1672–1770

Yearly Meeting Epistles: vol.1, 1672–1770

b.   Packets and bundles:

2Ai: Yearly Meeting Papers 1694–1819

2Aii: Printed Papers, 17th and 18th centuries

2Aiii: Printed Yearly Meeting Epistles 1714–1804

2Aix: Miscellaneous Printed Tracts, 18th and 19th centuries

2Axii: Meeting for Sufferings Papers, 18th and early 19th centuries

2Axxvii: MS Yearly Meeting Minutes and Epistles sent to the Quarterly Meetings, 1710–1826

2Axxxiii: Lancashire QM loose minutes

2Axxxv: Early loose papers of minutes, Lancs Quarterly Meeting and Lancaster Monthly Meeting

2Axxxvi: Miscellaneous late 17th and 18th century Quarterly Meeting and Monthly Meeting papers

2Axli: Note and Minute Books, 17th–20th centuries

2Bi(a): Miscellaneous Lancaster Monthly Meeting letters and papers 1700–1818

2Bii: Testimonies of Disownment, Lancaster Monthly Meeting

2Bxv: Lancaster Monthly Meeting Papers on discipline and tithe testimony 1671–1803

2Bxvi: Lancaster Monthly Meeting sufferings for tithes

2Bxvii: Papers detailing imprisonments and confiscations

2Bxxv: Early Lancaster Monthly Meeting letters and papers
2Bxxvi: Miscellaneous late 17th and 18th century papers

2. Lancaster Public Library (LPL)

MS 108: Lancaster Corporation, lists of officials and burgesses
MS 208: Lancaster Corporation, enrolment books of apprentices with
    orders to freemen 1736–1754
MS 221: Borough of Lancaster, Court: Orders 1710–1758; Oaths sworn,
    1712–1784
MS 2895: Manuscript Book, including list of corporation officials
    1709–1829
MS 5005–13: Election returns, 1679–1746
MS 5447: Papers relating to the case of Lambert v Cumming 1722
MS 5461–68: Letters from Thomas Cumming to Edward Cumming
MS 5376, 77, 79: Summonses, Lambert v Cumming 1722
MS 5469–74: Letters to Edward Cumming 1726–1745

3. Library of the Society of Friends, London (LSF)

Book of Cases: vol.1, 1661–1695; vol.2, 1695–1738; vol.3, 1739–1806
Great Book of Sufferings: vols.1, 3, 5, 7, 8, 11, 14, 16–21, 1650–1750
London Yearly Meeting Minutes: vols.1–9, 1672 1747
London Yearly Meeting Epistles Received: vol.1, 1683–1706; vol.2,
    1705–1738; vol.3, 1736–1758
London Yearly Meeting Epistles Sent: vol.1, 1683–1703; vol.2,
    1704–1738; vol.3, 1738–1756
Minutes of the Meeting for Sufferings: vols.1–28, 1675–1749
Morning Meeting Minutes: vol.1, 1673–1692; vol.2, 1692–1700; vol.3,
    1700–1711; vol.4, 1711–1734
Six Weeks Meeting Minutes: vol.3, 1695–1698; vol.4, 1698–1704
Westminster Monthly Meeting Minutes: vol.2, 1690–1701; vol.3,
    1701–1712
Swarthmore Monthly Meeting Minutes: vol.1, 1668–1674; vol.3,
    1691–1715; vol.4, 1715–1762
Swarthmore Women's Monthly Meeting Minutes: vol.1, 1671–1700;
    vol.2, 1700–1717; vol.4, 1731–1771
Swarthmore Particular Meeting Minutes: vol.1, 1699–1722; vol.2,
    1722–1756
Swarthmore Women's Particular Meeting Minutes: vol.1, 1712–1755
Bound MSS Portfolio series (numbered), vols.2, 7, 13, 14, 16, 17, 20, 23,
    25, 26, 27, 31, 36, 41, 42
Abraham MSS
Crossfield MSS
Dix MSS
Gibson MSS, vols.1, 3

Gibson T S (Life of Thomas Storey with Original Letters)
John Thompson MSS
Kelsall MSS
Miller MSS
Original Records of Sufferings, vol.3
Spence MSS vol.3
Thirnbeck MSS
MSS vol.77, Thomas Gwin's Journal

4.   Public Record Office, Kew, Surrey

CUST 31/1 Abstract of Customs General Orders, 1700–1736
CUST 32/1 Treasury to Board, Orders and Warrants, 1707–1811
CUST 41/1–2 Opinions of Council 1701–1738
CUST 47/66 Excise Board & Secretariat Minutes April–July 1711
CUST 81/70 Outport Records Lancaster: Board to Collector 1715–1726
CUST 81/72 Outport Records, Letter Book, Lancaster 1715–1728
T 4/9 Treasury Reference Book of Petitions 1711–1715
T 27/20/21 Treasury, Out Letters General 1711–1713

5.   Scottish Record Office, Edinburgh

CH 10/3/55 (unnumbered bundle) Papers relating to Aberdeen Burgess
   Oath 1699–1714

PRINTED SOURCES

a.   Works published before 1850

Advice to Church Wardens, Respecting the usual Oath administred to them in the Ecclesiastical Courts etc. (no place, c.1740)

The Ancient Testimony and Principle of the People Called Quakers Renewed with Respect to the King and Government, and touching the Present Association (London, 1695/96)

Atkinson, Thomas, *The Christian Testimony Against Tythes, In an Account of the great Spoil and Rapine committed by the Bishop of Chester's Tythe Farmer at Cartmell in Lancashire: upon the People there called Quakers, in the years 1677 and 1678* (no place, 1678)

Atkinson, Thomas, *An Exhortation to all People* (no place, 1684)

Barclay, A.R., *Letters etc. of Early Friends; illustrative of the History of the Society from nearly its origin, to about the period of George Fox's decease ...* (London, 1841)

Barclay, John, *Diary of Alexander Jaffray ... to which are added Particulars of his Subsequent Life given in connexion with Memoirs of the Rise, Progress, and Persecutions, of the People Called Quakers in the North of Scotland* (2nd. ed., London, 1834)

Barclay, Robert, *An Apology for the True Christian Divinity as the same is held forth, and preached by the people, Called in Scorn, Quakers; Being a full explanation and Vindication of their Principles and Doctrines* ... (6th ed., London, 1736)

Beekham, Edward, and Meriton, Henry, and Topcliffe, Lancaster, *A Brief Discovery of some of the Blasphemous and seditious Principles and Practises of the People, Called Quakers: Taken out of their most Noted and Approved Authors* (London, 1699)

Bellers, John, *An Essay Towards the Ease of Elections of Members of Parliament* (London, 1712)

Benson, Gervase, *A True Testimony Concerning Oaths and Swearing etc... and the command of Christ, Swear not at all, manifested to be an universal prohibition of all Oaths and Swearing whatsoever, to his Disciples* (London, 1669)

Benson, Gervase, *A Second Testimony Concerning Oaths and Swearing ... Wherein is fully cleared the command of Christ, and Practice of the Apostles concerning Swearing* ... (London, 1675)

Besse, Joseph, *A Collection of the Sufferings of the People called Quakers, from the Testimony of A Good Conscience, from The Time of their being first distinguished by the Name in the Year 1650 to the Time of the Act, commonly called the Act of Toleration* ... (2 vols., London, 1753)

Billing, Edward, *A Word of Reproof, and Advice to my late Fellow-Souldiers and Officers of the Engish, Irish, and Scotish Army; With some Inrhoad made upon the Hireling and his Mass-house, University, Orders, Degrees, Vestments, Poperies, Heathenism, etc* ... (London, 1659)

The Book of Oaths and the Severall forms thereof, both antient and modern (London, 1715)

A Brief Representation of the Quakers Case of Not Swearing; and why they might have been, and yet may be Relieved therein, by Parliament (London, 1694)

Bugg, Francis, *Some Reasons Humbly offered against the Quakers unreasonable Request, touching Elections of Members to serve in Parliament* (London, 1708)

Burnet, Gilbert, *History of His Own Time From the Restoration of King Charles II to the conclusion of the Treaty of Peace at Utrecht* (4 vols., London, 1815)

The Case of the People called Quakers relating to Oaths and Swearing, presented to the serious consideration of the King and both Houses of Parliament (no place, 1673)

The Case of the People Commonly Called Quakers, with some reasons humbly offered to the tender consideration of the Members of the House of Commons ... that their Solemn Affirmation may be allowed without Swearing in the Courts of Chancery and Exchequer (no place, 1696)

The Case of the People called Quakers, Humbly offer'd to the Parliament, in Relation to the Perpetuating the Bill for the more easie Recovery of small Tythes (no place, 1704)

The Case of some Thousands of the People called Quakers, in Great Britain, who conscientiously Scruple the present Affirmation (no place, 1721?)

The Case of the People called Quakers, with Respect to many of their Friends in South Britain, and their Friends in general in North Britain, who conscientiously scruple the taking of the present Affirmation (no place, 1721?)

Claridge, Richard, *More Reasons against the Bill to prevent the Growth of Schism, etc.* (no place, 1714?)

Crook, John, *Tythes No Property to, nor Lawful Maintenance for a Powerful Gospel-preaching Ministry* (London, 1659)

Crook, John, *The Case of Swearing (at all) Discussed, With several objections answered, the Primitive Practises therein asserted out of several ancient authors; together with several Presidents out of the Book of Martyrs...* (London, 1660)

Crook, John, *Sixteen Reasons drawn from the Law of God, the Law of England, and Right Reason, to shew why diverse Christians (called Quakers) refuse to swear at all* (London, 1661?)

Crook, John, *An Apology for the Quakers, Wherein is shewed How they Answer the Chief Principles of the Law, and Main ends of Government; with several reasons why they deserve the Liberty of their Consciences in the Worship of God ...* (London, 1662)

The Cry of Oppression In a Few Instances of the late Distresses and Levies made upon some of the peaceable People, called Quakers, in the Counties of York and Lancaster, On Account of their tender consciences, and for their Religious Meetings, briefly stated (London, 1683)

The Cry of Oppression, Robert Salthouse and John Fell of Ulverstone in the County of Lancaster, being Prosecuted by John Woods, of Dalton, Impropriator etc. (no place, 1698?)

Dalton, Michael, *The Countrey Justice, containing the practice of Justices of the Peace out of their Sessions ...* (8th ed., London, 1682)

Davis, Joseph, *Digest of Legislative Enactments, Relating to the Society of Friends, commonly called Quakers, in England ...* (2nd ed., London, 1849)

A Declaration From the People call'd Quakers to the King, and Both Houses of Parliament, Then Sitting at Westminster, what they can say instead of an oath (no place, 1700?)

A Declaration from the People of God, called Quakers, against all Seditious Conventicles, and dangerous Practises of any who under colour, or pretence of tender Conscience, have, or may contrive Insurrections ... (no place, 1670?)

Edmundson, William, *A Journal of the Life, Travels, Sufferings, and Labour of Love in the Work of the Ministry of the Worthy Elder, and Faithful Servant of Jesus Christ William Edmundson ...* (London, 1715) ,

Ellwood, Thomas, *The Foundation of Tythes Shaken; And the Four Principal Posts (of Divine Institution, Primitive Practise, Voluntary Donations, and Positive Laws) on which the nameless Author of the Book, called, The Right of Tythes Asserted and Proved, hath set his pretended Right to Tythes, Removed, in a Reply to the said Book* (no place, 1678)

Fell, Leonard, *An Epistle for the Strengthening and Confirming of Friends in their Most Holy Faith* (no place, 1670)

Fell, Leonard, and Addamson, Willm., *The Persecution of them People they call Quakers in several places in Lancashire* (London, 1656)

Fell, Margaret, *A Brief Collection of Remarkable Passages and Occurrences Relating to the Birth, Education, Life, Conversion, Travels, Services, and Deep Sufferings of that Ancient, Eminent, and Faithful Servant of the Lord, Margaret Fell; but by her Second Marriage, Margaret Fox* (London, 1710)

A Few Instances of the Severe Prosecutions in the Exchequer for Tythes of small value, Humbly offered to the Parliament (no place, 1705?)

Fox, George, *To the Flock of Christ, everywhere to be read in their Assemblies* (London, 1681)

Fox, George, *A General Epistle to Friends, London, 17th of 8th Month, 1688* (no place, 1688)

Gough, John, *A History of the People Called Quakers, from their first Rise to the present Time, Compiled from Authentic Records ...* (4 vols., Dublin, 1789–1790)

Haydock, Eleanor Junior, *A Visitation of Love, in The Good-Will of God; to the Professors of the Holy Truth; Containing, Lamentation over, and Warning to Backsliders and Unfaithful* (London, 1712)

Haydock, Roger, *A Collection of the Christian Writings, Labours, Travels and Sufferings of that Faithful and Approved Minister of Jesus Christ, Roger Haydock ...* (London, 1700)

Hubberthorn, Richard, *The Good Old Cause Briefly Demonstrated, with Advertisements to authority concerning it; To the end All Persons may see the Cause of their Bondage, and way of deliverance* (London, 1659)

Hubberthorn, Richard, *A Collection of the several Books and Writings of that Faithful servant of God, Richard Hubberthorn, Who Finished his Testimony (being a Prisoner in Newgate for the Truth's sake) the 17th of the 6th Month 1662* (London, 1663)

Journal of the House of Commons (London) vols.11–22

To the King and both Houses of Parliament, Now Sitting at Westminster (London, 1666)

Latye, Gilbert et al., *A Salutation or Testimony of True and Brotherly Love, as it did arise in our Hearts, unto all as are concerned therein* (London, 1672)

London Yearly Meeting, *Extracts from the Minutes and Advices of the Yearly Meeting of Friends held in London from its first institution* (2nd. ed., London, 1802)

London Yearly Meeting, *Epistles from the Yearly Meeting of Friends, Held in London, to the Quarterly and Monthly Meetings in Great Britain, Ireland and Elsewhere, from 1681 to 1817* (London, 1818)

London Yearly Meeting, *Extracts from the Minutes and Advices of the Yearly*

Meeting of Friends held in London ... Supplement to the second edition (London, 1822)

To the Lords and Commons in Parliament assembled, An Account of some late and present Sufferings, of some of the People called Quakers (for Tythes) (no place, 1700)

Meeting for Sufferings, *An Epistle from the Meeting for Sufferings...to Such Friends in England and Wales, or elsewhere, as are or may be concerned in the Favour granted by the Government for the Ease of Friends, from the Great Oppression of Oaths ...* (London, 1696)

Meeting for Sufferings, *Epistle from the Meeting for Sufferings, An answer to An Essay upon the Vth Matthew ...* (no place, 1714)

Meeting for Sufferings, *Epistle from the Meeting for Sufferings, An answer to Primitive Simplicity Demonstrated ...* (no place, 1715)

Milner, Richard, *A Few Words to the King and both Houses of Parliament, Worthy their consideration in a weighty Concern; to wit, the effect of the Execution of the late Act, made against Meetings and Conventicles, so called; through which very many of the Innocent Peope of God have and do deeply suffer* (no place, 1675)

Mollineux, Henry, *Antichrist Unvailed, by the Finger of God's Power; and His Visage Discovered by the Light of Christ Jesus; and his Ministers, Members, Works, and Lying Wonders Manifested by the Spirit of God ... Written in the Love of God by a Prisoner (at Lancaster Castle) for the Testimony of Truth ...* (London, 1695)

Mollineux, Henry, *An Invitation from the Spirit of Christ, to all that are a Thirst, to come and Drink of the Waters of Life ... Written by one, Who hath for a long time been deeply Distressed with Thirst after the water of Life; but through Mercy, hath obtained satisfaction thereby ...* (London, 1696)

Mollineux, Henry, *Popery Exposed by its own Authors, and Two Romish Champions Checked, for their hot and rash Onsets and Attempts against the People called Quakers ...* (London, 1718)

The Oath of a Constable, so far as it relates to apprehending Night Walkers and Idle Persons, etc. (London, 1707)

The Parliamentary History of England from the Earliest Periods to the Year 1803 ... (23 vols., London, 1811–1820), vols.7, 9

Patchett, Francis, *Living Words through a Dying Man; being a Melodious Song of the Mercies and Judgements of the Lord ... By one who died a Prisoner for the Testimoney of Jesus, Francis Patchett* (no place, 1678)

Pearson, Anthony, *The Great Case of Tithes Truly Stated, Clearly Open'd and fully Resolv'd ...* (6th ed., London, 1732)

Pearson, Anthony, *Reasons given for refusing to pay Tithes to Priests or Impropriators* (no place, 1700?)

Penn, William, and Meade, William, *The People's Ancient and Just Liberties Asserted, in the Tryal of William Penn, and William Meade, At the Sessions, held at the Old Baily, in London, the first, third, fourth and fifth of Sept. 70 ...* (London, 1670)

Penn, William, *Considerations on the Bill Depending for Preventing Occasional Conformity* (London, 1703?)

Penn, William, *The Proposed Comprehension, Soberly and not Unseasonably Considered* (London, 1672)

Penn, William, *The Select Works of William Penn* ... (3 vols., 4th ed., London, 1825)

Raven, John, *The Substance of a Discourse, some time since Betwixt a Countryman, a Justice of the Peace, and a Counsellor at Law in the County of Essex (all yet Living) concerning Tithes* ... (London, 1701)

Redford, Elizabeth, *A Warning from the Lord to the City and Nation in Mercy to the People, to see if they will yet seek him* (no place, 1695)

Redford, Elizabeth, *A Warning, a Warning from the Lord, in Mercy to the People, to see if they will yet seek him* (no place, 1696)

Redford, Elizabeth, *The Love of God is to Gather the Seasons of the Earth and their Multitudes into Peace* (no place, 1700?)

Redford, Elizabeth, *The Widow's Mite, Humbly offer'd, not imposed; shewing why the seventh Day of the Lord's Rest is to be kept in Christ* (no place, 1715?)

Rigge, Ambrose, *A Few Propositions offered to the King and his Council; by way of Querie, to be seriously weighed by them, being things which highly concerns the King and the whole Kingdom* ... (no place, 1664?)

Rigge, Ambrose, *A Faithful Testimony against Extravagant and unnecessary Wiggs* (London, 1699)

Rudd, Thomas, *An Account from the City of Chester, of A Barbarous Persecution Inflicted Upon one of the King's Peaceable Subjects, commonly called a Quaker. Only for his Lamenting the great Sin of Pride, and calling the People to Repentance* (London, 1700)

Rudd, Thomas, *The Cry of the Oppressed for Justice: or, The Case of Thomas Rudd, who was Imprisoned and Whipped through the several streets of the Town of Leverpool, in the County of Lancaster ... for going through the streets thereof, and exhorting the People to Fear God* ... (London, 1700)

Rudd, Thomas, *A Lamentation Over, and Further Warning to England's Inhabitants, before the day of the Visitation of many of them be wholly over* (no place, 1702)

Sheppard, William, *The Offices and Duties of Constables, Borsholders, Tything-men...and other lay-ministers, Whereunto are adjoyned the severall offices of Church Ministers and Church Wardens* (London, 1652)

Some Few of the Quakers Many Horrid Blasphemies, Heresies And their Bloody Treasonable Principles Destructive to Government Delivered to the Members of Both Houses of Lords and Commons ... (London, 1699)

Some Reasons Humbly offered ... why the Quaker's Affirmation should not pass instead of an Oath at future Elections of Parliament (London, 1708?)

Some Reasons offer'd with Submission on behalf of the Preachers among the People called Quakers, for their Exemption from being Taxed as such in the Poll Bill (no place, 1692?)

Speed, Thomas, *Reason against Rae: Being some Animadversions upon a late*

Scurrilous Libel Prefix'd to a Sermon Preach'd Nine and thirty Years ago ... (London, 1691)

The Statutes of the Realm, Printed by Command of His Majesty King George the Third In Pursuance of an Address of the House of Commons of Great Britain (9 vols., London, 1810–1822)

Story, Thomas, *A Journal of the Life of Thomas Story: containing an Account of his Remarkable Convincement ... and also, of his Travels and Labours in the Service of the Gospel: with many other occurrences and Observations* (Newcastle, 1747)

The Suffering Case and Complaint of the People Called Quakers: concerning some under execution of the late Poll Acts etc. (no place, 1692?)

Tillotson, John, *The Works of the Most Reverend Dr John Tillotson, Late Lord Archbishop of Canterbury* (10 vols., Edinburgh, 1772), vol.2

Whitehead, George, *The Case of the Quakers concerning Oaths, Defended as Evangelical* ... (no place, 1675)

Whitehead, George, *A Christian Epistle to Friends in General of weighty concern, for their present and future Peace and Safety from the Soul's Adversary's subtil Devices and Snares of Death* ... (London, 1689)

Whitehead, George, and Crisp, Stephen, *A Christian Reprehension of Confusion, Ranterism, Cruelty, and Opposition to Spiritual Order and Christian Liberty in Brief Reflections* ... (London, 1690)

Whitehead, George, *Christ's Lambs Defended from Satan's Rage, In a Just Vindication of the People called Quakers, Their Christian Sincerity, Innocency and Respect to the Civil Government, and the Good Ends thereof* ... (London, 1691)

Whitehead, George, *An Epistle of True Christian Love to all Friends called (or reputed) Quakers, who profess the True Light, To Remind them of the beginning and Progress of the Lord's Work and Ministry in our Day* ... (London, 1707)

Whitehead, George, *A Brief Epistle for Unity and Good Order among all Friends professing the blessed Truth* (London, 1708)

Whitehead, George, *The Christian Progress of that Ancient Servant and Minister of Jesus Christ, George Whitehead, Historically Relating his Experience, Ministry, Sufferings, Trials and Service in Defence of the Truth, and God's Persecuted People, commonly called Quakers* ... (London, 1725)

Widders, Robert, *The Life and Death, Travels and Sufferings of Robert Widders of Kellet in Lancashire, who was one of the Lord's Worthies, together with several Testimonies of his Neighbours and Friends concerning him* (London, 1688)

b.   Works published after 1850

Abbatt, Dilworth, *Quaker Annals of Preston and the Fylde 1653–1900* (London, 1931)

Aston, T., *Crisis in Europe 1560–1660, Essays from 'Past and Present'* (London, 1965)

Atton, Henry, and Holland, Henry, *The King's Customs, an account of Maritime Revenue and Contraband Traffic in England, Scotland and Ireland from the earliest times to the year 1800* (2 vols., London, 1910)

Baker, Derek (ed.), *Studies in Church History, vol.10* (Oxford, 1973)

Barbour, Hugh, *The Quakers in Puritan England* (London, 1964)

Barbour, Hugh and Roberts, Arthur (eds.), *Early Quaker Writings 1650–1700* (Grand Rapids, Michigan, 1973)

Bartholomew, John & Son Ltd., *Gazetteer of the British Isles* (Edinburgh, 1966)

Bauman, Richard, *Let Your Words be Few: Symbolism of speaking and silence among seventeenth-century Quakers* (Cambridge, 1983)

Blackwood, B.G., *The Lancashire Gentry and the Great Rebellion 1640–1660* (Chetham Soc., 3rd series, 25, 1978)

Bouch, C.M.L., *Prelates and People of the Lake Counties. A History of the Diocese of Carlisle* (Kendal, 1948)

Braithwaite, Alfred W., *Thomas Rudyard Early Friends' "Oracle of Law"* (JFHS supp.27, London, 1956)

Braithwaite, William C., *Spiritual Guidance in the Experience of the Society of Friends* (Swarthmore Lecture, London, 1909)

Braithwaite, William C., *The Beginnings of Quakerism* (London, 1912)

Briathwaite, William C., *The Second Period of Quakerism* (London, 1919)

Brewer, John, and Styles, John (ed.), *An Ungovernable People: The English and their law in the seventeenth and eighteenth centuries* (London, 1980)

Brinton, Howard H., *The Religious Philosophy of Quakerism: The Beliefs of Fox, Barclay, and Penn As Based on the Gospel of John* (Wallingford Penn., 1973)

Brockbank, Elisabeth, *Richard Hubberthorne of Yealand: Yeoman – Soldier – Quaker 1628–1662* (London, 1929)

Brownbill, John, *A Calendar of Charters and Records belonging to the Corporation of Lancaster* (Lancaster, 1929)

Browning, Andrew (ed.), *Memoirs of Sir John Reresby* (Glasgow, 1936)

Burbidge, P.G., *Notes & References* (Cambridge, 1952)

Cadbury, Henry J., *Narrative Papers of George Fox* (Richmond, Indiana, 1972)

Calendar of State Papers Domestic Series, (London) 1660–1704

Capp, B.S., *The Fifth Monarchy Men, A Study in Seventeenth Century English Millenarianism* (London, 1972)

Chetham Miscellanies vol.VII, (Chetham Soc., n.s. 109, 1945)

Clark, George, *The Later Stuarts 1660–1714* (2nd ed., Oxford, 1956)

Clemesha, H.W., *A History of Preston in Amounderness* (Manchester, 1912)

Cockburn, J.S., *A History of English Assizes 1558–1714* (Cambridge, 1972)

Coward, Barry, *The Stanleys Lords Stanley and Earls of Derby, 1385–1672, The origins, wealth and power of a landowning family* (Chetham Soc., 3rd series, 30, 1983)

Cragg, Gerald, *The Church in the Age of Reason 1648–1789* (revised ed., London, 1970)

Cranston, Maurice, *John Locke, a biography* (London, 1957)

Crossfield, Helen G., *Margaret Fox of Swarthmoor Hall* (London, 1913)

Cruickshanks, Eveline, *Ideology and Conspiracy: Aspects of Jacobitism, 1689–1759* (Edinburgh, 1982)

Cunliffe Shaw, R., *Kirkham in Amounderness, The Story of a Lancashire Community* (Preston, 1949)

Dickens, A.G. (ed.), *The Courts of Europe, Politics, Patronage and Royalty 1400–1800* (London, 1977)

Dickenson, H.T., *Walpole and the Whig Supremacy* (London, 1973)

Dickenson, H.T., *Liberty and Property, Political Ideology in Eighteenth-Century Britain* (London, 1977)

Dictionary of National Biography (63 vols., London, 1885–1900)

Doncaster, L. Hugh, *Quaker Organisation and Business Meetings* (London, 1958)

Evans, Eric J., *The Contentious Tithe: The tithe problem and English agriculture, 1750–1858* (London, 1976)

Evans, John T., *17th Century Norwich: Politics, Religion and Government 1620–1690* (Oxford, 1979)

Farrer, William, and Brownbill, J., *The Victoria History of the County of Lancaster* (8 vols., London, 1906–1911)

Fishwick, Henry (ed.), *Lancashire and Cheshire Church Surveys 1649–1655* (Record Society of Lancashire and Cheshire, 1, 1879)

Fishwick, Henry (ed.), *The Note Book of the Rev. Thomas Jolly A.D. 1671–1693* (Chetham Soc., n.s.33, 1895)

Floud, Roderick, *An Introduction to Quantitative Methods for Historians* (London, 1973)

Frost, J. William, *The Quaker Family in Colonial America: A Portrait of the Society of Friends* (London, 1973)

Gandy, Wallace (ed.), *Lancashire Association Oath Rolls, A.D. 1696* (London, 1921)

Gatrell, V.A.C., and Lenman, Bruce, and Parker, Geoffrey (eds.) *Crime and the Law. The Social History of Crime in Western Europe since 1500* (London, 1980)

Glassey, Lionel K.J., *Politics and the Appointment of Justices of the Peace 1675–1720* (Oxford, 1979)

Green, J.J. (ed.), *Souvenir of the Address to King Edward VII, 1901: The right of the Society of Friends to present addresses in person to the sovereign 1654–1901* (London, 1901)

Grubb, Isobel, *Quakerism in Industry before eighteen hundred* (London, 1930)

Haigh, Christopher, *Reformation and Resistance in Tudor Lancashire* (Cambridge, 1975)

Haller, William, and Davies, Godfrey, *The Leveller Tracts 1647–1653* (New York, 1944)

Hancock, Thomas, *The Peculium; An Endeavour to throw light on some of the causes of the Decline of the Society of Friends ...* (London, 1859)

Harding, Alan (ed.), *Law Making and law makers in British History Papers presented to the Edinburgh Legal History Conference, 1977* (Royal Historical Society Studies in History Series no.22, London, 1980)

Harrison, J.F.C., *The Second Coming. Popular Millenarianism 1780–1850* (London, 1979)

Hatton, Ragnhild, *George I Elector and King* (London, 1978)

Heal, Felicity, and O'Day, Rosemary (eds.), *Church and Society in England, Henry VIII to James I* (London, 1977)

Henning, Basil Duke, *The House of Commons 1660–1690* (3 vols., London, 1983)

Heywood, Thomas (ed.), *The Norris Papers* (Chetham Soc., 9, 1846)

Heywood, Thomas (ed.), *The Diary of the Rev. Henry Newcome, from September 30, 1661 to September 29, 1663* (Chetham Soc., 18, 1849)

Hill, Christopher, *Economic Problems of the Church from Archbishop Whitgift to the Long Parliament* (Oxford, 1956)

Hill, Christopher, *Society and Puritanism in Pre-Revolutionary England* (revised ed., London, 1969)

Hill, Christopher, *The World Turned Upside Down: Radical Ideas during the English Revolution* (Penguin ed., London, 1975)

Hill, Christopher, *Change and Continuity in Seventeenth-Century England* (London, 1974)

Hill, Christopher, *The Experience of Defeat. Milton and Some Contemporaries* (London, 1984)

HMC Twelfth Report, Appendix, Part VI, *Manuscripts of the House of Lords 1689–1690* (London, 1889)

HMC Twelfth Report, Appendix, Part VII, *The Manuscripts of S H Le Flemming Esq of Rydal Hall* (London, 1890)

HMC Thirteenth Report, Appendix, Part V, *Manuscripts of the House of Lords 1690–91* (London, 1892)

HMC Fourteenth Report, Appendix, Part IV, *The Manuscripts of Lord Kenyon* (London, 1894)

Holden, Joshua, *A Short History of Todmorden* (Manchester, 1912)

Holmes, Geoffrey, *Britain After the Glorious Revolution 1689–1714* (London, 1969)

Holmes, Geoffrey, *The Trial of Doctor Sacheverell* (London, 1973)

Hoon, Elizabeth, *The Organisation of the English Customs System, 1696–1786* (Newton Abbot, 1968)

Horwitz, Henry, *The Parliamentary Diary of Narcissus Luttrell 1691–1693* (Oxford, 1972)

Horwitz, Henry, *Parliament, Policy and Politics in the reign of William III* (Manchester, 1977)

Manuscripts of the House of Lords, vol.II, 1695–97 (n.s., London, 1903)

Manuscripts of the House of Lords, vol.IV, 1699–1702 (n.s., London, 1908)

Manuscripts of the House of Lords, vol.IX, 1710–1712 (n.s., London, 1949)

Manuscripts of the House of Lords, vol.XII, 1714–1718 (n.s., London, 1977)

Hughes, T. Cann (ed.), *The Rolls of the Freemen of the Borough of Lancaster*

1688–1840, Part I (Record Society of Lancashire and Cheshire, 87, 1935)

Hughes, T. Cann (ed.), *The Rolls of the Freemen of the Borough of Lancaster 1688–1840, Part II* (Record Society of Lancashire and Cheshire, 90, 1938)

Hunt, Norman C., *Sir Robert Walpole, Samuel Holden, and the Dissenting Deputies* (London, 1957)

Hunt, Norman C., *Two Early Political Associations, The Quakers and the Dissenting Deputies in the age of Sir Robert Walpole* (Oxford, 1961)

Jones, J.R. (ed.), *The Restored Monarchy 1660–1688* (London, 1979)

Jones, Rufus M., *The Later Periods of Quakerism* (2 vols., London, 1921)

Jones, Rufus M., *The Quakers in the American Colonies* (London, 1923)

Jones, W.J., *The Elizabethan Court of Chancery* (Oxford, 1967)

Kenyon, J.P., *The Stuarts A Study in English Kingship* (London, 1958)

Kenyon, J.P., *Revolution Principles. The Politics of Party 1689–1720* (Cambridge, 1977)

Kitson Clark, G., *Guide for Research Students Working on Historical Subjects* (Cambridge, 1965)

Lacey, Douglas R., *Dissent and Parliamentary Politics in England 1661–1689, A Study in the Perpetuation and Tempering of Parliamentarianism* (New Brunswick, NJ, 1969)

Ladurie, Emanuel Le Roy, and Goy, Joseph, *Tithe and Agrarian History from the Fourteenth to the Nineteenth Centuries* (Cambridge, 1982)

Latham, Robert, and Matthews, William (eds.), *The Diary of Samuel Pepys* (11 vols., London, 1970–83)

Lenman, Bruce, *The Jacobite Risings in Britain 1689–1746* (London, 1980)

Lloyd, Arnold, *Quaker Social History 1669–1738* (London, 1948)

Locke, John, *The Second Treatise of Government ... and A Letter Concerning Toleration* (ed. J.W. Gough, Oxford, 1956)

Locker Lampson, S., *A Quaker Post-Bag, Letters to Sir John Rode of Barlbrough Hall, In the County of Derby ... 1693–1742* (London, 1910)

Essays in History and Political Theory in Honor of Charles Howard McIlwain (Cambridge, Mass., 1936)

Macpherson, C.B., *The Political Theory of Possessive Individualism. Hobbes to Locke* (Oxford, 1962)

Madge, Sidney J., *The Domesday of Crown Lands. A Study of the Legislation, Surveys, and Sales of Royal Estates under the Commonwealth* (London, 1938)

Marshall, J.D. (ed.), *The Autobiography of William Stout of Lancaster 1665–1752* (Manchester, 1967)

Marshall, J.D., *Lancashire* (Newton Abbot, 1974)

Miller, John, *Popery and Politics in England 1660–1688* (Cambridge, 1973)

Miller, John, *James II a study in kingship* (Hove, 1977)

Milligan, Edward H., and Thomas, Malcolm J., *My Ancestors were Quakers How can I find out more about them ?* (London, 1983)

Mingay, G.E., *The Gentry: the Rise and Fall of a Ruling Class* (London, 1976)

Moore, Emily E., *Travelling with Thomas Story. The Life and Travels of an Eighteenth-Century Quaker* (Letchworth Garden City, 1947)

Morland, Stephen C. (ed.), *The Somersetshire Quarterly Meeting of the Society of Friends, 1668–1699* (Somerset Record Society, 75, 1978)

Mortimer, Russell (ed.), *Minute Book of the Men's Meeting of the Society of Friends in Bristol 1686–1704* (Bristol Record Society, 30, 1977)

Mortimer, Jean, and Mortimer, Russell (eds.), *Leeds Friends' Minute Book 1692–1712* (Yorkshire Archaeological Society, 139, 1980)

Morton, A.L., *The World of the Ranters: Religious Radicalism in the English Revolution* (London, 1970)

Mullett, Michael, *Early Lancaster Friends* (Lancaster, 1978)

Mullett, Michael, *Radical Religious Movements in Early Modern Europe* (London, 1980)

Napier, A. (ed.), *The Theological Works of Isaac Barrow, D.D.* (9 vols, Cambridge, 1859), vol.2

Nickalls, John L. (ed.), *Journal of George Fox* (revised ed., London, 1975)

Nightingale, B., *Early Stages of the Quaker Movement in Lancashire* (London, 1921)

O'Day, Rosemary, *The English Clergy. The Emergence and Consolidation of a Profession 1558–1642* (Leicester, 1979)

O'Day, Rosemary, and Heal, Felicity (eds.), *Princes and Paupers in the English Church 1500–1800* (Leicester, 1981)

Ogg, David, *England in the Reign of Charles II* (2nd ed., 2 vols., Oxford, 1956)

Pape, Thomas, *Charters of the City of Lancaster* (Lancaster, 1952)

Parkinson, Richard (ed.), *The Life of Adam Martindale, Written by himself...* (Chetham Soc., 4, 1845)

Parkinson, Richard (ed.), *The Autobiography of Henry Newcome* (Chetham Soc., 26 & 27, 1852)

Parkinson, Richard (ed.), *The Private and Literary Remains of John Byrom* (Chetham Soc., 40, 1856)

Penney, Norman (ed.), *The First Publishers of Truth. Being early Records, now first printed, of the Introduction of Quakerism into the Counties of England and Wales* (London, 1907)

Penney, Norman (ed.), *Extracts from State Papers Relating to Friends 1654–1672* (London, 1913)

Penney, Norman, *The Household Account Book of Sarah Fell of Swarthmoor Hall* (Cambridge, 1920)

Pennington, Donald, and Thomas, Keith (eds.), Puritans and Revolutionaries, Essays in Seventeenth-Century History Presented to Christopher Hill (Oxford, 1978)

Peyton, S.A. (ed.), *Minutes of Proceedings in Quarter Sessions held for the Parts of Kesteven in the County of Lincoln 1674–1695* (Lincoln Record Society, 25, 1931)

Phillips, C.B., *Lowther Family Estate Books* (Surtees Society, 191, 1979)

Pink, W. Duncombe, and Beavan, Alfred B., *The Parliamentary Represen-*

tation of Lancashire (County and Borough) 1258–1885, with Biographical and Genealogical Notices of the Members etc. (London, 1889)

Plumb, J.H., *Sir Robert Walpole, The King's Minister* (London, 1960)

Plumb, J.H., *The Growth of Political Stability in England 1675–1725* (London, 1967)

Quintrell, B.W., *Proceedings of the Lancashire Justices of the Peace at the Sheriff's Table During Assize Week 1578–1694* (Record Society of Lancashire and Cheshire, 121, 1981)

Richardson, R.C., *Puritanism in north-west England. A regional study of the diocese of Chester to 1642* (Manchester, 1972)

Rope, W.O., *Materials for the History of the Church of Lancaster* (4 vols., Chetham Soc., n.s. 26, 31, 58, 59, 1892–1906)

Roper, W.O., *Materials for the History of Lancaster* (parts 1 & 2) (Chetham Soc., n.s. 61 & 62, 1907)

Ross, Isabel, *Margaret Fell, Mother of Quakerism* (London, 1949)

Rowntree, John Stephenson, *Quakerism Past and Present: being An Inquiry Into the Cause of its Decline in Great Britain and Ireland* (London, 1859)

Rowntree, Joshua (ed.), *John Wilhem Rowntree Essays and Addresses* (2nd ed., London, 1906)

Russell, Conrad, *The Origins of the English Civil War* (London, 1973)

Scholfield, M.M., *Outlines of an Economic History of Lancaster from 1680 to 1860: Part 1, Lancaster from 1680 to 1800* (Transactions of the Lancaster Branch of the Historical Association, 1, 1946)

Sedgewick, Romney, *The House of Commons 1715–1754* (3 vols., London, 1970)

Shapiro, Barbara J., *Probability and Certainty in Seventeenth Century England* (Princeton, NJ., 1983)

Shearer, Muriel M., *Quakers in Liverpool* (Liverpool, 1982)

Smith, Joseph, *A Descriptive Catalogue of Friends' Books, or Books Written by Members of the Society of Friends. Commonly Called Quakers, From their First Rise to the Present Time ...* (2 vols., London, 1867)

Somervell, John, *Some Westmorland Wills 1686–1738* (Kendal, 1928)

Taylor, Ernest E., *The Valiant Sixty* (London, 1947)

Thistlethwaite, Pearson, *Yorkshire Quarterly Meeting (of the Society of Friends) 1665–1966* (Harrogate, 1979)

Thomas, Keith, *Religion and the Decline of Magic, Studies in Popular Beliefs in Sixteenth and Seventeenth-Century England* (Penguin ed., London, 1973)

Vann, Richard T., *The Social Development of English Quakerism 1655–1755* (Cambridge, Mass., 1969)

Vernon, Anne, *A Quaker Business Man, The Life of Joseph Rowntree 1836–1925* (London, 1958)

Vipont, Elfrida, *George Fox and the Valiant Sixty* (London, 1975)

Walker, David M., *The Oxford Companion to Law* (Oxford, 1980)

Ward, W.R., *The English Land Tax in the Eighteenth Century* (London, 1953)

Watts, Michael, *The Dissenters, from the Reformation to the French Revolution* (Oxford, 1978)

Webb, Maria, *The Fells of Swarthmoor Hall and their Family* ... (London, 1865)

Webb, Maria, *The Penns and Penningtons of the Seventeenth Century in their Domestic and Religious life* (London, 1867)

Weeks, W.S., *Clitheroe in the Seventeenth Century* (Clitheroe, 1923)

Western, J.R., *Monarchy and Revolution, The English State in the 1680's* (London, 1972)

Williams, Basil, *The Whig Supremacy 1714–1760* (2nd ed., Oxford, 1962)

c.   **Articles**

Alsop, J.D., 'Manuscript Evidence on the Quakers Bill of 1722', *JFHS*, 54 (1980), pp.225–258

Anderson, Alan B., 'A Study in the Sociology of Religious Persecution: The First Quakers', *Journal of Religious History*, 9 (1977), pp.247–262

Armitt, M.L., 'Fullers and Freeholders of the Parish of Grasmere', *TC&WA&AS*, n.s. 8 (1908), pp.136–205

Awtry, Brian G., 'Force Forge in the Seventeenth Century', *TC&WA&AS*, n.s. 77 (1977), pp.87–112

Axon, W.E.A. 'The Pemburtons of Aspull and Philadelphia, and some Passages in the Early History of Quakerism in Lancashire', *TLCAS*, 30 (1912), pp.153–163

Barbour, Hugh, 'William Penn, Model of Protestant Liberalism', *Church History*, 48 (1979), pp.156–173

Beattie, J.M., 'The Court of George I and English Politics, 1717–1720', *English Historical Review*, 26 (1911), pp.26–37

Beckett, J.V., 'The Lowthers at Holker: Marriage, Inheritance and Debt in the fortunes of an Eighteenth-century landowning family', *THSLC*, 127 (1977), pp.47–64

Bennet, G.V., 'Robert Harley, The Godolphin Ministry and the Bishopric Crisis of 1707', *English Historical Review*, 82 (1967), pp.726–746

'Bishop Nicolson's Diaries, part 4', *TC&WA&AS*, n.s. 4 (1904), pp.1–70

Bitterman, M.G.F., 'The Early Quaker Literature of Defence', *Church History*, 42 (1973), pp.203–228

Blackwood, B.G., 'Agrarian Unrest and the Early Lancashire Quakers', *JFHS*, 51 (1965–1967), pp.72–76

Blackwood, B.G., 'The Lancashire Cavaliers and their Tenants', *THSLC*, 117 (1965), pp.17–32

Blackwood, B.G., 'The Catholic and Protestant Gentry of Lancashire during the Civil War Period', *THSLC*, 126 (1976), pp.1–29

Blackwood, B.G., 'The Economic State of the Lancashire Gentry on the Eve of the Civil War', *Northern History*, 12 (1976), pp.53–83

'Sir Roger Bradshaigh's Letter Book', *THSLC*, 63 (1911), pp.120–173

Braithwaite, Alfred W., 'Early Tithe Prosecutions: Friends as Outlaws',

JFHS, 49 (1960), pp.148–156

Braithwaite, Alfred W., 'Early Friends and Informers', *JFHS*, 51 (1965–1967), pp.107–115

Braithwaite, Alfred W., 'Early Friends' Testimony against Carnal Weapons', *JFHS*, 52 (1969), pp.101–105

Brockbank, Elisabeth, 'The Story of Quakerism in the Lancaster District', *JFHS*, 36 (1939), pp.3–20

Browne, George, 'The Advowson and some of the Rectors of Windemere since the Reformation', *TC&WA&AS*, n.s. 9 (1909), pp.41–77

Burgess, John, 'The Quakers, The Brethren and the Religious Census in Cumbria', *TC&WA&AS*, n.s. 80 (1980), pp.103–111

Cadbury, Henry J., 'The First Publishers of Truth in Lancashire', *JFHS*, 31 (1934), pp.3–19

Carroll, Kenneth L., 'Quaker Attitudes towards Signs and Wonders', *JFHS*, 54 (1977), pp.70–84

Clark, Richard, '"The Gangreen of Quakerism"; An Anglican Anti-Quaker Offensive in England after the Glorious Revolution', *Journal of Religious History*, 11 (1981), pp.404–429

Challinor, P.J., 'Restoration and Exclusion in the County of Cheshire', *Bulletin of the John Rylands Library*, 64 (1981–82), pp.360–385

Cole, Alan, 'The Social Origins of the Early Friends', *JFHS*, 48 (1956–1958), pp.99–118

Collingwood, R.G. (ed.), 'Bishop Nicolson's Diaries, Part 6', *TC&WA&AS*, n.s. 35 (1935), pp.80–145

Collingwood, W.G., 'A Book of Old Quaker Wills', *TC&WA&AS*, n.s. 29 (1929), pp.1–38

Coward, Barry, 'The Social and Political Position of the Earls of Derby in later Seventeenth Century Lancashire', *THSLC*, 132 (1982), pp.127–154

Cowper, H.S., 'The Kirkbys of Kirkby in Furness in the Seventeenth Century', *TC&WA&AS*, n.s. 6 (1906), pp.97–127

Dickinson, R.F., 'Tithing Customs in West Cumberland in the Eighteenth Century', *TC&WA&AS*, n.s. 60 (1960), pp.130–134

Dilley, R.S., 'Some Words used in the Agrarian History of Cumberland', *TC&WA&AS*, n.s. 70 (1970), pp.192–204

Docton, Kenneth, 'Lancaster: 1684', *THSLC*, 109 (1957), pp.125–142

Downie, J.A., 'The Disenfranchisement of Christopher Musgrave, MP., by Carlisle Corportion in 1692', *TC&WA&AS*, n.s. 75 (1975), pp.174–187

Evans, Eric J., '"Our Faithful Testimony" – the Society of Friends and Tithe Payments, 1690–1730', *JFHS*, 52 (1969), pp.106–121

Evans, Eric J., 'Some Reasons for the Growth of English Anti-Clericalism c.1750–1830', *Past and Present*, 66 (1975), pp.84–109

Feiling, Keith, 'Clarendon and the Act of Uniformity 1662–1663', *English Historical Review*, 44 (1929), pp.289–291

Fell, John, 'Some Illustrations of Home Life in Lonsdale North of the

Sands in the 17th and 18th Centuries', *TC&WA&AS*, 11 (1891), pp.368–398

Fishwick, Henry, 'Quaker Lancashire Literature of the Seventeenth Century', *TLCAS*, 5 (1887), pp.105–116

Forde, Helen, 'Friends and Authority: a consideration of attitudes and expedients, with particular reference to Derbyshire, *JFHS*, 54 (1978), pp.115–127

Forster, Ann M.C., 'The Oath Tendred', *Recusant History* 14 (1977–1978), pp.86–90

Galgano, Michael J., 'Iron Mining in Restoration Furness: The Case of Sir Thomas Preston', *Recusant History*, 13 (1975–1976), pp.212–218

Gaythorpe, Harper, 'Swarthmoor Meeting-house, Ulverston: A Quaker Stronghold', *TC&WA&AS*, n.s. 6 (1906), pp.237–283

Goodwin, Ellen K., 'Caldbeck Parish Registers', *TC&WA&AS*, 9 (1888), pp.1–13

Hall, David J., 'Membership Statistics of the Society of Friends, 1800–1850', *JFHS*, 54 (1969), pp.97–100

Harris, Mary Dormer, 'Memoirs of the Right Hon. Edward Hopkins, M.P. for Coventry', *English Historical Review*, 34 (1919), pp.491–504

Heatherington, Lewis, 'The Quaker Jesuite', *TC&WA&AS*, n.s. 5 (1905), pp.106–114

Horle, Craig, 'Quakers and Baptists, 1647–1660', The Baptist Quarterly 26 (1976), pp.344–362

Horle, Craig, 'Judicial Encounters with Quakers, 1660–1688', *JFHS*, 54 (1977), pp.85–100

Hurwich, Judith Jones, 'The Social Origins of the Early Quakers', *Past and Present*, 48 (1970), pp.156–162

Ironfield, Christine, 'The Parish of Chipping during the Seventeenth Century', *THSLC*, 127 (1977), pp.25–46

James, Margaret, 'The Political Importance of the Tithes Controversy in the English Revolution, 1640–60', *History*, n.s. 26 (1941), pp.1–18

Jones, G.P., 'The Decline of the Yeomanry in the Lake Counties, *TC&WA&AS*, n.s. 62 (1962), pp.198–223

Kent, Joan, 'The English Village Constable 1580–1642: The Nature and Dilemmas of Office', *Journal of British Studies*, 20 (1981), pp.26–49

'Lancashire Recusants and Quakers', *THSLC*, 64 (1912), pp.309–319

Macpherson, C.B., 'The Social Bearing of Locke's Political Theory', *The Western Political Quarterly*, 7 (1954), pp.1–22

Marshall, J.D., 'The Domestic Economy of the Lakeland Yeoman 1660–1749', *TC&WA&AS*, n.s. 73 (1973), pp.190–219

Marshall, J.D., 'Agrarian Wealth and Social Structure in Pre-Industrial Cumbria', *Economic History Review*, 2nd series, 33 (1980), pp.503–521

Milligan, Edward H., 'Unchronicled Barchester – And a few recent Chronicles of our local Meetings', *The Friends Quarterly*, 22 (1980), pp.325–334

Mingay, G.E., 'The Agricultural Depression 1730–1750', *The Economic History Review*, 2nd. series, 8 (1955–1956), pp.323–338

Morgan, Nicholas J., 'Lancashire Quakers and the Oath 1660–1722' *JFHS*, 54 (1980), pp.235–254

Mortimer, R.S., 'Bristol Quakers and the Oath', *JFHS* 43 (1951), pp.72–77

Mullett, Michael, 'The Politics of Liverpool, 1660–1688', *THSLC*, 124 (1972), pp.31–56

Mullett, Michael, '"To Dwell Together in Unity": The Search for Agreement in Preston Politics, 1660–1690', *THSLC*, 125 (1974), pp.61–81

Mullett, Michael, 'Conflict, Politics and Elections in Lancaster, 1660–1688', *Northern History*, 19 (1983), pp.61–86

Murphy, James, 'The Old Quaker Meeting House in Hackins Hey Liverpool', *THSLC*, 106 (1954), pp.79–98

Muschamp, Robert, 'Historical Notes on the Society of Friends or Quakers in Manchester in the Seventeenth Century', *TLCAS*, 31 (1913), pp.45–62

Muschamp, Robert, 'The Forty-Five', *JFHS*, 21 (1924), pp.13–19

Muschamp, Robert, 'The Society of Friends in the Lancaster District in the Seventeenth Century', *TLCAS*, 42 (1926), pp.21–41

Muschamp, Robert, 'The Society of Friends in the Bolton District', *TLCAS*, 45 (1928), p.32–43

Muschamp, Robert, 'The Society of Friends in the Seventeenth Century with a few later Notes', *TLCAS*, 46 (1929), pp.78–92

Muschamp, Robert, 'The Society of Friends, Bury District in the Seventeenth Century', reprinted from the *Bury Guardian*, (1933)

Muschamp, Robert, 'Friends Disused Burial Grounds in Lancashire', *TLCAS*, 53 (1938), pp.131–139

O'Malley, Thomas P., 'The Press and Quakerism, 1653–1659', *JFHS*, 54 (1979), pp.169–184

O'Malley, Thomas P., '"Defying the Powers and Tempering the Spirit". A Review of Quaker Control over their Publications 1672–1689', *Journal of Ecclesiastical History*, 33 (1982), pp.72–88

Porteus, Thomas C., 'Roger Haydock of Coppull – A Brief Biography and Ten Original Letters', *TLCAS*, 52 (1937), pp.1–66

Ransome, Mary, 'Church and Dissent in the Election of 1710', *English Historical Review*, 56 (1941), pp.76–89

Rawlinson-Ford, J., 'The Customary Tenant-right of the Manors of Yealand', *TC&WA&AS*, n.s. 9(1909), pp.147–160

Reay, Barry, 'The Quakers and 1659: two newly discovered broadside by Edward Burrough', *JFHS*, 54 (1977), pp.101–111

Reay, Barry, 'Quaker Opposition to Tithes 1652–1660', *Past and Present*, 86 (1980), pp.98–120

Reay, Barry, 'The Social Origins of Early Quakerism', *Journal of Interdisciplinary History*, 11 (1980), pp.55–72

Reay, Barry, 'Popular Hostility towards Quakers in mid Seventeenth-century England', *Social History*, 5 (1980), pp.387–407

Reay, Barry, 'The Authorities and Early Restoration Quakerism', *Journal of Ecclesiastical History*, 34 (1983), pp.69–84

Ross, Isabel, 'Lancashire Women's Quarterly Meeting Minute Book', *JFHS*, 35 (1938), pp.40–43

Russell, Conrad, 'Arguments for Religious Unit in England, 1530–1650', *Journal of Ecclesiastical History*, 18 (1967), pp.201–226

Saxon-Snell, Beatrice, 'The Making of Thomas Ellwood,', *JFHS*, 36 (1939), pp.21–49

Scholfield, Maurice M., 'The Letter-Book of Benjamin Satterthwaite of Lancaster, 1737–1744', *THSLC*, 113 (1961), pp.125–167

Sharpe-France, R. 'A High Constables Register, 1681', *THSLC*, 107 (1955), pp.55–81

Straka, Gerald, 'The Final Phase of the Divine Right Theory in England, 1688–1702, *English Historical Review*, 77 (1962), pp.638–658

Sykes, Norman, 'Bishop Gibson and Sir Robert Walpole', *English Historical Review*, 44 (1929), pp.628–633

Sykes, Norman, 'The Cathedral Chapter of Exeter and the General Election of 1705', *English Historical Review*, 45 (1930), pp.260–272

Taylor, Ernest E., 'The First Publishers of Truth', *JFHS*, 19 (1922), pp.66–81

Thompson, Sylvanus P., 'John Wilhelm Rowntree', *Friends Quarterly Examiner*, (1905), pp.258–268

Vann, Richard T., 'Quakerism and the Social Structure in the Interregnum', *Past and Present*, 43 (1969), pp.71–91

Vann, Richard T., 'Rejoinder to Judith Jones Hurwich', *Past and Present*, 48 (1970), pp.162–164

c.   **Unpublished theses**

Anderson, Alan B., 'Lancashire Quakers and Persecution', (University of Lancaster, MA thesis, 1971)

Beckett, J.V., 'Landownership in Cumbria, c.1680–1750', (University of Lancaster, Ph.D. thesis, 1975)

Blackwood, Bruce G., 'Social and Religious Aspects of the History of Lancashire 1635–1655', (University of Oxford, B.Litt. thesis, 1956)

Clarkson, L.A., 'The Leather Industry in the Seventeenth Century', (University of Nottingham, Ph.D. thesis, 1961)

Evans, Eric, 'A History of the Tithe System in England 1690–1850', (University of Warwick, Ph.D. thesis, 1971)

Forde, Helen, 'Derbyshire Quakers 1650–1761', (University of Leicester, Ph.D. thesis, 1978)

Hopkins, R.A. 'Aspects of Jacobite Conspiracy in England in the Reign of William III', (University of Cambridge, Ph.D. thesis, 1981)

Hopkinson, R., 'Parliamentary Elections in Westmorland and Cumberland

1695–1723 ', (University of Newcastle, Ph.D. thesis, 1973)

Hurst, P., 'Family Continuity in the Representation of the North-West Counties in the Seventeenth Century', (University of Lancaster, M.Litt. thesis, 1980)

King, W., 'The Economic and Demographic Development of Rossendale', (University of Leicester, Ph.D. thesis, 1979)

Phillips, C.B., 'The Gentry in Cumberland and Westmorland 1600–65', (University of Lancaster, Ph.D. thesis, 1974)

Quine, E.K.L., 'The Quakers in Leicestershire 1648–1780', (University of Nottingham, Ph.D. thesis, 1972)

Spurrier, William Wayne, 'The Persecution of the Quakers in England 1650–1714', (University of North Carolina, Ph.D. thesis, 1976)

Wahlstrand, J.M., 'The Elections to Parliament in the County of Lancashire 1685–1714', (University of Manchester, MA thesis, 1956)

Wrightson, Keith, 'The Puritan Reformation of Manners, with Special Reference to the Counties of Lancashire and Essex, 1640–1660', (University of Cambridge, Ph.D. thesis, 1974)

For a complete list of Ryburn books
please write to Ryburn Publishing
Tenterfields   Luddendenfoot
Halifax HX2 6EJ   England

Ryburn